WRITING
ESSENTIALS

Raising Expectations and Results
While Simplifying Teaching

REGIE
ROUTMAN

HEINEMANN
Portsmouth, NH

Heinemann
A division of Reed Elsevier Inc.
361 Hanover Street
Portsmouth, NH 03801–3912
www.heinemann.com

Offices and agents throughout the world

The author and publisher wish to thank those who have generously given permission to reprint borrowed material:

Letter to Fourth-Grade Students at Swanson Elementary School reprinted by permission of Margaret Planner, Ph.D., Assistant State Superintendent, Division for Reading and Student Achievement, Wisconsin Department on Public Instruction.

"Anthem" by Leonard Cohen. Copyright © 1993 Sony/ATV Songs LLC. All rights administered by Sony/ATV Music Publishing, 8 Music Square West, Nashville, TN 37203. All Rights Reserved. Used by permission.

Library of Congress Cataloging-in-Publication Data
Routman, Regie.
   Writing essentials : raising expectations and results while simplifying teaching / Regie Routman.
      p. cm.
   Includes bibliographical references and index.
   ISBN 0-325-00601-6 (alk. paper)
   1. English language—Composition and exercises—Study and teaching.   I. Title.
LB1576.R7585 2005
372.62'3—dc22   2004020939

Editor: Lois Bridges
Production management: Patricia Adams
Production coordination: Abigail M. Heim
DVD production: Kevin Carlson
Typesetting: Gina Poirier
Cover design: Lisa Fowler
Cover photography: Terri S. Thompson
Manufacturing: Louise Richardson

About the Cover: Regie Routman conducts a one-on-one conference in a classroom during a weeklong writing residency.

Printed in the United States of America on acid-free paper
08   07   06   RRD   3   4   5

WRITING
ESSENTIALS

For my father, Emanuel
And for Peter and Claudine

Contents

3   Share Your Writing Life 35

Two   Teaching Essentials

4   Raise Your Expectations 53

Optimal Learning Model	
Who *Holds Book/Pen*	*Degree of Support*
Teacher /Student	DEMONSTRATION
Teacher /Student	SHARED DEMONSTRATION
gradual handover of responsibility	
Student /Teacher	GUIDED PRACTICE
Student /Teacher	INDEPENDENT PRACTICE

Five   ## Teaching in Action: Lesson Essentials

Five-Day Lesson Plans

Teaching Points: Conference Video Clips 336

Appendices

A Note About Notes and Other Resources

To keep the text clean and unencumbered, all references to research, ideas, authors, and quotations requiring explanation or further discussion are listed in a notes section beginning on page A-22 in the end matter. The notes are divided by chapter and sequenced consecutively by page number. Sources and/or elaboration, including bibliographic information to help you find referenced material easily, are presented after a brief identifying phrase or statement linked to the text. Simple reference citations not requiring annotation are contained in the references section beginning on page A-46.

Any statement or concept not attributed is based on my own teacher-research, observations, and more than thirty-five years of teaching experience. To keep the book itself to a manageable length, the notes also provide additional recommended resources and references for information and self-study.

Brief definitions of terms that may not be fully explained in the text are included beginning on page A-16. In addition, practical, how-to support to implement the structures and procedures described in the text are provided in the sample five-day lesson plans beginning on page 292; enclosed DVD containing video clips of my conferences with writers in the classroom, along with detailed accompanying commentary beginning on page 336; and a companion website, www.heinemann.com/writingessentials, offering classroom writing forms, student drafts to use as models, a genre information chart, and new and updated information on literacy education.

Acknowledgments

Thanks are due to the many teachers, principals, children, friends, and family that have made all the hard work of this book possible and gratifying. In particular, I am grateful for the collaboration and collegiality of the marvelous staffs at the schools in which I have worked in for the past five years: Adams Elementary in Mesa, Arizona; Huntsville Elementary in Huntsville, Ohio; Burnt Bridge Creek Elementary in Vancouver, Washington; Sulphur Springs Elementary in Tampa, Florida; Lakeside Elementary in Chattanooga, Tennessee; Arapahoe Ridge Elementary in Westminster, Colorado; Swanson Elementary in Brookfield, Wisconsin; Rio Grande School in Santa Fe, New Mexico; Rummel Creek Elementary in Houston, Texas; Ardmore Elementary in Bellevue, Washington. I am humbled and privileged to continue to teach and learn with so many fine educators. Much of their excellent work is included in this book.

I depend on willing readers for honest and helpful feedback to make the text readable, clear, and useful. Diane Levin, Kari Oosterveen, Karen Sher, and Gail Westbrook read the entire text with sensitivity and care and gave thoughtful comments and suggestions. For their generous time and feedback, I am most appreciative. I am very grateful to Richard Allington for his carefully considered response to the chapters on research and assessment. Thanks also go to Darcy Ballentine, Monica Carrera-Wilburn, Sandy Garcia, Devon Isherwood, Melinda Jennings, Marilyn Jerde, Cami Kostecki, Sue Mikulecky, Beth Petrie, and Millie Rable for responding to portions of the text. And I extend a special thank you to Donald Graves for his ongoing response and encouragement.

In addition, the following people provided me assistance with research and/or sent materials/resources, responded to a request for help, or responded to a brief section of text: Linda Benedict, Mark Bergmann, Cindy Coronado, Nancy Curry, Marquita Curry, Debbie Fowler, Tom Fuller, Lindsey Gandolfo, Diane Gillespie, Patty Hughes, Terry Lamp, Royce Lindner, Nancy McLean, Cindy Marten, Diane Mattern, Donna Maxim, Lea Payton, Bryna Osborne, Sheila Pearce, Gloria Pipkin, Kristen Potter, Marilyn Robbins, Carole Robinson, Cathy Roth, Allyson Secord,

Bobbi Selig, Sharon Sharadin, Terri Smith, Susan Thaney, Andrew Thomas, Terri S. Thompson, Bob Torrens, Marlene Tucker, Lindy Vizyak, Linda Wold, Robin Woods, Victoria Young, and Linda Zarkovich. Many thanks to Kären York for tracking down hard-to-find research and for her willingness to do so. Appreciative thanks to teacher-librarian Marcie Haloin for creating the genre tables, to JoAnne Piccolo for shooting the video clips in classrooms, and to Rhett Johnson and Joel D'Alessandro for their follow up video and DVD work.

I am indebted to the Heinemann "dream team." So many people worked long and hard to create and produce *Writing Essentials*. First of all, heartfelt thanks go to my dear friend and terrific editor, Lois Bridges. Lois' insights, energy, brilliance, and generosity are woven through my text. As well, editor Alan Huisman is a writer's precious gift. Alan's honesty, tough questions, and remarkable editing talents made this a stronger book. Abby Heim, production manager, has been extraordinary in coordinating efforts to produce a beautiful book. I appreciate her "can-do" spirit, her flexibility, and her meticulous attention to detail. I am also thankful for the work of production assistant Donata Luz, and for Patty Adams who has worked tirelessly to ensure that every page was formatted correctly and that no detail was overlooked. Lisa Fowler deserves special recognition for choreographing the lesson plans design and creating my beautiful cover. I appreciate her great talent and enthusiasm. Typesetter Gina Poirier worked long and hard to lay out the book in a pleasing, easy-to-access fashion. And Diane Brenner helped create a useful index. To Kevin Carlson, grateful thanks for developing our DVD with great skill, good humor, and patience. Always I thank Maura Sullivan for her smart guidance on a wide range of issues at the exact moment her expert help is needed. And I appreciate Pat Carls' on-target marketing efforts. Others at Heinemann continue to support my efforts as well: Lesa Scott, Leigh Peake, Mike Gibbons, Tracy Heine, Vicki Boyd, Cherie Bartlett, Pat Goodman, Kristine Giunco, Louise Richardson, Eric Chalek, Jen Andrews, and Doria Turner.

I am fortunate to have had the support and encouragement of wonderful friends and colleagues throughout the writing of this book. I especially depend on and treasure my lifelong friendship with Harriet Cooper. I am also blessed to have Jenifer Katahira, loving friend and colleague in my life. As well, Sheila Valencia is an esteemed friend. Our conversations and her keen insights enrich my life and helped shape this book. Judie Thelen's friendship is dear to me, along with her love and good humor. Special thanks to Bonnie Campbell Hill for her kind friendship and her support on multiple fronts. I am also grateful to talented educator and loving friend Claudia Mason for her caring friendship. And I depend on my dear friend Judy Wallis for our thoughtful conversations on all matters, both professional and personal.

Finally and most importantly, I could not have written this book without the generous love and kindness of my husband, Frank. For him, especially, I am most grateful.

September 2004

WRITING
ESSENTIALS

One

The Essential
Writing Life

*I WANT STUDENTS TO WRITE WITH
PASSION AND EASE. I WANT THEM
TO BE MOTIVATED, CONFIDENT
WRITERS WHO SEE WRITING AS
AN EVERYDAY, USEFUL, EVEN
ENJOYABLE TOOL.*

3-10-04

Well, he does NOT!
If ... ark and I have
... Oliver to get
... earwash in his
... ears. We put some of
the wash in a syringe.
A syringe is kind of
like a ...

1. Simplify the Teaching of Writing

The great artist is the simplifier.
—Henri Frederic Amiel

It was the first thing Monday morning. I was about to begin a residency, a week of demonstration teaching and coaching in a school that had hired me to improve student writing. Specifically, the teachers and principal wanted help getting students to write coherent-enough paragraphs to pass the state writing test. A group of frustrated and anxious teachers were lamenting how poorly their students wrote. In spite of heightened attention to teaching the school's fourth graders how to write a topic sentence with supporting details, the students' writing had gotten worse over the past few years (or so the declining test scores seemed to indicate). And it was not just students' ability to construct a meaningful paragraph that was lacking. Their spelling, grammar, and punctuation were worse, too. These teachers told me that the harder they worked on teaching writing, the more resistant their students became.

Increasingly, schools' requests for my teaching residencies focus on writing: "Our test scores are low, and we're under pressure to bring them up," or, "How do we get students to revise, spell words correctly, and use proper grammar?" When I inquire, I find there has been lots of focus on skills, practice exercises, and writing to a prompt. Often, teachers have been trained to use writing formulas and templates. The kids learn how to use these tools but aren't able to apply them to other kinds of writing. And, sadly, there is rarely any talk about making writing enjoyable for children or writing for real readers. Students find writing tedious, and teachers dread trying to teach it.

Why *Writing Essentials?*

I want students to write with passion and ease. I want them to become motivated, confident writers who see writing as an everyday, useful, even enjoyable tool. I want the same for teachers. I want teachers who focus on writers and writing, not on procedures and prompts. I want the test pressure eliminated—or at least greatly reduced. I want to make teachers' lives easier and more enjoyable. I want to bring sanity, common sense, and joy back into writing classrooms.

Excellent and enjoyable writing needs to become central to the everyday life of the classroom. Based on my work in classrooms, I now have thoroughly tested methods for accomplishing this. I also have supporting data demonstrating that students successfully transfer their writing skills to high-stakes writing tests when we focus on teaching writing well for authentic purposes and real readers.

Unfortunately, most of us educators still don't trust that excellent teaching and assessing, daily writing, and writing enjoyment will translate to success on the writing tests. Pressured by a demand for higher test scores along with our collective lack of knowledge and confidence in how best to teach writing, we understandably succumb to the latest program or newest method.

There is another way. We can become knowledgeable writing teachers and advocates of best writing practices. We can give writing the central, meaningful, enjoyable place it deserves in the curriculum and in our lives—crucial for planning, thinking, communicating, reflecting, congratulating, speculating, and on and on. Teaching writing well gives our students a lifetime gift, helps bring joy and empowerment back into our classrooms—and results in high test scores, too. Let our journey begin.

I have written this book to:

- ☐ Make writing more purposeful, manageable, and joyous for you and your students.
- ☐ Raise your expectations for what your students can do.
- ☐ Show you how to teach the "skills" effectively and efficiently.
- ☐ Ensure writing success for *all* students.

- ☐ Demonstrate how to conduct effective, enjoyable writing conferences.
- ☐ Help you prepare your students for high-stakes testing in a sane and sensible manner.
- ☐ Share the latest writing research.
- ☐ Increase your confidence and competence as a writer and as a teacher of writing.
- ☐ Help you focus on what's really essential.
- ☐ Give you lots of practical, easy-to-do strategies for teaching writing well.
- ☐ Show you how to teach more effectively in less time.

Simplify Teaching and Increase Results and Enjoyment

One of my main purposes in writing this book is to make teaching writing easier, more manageable, and more fun. Over and over again, I have been taken aback by how little we really expect of students, how much time gets wasted, how little pride and enjoyment students take in their writing, and how much our testing culture has influenced how we teach writing.

Teaching writing is a serious problem in many schools. We are overfocused on procedures, processes, genres, and testing and underfocused on thinking, communicating, inquiring, and exploring language.

Although teaching writing well is a complex art, we have made it far more difficult than it needs to be. Let me be very clear here. I am not talking about lowering expectations or standards, just the opposite. My aim is to raise expectations while streamlining the teaching of writing to essential elements and manageable procedures. Then we and our students can maintain the energy, commitment, and positive attitude that are necessary to produce writing worth reading.

A personal story illustrates my point. Recently, I was staying at a hotel and getting ready to deliver the morning keynote address at a state literacy conference. As is my usual custom, I planned to shower and wash my hair before dressing. As I leaned into the shower stall and turned on the water, water shot out with great force from multiple spigots. Temporarily blindsided, I was instantly drenched from head to toe. A second attempt yielded the same results. I called the front desk for help, and the maintenance man appeared. After ten minutes of fiddling with the various knobs, he was unable to adjust the shower so water came out only from the top spigot. I called the front desk again, and thirty minutes later when the housekeepers reported for work, the manager sent two of them to solve the problem. With the assistance of the maintenance man, they worked for twenty minutes to get the shower functioning properly.

Feeling stressed and helpless about being able to work the shower by myself, I called the manager: "I will want to take a shower again tomorrow. Do you have any written directions?" Within minutes, a full page of instructions (see below) appeared under my door, a clear sign that many others had experienced similar problems. I quickly looked over the page and became immediately frustrated by the amount of print and the complexity of the directions. I never did read through it all, and I never took a shower the following day.

My shower experience is a metaphor for what happens when tasks seem too difficult and overwhelming. Most of us—teachers and students alike—just give up in frustration and exhaustion. Such resignation seems particularly true with

---

Shower Instructions

1. Turn on the water by turning the Water Flow Valve to the left.
2. Water will begin to poor from the spigot.
3. Set the desired water temperature by turning the temperature valve.
4. Pull the knob up on the spigot to start the shower flow.
5. Each corresponding indentation on the shower controls represents what heads will flow.
   a. Upright - Shower only
   b. One turn right – Wand Only
   c. Two turns right – Shower and Wand
   d. Three turns right – Three Lower Heads
   e. Four Turns right – Shower and Lower Heads
   f. Five Turns right – Wand and Lower Heads

   (Each shower may be calibrated differently and the positions as described above may not be the exact positions of the knob while the corresponding heads flow, however with each turn of the knob a different set of heads will flow in one of the above configurations.)

To turn the shower off you turn the water flow knob to the right, the knob on the spigot will automatically drop and the water flow from all heads and the spigot will stop.

regard to writing, an activity in which we start with a blank page (or screen) and literally have to create something out of nothing more than our own thoughts. It takes enormous energy, courage, confidence, and skill, not to mention a positive attitude.

If all of our students are to become successful writers, then from the day they enter school they—and we—must see the process as doable, manageable, and enjoyable. We need to simplify the process while raising our expectations and achieving better results. My aim is to show you many possibilities, pique your curiosity, inspire you to take risks, and increase your confidence, competence, and joy as a teacher and assessor of writing.

Become More Knowledgeable About How to Teach Writing

During a recent school residency, the teachers told me that over the past six years, their district had adopted and abandoned four different writing programs. All the teachers had recently been trained in using the latest program, and they were feeling exasperated about having to spend time learning yet another new approach. And therein lies the problem. Rather than developing professionally into better writing teachers, these teachers were learning how to use a program. The latest program involved learning a "writing method" for "teaching basic writing skills." It was essentially a square template, with writing a topic sentence in the center, adding four supporting statements around that, and then copying all the information into a paragraph below. Certainly, such a template can be a useful organizational tool, but as the mainstay of the entire writing program, it was, at best, a limited resource.

By contrast, in the districts where students are excellent writers who write for real purposes and audiences—and publish their writing—no particular program is being taught. In classrooms in these districts, knowledgeable teachers teach writing every day. Students write coherent texts (not practice exercises) and get helpful and respectful responses. Productivity and enjoyment are high, and so are the test scores.

We educators will remain at the mercy of published programs and formulaic mandates until we become knowledgeable about how to teach writing well. To be effective writing teachers, we must become aware of our beliefs and how they drive our teaching and assessing. We must also be writers ourselves (see Chapter 3) and advocate for saner teaching of writing.

Examine Your Beliefs

Our beliefs drive our teaching practices even if we don't articulate those beliefs to others or even ourselves. One of the reasons lasting change takes so long is that our beliefs are slow to change. Until we recognize our beliefs, question them, challenge them in the light of new information, research, and experiences, nothing much happens. We may add a new activity or program, but the change is only on the surface. Effective teachers are always examining, evaluating, and refining what they believe as a first step to improving and refining instructional practices. A list of my key beliefs is shown below.

TOP FIVE THINGS I DO TO ENSURE STUDENTS BECOME EXCELLENT WRITERS

- ☐ Demonstrate that I am a writer *who always writes with a reader in mind* (sometimes that reader is myself) and make my writing and thinking processes visible.

- ☐ Connect writing to reading through literature; notice what authors (including student authors) do.

- ☐ Guide students to choose topics they care about (by offering them choice within structure) and give students time to talk and write about them.

- ☐ Teach students the strategies they need to draft, revise, edit, polish, and publish.

- ☐ Rely primarily on regular conferences with students to assess and evaluate: note strengths, give feedback, teach, and set mutual goals.

This list reflects my current thinking, which is always evolving. It is not the "right" list, but it is based on my strong beliefs, which come from many years of experience as a teacher, writer, observer of children, collaborator with colleagues, and thoughtful reader of writing research.

Use my list as a springboard for thinking about your own beliefs and practices. And make a point of talking about your beliefs and practices with your colleagues. Strong, trusting collegial relationships make it more likely that teachers will take risks and change their beliefs.

Use Your Beliefs to Assess Your Teaching

During a residency in Houston, Texas, after just three days of seeing what students could accomplish as writers, many teachers began to shift from believing that teaching should proceed part-to-whole (skills first) to believing that it worked best moving whole-to-part-to-whole (meaning first, with skills integrated to make meaning clear). Articulating their evolving beliefs with one another helped them clarify their thinking and start to change their process. See below.

ONE SCHOOL'S EVOLVING SHARED BELIEFS ON WRITING

☐ Quality is more important than quantity.

☐ In kindergarten, peer sharing is more valid than peer conferencing.

☐ You have to teach in order for writing to improve.

☐ There are lots of ways to prewrite.

☐ Don't dwell on the rubric in isolation.

☐ Students need to see their teachers as writers first.

☐ Having students talk before they write makes it easier for them to work.

☐ Good sharing of writing is really a public conference.

☐ Direct teaching of skills is part of writers workshop.

☐ Peer conferencing needs to be modeled and done well to be useful.

☐ Our writing program needs to celebrate student's writing and not be driven by the 6 traits.

☐ "It's really pointless to have those practice sheets."

☐ Nonfiction has to be taught.

☐ It's fine for a student to write in depth on the same topic for an extended time if student chooses to do so.

☐ Writing doesn't have to be painful for the teacher or student.

☐ Modeling an entire piece gives students a clearer understanding of what is expected.

☐ Students need time to think before they write.

☐ Writing down a child's oral thoughts helps him organize before writing.

☐ All writing doesn't need to be graded.

WHAT WE DO TO GET EXCELLENT WRITERS:
A PART-TO-WHOLE BELIEF SYSTEM

☐ Use commercial texts for grammar and spelling.

☐ Ability-group for spelling and vocabulary.

☐ Have weekly writing to a directed prompt.

☐ Have kids critique each other's work.

☐ Edit papers at home and have parents edit with students.

☐ Teach isolated lessons (commas in a series, quotation marks, and so on).

Compare the evolving beliefs and practices of teachers at one school (see page 9), to those in the box above, which are the beliefs of teachers in a school that has a part-to-whole belief system (and, not coincidentally, low test scores that have "not budged from year to year" in spite of attention to "the test").

Where does your school fit in? Use these charts and the writing exercise "Writing Process: Agree or Disagree" (Appendix A) to get conversations going in your school.

Meet a Teacher Who Changed

Terry Lamp is a fourth-grade teacher with twelve years of experience teaching grades 1 through 4, most recently a grade 3–4 loop: he teaches the same students in grades 3 and 4, then moves back to a new class of third graders. Terry calls himself the "extreme makeover."

Based on his own education, Terry's teaching of writing included directed assignments with little student choice:

☐ Daily oral language exercises.

☐ Five-paragraph papers.

☐ "Huge" projects—such as animal reports and autobiographies—that took months to complete.

☐ A focus on correctness and conventions.

While Terry didn't know what a good writing program looked like or how to get the kids to love writing, he was ready for change. "I hated the projects and so did the kids."

Terry started to read professionally, talk more with his colleagues, and question his beliefs. Also, over a three-year period, he observed the demonstration lessons I taught in an ongoing school residency. Seeing those lessons, trying things out for himself with support and coaching, and being part of schoolwide conversations about aligning writing standards to teaching, made him believe, "I can do that."

Initially he found the transition "rough going," but he knew he was doing a better job of teaching because "the kids' writing was getting better and they were enjoying it more." He added three components to teaching writing that were new for him:

- ☐ Modeling writing for and with students.
- ☐ Having conferences with students.
- ☐ Celebrating students' writing.

Terry continues to have his students write every day because he sees so much success as a result. He acknowledges that the optimal learning model (see below and the inside front cover), which I use with the adults I teach as well as with children, was an important factor in his growing competence.

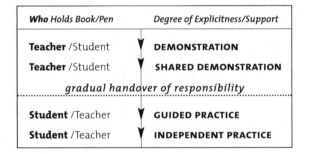

Who Holds Book/Pen	Degree of Explicitness/Support
Teacher /Student	▼ **DEMONSTRATION**
Teacher /Student	▼ **SHARED DEMONSTRATION**
gradual handover of responsibility	
Student /Teacher	▼ **GUIDED PRACTICE**
Student /Teacher	▼ **INDEPENDENT PRACTICE**

The Optimal Learning Model

In the optimal learning model, students:

- ☐ Explicitly see writing taught (observe demonstration teaching).
- ☐ Work with an expert teacher, side by side (take part in shared and guided experiences).
- ☐ Try it out on their own (practice independently).

In addition, having lots of professional conversations and observing in in lots of classrooms at his and other grade levels provided great support as he reflected on his continuing professional development.

It's a joy to observe and coteach with Terry today. The writing in his classroom is purposeful, his writing demonstrations and conference techniques are excellent, and his students are competent, confident writers "who see themselves as writers and enjoy their craft."

Meet the Leadership Team

Lasting change depends on strong leadership, not just from the principal but from teachers, too. At Burnt Bridge Creek Elementary School, in Vancouver, Washington, principal Melinda Jennings and teacher representatives from each grade level took responsibility for improving the way writing was being taught. Spurred by low test scores and a Bill & Melinda Gates Foundation grant, the school brought me in for a series of writing residencies during a four-year period, in which time the staff moved from stressful, complex teaching of writing to enjoyable, more meaningful teaching. Both expectations and results increased. How did this happen?

While my demonstration teaching and coaching made an impact, my visits served mostly as a catalyst. It was—and continues to be—conducting ongoing professional conversations, examining and discussing children's writing within and across grade levels, changing beliefs and practices based on increased professional knowledge, and observing what kids are capable of at every grade level that caused teachers to change how they teach writing and to expect far more from their students. As teachers became more knowledgeable, competent, and confident, so did the students. Principal Melinda Jennings comments:

> We wrestled with our rubrics and state standards, said a collective "Got it!" and then we put the joy back in teaching. We simply focused on "what good writers do" and "what makes good writing" in every classroom. Our expectations for what our students can do went way up. Teacher and student confidence grew, and the writing got better and better. Now writing time is everyone's favorite part of the day. And all of the grade-level expectations and state standards for writing are visible in our children's work.

Teach What's Essential

The question we need to be asking is, *how can I teach writing so that all students become effective and joyful writers and communicators?* not, *what does the best writing program look like?* or *what skills should I be teaching?* Teaching the skills is crucial, certainly, but those skills need to be taught because the writer needs them to convey a message, not because they are on a checklist or in a prescribed "scope and sequence" program.

Also, and this is so important, *the skills and strategies that writers use are the same across the grade levels;* their depth and sophistication are what increase. All of the writing essentials that follow are taught and retaught, beginning in kindergarten. What advance are the writer's control, application, and competent use of these "skills," through demonstrations, guidance, support, practice, feedback, and authentic use.

12 Writing Essentials for All Grade Levels

Teach these essentials well in connection with any purposeful writing, and, with guidance, students will be able to use them in whatever form of writing they do:

- ☐ **Write for a specific reader and a meaningful purpose.** Write with a particular audience in mind (this may be the author herself or himself) and define the writing task.

- ☐ **Determine an appropriate topic.** Plan the writing, do the necessary research, narrow the focus, decide what's most important to include.

- ☐ **Present ideas clearly, with a logical, well-organized flow.** Structure the writing in an easy-to-follow style and format using words, sentences, and paragraphs; put like information together; stay on the topic; know when and what to add or delete; incorporate transitions.

- ☐ **Elaborate on ideas.** Include details and facts appropriate to stated main ideas; explain key concepts; support judgments; create descriptions that evoke mood, time, and place; and develop characters.

- ☐ **Embrace language.** "Fool with words"—experiment with nouns, verbs, adjectives, literary language, sensory details, dialogue, rhythm, sentence length, paragraphs—to craft specific, lively writing for the reader.

- ☐ **Create engaging leads.** Attract the reader's interest right from the start.

- ☐ **Compose satisfying endings.** Develop original endings that bring a sense of closure.

- ☐ **Craft authentic voice.** Write in a style that illuminates the writer's personality—this may include dialogue, humor, point of view, a unique form.

- ☐ **Reread, rethink, and revise while composing.** Assess, analyze, reflect, evaluate, plan, redraft, and edit as one goes—all part of the recursive, nonlinear nature of writing.

- ☐ **Apply correct conventions and form.** Produce legible letters and words; employ editing and proofreading skills; use accurate spelling, punctuation, capitalization, and grammar; adhere to the formal rules of the genre.

☐ **Read widely and deeply—and with a writer's perspective.** Read avidly; notice what authors—and illustrators—do; develop an awareness of the characteristics of various genres (fiction, poetry, persuasive pieces) and how those genres work, and apply that knowledge and craft to one's own writing.

☐ **Take responsibility for producing effective writing.** Consider relevant responses and suggestions and willingly revise; sustain writing effort; monitor and evaluate one's own work and set goals; publish, when possible and appropriate, in a suitable and pleasing presentation style and format; do whatever is necessary to ensure the text is meaningful and clear to the reader as well as accurate, legible, and engaging.

These 12 writing essentials are applicable from kindergarten through high school and beyond. *Since we teach the same writing skills and strategies from grade to grade, we don't need a separate list for each grade level.* (Teaching Beyond the Standards on pages 150–151 illustrates this point.)

The factors that change are:

☐ The amount of excellent support the student needs (demonstrations and explicit teaching).

☐ The complexity of texts the student composes.

☐ The variety of forms or genres the author attempts.

☐ The learner's level of independence.

While students do need to know and understand the particular qualities of each genre (and we need to teach them), successful writing in a specific genre involves applying what students know about all effective writing. Research suggests that "the strategies of production are generalizable to other comparable tasks. When instruction is aimed at developing a particular narrative, students may not learn those strategies of production for use independently." That is, when we focus too closely on the genre—rather than on producing excellent writing—students may not transfer what they learn to other forms of writing. (See genre teaching perspectives on pages 190–193).

Teach Writing the Way Real Writers Work

When I sit down to write, here's what I'm thinking about:

☐ *What do I want to say?*
☐ *How can I say it clearly?*

☐ *How can I explain important ideas so my readers will feel convinced and confident enough to think about them (and try them out)?*

☐ *How can I write so that I will engage and interest my audience?*

In other words, I am thinking about who I'm writing for, about clarity and brevity, about organizing my material logically, about writing in an accessible and friendly style, about what's most important to say and how to say it. In the process of getting the words down, I will write short and long sentences, fuss over word choice, put in transitions, and maintain a personal tone. But I am doing all these things in service to my reader(s).

Teaching writing by focusing on the parts—spending weeks teaching sentence fluency or transitions or voice, for example—is not how writers work. Something is amiss in our writing classrooms when most of our time is spent on bits and pieces and exercises. I have never:

☐ Written two short sentences and thought, *now I need a long one.*

☐ Thought to myself, *my voice is missing here, and I need to add it.*

☐ Worried about editing when I'm getting my ideas down.

☐ Thought to myself, *I need to write a topic sentence and add supporting details.*

While we do, of course, need to teach writing explicitly—to include all the individual skills and techniques that go into producing clear, excellent, engaging communication—we are far more productive as teachers of writing when we embed that teaching in writing for purposes and audiences that students understand and value. When we start with a whole piece of writing for an intended reader, we can then look at the parts and connect them back with the whole. Whole-to-part-to-whole is much easier for teachers and students than part-to-whole-to-part.

Be Explicit—Show Students How

Explicit instruction goes hand in hand with meaningful teaching and cannot be left to chance. One teacher spoke for many when she said, "I just kind of go with the students who get it and hope the others will eventually catch on." The lucky ones will, but it is our job to teach *all* students.

Showing students *how* to write makes more sense to them when they understand and value *why* they are writing. Certainly, effective writing defies a cookie-cutter model, but our students do need to see and experience the thinking that goes into producing effective writing. Here are some of the ways:

☐ **Think aloud as we write** (or visualize or illustrate or set up a chart).

☐ **Think aloud as we read aloud** (commenting on the language—choice of words, impact, usage).

☐ **Notice what authors and illustrators do** (include student authors and illustrators).
☐ **Think and write with students.**
☐ **Analyze effective writing.**
☐ **Show examples of a particular writing genre.**
☐ **Establish criteria for excellent writing.**
☐ **Compare successful and unsuccessful pieces of writing.**
☐ **Discuss and note what makes a piece of writing "work."**
☐ **Evaluate a piece of writing** (whether one's own or someone else's), noticing strengths and weaknesses, and figuring out how to move forward.
☐ **Celebrate and publish writing.**

All of these techniques are discussed and demonstrated throughout this text. As noted in the optimal learning model (page 11), these demonstrations include teacher modeling (writing and thinking aloud), shared writing, and thinking aloud before students attempt to write on their own, either with teacher guidance or independently.

Simplify

The older I get, the greater effort I make to get rid of the clutter, literally and figuratively. *What's most important? What can I do without? What's absolutely essential?* In my life and in my teaching I ask these questions over and over. My husband Frank strives to do the same thing as an artist. As teachers we must be artists too, making those same judgments, asking those same questions, and choosing wisely the essentials that shape our classroom canvases so they are rich in detail, color, and form and inviting and accessible to all learners.

A major purpose of this book is help you develop and refine your beliefs and practices for teaching writing effectively and in a way that is sensible and enjoyable. By reducing the clutter in our teaching lives—the overplanning, the unnecessary activities, the paper load, all the "stuff" that takes our time and energy and does little to improve teaching and learning—we bring joy back into our work. Nothing I do in classrooms is difficult or draining. As you read this book and get ideas, you will be thinking, *I can do that, too.*

Focusing on writing essentials empowers us teachers to empower our students. Focusing on what's most important gives us time to live and enjoy our lives more, in and out of school. And what's more essential than that?

2. Start with Celebration

*I did it for the pure joy of the thing. And
if you can do it for joy, you can do it forever.*
—Stephen King

I am working with a fourth-grade class during the week before Valentine's Day. My primary goals have been for the students to see writing as enjoyable and themselves as successful writers. The classroom teacher and I have not discussed traits, rubrics, grades, standards; yet we have taught and addressed everything connected with these assessment tools.

When I read the first drafts (see examples on page 201), each paper touches my heart. Every piece of writing has a lead, is well organized, speaks to the designated reader, and would receive a passing score of 3 or 4 if it were scored against the state rubric (a judgment made by the K–12 language arts coordinator and several teachers). It takes ninety minutes to share every paper. No student talks out of turn or needs to be called to order. They are totally engaged in one another's work. Teachers later comment with surprise, "They sat for ninety minutes!" I didn't thank the students for their attention;

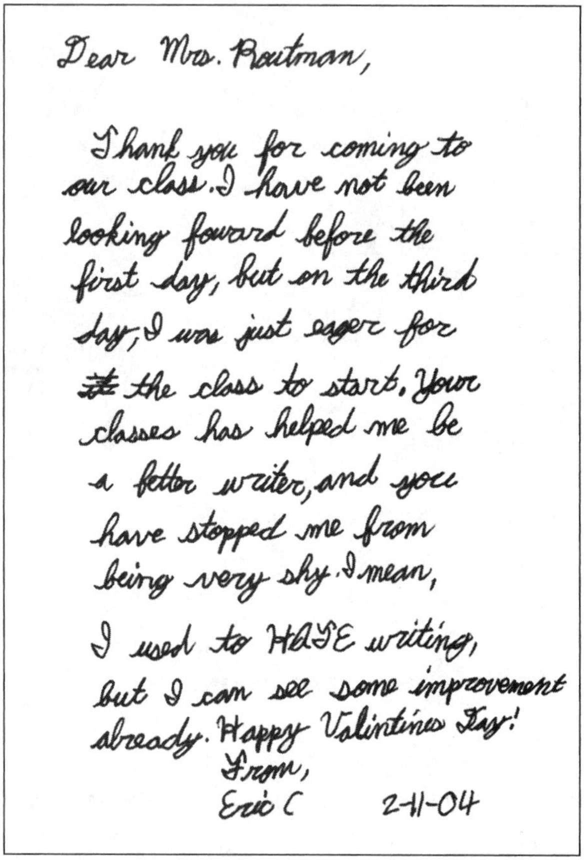

Dear Mrs. Raitman,

Thank you for coming to
our class. I have not been
looking foward before the
first day, but on the third
day, I was just eager for
the class to start. Your
classes has helped me be
a better writer, and you
have stopped me from
being very shy. I mean,
I used to HATE writing,
but I can see some improvement
already. Happy Valintines Day!
        From,
        Eric C   2-11-04

A student begins to see himself as a writer and finds writing enjoyable.

I expected it. Celebration made it easy for them to stay engaged, to see themselves as writers. (Later Eric, an English language learner and reluctant writer, wrote me the letter shown above.)

The celebration of children's writing needs to move right up front to become a major teaching goal. Too many of our students find writing painful, and much of that pain comes from too much concern with correctness at the expense of enjoyment. Enjoyment and writing have not coexisted, and they must do so if all our students are to become proficient writers. We are much more apt to do optimum work when we know our best efforts will be supported and celebrated and when we believe we can succeed.

Celebration benefits us teachers, too. Principal Melinda Jennings, in Vancouver, Washington, begins every staff meeting with celebrations of children's writing. Teachers bring student samples and read them aloud as they project them on a screen. Those celebrations generate schoolwide conversations about quality and what kids are capable of and get everyone "on the same page." Teachers are often inspired by the high-quality writing being done in their colleagues' classrooms.

Change the Status of Kids in the Classroom

Ari, who I've been told is dyslexic, tells me on the first day of a residency, "I hate writing." She is not a risk taker and doesn't believe she has anything to write about. Each day during optional sharing, her back is to the front of the room and she wedges herself between desks so she is almost invisible. But on the next to the last day of my residency, she positions herself almost face forward. After seeing other writers, especially Allen, a special education student, struggle and then be celebrated and affirmed, she finally writes, and effortlessly at that, two-and-a-half pages in just fifteen minutes, a triumph for her.

Celebrate your students' risk taking. Ask, *Who tried something new? Who rewrote a part that didn't work? Who has a great lead?* What we choose to celebrate sends a message about what we value, and that must be more than correct form and conventions if students are to say anything worthwhile.

Writing success has the power to transform kids, literally. They see themselves differently and more confidently, and their peers see them that way, too. I have seen a child grow taller right before my eyes because he now sees himself as a writer. He looks different. He holds his head higher, volunteers more in class, takes more risks, becomes less disruptive. This has happened so many times over the past several years that I have come to see writing success as transformative to the lives of students and to classrooms. Students who have been outside the classroom community are brought in as full-fledged members. For proof we need only look at the stories of Ari (above), Owen (page 22 and 292–304), Cory (pages 78–80), and Max (see the video clip and related notes on the accompanying DVD).

Turn Kids into Writers

I am working with a class of second graders and quickly learn that neither the students nor their teachers take much joy in writing. The requirements—personal narratives, reports, summaries, and more—are dutifully ground out but without much pleasure. Students see writing as performing for the teacher, generating something to fill up the nearest bulletin board, or preparing for high-stakes tests.

When I ask these second graders what they dislike about writing, Owen says, "It gives me a hand ache," and many students chime in that their hands get tired. I change my plans. Instead of writing a friendly letter this week, we will focus on the joy of writing. My planning is mostly, *how can I engage these students so they want to write and enjoy writing?* I know from years of experience that if students invest their minds and hearts in their writing, I can teach them everything they need to know about writing well. Truly, the hardest part is finding and creating a topic and purpose that will get them excited about writing. Once I do that, always going from whole-to-part-to-whole, the skills will follow.

Kids enter kindergarten loving school and full of the promise of possibilities. They see themselves as writers even if that writing is drawing and scribbling. Don Graves puts it best in the very first words of his landmark *Writing: Teachers and Children at Work*: "Children want to write." It is our job to ensure they don't lose that positive I-am-a-writer spirit.

However, as early as first grade, many children already dislike writing. Often, we kill off their writing spirit and energy with all the "stuff" we give them, all the talk of requirements, the lack of choice, the overfocus on correctness, and the pressure to do well on high-stakes tests. They become avoidance writers—that is, they write only what is required and take no pleasure or satisfaction in the task. Justin is typical. He handed me the letter shown below on the first day of our week together in his fifth-grade classroom. There would be no way I could

---

3MAR03

Dear Mrs. Routman,

    I want to tell you about my writing career.

    In first grade and second I knew how to write really good. My writing was full of imagination. My first story was about a garbage truck. I still have it!

    When I went to the third grade, I didn't like writing anymore. It started to get really boring. In first and second grade I got to write freely. In third grade we had to write about things that I didn't want to write about. I lost interest. Since then I've figured out that I like drawing and creative stuff.

    I hope that you get me interested in writing again!?!?

                Sincerely,
                Justin R.

improve Justin's writing abilities until he changed his perception of writing and how he viewed himself as a writer.

It takes so little to turn a student into a writer: a human connection, teacher modeling, supportive conversations before writing begins, an appreciation of the student's efforts, sincere affirmation, real writing for a purpose, and a reader that the student values. Teaching skills in isolation does not make students writers; neither does teaching to the test. And breaking writing into bits and pieces robs children of the joy of writing. When you ask students, "What makes good writing?" or "What makes this passage the author wrote memorable?" avoidance writers answer, "It has good spelling, handwriting, and punctuation." To which I reply, "But you couldn't *see* that as I read aloud. Listen again, what do you hear that makes the writing outstanding?"

Make Sure Writing Is Meaningful, Not Just Correct

One first-grade teacher found out she was emphasizing correctness and mechanics over content, ideas, and enjoyment when she asked her first graders to give her an idea for a class story they would write together.

Derrick said, "Always end with a period."

"Yes, that's true," she affirmed, "always use periods at the end of a sentence." Then she tried to get back on track. "What's another good idea for our story?" Another child volunteered, "Always start a sentence with a capital and remember to space."

This teacher recalls, "They said this while sitting on the floor looking at me, waiting for the writing 'fun' to begin. *Poor babies,* I thought. I had been so focused on the rubric and end-of-the-year writing scores that I drained the creativity right out of them."

When students get used to writing that is enjoyable and for a real purpose and audience, the results are quite different. In a fourth-grade class, when I ask, "How many of you like to write?" only a few students raise their hand. But, at the end of the week, after we have written "special moments" valentines (see page 201) to give to a friend or family, I ask the question again, and all the hands go up. "What do you like about it?" I ask them.

"It was easy. We got to choose what we wrote about."
"We already know a lot about what we would write about."
"We watched you write and saw your draft."
"We had time to think before we wrote."
"We got to talk and that helped."

Meet a Writer

Everyone knows a student like Owen. Owen entered second grade as a struggling reader and writer—according to his teacher, the lowest-performing student in the class. He spent much of first grade filling in one or two words at the end of sentences on a worksheet, so the teachers observing our lesson are surprised when he volunteers to talk about his "secrets" story. I deliberately choose him knowing he is "hard" and that the teachers will want to see how I work with him. (Truth be told, they also love to watch me squirm a bit.)

No one is prepared for what Owen accomplishes. After a scaffolded conversation with me (included in the five-day lesson plan Secrets of Second Graders, on pages 292–304), he is very focused and totally engaged for more than thirty minutes, and he doesn't want to stop writing. His finished draft (see below) has all the components of "good" writing—he has a lead, coherence, humor, organization, a satisfying ending—and I have not specifically mentioned these things. I have simply valued his story and helped him tell it.

Owen drafts his first complete story

WATCHING TV

One night when I was 5 I was watching TV in bed with the lights off. It was past my bed time. I heard Mom's footsteps in the kitchen. I jumped out of bed. I turned the TV off. She was checking on me. I pretended to be asleep. "Owen, were you watching TV?" I kept pretending to be asleep. Mom went back to the kitchen. Then when I got out of bed, I caught mom watching TV.

Start with a Story I always start with a story. In the residency work I do, I have a new first day of school almost every month. Stories are how I bond with kids—the stories I tell and read and write, the stories we write and then read together, the stories students tell and write. From "You won't believe what happened" to "Let me tell you about the time . . . ," stories are how we relate to one another in the world and form the necessary bonds that build trust. Family stories and traditions, everyday happenings—stories about our lives—are easy "hooks" for children to grab on to.

I want all students to be successful writers from day 1, and they are. Even students from low socioeconomic backgrounds with little knowledge of how written language works, can and do acquire that knowledge in school, especially when they have rich opportunities to hear and respond to stories.

Use Stories as a Springboard for Teaching and Learning

As kids listen to stories and sometimes dramatize them or draw them, they get ideas of their own—original ones or adaptations. Let students know stories happen everywhere—at home, in school, on the playground, on the bus, in the imagination. Stories get us going in our writing. One student, on meeting her teacher years later as an adult, told her, "What I remember most about our year together were the stories you told."

Through stories, we can teach and develop:

- ☐ Language and vocabulary.
- ☐ Listening and communication skills.
- ☐ Imaginative thinking.
- ☐ Comprehension.
- ☐ An appreciation for literacy.
- ☐ An awareness of story structure.
- ☐ An awareness of how to sequence ideas.
- ☐ An understanding of life and other cultures.
- ☐ An awareness of authors and illustrators and how they work

Acting out stories in dramatizations and Readers Theatre, at all grade levels, improves children's reading and writing and positively impacts their fluency, their ability to sequence and shape ideas, their understanding of how stories work, and their awareness of audience, to name just a few benefits. For English language learners of all ages, telling stories of their lives helps them develop their oral language facility, a necessity for writing and thinking clearly.

We also need to allow kids to experiment and play around with the pop culture stories in movies, video games, and sports. Many boys experience their greatest writing enjoyment and literacy growth when they can create their own pop culture stories, even though these stories appear to their teachers to be repetitive and sometimes gruesome.

Most of all, stories are fun, and fun is sadly missing from our classrooms these days. My four-and-a-half-year-old granddaughter, Katie, has already heard thousands of hours of stories and easily makes up her own. She adores stories of all kinds and will even sit still through rather lengthy chapter books like *Charlotte's Web* and *Charlie and the Chocolate Factory,* which contain few pictures. Even though she doesn't understand every word, she gets what the story is about and savors the language.

Ensure That All Your Students Hear Stories

Guard the time you have with your students. Kindergarten and first-grade teachers, especially, need to be strong advocates for keeping all students in the room during story time. Do your best to ensure that your students who most need to hear stories and rich language are not leaving the room for special classes when you are reading aloud and introducing shared language experiences. Hearing and talking about stories and creating our own are a great way to get kids' oral language going.

Oral language development and literacy skills are closely linked. Poor readers are less experienced as storytellers. Poor writers have good ideas but have difficulty with organization and structure. Stories are an entryway into reading and writing. Phonics and "the skills" only make sense once a student connects those skills with reading and writing real stories.

TRY IT APPLY IT

teaching tip

Journals

Avoid journal writing as morning seat work. Kids' writing gets worse. Kids don't need story starters; they need good teaching.

- Take stories apart with students and notice what makes them "good." Chart what the author did.

- Validate students' lives through regular journal writing in which students can tell the stories that matter to them.

- Take an objective look at your students' journals. Are they full of rich, detailed stories and topics they care about, or are they dutifully completing boring entries? One way to combat boring entries is by encouraging students to stick with the same story or topic for days or even weeks.

- Have an adult scribe (it doesn't always have to be you) take dictation for students who aren't ready to write (or aren't ready to write as much as they say) and then dramatize these students' stories. Talk about characters, setting, problem, etc. as the stories are being acted out.

- Publish class-authored and kid-authored stories regularly, and feature them in your classroom and school libraries.

Choose Your Topics Carefully

When I write in front of students and bonding with them is a major goal, I pick a story topic that:

- ☐ Is easy for students to relate to.
- ☐ Is appropriate to share with students.
- ☐ Is important to me.
- ☐ Lets students know more about me.
- ☐ Allows me to take some risks.

My topics are personal and commonplace and relate to everyday happenings: getting new glasses, having a hard time moving to a new place, taking care of my disabled father. Often, my stories are about things that happened when I was the students' age (see my "secrets" story on page 73 and my thinking/writing process in Teaching in Action: Lesson Essentials).

I always tell the story first before I write it. Saying the story out loud engages the students, lets me clarify my thinking, and reinforces the importance of conversation before writing. It also models the conversation—outer (with others) and inner (with yourself)—that I want students to have with their own writing.

Then, when I write, I make sure to include the details that fascinate. (Often I observe teachers tell a lively story and then just write down the bare-bones facts.) I pull out all the stops—recreating conversations, slowing down the writing with carefully chosen descriptive words, letting students in on my thinking and what I'm feeling. I try to emulate award-winning author Kate DiCamillo: "I put my heart on the page when I tell the story."

It is important to take a risk and share something personal about yourself that you are comfortable sharing. Our students will not easily share their life experiences in a meaningful, personal way until we share ours. If we write dry, boring stories when we model, we will get dry, boring stories from our students. If you have never written in front of your students before, take the plunge: they will appreciate your risk taking, and you will have a much clearer idea of what you are actually asking them to do.

Keep Your Students' Attention

I adjust the story I tell and the amount I write to the age and capacity of my students. I only write as much as I expect my students to write. It makes no sense to take the time to model a full page of writing when most of the students are able to write just a few sentences. Likewise, if the goal is for older students to

teaching tip

Keep It Clean!

Are your projected transparencies hard to read? Especially if you have an old overhead projector, clean the lens (as well as the glass top). You will need a small screwdriver to remove the lens in order to clean it, but you and your students will now be able to clearly see all the print on your screen.

**TRY IT
APPLY IT**

write and publish one excellent paragraph, model writing just one cohesive, interesting paragraph. (I write on a lined chart or projected transparency.)

Watch the clock. I always look at the time when I start. It's so easy to go on too long. I aim for ten or fifteen minutes, maximum. Otherwise, I lose students' attention, and I also lose precious time for students to write.

Focus on the content. You can't do everything at once. Avoid explaining why you're putting a capital letter here and a period there. And don't ask students, *What do I need here?* or *Why do you think I . . .?* This is your time to demonstrate, show possibilities, and get students excited about writing. Show your thinking out loud, and then just write. Write the words as you say them so students match your voice with the text.

With very young students, stretch out the sounds of the words as you write them. I tend not to ask students to help me spell words, because it slows the writing down too much, and my main purpose is showing good storytelling (although I will say, "*everyone, spell*-ing"—or whatever word or letter grouping we've been working on).

- Identify some topics that are easy for teachers and students to write about and that can help us bond with one another:
  - Start of school.
  - Special memory (summer, friendship, family, trip).
  - Best friend.
  - Family (parents, siblings, grandparents, other relatives).
  - Sports.
  - Pets.
  - Favorite movie, book, food, thing, place.
  - Being an expert.
- Pick a topic that resonates for you and that will let your students get to know you more. For example, if you write about being an expert, pick something like being a good friend or taking super-good care of your pet. What's important is that your modeling be everything you want your students' writing to be.

Write in Front of Your Students

The only preparation I do before writing is to think about what my topic will be and narrow that topic. Usually, I'll jot down three or four ideas on a sticky note. Here's my quick planning for writing about moving.

teaching tip

Talking through stories and possibilities before writing often helps to "find" the story you really want to tell.

After listing my subtopics, I think out loud, talking briefly about each one. Then I choose the one I most want to write about now and put a check mark next to it. (See page 63 for an example of a student circling her writing topic.)

I continue to make all my decisions in front of the students, beginning by saying something like this: *Kids, I'm going to be thinking out loud before I write and as I write my story. I'm doing that so that when you write you'll know what kind of thinking writers do.* Then I compose on a projected transparency or large (usually lined) chart.

> Moving to Seattle
> finding an apartment
> ✓ looking for a house
> taking care of my dad
> meeting new people
> feeling like home

Expand Personal Writing

teaching tip

Be sensible about illustrations. Some first grade journals, premade in the district, have room for pictures on every page; yet kids don't draw on every page and can use more writing space. Also, some children prefer to write first. As time goes on, have illustrating become an option.

Older students are often tired out from years of writing personal narratives. Besides journals, kids can write: brief memoirs from one period of their lives, photo-autobiographies, a moment from the timeline of their lives, favorite memories, snapshots (see Chapter 8), hero moments (see pages 323–329), friendly letters, cards, poems

Choose writing assignments (being sure to give lots of choice within an unobtrusive structure) that build classroom community and enjoyment and can become class publications. Some examples are:

- ☐ What we worry about.
- ☐ Our favorite places.
- ☐ A day we'll never forget.
- ☐ What we're experts at (what we're great at).
- ☐ The best thing we ever did.
- ☐ All about us.
- ☐ What we like (or dislike).
- ☐ Heart poems.
- ☐ Our pets.
- ☐ Secrets of second graders (kindergartners, whatever).

Connect Home and School Writing

Often the writing that students do freely at home (mostly stories and poems), which emerges from their own interests, far exceeds the quality of the work and effort they put into school writing, which they mostly see as mechanical and routine. Students will spend a substantial amount of time planning, writing, and revising when they are interested in the writing. See Taylor's writing on page 28.

Taylor's Writing: School/Home Contrasts

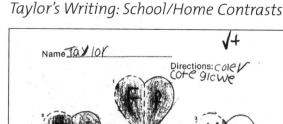

January, school writing

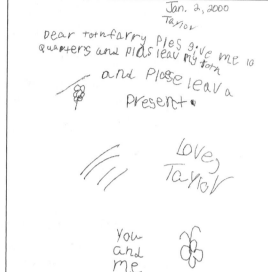

January, home writing

February, school writing

February, home writing

*The sun is very hot. It is on fire. The earth spins
around the sun. You do not need to worry that you
will spin around really fast some day.*

It's common sense that whenever we are able to engage students' interests, we will have higher-quality writing. Take a look at the work of kindergartner Taylor writing in school and writing at home (see page 28). Notice what she is being expected to do at school and independently chooses to do at home. The school writing is disconnected from her life and has no voice. It has been dutifully completed but without enthusiasm. The writing at home is more extensive, interesting, and of higher quality. Even the handwriting looks better, a typical outcome when students are invested in their writing. We teachers need to ensure that students experience the same interest and enjoyment in school writing. When we tap into students' interests, they are more likely to connect with all aspects of schooling.

Taylor, who is now ten years old and in fifth grade, says: "Give students choices! At one point in the day just let us do freewriting. I only got to do that once about every two weeks!"

See What Writers Do Well

My husband, Frank, is an artist. He "sees" the world in ways I am unable to. He looks very closely and misses little. As teachers, we need to view children's writing through a nurturing, positive lens and notice all the small and big things kids do well. Too often, we teachers are unable to "see" what children have accomplished. When we cannot, we lose them as writers. "We have to let children in on the secret of how powerfully they write."

See Their Brilliance

Independent writing time was coming to a close. These first graders were working on surprising stories, and I invited them to come and sit in the reading-writing corner and bring their stories. Those who wanted to could share. Wade brought his paper up to me before he sat down and said, "I've only written a little." He had written one sentence, crossed it out, and written it again. "Oh, that's fine," I said. "I can't wait to hear the start of your story." Those encouraging words prompted Wade to volunteer when I asked who would like to share, and I was able to build on what he had started so he could write more fluently the next day.

Such a simple thing. To recognize the writer for what he is attempting and help move him forward. I know that if Wade—or any student—can see himself as a writer, I can teach him all the skills he needs to know.

And this. After I read through the "heart" poems a group of students had written (the poems and lesson plan are on pages 305–315) and on the accompanying DVD), I was overwhelmed by the students' work. Assuming that the classroom teacher was as pleased as I was, I said to her, "Well, what did you think of the kids' poems?" I had expected her to comment on how powerful the writing was, and her answer floored me: "Well, they were a little better than the first ones." I practically screamed. "A little better. They were fabulous! I was knocked out by them." Now I understood why the students were not excited about writing and did not see themselves as good writers. This teacher would first need to "see" the worth of her students' writing before they would be able to see it.

Take a Leap of Faith

Cindy Coronado is a first-grade teacher in Westminster, Colorado, who had always been a "skills first" person. She admits that when a student did very little writing, she was not encouraging. As her beliefs began to change, she took a risk. Michael had written only "Happy Thanksgiving" on his paper after an entire writing period, and that had been copied from the board. While in the past she would have said, "That's not a story. You haven't done any work," she took a different tack and complimented him on his beginning. Then, as she helped him create his story through back-and-forth conversation and targeted questioning, she wrote his ideas and key words down on sticky notes. Feeling affirmed, Michael went back to his seat to complete his story. Rather than losing a writer, perhaps for the whole year, Cindy gained one.

Cindy had evidence of that success by the end of the school year. Michael's parents proudly told Cindy that, without any prompting, Michael now came home from school and wrote notes to family members. On his own initiative, he also wrote a thank-you note to his karate teacher. Cindy said, "I am so proud of the growth that he has made."

See the Light—Write Poetry

One day when I was having a difficult time writing and had been stuck behind my desk for hours, Frank said, "Come take a walk with me. Take time to see the light." From where I sat it was a cloudy day. However, one of the delights of moving to Seattle has been the extraordinary light—on the water, in the ever-changing skies, over the mountains, through the trees. I love that light, but I miss seeing it many days because I fail to slow down and take the time to see it.

Leonard Cohen has written:

> Ring the bells that still can ring.
> Forget your perfect offering.
> There is a crack in everything.
> That's how the light gets in.

I love that poem for what it says about life and teaching—being able to see the light, not searching for the silver-bullet program, appreciating what's here. I love writing and reading poetry for the same reasons. I can explore light and feeling and rhythm and anything on my mind as freely as I choose without worrying about perfect form. The president of the Poetry Foundation of America, which aspires to expand the audience for poetry, says, "Poetry helps us live better, helps us understand the human experience."

Of all the writing I have ever done with students, poetry brings the most joy, ease, and success for both students and teachers. I am not talking about poetry by formula here (acrostics, limericks, cinquain, haiku) but the kind of poetry most people in the world read and write—free verse. One of the best things about poetry is that kids get to play around with language and have fun with it. Such playfulness helps develop children's interest in language, which carries over to other forms of writing.

Once we've shown them the possibilities, students can write poems all year long, and they do: for special occasions such as holidays and Mother's and Father's Day, to summarize what they've learned, to record what they wonder and imagine, for themselves and for each other. My classes always publish a beautiful classroom anthology, which serves as a model for other classes (see pages 305–315 and the DVD).

Make Enjoyment Central to Teaching Writing—Let the Fun Begin

Marquita is a fourth grader who spent her entire school year preparing for the high-stakes writing test. I interviewed Marquita halfway through the school year, after her mother approached me about her writing. She was concerned about the way her daughter was being taught and graded and troubled that Marquita disliked writing so much.

At my first meeting with Marquita, she showed me some of the writing she did in school—daily oral language exercises and five paragraphs about a person from a "giant culture project." She described writing at school as having to "write a lot" and "to rewrite a whole lot." All writing was assigned; she never got to choose the topic. When I looked at the papers she brought me, I was struck by the teacher's comments and marks, in red and blue ink, all over her writing. Every comment was related to form and correctness: *not a sentence, need more detail, indent every paragraph*. All the misspelled words were circled; every error in grammar, punctuation, and capitalization was noted and corrected. I could not find one positive comment anywhere even though the content of Marquita's writing was adequate.

Here are some of the things Marquita told me as we talked:

- ☐ "When the teacher goes over my paper, she only checks spelling, not ideas."
- ☐ "I don't like daily oral language. I have to rewrite all the sentences when I make a mistake."
- ☐ "My teacher expects me to write a lot. But once I'm done she doesn't really help me learn that much. We write a draft. Then the teacher says, 'Check over your copy before you put it on the computer.'"

April 9, 2003

Dear Fourth Graders,

I don't like writing, and Mrs. Routman says you enjoy writing. I would like to know how it can be fun.

In class we have to do three or four pages of writing for one assessment. We do one assessment every week. My teacher puts a lot of red marks on my papers and barely says "great" or "nice job." She gives the kids a checklist, and, on it, it says you need seven to ten adjectives and five adverbs. It also says each sentence in a paragraph must start with a different word, and we can't have any dead words like "said." She makes us use a thesaurus to find better and more detailed words.

We never get to choose what we want to write about so we don't have many ideas. If we don't get much down, we have to go to study hall that goes on during recess. If we get half done, we take it home for homework.

I would appreciate it if you would tell me how writing can be fun. That would be great!

Sincerely,
Marquita

A student explains why she dislikes writing in school

April 15, 2003

Dear Marquita,

Writing can be alot of fun. Since your teacher makes you write about certain things. sometimes you can write stuff like poems, stories, comics, any kind of writing at your house and that can be alot of fun. I like writing because I can write my favorite-writing a comic. Sometimes I write poems or letters or auto-biographys, but my favorite thing to write is comics. Now here is a little comic strip for you to enjoy!

A.O.T.A.
Attack Of the Aliens

One night I saw a shooting star well t-hats what I thought it was.

The next day I saw a big hole in my backyard and...

I called the police they got here fast and... To be continued.

I hope you enjoyed the comic strip and I hope you have a nice day.

Sincerely,
Andy

April 15, 2003

Dear Marquita,

I know you don't like writing, but sometimes it can be fun! You just have to find what you do best.

Write in something that is personally yours. A diary would work. I use a diary. Write many things to see what you do best. Write a story, write poems, songs, comics, anything that you enjoy. Write nonsense, make your story come to life. Write about what makes you happy sad, or even mad.

Another thing you can do is quick writes. My class does them. A quickwrite is a short story done in a short period of time. This is something you may enjoy.

Sincerely,
Sarah P
Ms. Kari's class

April 18, 2003

Dear Marquita,

I heard that you are having problems writing, and I hope I can change that so you can have as much fun with writing as I have with my writing.

What I like about writing is I'm the one who makes the story funny, scary, or even dramatic. But my very favorite thing about writing is me having fun writing the story and knowing that the reader will have fun reading the story too. Writing is one of my favorite parts of the day because I get to write my thoughts on a piece of paper.

I hope that I helped you with making you have more fun with writing and enjoying writing as much as I like writing. Good luck!

Your friend,
Paige B

Fourth-grade students in Kari Oosterveen's class respond to Marquita's letter

I told Marquita, honestly, that I worked with lots of fourth graders and that her writing looked pretty good to me. She looked at me in disbelief. She was flabbergasted when I told her I knew lots of kids who loved to write: "I'm shocked that kids can like writing. I'd like to know how people actually have fun doing it."

Eager to change Marquita's negative perception of writing, I asked her if she would be willing to write to fourth graders at the school where I had just completed a writing residency. She wrote the draft shown on page 32 without any help and completed it in fifteen minutes. We sent her draft, along with a word processed copy I did "for free," to all the fourth graders in the other school. She received about fifty letters back (three of them are shown on page 33).

After Marquita had completed fifth grade, I spoke with her mom, Nancy Curry, who told me, "The letters helped Marquita know that it might be possible to enjoy writing. She got ideas from some of the kids' letters. As a fifth grader, she wrote songs on her own at home. She started writing again."

Unfortunately, I am seeing more and more students, like Marquita, who dislike writing. In the frenzy of our pressured testing culture, many teachers and administrators are overemphasizing correctness and teaching to the test. The result is that while many of our students can write to a prompt and pass the test, they do not know how to write in other forms and they rarely choose to write. They fail to see the power of writing—writing as thinking, writing as communicating, writing as having fun with language. They see writing as drudgery and themselves as workers, not writers.

All students, especially those who begin school with limited literacy skills, need to think of themselves as readers and writers, see the processes as meaningful, and have positive attitudes about literacy before they can successfully engage in literacy practices. More and more of our students are culturally and linguistically diverse and are at risk of educational failure, and these numbers are increasing. So we need to pay close attention to what works. And it's not more programs. These students are most successful with contextualized, social learning—not isolated drills and skills. Writing for actual communication is one of the most effective—and enjoyable—ways to bring them into the literacy community.

Certainly, my goal in *Writing Essentials* is to help your students pass the test, but that's the easy part. Really. If you teach writing well—if your students write for readers they value; if they put their minds and hearts into their work; if they are able to choose their writing topics; if they willingly revise, edit, and publish because they care about their readers; if they develop a spelling consciousness— they will become lifelong writers. And, that, dear reader, is my main goal—to become your collegial partner in transforming the teaching of writing so that students not only become proficient writers but also joyful and confident writers whose unique voices engage their readers. Teaching, supporting, and expecting kids to do their best is where the fun begins.

3. Share Your Writing Life

When I was younger I enjoyed writing a lot, but
I've done less and less of it as I've gotten older.
Also, somewhere along the way,
I've lost confidence in myself as a writer.
—Cami Kostecki, second-grade teacher

I know what you're thinking. You're not a writer, so maybe you'll just skip this chapter. Shift your thinking. You are a writer. Allow the possibility to sink in. Read on.

The simple fact is we have to see ourselves as writers if we are to teach writing well. This is no easy feat. Doing the task and feeling competent at it are two different things. One of the toughest parts of teaching writing is that, collectively, we teachers haven't had many positive writing experiences in our own schooling. Added to that, our knowledge of how to teach writing has been limited, through no fault of our own. Most colleges and universities still do not require or even offer writing courses as part of teacher education. Most of us have been left to fend for ourselves with few writing models, little confidence, and scant support. No wonder so many educators embrace published programs, even though most of them prove to be of so little help.

A terrific resource, however, is right at hand. All of us are writers, even though we often don't view ourselves as such. In the course of living and working, we write communications of all kinds: notes, cards, emails, faxes, lists, plans, parent newsletters, college papers, journals, letters, and more. When we begin to take a close look at how we think, compose, revise, edit, and publish, we inform our teaching.

One of the best ways to begin to view ourselves as writers is to write together as a staff. Writing together creates opportunities for closer collegial interaction, sensitizes us to how we teach writing in our classrooms, and increases our confidence as writers. When the writing purpose, audience, and topic are worthwhile to teachers, most discover that they are, in fact, able writers. As one fifth-grade teacher remarked after completing such a writing task, "I found out I'm as good a writer as my colleagues. That surprised me and also gave me more confidence."

Bond As a Staff by Writing Together

On one of my return visits to a school where the staff and I had been working on teaching writing for two years, the teachers felt ready to write themselves and requested we take the time to do so. Up until that time, the effort had seemed too risky for some. But now they all realized that if they were to teach writing well, they first needed to see themselves as writers and examine their own processes. I took the invitation as an opportunity to demonstrate my own writing process and, more important, to use writing as a way for me to bond with the staff and have them further bond with one another. Bonding as a staff is not just a "feel good" activity; staffs that are more collegial and collaborative have higher achievement in writing and reading.

To begin, I talked, thought aloud, and wrote in front of them about a school memory that changed me. I deliberately chose an experience in which I had felt vulnerable. If I want teachers to be risk takers, I need to be willing to take risks in their presence so they can do the same when writing in front of their students.

The memory I chose was of a final exam I took in a philosophy of education course in graduate school. As one part of the exam and without advance notice, we were asked to write our own test question and answer it. It was the first time I could remember being asked by a teacher what I thought was important. It had a profound effect on me. I relished deciding on and constructing an important question that would demonstrate my knowledge of important content. The experience stretched me, made me feel smart, and gave me confidence. I did well on the test, but that seemed less important than the opportunity to think about and synthesize what I deemed most significant.

After I wrote my draft in front of them, I gave the teachers some time to think about what they might write. Then, in front of the whole group, I talked with one teacher about the incident she remembered. This public conversation (*What happened? Why is it important to you? How did the experience change or influence you?*) was a model both for how these teachers might think about this particular writing experience and for how I interact with students before they write. (See pages 336–350 in lesson plans for an example of such a conversation.) Next, sitting together at tables, each teacher told his or her story as the listeners asked for clarification and gave affirmation. After telling their story of a school memory, the teachers began to write them down. Finally, several teachers shared what they had written.

What we did adheres to an optimal learning model (see inside cover page and the schematic shown on page 11), which I use in all my teaching:

- ☐ Demonstration (my writing and thinking aloud).
- ☐ Shared demonstration (my conversation with the single teacher).
- ☐ Guided practice (the teachers' conversations with one another as they shared their stories).
- ☐ Independent practice (each teacher writing his or her story individually).
- ☐ Celebration and sharing.

Observe What You Do and Note the Teaching Implications

I asked these teachers to be *metacognitive* as they wrote; that is, to observe and think about their own writing habits, needs, and thoughts in the process of writing. Noticing and valuing our own behavior has the power to inform and transform our teaching. What works for us as writers is important to bring into the classroom. Here are some of the statements teachers made about the experience:

- ☐ "Talking before writing helped."
- ☐ "Listening to others' stories gave me ideas."
- ☐ "I became aware of how messy my draft was. Yet, I always require neatness from my students."
- ☐ "When I read my piece out loud, it sounded better than if someone else read it. It also helped me see where I wanted to make changes."
- ☐ "I kept thinking about putting in voice and elaboration, and it distracted me. Then, I just wrote, and the writing flowed."

After writing together as a staff, several teachers said they would now change their classroom practices to:

☐ Make more time for conversation around writing.

☐ Focus more on the content and less on the messiness of the draft.

☐ Encourage students to read their writing aloud (to themselves, a peer, or the teacher) as part of writing and revising.

☐ Stop emphasizing writing as discrete elements (voice, detail, transitions, etc.).

These teachers were also struck by how much closer they felt as a staff. When many teachers volunteered to read their pieces aloud, the room grew quiet. Their writing revealed diverse, unique voices. Many of the stories touched our hearts. When someone, regardless of age or profession, writes something of importance and reads it aloud, the audience pays attention because its members are personally moved by the writing.

As part of this residency, we published a booklet containing everyone's story. On the final day, we read the booklet aloud, and there was silence and awe in the room. Almost every school memory was sad or painful. We came to know one another better. Teachers spontaneously approached their colleagues to say how sorry they were for what had happened in the past or how the writing had filled them with emotion. (Inadvertently, two teachers' wonderful pieces were omitted from the final booklet. Their disappointment showed us all the power of publishing and the need for care and sensitivity to every writer.)

Make Time for Your Staff to Write Together

In most schools, teachers are not eager to write and are always pressed for time. To help make the writing I want teachers to do easy and fast, I've come up with something I call "snapshot writing." These are short, personal pieces (revealing something that colleagues don't know about you), written in about fifteen minutes or so and, later, published in a booklet. This on-demand writing is similar to what we often ask of our students. We give an assignment, perhaps a prompt, and expect them to write on the spot.

- Give us a snapshot: write something about yourself the staff doesn't know, some little thing that tells us more about you.

- Use the following teachers' observations of their own writing process to think about your writing and teaching:

  - *I did lots of rereading to get ideas, for flow.*
  - *I was frantic at first (because of the teacher audience). I didn't know what I was going to write about.*
  - *It was hard to get started. I needed planning time. Made me think of my kids.*
  - *Once I got the first few sentences down, I was fine.*
  - *I focused on organization as I wrote.*
  - *I learned it didn't need to be a big production.*
  - *I was surprised at how much writing got done in just ten minutes.*
  - *I chose a "safe" topic (I'm a new teacher; I'm not part of the community yet; I'm still getting to know the staff).*

Whenever I use the snapshot exercise, many teachers feel pressured by the short time frame, and some are reluctant to share after hearing their colleagues' stories, thinking, *mine's not as good as theirs.* One time all the examples I used were humorous, and some teachers were afraid to write a serious piece. So I've learned that it's important to model many possibilities before teachers write.

In all the schools where we've written these snapshots together as a staff, the results have been very positive. We get to know colleagues better, we trust one another more, we take risks as writers, and we examine our own processes. My snapshots have included my mania for shoes, stage fright at public speaking (see next page), and being painfully shy as a child. Other teachers have written about sneaking out at night in high school, getting a speeding ticket, cross stitching to relax, being addicted to weather reports (see next page), and singing with a rhythm-and-blues band.

Every time I lead a whole-staff writing exercise like this, afterward I ask, "What would have happened if I had said to you just before you wrote: don't forget to paragraph, use excellent word choice, vary the length and structure of your sentences, and be sure to get your voice in there?" Without exception, every teacher and principal has said, "I wouldn't have been able to write." A teacher in Houston, Texas, commented: "This was so revealing and informative. I always tell my kids, 'Read your papers over and look at your word choice.' But I found I liked my writing just as it was and didn't want to change my words. This experience will change my focus with my students."

Each staff writing ends with sharing. With snapshot writing, five staff members can share in just five minutes. We don't comment or criticize, we celebrate—we listen to each piece and applaud it. Celebration helps us feel like successful writers.

Partly Cloudy

We interrupt this regularly scheduled writing for a weather report. Oh goody, the weather is on. I admit it. I'm addicted to watching the weather. I especially like Mike Nelson-Channel 9. I have even gone as far as watching the four o'clock weather and then watch the nine o'clock weather too, you know, just to be sure. O.K. call me crazy, but call me when the weather is on!

By
Debbie Fowler

STAGE FRIGHT
Regie Routman

I get incredibly nervous every time I speak before a large audience. I don't sleep the night before, I have an upset stomach, I have trouble eating; in short, I'm a total wreck. It's only after I begin speaking that my nervousness disappears and my confidence returns. I actually enjoy public speaking very much once I'm actually doing it. But, before I start to speak, I am nothing but jitters—even after all these years.

Two pages from "Our Stories Come to School"

Arapahoe Ridge Elementary School teachers in Westminister, Colorado, reading their pieces aloud. Teachers publish these in "Our Stories Come to School"

Examine Your Life as a Writer

Many teachers ask, in regard to teaching their students, "Should I begin with paragraphing, voice, organization?" or something to that effect. But think about how you begin when *you* are starting to write. My hunch is you begin, as I do, with your reader in mind, whether you're writing a newsletter to parents, a letter to a friend, a query to a company, or a note to your partner.

The next time you sit down to write, examine your process:

- [ ] What are you thinking about while you are composing?
- [ ] What exactly do you do to plan, to get started, to continue when you get stuck, to complete your piece?
- [ ] What do you focus on as you are writing?
- [ ] What does the process look like for you? Do you write straight through? stop to reread? revise as you go? look up information? edit?

Apply what you do as a writer to teaching your students.

Look at Your Writing Practices

Some years ago, when a few kindergarten teachers and I were reexamining the predominance of journal writing to the exclusion of other forms of writing in our classrooms, I recorded all the writing I did for one month and used my findings to adjust my teaching practices. I added poetry, notes, cards, letters of all kinds, book reviews, and advice to others to our kindergarten writing curriculum (as well as to that of all other grades). The students, who had previously struggled with writing or complained about "doing journals," blossomed. I also looked at my own writing practices and used what I do to influence how I taught.

MY WRITING PRACTICES

- [ ] Write every day.
- [ ] Write what I care about.
- [ ] Write for a purpose and audience that matters.
- [ ] Write to think, discover, and communicate.
- [ ] Plan and organize before I write, as I go along, and after I write.
- [ ] Think about my writing-in-process throughout the day.
- [ ] Revise, polish, proofread, and edit.
- [ ] Seek and consider response.
- [ ] Write in various genres.
- [ ] Work on more than one piece of writing at a time.
- [ ] Write mostly letters, cards, notes, memos, lists, emails.
- [ ] Write poetry for myself and others.
- [ ] Keep writer's notebooks.
- [ ] "Read like a writer" (notice what authors do).

TRY IT APPLY IT

Look at Your Writing Practices

- Look at the writing you are teaching and assigning students. Make sure it is not all just school-based writing.
- Take an inventory of the writing you've done this past week or month. How does what you wrote impact what and how you teach about writing?
- Make your own "My Writing Practices" list. Does it align with what you do in the classroom?

Tell Students Why You Write

Our students need to see that our purpose for writing is genuine, that we write with readers in mind even if the readers are ourselves. Students need to know why good writing matters and why conventions have to be correct.

I bring in letters about to be mailed, show the writing paper I use, perhaps read a sentence or two. Kids are always surprised that writing is a real-life activity. When I write letters with students (see pages 200–203), someone always asks, "You mean we're really going to mail these?"

Think About Keeping a Teacher Reflection Notebook

Part of being a writer and teacher is being a teacher–researcher. I am always asking questions, listening, observing, speculating, changing, clarifying, raising new questions for myself and other teachers. I jot down my thinking—so I don't lose it and can return to it later—in an ordinary spiral notebook I always carry with me. In writing this book, I went back to my notebooks and reread, questioned, rethought, and came to new conclusions. Teachers find that recording ideas while they are fresh reduces planning time and increases teacher effectiveness.

Write to Learn

Writing enhances thinking and helps develop it. Most of us don't understand this sophisticated concept—writing as thinking—until we experience it as writers ourselves. Our students think writers have all the information in their heads and just put it all down. Don't we wish it were so! I didn't learn that you write to figure out what you know and don't know, to problem-solve, organize, and work through confusions until I did lots of writing.

Two gifted authors of many acclaimed books tap into this phenomenon. Toni Morrison says, "I write out of ignorance. . . . It's what I don't know that stimulates me. I merely know enough to get started." And Wallace Stegner notes, "We do not write what we know; we write what we want to find out." You are in good company if writing is hard for you and you don't know what you're going to say till you "mess around" with thinking on the page. That is how writers work. Let your students in on that writing secret.

- Bring in correspondence you're about to mail. Tell students why you wrote the pieces, and describe your process. Seal stamped letters in front of them.
- Print out emails and faxes you sent and show your students. (You don't have to read them aloud.)
- Save notes, jottings, lists, plans, and show them to your students.
- If you keep a journal, diary, or reflection notebook, let your students know. (You can show it to them without reading from it.)
- Show examples of how you used writing to figure out what you wanted to say.

Connect Your Reading Life with Writing

Good writers are good readers. Make the connection for and with your students. Talk about books you are currently reading and what you plan to read next; talk about how you browse, choose, and read books and how you organize your home library. I also talk about how, what, and why I read and how that reading impacts my writing. I let students know that I keep a reading record and make an effort to read a variety of good literature, that I cannot work effectively as a writer without being an avid reader. I show the books I am currently reading and about to read. I show the writing I am currently doing. I let students know I pay attention to what authors do.

I also show students my writing notebook, in which I record inspiring and beautifully written passages so I can go back to them for the pleasure of rereading them (and perhaps to borrow an idea for my own writing). I let students know I notice how authors craft their writing because I find great writing fascinating and because I am always looking to become a better writer.

How I use reading and writing in my life greatly impacts what I do in the classroom. Classroom writing pieces that have grown directly from my reading habits include:

- ☐ Creating a top-ten list of favorite books (and revising it monthly).
- ☐ Book reviews (there are no book reports except in school).
- ☐ Book blurbs.
- ☐ Stories.
- ☐ Poems.
- ☐ Letters (to an editor or person you hope to influence).
- ☐ Author profiles.
- ☐ Keeping a notebook—quotations of memorable writing.

TRY IT APPLY IT

- If you are not an avid reader and do not see yourself as a writer, work on changing that. Start a book group/writing group with your colleagues.

- How does what you read impact how and what you write? Discuss your findings with colleagues. What are the teaching implications?

- Discuss with your students, "Who are our favorite authors? Why? What do we notice about their writing? What are the possibilities for our writing?" Keep a classroom chart of your findings.

Find Your Own Voice

There's lots of talk and emphasis on putting voice—the writer's unique personality made visible on the page—into writing. And while, clearly, writing is far more interesting to read when we sense the writer behind the writing, we need to be cautious that we don't teach voice as an end in itself (see the story of Andrew, on page 146). It's become common practice to spend weeks devoted to teaching kids how to write with voice. Students dutifully do what we ask them to, but little of this transfers to their everyday writing. As one student told me, "I know what my teacher wants, so I do it because she asks for it." Clearly, this is not what we're after. We want students to put voice into their writing because they value their reader and their writing purpose, know about the craft of writing, and want to put their unique stamp on what they're trying to say.

Donald Graves once said, "You can't expect students to write with voice until the teacher has one." Notice what you do when you write. Are you thinking about putting voice into your writing, or are you thinking about how best to communicate with and engage your reader? My hunch is that like me, you are focusing on your message and that your voice comes through because you are writing something of importance and that you care about your reader (even if that reader is yourself).

Donald Murray, Pulitzer prize–winning author and prolific writer and journalist, advises us on how to develop our own voice. Read aloud as you are writing and after you write. Notice the qualities that feel right to you and choose one and develop it.

"[Those qualities] are you, and your task, as an artist, is to bring your vision of our world to us in your own words. Start today. . . ."

Use Writing to Bond with Your Students

Through demonstrating our own writing process in front of students, doing lots of shared writing, and choosing writing topics we think will help us all bond, we go a long way toward fostering excellent writing habits in our classrooms. Just as important, such writing is powerful for building a classroom community—that is, a safe haven where all the voices are heard, known, and respected, even those of the writers who struggle most.

At the start of the school year, especially, writing is a powerful way to get to know your students, have your students get to know you, and set a positive, enjoyable tone for the writing classroom. When students enjoy writing, feel successful, and understand and value its purpose, they stop asking, "How long does it have to be?"

Try the start-of-the-year writing exercise below, (see my modeling on page 46), the "secrets" lesson (see pages 292–304), or the "heart poems" lesson (see pages 305–315) to begin bonding with your students.

Let Students See You Struggle

One of the most powerful ways for students to grow as writers is to watch you write—to observe you plan, think, compose, revise, and edit right in front of them, pretty much off the cuff. Very few of us just write down page after flowing page. Students need to see and hear our in-the-head thinking as we change our mind, "mess up," make adjustments, do everything "real writers" do. Remember what Nancie Atwell says, "You only have to write a little bit better than your students for them to take something away from your writing." Even if you are terrified to write, keep that wise statement in mind, and give writing in front of your students a try. Fourth-grade teacher Darcy Ballentine notes, "I always felt like I had to have everything perfect *before* I wrote so the kids could 'get it,' but it's the actual struggle that helps them learn."

In a recent workshop for teachers and principals, the participants and I focused on starting the year by writing poetry. Before expecting them to write a

---

WRITING EXERCISE FOR START OF SCHOOL YEAR

Choose 1

Add simple criteria for you and your students.

Go through writing process (note how you plan, write, confer, edit—insights for teaching)

- ☐ About yourself (for class book)
- ☐ Recent favorite book (for bulletin board of favorite books)
- ☐ **"Capture a moment" from the summer (class book)**
- ☐ The meaning of your name (book of names/nicknames)
- ☐ Your favorite room (could be illustrated and labeled)

CAPTURING A MOMENT FROM THE SUMMER

Criteria:

- ☐ What happened?
- ☐ Why remember it?
- ☐ How did it make you feel?

(Show draft [written in 5–7 minutes]. If I can complete a paragraph in 5 minutes, then students can do so in 10 minutes.)

> "We made it to the top, and we hadn't been sure we could do it. Now the feeling was glorious, and the view breathtaking. We were at the end of a two-and-a-half-mile-steep trail on Mt. Rainier. We looked around and below and saw meadows of wild flowers bursting with color, a shimmering lake, an eagle soaring overhead in a cloudless blue sky, and an unobstructed view of the majestic mountain. What a perfect reward for our hard climb."

Observations of my process:

- ☐ Reread as I went along—helped my composing, made cross-outs and changes and additions.
- ☐ Realized I needed an ending sentence, hard to do, required time, rest flowed easily, had to reread many times and am still not satisfied with ending I wrote.
- ☐ Topic sentence is in the middle (third sentence).

(My modeling for teachers before they wrote about their own moment and observed their own writing process.)

---

poem themselves, I wrote two short ones on the spot, and we also wrote one poem together in a shared writing demonstration (for a discussion of shared writing, see Chapter 5).

Several participants who had never before written a poem later told me that seeing my struggle gave them the confidence to write their very first poem. As one principal put it, "When I saw you, an accomplished writer, have trouble deciding what to say and how to say it, I thought to myself, *Maybe I can do this.*"

Lastly, don't be afraid to be yourself. Students are more likely to find their own voices when our true voices come through. One teacher told me, "I've never thought of myself as a good writer so I tried to impersonate what I thought a good writer would do. I finally realized I needed to be me."

Do Your Composing "On the Spot"

Many teachers do their demonstration writing behind the scenes. As conscientious teachers who are at the same time fearful about writing, they want to do their modeled writing ahead of time, to be prepared. Then, they show students the finished writing as part of their demonstration or minilesson. This robs students of the opportunity to see real-life writing in process and diminishes the learning possibilities.

Just as important, such overplanning creates unnecessary work for the teacher. Use that time instead to enrich your life—visit with a friend, take a walk, read a book, cook a favorite dish. These activities will leave you with more energy and enthusiasm for the hard work of teaching.

One more point. When we try to simulate writing "on the spot" by copying writing we have already done onto a chart or projected transparency, the lesson we teach is one of accurately copying the message rather than authentically composing it. What our students need to see demonstrated is exactly what we are asking them to do—write on demand, within a set time.

Get to Know Writing as a Recursive Process

When you begin to trust what you do as a writer, you will become a better writing teacher. You will notice that writing is recursive, not linear. Recursive means "to go back"; it includes the hesitating, reformulating, rewriting, and looking ahead we do when we write. That is, as we write we continue to plan or prewrite, draft, make changes as we reread, edit as we go along, all in the process of getting our thoughts down.

Be Realistic About Planning Before Writing

While planning before and during writing is a necessity, that planning rarely needs to be elaborate or time-consuming. In fact, most of the writing we do requires quick planning. For almost all demonstrations that I do—including the poetry writing I just described—I jot down a few notes/key ideas on a sticky note, just bare-bones information to help me get started. Taking a look at how and what we plan as adult writers can be very helpful to our teaching practices.

For example: in order to understand better what students are expected to do on the required state writing test, an entire elementary faculty and I responded to a writing prompt from a former state test. To our surprise, we found that not one of us made a graphic organizer as a way to plan our writing. Most of us did some kind of brainstorming or listing of ideas. Again, when these same teachers did the start-of-the-year writing exercise on pages 45–46, no one produced any kind of written plan. They all planned as they went along, visualized what they wanted to say, or just began to write.

These were eye-opening experiences, because many of these teachers spent a lot of time teaching—and expecting—all students to make some sort of visual organizer or elaborate plan for every piece of writing. Teaching planning devices is necessary, but do take a careful look at your own prewriting/planning techniques and apply common sense to the whole process (pages 179–184 contain a discussion on prewriting techniques).

Observe Your Composing Process

Even professional writers are rarely able to produce final copy in a first draft. For most of us, myself included, the composing process is difficult and complex. One of the reasons I always try to get teachers to write is so they experience what it is they are asking students to do. The writer is always making decisions and reviewing as she goes along, and many of these decisions are made quickly during the act of writing:

- ☐ *How should I begin?*
- ☐ *Should I say it this way or that way?*
- ☐ *Will it sound better if I change this word, this line?*
- ☐ *I better reread this to figure out what to say next.*
- ☐ *I need to reread again to hear how it sounds.*
- ☐ *Will my reader be pleased with the way I'm saying this?*
- ☐ *Does this make sense?*
- ☐ *Have I been too wordy, repeated myself, rambled?*
- ☐ *What can I leave out? What's still missing that I need to add?*

In making these decisions, the writer, among other things, considers the following:

WHAT A WRITER DOES
- ☐ Rereads, often out loud, a few times to get an idea of what to say next.
- ☐ Thinks ahead to what to say next.
- ☐ Moves things around to see if the text sounds better one way or another.
- ☐ Adds headings and starts new paragraphs to make it easier to follow.
- ☐ Goes back to the beginning to check for coherence and where to go next.
- ☐ Rereads, out loud or silently, to hear what's missing, what's confusing, what doesn't seem to work, what's working well—all under the umbrella of *will this work for my reader?*

All of this composing and revisiting of the text requires energy, confidence, and much writing practice—all the more reason we have to ensure immediate success for all writers. Our students are more likely to experience such success when they see us write and think of us as writers.

Observing our own writing process helps us decide what to emphasize with our students. When I seek response from colleagues and the first thing they comment on is grammar or spelling or where I need to improve, I am deflated. I want to know what the reader likes and how the reader was impacted by the writing before hearing suggestions.

My own memory of being edited too soon makes it easy for me to delay the editing focus until *after* students have a clear message to a reader. Every time I gave a book chapter draft to a colleague for response and she or he marked up my draft with corrections of grammar, spelling, and conventions, I was distracted from giving my full attention to improving the content. Once those correction marks were on the paper, I found them hard to ignore. They also drained my energy, because I felt I had to attend to both content and mechanics as I reworked the writing.

TRY IT APPLY IT

- ✐ Deliberately notice what you do as you compose. Are you doing one thing at a time or are you working on ideas, word choice, and organization interactively? How are you handling voice? Are you thinking about sentence fluency? When and how do you do most of your editing? What does all this mean for your teaching?

- ✎ When you write aloud in front of kids be sure that you don't just write but that they hear your thinking before you put pen to paper and as you are writing.

- ✐ If it is difficult for you to write in front of your students, first observe a colleague you trust.

- ✐ If you are new to writing aloud in front of your students, make a copy of the decisions list on page 48 and keep the list in front of you at first as a helpful guide for knowing what to say and do.

Increase Your Writing Enjoyment

Before students can enjoy writing, we teachers need to enjoy it. Chances are, your memories of school writing may not be positive. I still cannot use a red pencil—ever—when I'm working with students because it reminds me of all those teacher correction marks on my papers.

A teacher who did not see herself as a writer wrote to me about her change in attitude:

> I have continued to model myself as a writer in class. This has made me enjoy writing again. I love sharing my own stories with my class. I am even beginning to write to family and friends again. One of my friends and I have started to keep a traveling journal.

Start by writing with your colleagues. Close your door and think and write aloud in front of your students. Write fewer emails and more letters. Write a note complimenting a colleague or remembering a birthday. Pen the words yourself. Lose yourself on the page. You are a writer. Envision yourself as a writer.

Two

Teaching Essentials

BEING ABLE TO WRITE WELL NOT ONLY MAKES STUDENTS MORE EFFECTIVE COMMUNICATORS, IT ALSO GIVES THEM MORE ENJOYMENT, PRIDE, AND INDEPENDENCE, AND THAT, IN TURN, INCREASES THEIR MOTIVATION TO WORK HARDER AND DO WELL. COMPETENCE LEADS TO CONFIDENCE, WHICH LEADS TO WANTING TO WRITE.

4. Raise Your Expectations

*The question is not, Is it possible to educate all
children well? but rather, Do we want to do it badly enough?*
—Deborah Meier

I have never worked in a school or classroom where the expectations for students are too high. The more I teach kids, the more I become aware of how much they can achieve. Children continue to surprise and amaze me with their capacity to learn and assume responsibility. I keep expecting more from them based on what I see they can do, and they rise to meet those expectations.

Why are our expectations for what students can achieve almost always so low? Often we hold flawed assumptions about what students can and cannot do. When I work in classrooms where I don't know the students, the teacher will often approach me after the lesson and say, "I didn't know he could do that." And I respond, "I didn't know he couldn't."

When I speak of raising expectations, I am not talking about adding more skills or more work. Nor am I talking about long lists of "narrow" standards or elaborate and extensive writing projects that exhaust both students and teachers. Higher-quality work is not by definition long. Raised expectations mean that students learn what it means to explore writing in depth.

When they experience what good writing is and realize they are capable of it, they are finally able to judge when their writing is superficial and uninteresting and when they have hit the mark. Being able to write well not only makes students more effective communicators, it also gives them more enjoyment, pride, and independence, and that, in turn, increases their motivation to work harder and do well. Competence leads to confidence, which leads to wanting to write.

When my father suffered a debilitating stroke, there were very few expectations for his recovery. Not knowing how severe his stroke was and relying on what I observed myself, I expected him not only to live but to learn how to live productively. Although he was not expected to be able to feed himself, comb his hair, talk, make jokes, respond to questions, voice his needs, sign his name, or read, he learned to do those things and more—in large part because we had those expectations for him, verbalized what those expectations and goals were, and worked with him and the nursing home staff to advocate for and provide whatever was necessary to make his achieving them a reality.

One-and-a-half years after my dad's stroke, his language skills continued to improve, even though I had been told there is no improvement beyond the first six months, especially after a stroke as severe as the one he had suffered. Ongoing love and support, along with caring interactions with Frank and me, other family members, friends, and the nursing home staff, made his improvement possible. I see my dad as the ultimate disabled, struggling learner, yet his accomplishments have far exceeded the low expectations originally held for him. The same is possible for our students. We need to "see," literally, what's possible.

Change the School Culture of Low Expectations

Many schools continue to support a culture of lowered expectations, especially for minority and poor students. It is well-documented that minority students as a group experience a curriculum of lowered expectations and less rigor. Students who can't write proficiently have fewer opportunities to succeed. However, once students become successful writers, they are able to apply those skills, that fluency, across the curriculum—thus achieving more, as well as being able to pass high-stakes tests (see Cory's story, on pages 78–80).

I also encounter lowered expectations at affluent schools. Their students' high-test scores breed complacency and lack of innovation. Students write with accuracy, but the writing is often not worth reading. More important, far too many students dislike writing and see it as a "school thing for the teacher." At these schools as in all schools, I begin teaching writing by focusing on enjoyment and on a real, valued reader.

Take Action to Raise Writing Expectations

Raising expectations regarding our students' ability to write is not just a school issue, it is also an important political issue. The public judges educators by how well their students write. Parents, businesspeople, and politicians especially notice poor spelling, sloppy handwriting, bad grammar, and missing punctuation. We need to be sticklers with any work that goes public: published letters or stories, the class news magazine, work posted on a classroom bulletin board or school wall.

You will want to meet as a staff or grade-level group and decide what quality of work is acceptable. For example, look at the letter below that Gillian, a second grader, wrote to her grandfather in school in March of second grade. Is it commendable, acceptable, or in need of improvement?

I have shown this letter to thousands of educators. Without exception, at least half of every group believes it is fine for the letter to be sent from school as is, that young students cannot be expected to edit their work. I am always unsettled by this response. My own work with second graders has taught me that they

Friendly Letter

5|5 General MotorsR
Milford MI 48381
March 1, 2001

Dear Bopa,
Were geting in to Letter Writing
at school. And were lerning
2 diget Math problums.
Were lerning also how to
do Rers.uf and were lerning
about dr. Seuss. please write
back!

Love
Gillian

can write short, final copy that has voice, interesting detail, legibility, and correct spelling and punctuation. According to Gillian's mom, "Gillian has come a long way since she wrote that letter. In second grade, her teacher never made her correct anything. Now that her teachers expect it and teach it, she writes with more care and tries her best to spell things correctly."

While there is no right answer here, it is important to set schoolwide expectations that are both reasonable and rigorous and that are clearly articulated. Then, we need to ensure that students, teachers, parents, administrators, and the public know about these expectations. (Appendix J contains an example of how one teacher told parents about her editing expectations.) In schools whose students are good readers and writers, the students, teachers, administrators, and parents all know, value, and work toward common goals and worthy schoolwide aims.

In one school in which I worked with teachers to improve the teaching of writing, one of the first-grade teachers said,

> "No way! My kids won't be able to do that." That's exactly what I thought when I watched second-grade students revising and editing their own work and was told first-grade students can do this too. But, oh, my gosh! They did it even at the beginning of first grade. It's amazing what high expectations and explicit teaching can do.

Expect Excellence

I work the same way in high-poverty schools and schools where students' language, culture, and experiences make learning a challenge as I do in more privileged schools. All students, advantaged or disadvantaged, go through similar stages of literacy development. Therefore, they need the same excellent instruction, not different instruction. Disadvantaged students just need more of it: more demonstrations, more shared experiences, and more guided practice in order to become successful independent learners.

We sometimes further disadvantage students by feeling sorry for them (*Poor baby*) and expecting less, accepting minimal participation and effort (*You know, he has had such a hard life*). I never give up on a child; it is never okay for a student not to write or not participate—no matter what the child's background. It is also not okay to rely on scripted, one-size-fits-all programs in our poorest schools while our more affluent ones can choose the best materials and strategies to teach their students.

Students achieve faster, more easily, and on a higher level when they find the lessons and materials interesting, relevant, and challenging. I use the highest-quality materials I can provide. Worksheets aren't good enough. The students who can do them don't need them, and the ones who struggle with them feel defeated by the red marks, which only reinforce their feelings of inadequacy. Worksheets foster mediocrity.

Mediocrity is not an option. Why do we persist in thinking that just squeaking by is all right for some of our students? It will not get our students where they need to go. Students know when we think they are smart and capable, and with our help, they rise to the occasion. When expectations are high, the work is interesting, and sufficient demonstrations and support are provided by knowledgeable teachers, *all* students succeed—the second language learners, the students with learning disabilities, all writers who struggle.

A fact not to be minimized is that these high expectations must be accompanied by close, trusting relationships in which students bond with the teacher and feel safe to take a risk. Students need to know that their approximations—as they are trying out and learning along the way—are welcomed and accepted.

Nurture and Nudge

Working with first-grade teacher Gail Westbrook during my third year at her school, I am impressed with the quality and fluency of all her students' writing. Their journal stories are lively, elaborate, and full of voice. Their handwriting is legible. Most students easily write a page or more in fifteen minutes. They write every day for about thirty minutes. Gail also models her own writing and has conferences with several students every day.

Gail attributes her students' excellent writing to:

- ☐ **Reading aloud at least three texts a day** (fiction and nonfiction picture books as well as an ongoing chapter book). Gail reads to her kids first thing in the morning, right after lunch, and last thing in the afternoon. She focuses on language and how authors use words. For example, she and the students identify interesting vocabulary, and the kids brainstorm other words that mean the same thing (like *peculiar*, in Dr. Seuss's *The Sneetches*, and *immense*, in his *Horton Hatches the Egg*). They also note "golden lines" (sentences they can picture) and playful language.
- ☐ **Writing poetry.** Playing around with language by hearing and writing poems early in the year gives students facility with words. Gail focuses on using one's senses and on "feeling" words, rhythm, and rhyme.
- ☐ **Having good peer models.** Seeing the writing of other students has a very powerful effect on community and trust. Students begin to take risks when they see peers take risks in their writing.
- ☐ **Focusing on audience.** Before, Gail says, "I had not made audience a focus. This is the biggest change in my teaching. Once the students start to consider the reader/listener, their writing just expands."

☐ **Modeling frequently.** Gail writes and thinks aloud several days a week and also relies on frequent shared writing.

☐ **Intentional teaching.** Gail's teaching is explicit and deliberate. She relies on what she calls the "efficiency of context" to teach skills within purposeful writing contexts.

☐ **Holding high expectations for all students.** "This sends the message that I believe in their ability and value their writing. They are worthy of that expectation."

So Gail and I raise our expectations for her students still further. With her students, Gail has created an excellent chart (see box, What Makes Our Writing Interesting?) that delineates quality writing. Now we ask them to define "tell more" based on what they are already doing in their writing (see the following box, What Does It Mean to Write More/Tell More?). Together we come up with a list (see box below). Almost immediately amazing things begin to happen. Many students cross out words and add more precise ones; others think more about their ending and craft a better one; and everyone writes with more specificity, supporting ideas with appropriate examples.

WHAT MAKES OUR WRITING INTERESTING?

☐ Include something funny (use humor).
☐ Make it easy to read—use spaces, neat handwriting.
☐ Tell feelings.
☐ Don't be afraid of big words (sound them out).
☐ Use interesting words.
☐ Make sure to have a lot of sense.
☐ Write more—tell more.

WHAT DOES IT MEAN TO WRITE MORE/TELL MORE?

☐ Tell what it is (give examples).
☐ Describe (give a picture to the reader!).
☐ Tell when.
☐ Tell why.
☐ Tell where.
☐ Tell how (directions).
☐ Tell what happens.
☐ Tell your feelings.
☐ Tell more to make it BETTER (not just longer)!

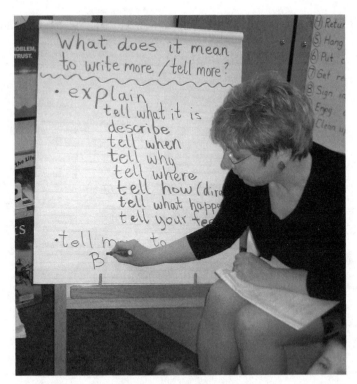

First-grade teacher Gail Westbrook uses shared writing to chart expectations

Most of the other first-grade writing in Gail's school has the same high quality, but it was not always like this. On my first visit to the school, first-grade teachers' expectations for quality, legibility, quantity, spelling, and content were much lower. Seeing what students could actually accomplish raised expectations schoolwide. Higher expectations and explicit teaching changed our definition of "average" (see pages 60–64).

Establish Schoolwide Expectations for Quality

When Gail and I shared our work with the whole staff, we talked about how what these first graders are working on is what we want all our students to do. Being able to explain clearly is a necessary, lifelong literacy skill.

In particular, "explain your thinking" has been a goal of the school's fourth-grade teachers. When a fourth-grade teacher and I reviewed the high-stakes writing tests of students who had failed, we realized that many wrote well but did not follow the test's directions: "Write several paragraphs *explaining* to your teacher the reasons why you like doing. . . ."

Four First-grade Writers Show What It Means to Write More/Tell More

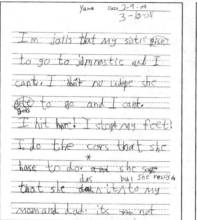

I'm jealous that my sister gets to go to gymnastics and I can't. I don't know why she gets to go and I can't. I hit her! I stamped my feet! I do the chores that she has to do. I clean the room and the

kitchen and I clean the living room and the bathroom. Yuck, gross, icky. That's the sickest part of it. She says to my mom and dad that she does it but she really doesn't. It's not FAIR!!! Well, now

it's fair! Cause she can't go because she already has a job. It's selling newspapers. So now I am happy that she didn't get to go.

Yana, average-performing student, English language learner. Grade 1, March 2004

Yesterday I was so-o-o- exhausted after school when I got off the bus my mom had to carry me in my room. [First line of story that goes on for a few days.]

Last night I exploded and it was bigger than a hotel. It was my bedtime. I yelled! My face was as red as a meteor. When my mom touched my face it burned her finger. Kwow!!!

I have excema. Excema is when you have red spots that itch a lot. The first time I had excema I was 4. I do not like excema. It is too itchy for me. [Start of story that continued for a few days.]

Montana, strong writer

Jason, most struggling writer in the class

A. J., struggling writer, low confidence

Teaching what explaining means in first grade and continuing to work on it in the following grades ensures that students will no longer find writing explanations difficult. Having done it for years, they will have internalized what it means to explain and will automatically apply what they know from years of practice.

On pages 62–64 are first-grade journal writing samples from low-performing and average-performing students in this school over a three-year span. See also the writing of Julia, an English language learner, and observe her growth from early first grade to mid-third grade where she no longer looks like an "average" writer. Notice the improvement in content, spelling, handwriting, word choice, and more.

First week in September, grade 1:

"I am play slide" [the words she read back to her teacher]

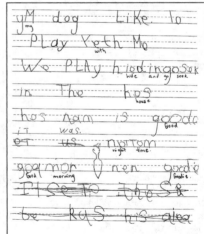

First week in February, grade 1, continuing a story (2 days of writing):

My dog died. I miss him. My dog is a good big dog. My dog has brown spots. The rest of him is dark brown. He has a pink nose. He has blue eyes.

My dog likes to play with me. We play hide and go seek in the house. His name is Goody.

Michele's writing in September and February: one "low performing" student's progress

The Results of Raising Expectations Spanning Three School Years

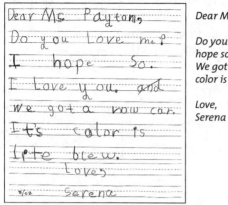

Dear Mrs. Payton,

Do you love me? I hope so. I love you. We got a new car. Its color is light blue.

Love,
Serena

June 2002, Serena

My grandpa died because he never uses medicine. He doesn't use vitamins because he forgot to take some. I was upset. My little sister was upset too. I was crying. My sister was yelling and crying.

May 2004, Marco

Typical Grade 1 writing samples by struggling writers (low performing)

June 2002, Lindsey

Dear New Teacher,

I'm a good student. And I have blue eyes and I have short hair. Do you? And I have a sister who is 10 years old. And she bosses me around. I'm so glad I'm in your class.

Your New Student,
Lindsey

SEASIDE

"Are we going to Seaside?" I said. Dad said, "If you be quiet, we will. We're going." "We're going," me and my sister said. We were driving for an hour when me and my sister got hungry and thirsty. So we stopped at a gas station. We got beef burgers and soda pops.

When we got there we walked down to the beach. When we got back we went to Seaside Candy Man and got ice cream. Then we went swimming. I wore a life vest. We went to Seaside Candy Man again for salt water taffy. And that is how our day went at Seaside.

May 2004, Jackie

Writing samples by typical students (average performing)

One English Language Learner's Progress from Grade 1–Grade 3

Grade 1, June 2002

Dear Mrs. Pearce,

I speak Chinese. What do you speak? I'm looking forward to second grade. I feel scared of it. I want to learn times.

Love,
Julia R.

Grade 2, June 2003

Narrowing her topic, Me and Akari

- Mall Finding (?)
- Play play
- Laughing together
- Jokes to tell
- First day we met (circle indicates she wants to begin with this subtopic)
- Talking on the phone
- Friends forever

The first day we meet, Akari and I were shy. I asked her, "What do you speak?" She said "Japanese." I said "Chinese." We were best friends. Akari said "What's Chinese?" I said, "I speak it" so she said "Oh. Now I know." I said, "You rhyme words." "You are funny," Akari said. And that's how I met Akari. But she said, "I am not your friend. Just kidding." I laughed so much. I had so much fun. Then the bell rang. We ran to room 204. The end.

Grade 3, January 2004

CHRISTMAS SURPRISE

It was 12:00. Ring, ring, beep, beep.

"Just one minute please," I said, snuggling my head under my pink and white polka dot pillow and yanking my blanket to my head.

"Wake up sleepyhead," said my Mom with a big grin from ear to ear.

"Hmm. I thought. I saw that grin

before but who cares," and I went back to my pleasant sleep desperately. I felt so pooped from hearing my excel. I was so scared like after that I will fall. "Hey author, this is not excel so get back to the story." [self-monitoring, talking to herself]

"Christmas eve is here Julia. Tomorrow we will go to Spokane," said my dad.

I said, "Go away."

My mom pushed me out of bed and pulled me by my feet on the fuzzy carpet. I tried to reach my comfy bed but I missed. I kicked my cold feet to escape my mom. but I missed again. I started walking to see the lovely gifts.

Julia's writing progression from first to third grade

Now take a look below at Kelly's mid-year first-grade writing, deemed "exemplary" at another school. Kelly's mother is a second-grade teacher at Gail's school. When she learned that her "verbal and expressive" daughter's writing had been published and displayed in a place of honor, she commented:

> Several years ago, I would have considered this piece an example of successful first-grade writing, but my understanding of the writing process and what children are capable of has been altered dramatically through our school's writing residencies and our ongoing professional conversations. Kelly's story may contain many elements of good writing, but it's not indicative of what she's capable of communicating to the reader.

My animal is a cat. It loves to eat cat food. My cat lives in my house. I like my cat very much. I always pet her.

Kelly's letter, grade 1

An example of "good writing" by traditional school standards

I recently overheard a first-grade teacher say, "My goal is to have my students write three complete sentences with capitals and periods by the end of the year." They are capable of so much more! Years ago I figured out that we need to teach even our youngest students to write quality pieces along with correct conventions. For example, instead of moving on to a new topic every day, teach kindergartners to write a continuing story (see pages 207–210); teach first graders to reread their writing and "fix it up" by adding missing words and correcting the spellings of a few frequently used words (see page 60); teach second graders to "write small, that is, narrow their topic and elaborate" (see pages 292–304); and teach fourth graders to write persuasive pieces (see pages 330–335).

**TRY IT
APPLY IT**

✐ At your grade level and across grade levels, examine and discuss the preceding writing samples. What do you notice about organization, voice, elaboration, conventions—and about struggling writers? Set high expectations for what is "average" writing at your school.

✐ Encourage students to take risks as writers. Kelly, designated an "exemplary" writer has only used words she knows how to spell. Jason, the most struggling writer, has invented spellings for words such as "exploded" and "meteor." Discuss what this means for our teaching.

Remember That Quantity Matters

If you're reading everything your students write, they're not writing enough. Expect more. Kids become writers by writing every day, not by completing exercises *about* writing. Students who are excellent writers write a lot. First graders can write a full page in twenty minutes by the spring of the year. When I noticed one first grader wasting time, I raised the expectation and he met it. Then I said, referring to the page of writing he had just generated, "Now we know what you can do. Three words for a writing period is not acceptable. This is what we expect to see from now on."

Use freewrites, daily writing with lots of student choice, and writing across the curriculum. Students need fluency and endurance to pass high-stakes writing tests, and they can only attain that fluency and endurance by doing a great deal of writing.

Raise Your Expectations for Conventions

When students can read their own writing, spell most words correctly, and write with appropriate punctuation, the writing process speeds up—for both student and teacher. It is reasonable to expect even young students to spell some high-frequency words correctly.

I will never forget working midyear in a first-grade classroom and seeing most students writing *I* as *i* and *my* as *mi*. The teacher, conscientious and excellent in every way, didn't want to "interfere" with the students' writing. Insisting that these words and others could no longer be misspelled saved time, made writing easier to read, gave students a sense of accomplishment, and sent the message to parents that spelling matters—all important writing goals. See Appendix B.

Raise Your Expectations for Handwriting

In every school I visit, how and when to teach handwriting is an issue. Handwriting matters. Not being able to form letters easily constrains writing. That's common sense. If your energy is taken up forming letters, you're not able to concentrate on your message.

Even in our age of technology, a lot of the writing students do in school is still by hand. For example, students write high-stakes tests by hand. And, fair or not, handwriting quality impacts how scorers rate students' writing papers. Legible handwriting is also a political issue. We are judged, rightly or wrongly, by how our students' papers look. When they look beautiful, parents judge us to be effective teachers of writing. That's part of the reason I'm such a stickler for excellent handwriting and conventions in all published work.

I continue to be surprised—and sometimes alarmed and embarrassed—at the poor quality of handwriting that we teachers accept from students: sloppy journals with lots of graffiti, hard-to-read papers posted on bulletin boards or published in some other way. We can focus our writing instruction on quality writing and at the same time expect legibility.

When we raise our expectations and refuse to accept poor handwriting, kids' handwriting improves. If we want students to value handwriting and produce beautiful penmanship, we need to teach it, demonstrate it, value it, and—above all—give writers audiences they value, so that they're engaged and invested in their writing. I once received a group of letters from fifth graders asking me questions about being a writer. Had I not known the authors were fifth graders, I would have assumed they were second graders. The papers were a mess—poor handwriting and spelling, careless grammar, lots of pencil smudges, written on paper torn out of spiral notebooks. I immediately knew the writing was an assignment that had no meaning for them.

We need to take the time to demonstrate slow, careful letter formation, word spacing, and spelling verification—but without pressuring students. My everyday handwriting is messy and hard to read, but when I send a personal note, I slow down and take care. I want the reader to feel valued and to be able to read my message easily. Sloppy handwriting is disrespectful to the reader.

In a second-grade classroom where the students wrote letters to someone who had helped them and made their life easier in some way (see page 203), I spent a full twenty minutes setting the stage for excellent handwriting. First, we established expectations that we all agreed on. Next, using the same lined paper they would be using, I carefully copied the beginning of my revised letter right in front of them while speaking aloud.

Teacher Talk

☐ *I'm looking at our big chart that shows the format of the letter. I have to start writing the date in about the middle of the line. I have to make sure I spell* December *correctly, so I'm going to check letter by letter as I write it.*

☐ *I need to space between the month and the day and put a comma after* December 5.

☐ *I'm checking my paper for where to start* Dear. *I need to remember to capitalize it. D-e-a-r. I'm going to write Jenifer's name carefully. I know how to spell it.*

☐ *Now I'm going to begin my letter. I need to indent my first line right under the* r *in* Dear.

☐ *I'm looking at my draft and copying my words and spellings very carefully. I'm going to write slowly and really concentrate on my best handwriting.*

☐ *If I make a mistake, I'll just erase. Normally, we cross out, but that would be too messy. We want our cards to look as neat and beautiful as possible. Our best work shows we care about our readers.*

When the students placed their specially designed paper next to their revised and edited drafts, every student took the task seriously and did an excellent job. Even Jon, who struggled most often with letter formation, writing, and neatness, did his best handwriting to date (see his draft and final copy, page 203). Some of the teachers expressed surprise at how well the kids did, how they visibly made a great effort to slow down, how they concentrated and checked their work.

A few weeks after my visit, I received a personally designed thank-you note from each student, every one of them in excellent, legible handwriting. If we expect it, explain why it's important, demonstrate how to achieve it, and provide time for it, students almost always meet our expectations.

TRY IT
APPLY IT

*Raise Your
Expectations
for
Handwriting*

- Once you've taught cursive writing, you may want to let students print if handwriting is hard for them. What you're after is legibility. Research indicates that students need to be knowledgeable about styles of writing, not that cursive is preferable to printing.

- Have various kinds of beautiful writing paper available. Invite parents to donate writing paper, cards, and envelopes; and students to create their own. If you are fortunate enough to have the appropriate software, you and your students can design your own cards and keep them on hand.

- Check your students' published writing. Make sure that any work displayed in the classroom or principal's office has excellent handwriting, spelling, and conventions.

- When you conference with students, even on the run, teach letter formation when a student is having difficulty. (I also do this when students are writing on tiles and white boards.)

- Take a critical look at your students' daily handwriting. Have you given the message that handwriting doesn't matter?

- Make sure developing writers have an alphabet strip or chart close by to use as a resource/reminder for letter formation. Model for a small group of kids who need more practice. Have them practice forming letters on sand trays, in the air, on white boards.

Expect Legibility

Journals and writing notebooks are often a shambles. I am always baffled by teachers who will accept defaced covers, messy handwriting, scribbles, and poor spelling. These are, after all, books: writing books. When I see that lack of pride in workmanship, I say something like this: *Kids, I work in a lot of classrooms, and when I see such messy work, it tells me you're not taking pride or enjoyment in your writing. Let me show you what I expect.*

You may need to start all over again with new notebooks. When you hand them out, make sure you model how to write in them—format, spacing, letter formation, date placement, how to cross out, and so on. Let students know that you expect quality work and carefully thought-out cover decoration. Students do what we expect them to. When first-grade teacher Lindy Vizyak, of Westminster, Colorado, told her first graders she would no longer accept their sloppy handwriting and demonstrated what legibility "looked like," the handwriting of many of her students improved that same day.

Raise Your Expectations for Editing

Students, even young ones, can do most of the editing work themselves if they:

- ☐ Write for readers they value.
- ☐ Value the necessity for accuracy in published pieces.
- ☐ Understand that readers expect text to be error-free.
- ☐ Recognize that effective writing must have correct conventions, grammar, and spelling.
- ☐ Have realistic but rigorous editing expectations to meet.
- ☐ Have taken part in setting these expectations (see page 204).
- ☐ Know and understand exactly what they are to do.
- ☐ Can get feedback and assistance from their peers and their teacher.
- ☐ Know they will be held accountable for editing.
- ☐ Have seen editing demonstrations.
- ☐ See themselves as the final editors.

When I told a class of fourth graders I could not publicly share their beautifully written and illustrated heart poems anthology (see pages 305–315) because of spelling, punctuation, and grammar errors, they rose to the occasion and republished it without a single error. Now, I proudly share it with many teachers and students.

See That What Gets Published Is Perfect

Recently I worked with an intermediate-grade teacher. When I entered his room, a wall of book reviews caught my eye. They were presented just as they are in many bookstores. There was a copy of the cover of the book above a book review on a three-by-five card hanging on a ring attached to the bulletin board with a pushpin. Just as I do at my favorite bookstores, I picked up a few to read. The reviews themselves were well done because the class had been working on how to craft reviews (see pages 132–133), but I was distracted by the errors of spelling, punctuation, and capitalization as well as the sometimes messy handwriting.

I spoke with the students, praised what they had to say in the reviews, and then told them how their errors and poor handwriting had distracted me. Instead of being able to concentrate on what the reviewer had to say, I found myself focused on errors. I also told them that, as a reader, I expected to be able to read the message straight through, that one of the responsibilities of the writer is to make the text easily readable.

Why do we work so hard on writing with our students and then accept a less-than-exemplary final form? *Work published for a reader has to be as perfect as we can get it.* That's the way publishing works in the world. We need to have the same expectations for our students and help them learn how to assume that responsibility.

Rely on an Optimal Learning Model

Excellent instruction is not based on a set of procedures or skills or a list of standards, although those things can be helpful. Excellent instruction is based on an optimal model of learning. Learning happens best within a supportive community that offers many opportunities to observe, talk, listen, suggest, collaborate, try out, make choices, set goals, and evaluate. Relevance is a necessity here. Students will only feel the "need" to learn something if they see the task as significant. This is particularly true for our culturally and linguistically diverse learners.

Once teachers understand how the model works and how to apply it, teaching and learning become more explicit, effective, and enjoyable. Implementing the model lets us teach with higher expectations for what students can accomplish.

The model assumes that the purpose for writing is meaningful and useful and that students understand it. The model also requires a classroom that is a safe, relaxed, collaborative, and a social environment in which students are encouraged to approximate, take risks, and are validated for their efforts.

Who Holds Book/Pen	*Degree of Explicitness/Support*
Teacher /Student	DEMONSTRATION
Teacher /Student	SHARED DEMONSTRATION
gradual handover of responsibility	
Student /Teacher	GUIDED PRACTICE
Student /Teacher	INDEPENDENT PRACTICE

The Optimal Learning Model

Notice who is in charge at each stage in the model and who is holding the pen or book. The better job we do demonstrating—often in shared demonstrations—

the easier it is for students to apply what we have been teaching as we gradually "hand over" responsibility to them. When my teaching breaks down, it's almost always because my demonstrations have not been sufficient.

Demonstration

The teacher or expert shows precisely "how to do it" by initiating, modeling, explaining, thinking aloud, and writing aloud. Students observe the teacher planning, drafting, making choices, rereading, evaluating, revising, editing, and monitoring. They may be invited to participate in a limited way, but there is no pressure to perform. The teacher also demonstrates the satisfaction she takes in writing.

By modeling her own authentic writing in front of students, a teacher hopes learners will emulate but not imitate her. Students come to see the teacher as a writer rather than as a "talker-about-writing." The teacher or expert also demonstrates and calls attention to the author's craft—in literature, her own writing, selected students' writing—to model what excellent writers do to engage readers.

Shared Demonstration

The teacher is still in charge (and holds the pen), but now the children collaborate on the writing as much as they are able. Scaffolded conversations—as a class, in a small group, with a partner—are integral to the composing process. As learners interact and respond to create a joint text, the teacher "holds their hand," acknowledging, affirming, and encouraging participation and rich, coherent language. Learners also notice and acknowledge various authors' craft. The teacher observes what each learner is able to do and what additional teaching and supports are needed; this assessment is ongoing, and the teacher makes adjustments based on each learner's needs.

Shared demonstration is underused as a powerful teaching context for students of all grades. Yet it is through shared writing and scaffolded conversations before, during, and after writing that I do much of my teaching. Shared writing experiences (see Chapter 5) make it possible to write challenging text that no single child could write independently; they raise expectations for what's possible.

Guided Practice

The student is now in charge, holding the pen (or pencil) and attempting to apply what has been previously demonstrated and practiced with the direct support of the teacher and/or group. Students' guided practice writing is likely to be only as good as our demonstrations. Errors and approximations are expected as a normal part of the learning process. At the same time, however, students are encouraged to monitor their work and move toward independence.

The teacher or mentor is close by to validate, support, teach, and give feedback. However, there may be times when applied practice does not include direct supervision (when the teacher is guiding a small group or conducting a writing conference, for example). In these cases, the knowledgeable teacher builds in an evaluation to monitor student progress and help determine what further support/teaching is needed. (See the examples of summary writings on pages 128–132 and student conference forms on this book's website.)

Guided writing is not parallel to guided reading. Many teachers have told me, "We're supposed to do small-group writing instruction." When I ask why, they say, "Well, you know, like guided reading groups, we're supposed to do guided writing groups." The question I always ask is, *How is what you are doing helping kids become more proficient and independent—and joyful—writers?* We need to be thinking about why we're doing what we're doing. I do use small guided writing groups when I am teaching something like summary writing, questioning for literature discussion, or reciprocal teaching. Mostly, though, guided practice takes place during daily, sustained, whole-class writing. I am available to help during roving conferences, whole-class shares, and one-on-one conferences, and students also seek help from their peers.

Independent Practice

At this stage, learners have developed enough competence and confidence to be able to choose their own topics, problem-solve, and monitor and set goals for themselves with minimal assistance. Teacher intervention is just as likely to move a student to a higher level of writing development as help him with the task at hand. Students' reward for their successful writing is intrinsic—personal pride in their accomplishments and their ability to transfer what they know to new writing contexts. Noncompetitively, they enjoy demonstrating small improvements and achievements to the teacher as well as to peers and significant others (such as parents) for approval and affirmation.

Independent practice often occurs once we have taught students how to successfully write poetry, fiction, persuasive pieces, and so on. Students may also have gleaned writing strategies and techniques from extensive reading. Now learners choose to write in a particular form or genre and have the skills and confidence to be successful. Just as it is necessary to do a great deal of independent reading to become a competent reader, so too is it with writing.

Decide What Support Learners Need

When looking at the optimal learning model, pay more attention to the degree of support students need than to the teaching context. Ask yourself, *What support (demonstrations, practice, guidance, resources) do students need to succeed with minimal guidance, and how can I best provide it?* Almost always, additional demonstrations are in order, often shared demonstrations. But these shared demonstrations are not just co-writing projects.

For example, before students wrote their drafts for the "Secrets of Second Graders" lesson (see pages 292–304 and the accompanying DVD), I wrote my own story, "Stealing Stuffed Celery" (see below), thinking out loud, writing, and rewriting in front of them (see below and my thinking process on pages 294–295). However, that one demonstration was not enough of a model for them to go off and write. Shared writing wasn't appropriate, because there was no one classroom secret to write about. So instead, our shared demonstrations were two scaffolded conversations before writing (see pages 296–297 in the Teaching in Action section).

Or, again, in a science unit, after we did a piece of shared writing about the heart for a book about the human body (see page 114 and the DVD), the students were not yet ready to go off on their own to write. Next, as a class, we brainstormed topics for the complete book as well as the important content to include for each subtopic. Then, using our piece of shared writing as a model, students worked together in small groups, each group writing on just one topic.

My demonstration for writing for "secrets" stories

Sometimes I can only figure out the degree of support and explicitness needed when learning breaks down. For example, I was working with a group of first graders and did not get the quality work I expected. Even though I had thought about and written my own story aloud in front of them, I decided—after forty-five minutes of hard thinking—that my demonstration had been insufficient. We would need to do some shared writing before I could expect the students to write a story on their own.

Here's how my thinking went:

☐ *Why are the children's writing samples so ineffective?*
☐ *What have I failed to provide so students can be successful?*
☐ *What else do I need to do?*
☐ *Should I abandon the project and start again?*
☐ *Would additional demonstrations enable students to move forward?*
☐ *What's the best way to provide more demonstrations at this time?*

I decided (as I always do when I don't get good results) that the fault was mine. I told the students, *Kids, when I read your papers, I realized that I hadn't given you enough help to do a really great job with your writing. So today we're going to write a story together to give you more ideas for your own writing.*

We wrote a fictional story about their teacher being asleep in school (see below), and this thinking through and writing together made a huge difference in their next attempts. (See Create a Fiction Story Through Shared Writing, pages 99–104).

The beginning pages of our shared writing fiction story

Their teacher, Lindsay Gandolfo, said afterward, "That was the most productive writing workshop I've seen with my students. They all did their best writing, and they were all engaged."

A caution against overteaching. One of the mistakes many of us have made in teaching reading is to spend so much time demonstrating or teaching in small groups that the students don't have time to read; understandably, they never become very good readers. Keep the learning model in mind—remember that students need to spend most of their time writing independently. If they are to become excellent writers they have to spend most of a writing lesson composing continuous text, not participating in lessons and activities about writing.

Include More Shared Experiences

I strongly believe one of our primary roles as educators is to ensure that shared learning experiences (shared writing, shared reading, and scaffolded conversations) are a major component of everything we teach. Without those shared experiences, many of our learners will remain severely limited in their abilities and accomplishments. One demonstration is rarely enough. A personal story brings home the point.

For a recent "big" birthday, my son Peter and his wife Claudine generously gave me a state-of-the-art digital camera. Up until then, I had been using what I call a PHD camera (*push here, dummy*), which only required that the lens be open before I snapped the picture. I took all my photos on this inexpensive camera, including those I use in my books. I had wanted a better camera so I could get better quality and clearer shots, so this was a perfect gift.

Peter showed me how to use it ("Nothing to it, Mom"). For more than an hour, he demonstrated the various features as I looked on. Then he had to leave, and he wished me luck. I could turn the camera on and off, I could snap some photos, but that was about it. I didn't recall how to delete pictures or view the pictures I had taken. I didn't know what all the buttons and displays meant and had little idea of all the available options. When I first took the camera with me on a school residency, I asked a more experienced user to take pictures for me.

Six months went by. My confidence and competence hadn't budged much, even though I repeatedly referred to the user's guide and to a set of easy directions a kind teacher had written out for me. Now, at the start of a new school year, I was determined to learn how to use the camera effectively to document literacy learning and teaching in my school residencies.

Do More Hand-Holding

I did two things to increase my competence. First, I went to my local camera store and asked the manager if he would teach me how to use the camera in exchange for my having my photos developed there. He kindly agreed. Second, I asked a friend to spend a morning teaching me how to transfer photos from my camera disk to my computer's photo program and how to categorize and organize them.

With these many hours of hand-holding, I slowly became an able user of a digital camera. What I needed and finally received was the scaffolding, let's-do-it-together help: I observed the expert, who then invited me to try it out, trial and error, while he coached patiently at my side and assured me encouragingly that I could, in fact, succeed. I still needed lots of practice and guidance along the way, but those shared experiences gave me the knowledge and training I was missing.

In all those months that I was unable to use the camera successfully, I never confessed it to my son. When he asked how it was going, I fudged, saying I was getting the hang of it. I didn't want him to know I couldn't master this "simple" new camera. I was unable to tell him, "Look, I need you to come back, sit with me, show me the features of this camera over and over again, and help me while I try them out." Why didn't I do that? I was embarrassed, felt I was a slow learner, didn't want to bother him, and, most of all, didn't want him to think I was an inept user of technology.

I tell this story because I believe this is how our students often feel when learning new tasks. We may show them how to do it, even demonstrate our own thinking, reading, and writing, but unless we spend *lots of time doing the task with them*—explaining, modeling, encouraging, supporting, and guiding the learning-in-process, many of them will never develop the skills and confidence to master the task successfully. As a mostly confident adult, I was eventually able to ask for and receive the help I needed. Many of our students, however, are unable to make such a request. Lacking that critical support and scaffolding, many of them never do figure out what they know and don't know and what their questions are. Without that shared learning and experimentation, many never get on the path to becoming independent learners. They may learn by rote, but they don't learn how to learn.

I also tell this story to make a strong case for shared experiences. We teachers will rely on shared experiences (such as shared writing) only if we value their worth. Otherwise, we fill our classroom time with other activities.

> ### ADVANTAGES OF SHARED LEARNING EXPERIENCES FOR THE LEARNER
>
> ☐ Finds out what s/he knows.
>
> ☐ Finds out what s/he doesn't know.
>
> ☐ Is able to solve problems in a supportive atmosphere.
>
> ☐ Figures out the questions s/he needs to ask in the process of participating, thinking, and problem solving.
>
> ☐ Can try things out without fear of failure.
>
> ☐ Has a supportive other who demonstrates and with whom s/he can interact.
>
> ☐ Participates in interactive, responsive learning, which is the best way to attain achievement, versus telling, which does not raise one's achievement level.

Rely on Scaffolded Conversations

Rather than asking each student in the class, *What are you going to write about?* and getting only a few words about their topic, invite one or two students to have a public conversation with you. Such in-depth conversations will help expand everyone's language ability and story possibilities and are critical for our English language learners, who need to speak the language before they can write it. (See the photo of a scaffolded conversation, page 53, and pages 110 and 181–183.)

In the "Secrets of Second Graders" lesson, with the whole class looking on, I had a conversation with Owen, a struggling writer, and Madison, a strong writer. The lesson plan on pages 292–304 contains the conversations we had. Notice how much of what occurred in the scaffolded conversation appeared in their writing (see pages 22 and 342–347 for their drafts). These public conversations also triggered ideas in other students, and many wrote similar stories.

Then, before students went on to write, I had them spend a few minutes sharing their story with a partner. When it was time to write, I met at the front of the room with those few students who still weren't sure what they would write about. Once those students were off and writing—about five minutes later—I was free to roam around checking on how everyone was doing—to see who needed a quick conference, celebration, affirmation, and who was a good prospect to ask to share his story with the whole class.

teaching tip

Examples of Teacher Language

☐ *"That sounds just like a story. I'm going to write that down on a sticky note so you can remember it."*

☐ *"Slow that down so we can picture it."*

☐ *"Tell us exactly how…"*

☐ *"How big was it? Was it as big as a city bus or as big as a desk?"*

☐ *"What did you do/say then?"*

Focus on the Writer First

Respect for the writer as a person is paramount to teaching anything about writing. Whenever I lose sight of that principle, I lose whatever writing goals I had in mind, and I become ineffective as a teacher. Putting the writer first is of greatest importance, regardless of that writer's age. The following story is a case in point.

I was paying a return visit to a school where we had been focusing on writing. The teachers and principal had decided to spend the first day of our week together in grade-level meetings. Each hour of the day, I met and conversed with a different group of teachers about what they were doing, how they were teaching writing, and what their needs were. Since I had been brought into this school to increase the fourth-grade scores on the annual state test, I was feeling pressure to move things along. In one grade level, in particular, I unwittingly put teachers on the spot by questioning what they were doing. Rather than listening to them without judgment, I quickly jumped in and took over the conversation. All the trust I had carefully nurtured in previous visits quickly disappeared.

Fortunately, one of the teachers later approached me and told me how difficult it had been for her to take a risk in front of her colleagues and talk about how she was teaching writing and, then, how devastated she felt when I kept asking her why she was doing what she was doing. In my rush to "cover" more material, I acted insensitively to the people I was working with. Although I sincerely apologized, it took a lot of time, effort, care, and nonjudgmental listening to win back the teachers' trust. It was humbling to be reminded, once again, that without the learner's trust, it's impossible to teach.

Build Early Success for All Students, Including Writers Who Struggle

Fourth grader Cory saw himself as a failure. His teacher knew it; so did his classmates. When his teacher called on him to come up to the front of the class to have a public conference with me (with many teachers observing), I only knew, from glancing at his paper, that his writing was difficult to read. I didn't know anything about him as a student. But from the slouch of his shoulders and the pained look in his eyes, it was clear he wanted to be elsewhere and that he was expecting to hear what was wrong with his writing. If I was to help this student as a writer, I had to find something that he had done well and start from there. I had to validate his efforts so that he would want to continue to write.

I asked him to read aloud his piece on a family tradition so I could concentrate on his intended message. While he was reading I looked on with the sole purpose of finding out what he was trying to say and where he had been successful in saying it. I ignored his poor spelling and handwriting, the lack of punctuation, and the jumbled quality of the work. I concentrated only on finding what he had done well—even if it was just one sentence. Observing teachers later told me they were flabbergasted when my first comment to Cory was a positive one: *I can tell by this sentence exactly what your story is about. You let the reader know right away. That's what good writers do.* Cory's face registered immediate surprise. *How about if we move this sentence right up front? It's a fine beginning sentence. Is it okay if I do that?* Cory nodded. *Okay, I'm just going to cut this here and paste it there.*

Cory went back to complete his writing, and he worked diligently. At the next whole-class share, he volunteered to read his finished piece aloud. He was no longer the sad, defeated boy of a few days earlier. His eyes were shining and looked directly at his audience, his shoulders were straight, he was smiling broadly. He was, in fact, transformed—all because of one honest compliment that allowed him to see himself as a writer, perhaps for the first time in his school career.

Cory's draft after a public conference, grade 4

B-DAY

I like my birthday because I love going out to eat. My favorite place to eat is Elmdoes. I love their food.

It is a Chinese restaurant. You come in and sit at a table. The waiter comes and asks you what you want. I say, "I'll take nachos and cheese."

You get crayons, cups, and crossword puzzles. I love to do the crossword puzzles.

I'm happy because it is the first time I've gone out with my landlord.

Cory, who was classified as learning disabled and who was from a low socio-economic background, was reading two years below grade level in the fall according to standardized tests and was, according to his teacher, "easily frustrated, withdrawn, and not a reader or writer." However, after his writing success and as his teacher continued to build on his strengths, he ended the school year reading close to grade level as measured by standardized tests. He also scored a 4.0 (a passing grade) on the Tennessee Writing Assessment. His teacher, Margaret Phillips, wrote to me about his amazing progress, pleased and grateful that we had "empowered a young mind to realize his own potential and his own worth." She noted:

> He wrote like he was possessed. He could not get enough written down. He volunteered in class and the anger and fights lessened. He became a risk taker. He began doing his homework. His family even commented on the change. I now know I can reach those students that believe they cannot write.

Based on Cory's story and others like it, I am firmly convinced that until the student thinks of himself as a writer, no real improvement is possible. *"Try to focus more on what the child is trying to do and less on what we are trying to teach"* is very good advice.

Don't Underestimate the Power of Kindness

I have thought a lot about why it is always necessary to begin with a positive, hopeful comment. When the first remark we hear is a critical one, most of us feel disheartened. Our brain often shuts down, and what we hear is, *I'm a terrible writer. I knew it was true, and now it's confirmed.* It is the rare person who has the confidence to welcome criticism as an initial response. However, once we trust the person making the remarks, constructive criticism is usually welcome.

Making the first comment a positive one is a necessary act of kindness, and kindness goes a long way. Now the writer is thinking, *She sees something good in my writing. Maybe I'm not such a terrible writer after all.* Kindness makes it possible for us to try again. Kindness gives us energy to reinvest and take risks.

Even in the occasional case when the writer has wasted time and turned in a poor effort, in a conference with the student, I first say something along these lines: *I really want to be able to read your piece and understand what you're trying to say. I know you have smart things to say, but I'm having trouble understanding what you've done here. Let's talk about. . . .* If I say instead, *Don't waste my time. I can't read this. You haven't made any effort,* I have no chance at all of getting the student to invest in writing.

Leave the writer intact is always uppermost in my mind. I want the student to go back to his seat and feel okay about himself. I want the student to know I care about him and that I will support his efforts. I want the student to go on writing.

Demonstrate Respect for Students' Language and Culture

All children bring rich language and cultural resources into the classroom. It is our job not only to respect those experiences but also to use them as strengths from day 1. When a child is viewed as language deficient, teachers communicate less with that child. As Lisa Delpit reminds us, *"It is this teaching behavior and not the language of the child, no matter how different, that creates the problem for learners."* Our job is to recognize, value, and build on those experiences and do whatever is necessary to ensure each child meets success.

"Language works to *position* people in relation to one another." That is why the words we use with children are so critical if we are to position them for success. The longer I teach the more I believe that we can only teach a child when that child senses—through our words, gestures, and actions—our genuine caring, respect, and belief in his abilities. Relationships matter. It's why I don't work in classrooms for a day but for a week. I can teach a skill or activity in one lesson, but I can't get to know the children in one lesson.

Respond to the Writer

I pay little attention to a child's label and lots of attention to what the child is trying to do. I approach all students with the belief that they are capable and can learn. And so, not surprisingly to me, they all do—English language learners, special education students, learners who struggle.

I say to teachers: *Don't tell me who your special education students are, your learners who struggle, your behavior problems. I don't want to know.* There are usually some pleasant surprises. (For the story of some special ed students who succeeded, see pages 19, 69, and 221.)

In teaching writing, remember that you as a caring, knowledgeable teacher are responding to a live, sensitive person. Don't rely on formulas, checklists, traits of writing, a plodding sequence of steps in a book on writing. Listen with your heart as well as your mind, and you will know what to say and do. "Our decisions must be guided by 'What might help this *writer?*' rather than 'What might help this *writing?*'"

Do Not Accept Failure As an Option

Students need to know by our tone, voice, gestures, support, and expectations that failure is not an option and that we respect and value them, their experiences, and background. Our teaching style and demeanor toward our students determine their attitudes and efforts toward learning. In too many classrooms—where students may be disruptive, resistant, learning English as a second language, or have parents who have difficulty communicating with teachers—we give students permission to fail. We marginalize their access to the world of literacy and are too quick to accept failure. Instead, we need to demand success and believe in their capacity to learn, as well as advocate for the resources and support to make success possible. Often, that also means raising expectations for our own professional development.

Former Secretary of the Treasury Paul O'Neill kept a plaque on his desk that said, *WHAT WOULD YOU ATTEMPT TO DO IF YOU KNEW YOU COULD NOT FAIL?* That is the culture of high expectations and success we need to inculcate in all our schools. Students know when we believe they are capable. They feel our commitment. When they feel validated, they are willing to take a risk. They are just like us. When we feel worthwhile and valued, we are also more willing to take a risk and raise our expectations for what might be possible.

5. **Do More Shared Writing**

Language, written and oral, is the
foundation of learning and school achievement. All I do in
the classroom is driven by this belief. This hasn't changed throughout my
career, no matter where the proverbial pendulum is at any point in time.
—Karen Sher, kindergarten teacher

Of all the writing I do in classrooms, shared writing is one of my favorites. It's quick, fun, easy, efficient, and it's a great way to teach and engage all students, of all ages, in all aspects of oral and written language. When teachers add shared writing to their daily reading/writing program, students' enjoyment, confidence, and competence in reading and writing increase and their language skills grow.

In shared writing, the teacher and students compose collaboratively, the teacher acting as expert and scribe for her apprentices as she demonstrates, guides, and negotiates the creation of meaningful text, focusing on the craft of writing as well as the conventions. Texts can be short and completed in one session or long and written over several weeks.

Shared writing builds on what the teacher has already modeled through writing aloud and is the important scaffold students need in order to attempt their own successful writing. While shared writing can be done in pairs, in groups, or as a whole class, I use it most often with the whole class. I make sure the topic is engaging to students, and then I keep a lively pace throughout the lesson. The classroom, with all the children in front of me, is easy to manage, and I relish the opportunity to have every child participate and shine.

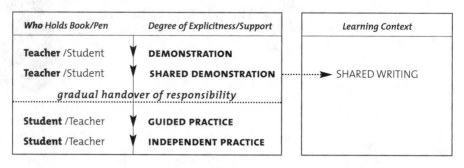

The Optimal Learning Model's Progression of Responsibility

Apply Principles of Instruction and Learning

Notice how shared writing fits into the optimal learning model. During shared writing you are holding the pen and guiding the writing while acting as an expert for your group of apprentices. Shared writing is the context in which the students gain the skills and confidence to "have a go" on their own, with guidance.

Although you want students to feel free to express themselves and fully participate, you also want to raise the standard by showing them what's possible in all aspects of writing—organization, clarity, word choice, legibility, tone, editing, and so on. It's a delicate balance, seeking and validating students' input while at the same time shaping their thoughts in a respectful, collaborative manner. It's the handholding stage, when you take over just enough to allow and encourage students to participate successfully in the writing process.

One of the most powerful aspects of shared writing (or reading) is that it is here that many students begin to figure out how written language works. Much of that learning occurs through the collaborative opportunities and social interactions that take place, not just through our explicit teaching. "As teachers we have to decide *what* to be explicit about for which students, and *when* to be explicit about it."

In shared writing, the teacher does not place expectations for correctness on the students. He values the students, encourages and welcomes their attempts and responses, and supports their efforts, all of which contribute to the teacher-children bond. The teacher expands on the students' ideas, paraphrases their thinking, and demonstrates what cohesive writing looks like and sounds like.

Regardless of student age, shared writing needs to be a major part of every writing program. Shared writing is just as important in the intermediate grades and middle school as it is in the beginning grades.

Shared Writing Is Ideal for All Learners

For all learners, but especially for our English language learners, challenged learners, and economically underprivileged students, shared writing helps provide the rich oral language modeling that stimulates literacy development. Shared writing taps into students' interests. When work is interesting and students see and value its purpose, they are motivated to work harder.

When students of different ethnicities or nationalities have access to their own language and experiences—in print—the text is immensely meaningful and liberating. Bilingual texts that teacher and students have written together are engaging reading material (see example, page 118 and on DVD). Students not only love writing them, they can always read them easily. Teachers can also focus on phonics, word work, fluency, and other reading skills using these familiar texts.

Shared writing is a safe context in which struggling learners can shine. Students who are weak in organization, structure, and form are often strong in ideas. Receiving validation for their ideas in front of their peers builds students' writing confidence, a necessary prerequisite for becoming a writer.

Understand the Research That Supports Shared Writing

Social context is crucial for learning, and shared writing provides the safe, collaborative setting that promotes cohesive writing. The desire to share ideas and words is the impetus behind writing development.

A large body of research also indirectly supports using shared writing with students for whom English is not their first language. Five generic principles of instruction, all of them part of a shared writing experience, contribute to high levels of language and literacy for these students.

PRINCIPLES OF INSTRUCTION THAT SUPPORT ENGLISH LANGUAGE LEARNERS

1. Productive, collaborative learning among teachers and students. ("Learning is most effective when novices and experts work together for a common product or goal, and when they have opportunities to converse about what they are doing.")
2. Purposeful conversation rather than drills and decontextualized rules.
3. Contextualized teaching and curriculum that include and value experiences and skills of students' home and community.
4. Intellectually engaging curriculum of complex, challenging work.
5. Instructional conversation in which students question and share their ideas and knowledge.

Link Shared Writing to Reading

Shared writing is a powerful way to connect reading and writing and improve both reading and writing skills. Beginning in kindergarten and in every grade thereafter, we can use shared writing to teach conversation, humor, character development, interesting beginnings—everything authors do. As I scaffold and shape kids' writing, I make connections to reading: *The text we're writing together will become a reading text for us and others, so we want to do our best thinking and writing. Let's think together about all the great things we've noticed that authors do when they write.*

Shared-writing texts, which can take the form of narratives, lists, charts, booklets, poems, pamphlets, newsletters, worksheets, and so on, can become reading texts for:

- ☐ Shared reading.
- ☐ Guided reading.
- ☐ Independent reading.
- ☐ Their intended reader(s).

They can also become classroom resources:

- ☐ Criteria for writing, editing expectations, etc. (for examples, see the charts on pages 58, 117, and 204).
- ☐ The basis of writing extensions and skills work (see page 94).
- ☐ Springboards for further student writing (see page 111).

To check whether students are following along with the text (orally, visually, or both), I often ask a student to lead the rereading of our shared writing (see photo page 113). That frees me to notice each student and when necessary, refocus attention with a gentle nudge, look, or hand signal.

Frequent rereading of texts they have taken part in writing is also a terrific strategy for improving the fluency, reading skills, and confidence of developing readers, English language learners, and readers who struggle.

Teachers are often surprised by the power of shared writing. Sheila Pearce, who teaches a combination grade 2/3, found shared writing a perfect vehicle for teaching book reviews (see page 132), which require students to be able to identify the main idea of a story and briefly summarize it. She notes, "I have been so pleased with not only the increase in writing skills, but also the boost in reading comprehension skills."

And sixth-grade teacher Royce Lindner of Brookfield, Wisconsin, found that using shared writing to identify the problem and main character in *Holes*, by Louis Sachar, produced a better example than the one he had first created (and later showed to students for comparison). (Both examples are shown below.) Royce also noted that:

- ☐ Students who rarely participated consistently added their ideas.
- ☐ The shared writing was more detailed than the teacher's writing.
- ☐ All students were engaged.
- ☐ He felt more effective as a teacher. "I was able to capture teachable moments rather than trying to lead students into them."

Use Interactive Writing Wisely

Interactive writing is a form of shared writing in which the teacher and a student or students share the pen. The student writes the letters he or she can write, the teacher writes the rest.

Holes by: Louis Sachar (teacher created)	*Holes* by: Louis Sachar (shared writing with students)
In the story, Stanley's main problem is that this great-great grandfather forgot to keep a promise to a lady by the name of Madame Zeroni. This brought a curse to all of the Yelnats men. Stanley fell victim to the curse when he was wrongly accused of stealing a pair of shoes. To serve his sentence he was sent to a miserable place called, Camp Green Lake.	The main problem in this story began when Stanley's great-great grandfather forgot to keep a promise to Madame Zeroni. In exchange for help in his love life, Stanley's great-great grandfather agreed to carry Madame Zeroni up a mountain and sing to her while she drank from the stream that flowed uphill. Because he forgot to do this, the Yelnat's name was cursed. Stanley's great grandfather was robbed by Kissin' Kate Barlow, and his father is a failure as an inventor. The curse affected Stanley because when he was in the wrong place at the wrong time, he was convicted of stealing a pair of shoes he never really stole. As a punishment, he was sent to Camp Green Lake to work off his "crime."

The power of shared writing—the review created by students through shared writing outshines the teacher's

teaching tip

Even though just one person is designated to write on the class chart, have the others each write on a whiteboard using a dry mark pen and eraser. All the kids are engaged, and you can quickly assess individual students.

I use interactive writing occasionally with individuals and small groups, when it seems appropriate, but rarely with a whole class, because it's too time consuming and distracting. As a student comes up to the front of the room to write his letters or words, he invariably trips over someone, and I've lost the attention of the class.

Use your professional common sense. Choose interactive writing if it's the best way to meet your students' needs. Is it the best use of this time for what you want and need to teach? Or is there another way you can do this faster and more efficiently? Even with a small group, I am more likely to use shared writing, because it's faster and I can accomplish much more writing, teaching, and rereading within a short time.

Implement Shared Writing

Using shared writing, with our students around us to offer ideas and support, we can try out writing in a nonthreatening way. The framework below will help you put shared writing into practice. (See Observe Shared Writing in Action, pages 99–111.)

CONCISE FRAMEWORK FOR A SHARED WRITING LESSON

- ☐ Alone or collaboratively with your students, choose a meaningful topic.
- ☐ Discuss why you are doing the shared writing and who the audience is.
- ☐ Brainstorm possibilities for what content will be.
- ☐ Write a title.
- ☐ Get started immediately. Ask for or suggest a beginning sentence. *Who has a good beginning sentence? How about if we say it this way?*
- ☐ Say the words as you write them.
- ☐ Shape students' language. Accept everything you can. (Revise later.)
- ☐ Move along quickly so students stay engaged. Stop after ten or fifteen minutes; it's hard to concentrate longer than that. You can continue the next day.
- ☐ Focus on meaningful language and logical organization. *Does this make sense? How can we say this in a way that's clear to the reader? What should we say next?*
- ☐ Look for opportunities for all students to participate.
- ☐ Stop and reread as you go in order to decide what to write next, to hear what you've already written, to make changes that clarify and strengthen the text. Point to the words as you read so students can follow along easily.

Many teachers are terrified of writing. Because our own writing as students focused on its editorial aspects rather than on its creative, composing facets, we emphasize the same with our students and turn them off to writing. Shared writing boosts our confidence, new and experienced teachers alike.

TEACHING TIPS TO GO ALONG WITH SHARED WRITING FRAMEWORK AND LESSONS

☐ **Choose a Meaningful Topic**

- Show enthusiasm for the topic. Tell why you're excited about it. (See the Teacher Talk entry on page 92.)
- Write for a real audience. (See the examples on page 106.)

☐ **Say the Words as You Go**

- Use shared writing to teach phonics and phonemic awareness. As you scribe the words, stretch out the sounds slowly. Clap the number of syllables in a word.

☐ **Shape Students' Language**

- If a student is faltering with words and having difficulty making herself understood, gently guide and encourage her: *Are you saying . . . ? I want to be sure I am understanding you; try saying that again. What you have to say is important; take your time.*

☐ **Move Along Quickly**

- To keep kids engaged, pause as you are writing and say *"Everyone, quickly spell . . . "* [choose a word they can spell, like *and* or *going*] or *"Read this line with me."*
- Decide what's most important to focus on for this lesson: Getting ideas down? Hearing many students' voices and ideas? Rereading and reorganizing? Editing? Polishing? Choose one or two.
- Time yourself. Stop after ten to fifteen minutes.
- Accept ideas from two or three students, then quickly pull things together: *Let's say it like this. . . .*
- When everyone wants to tell a story about pets, moving day, siblings, hobbies, favorite toys, and so on, save time by asking students to write their stories instead. Then create a class book. Write the introductory page together (see the example on page 116.)

☐ **Look for Opportunities for All Students to Participate**

- Start a story or text together as a class, and then say *"What if the story went this way?"* or *"What do you think is a better [or different] idea for this part?"* Have kids continue the class-generated story on their own or with a partner and write their own ending.

teaching tip

Keep Up a Lively Pace

It's easier to keep students engaged if your lesson moves along quickly. I am not talking about keeping a frantic pace but rather about teaching with a sense of urgency—that is, making every moment count by implementing effective teaching and assessing practices. Often, if you ignore initial behavior problems, disruptive students will participate appropriately without being told.

- Value all students' language and culture.
- If a student raises his hand to contribute and then doesn't know what to say, try: *I can tell you're thinking about this. Think some more, and I will come back to you.* Later, if he is still unable to speak, try: *Jason, tell us what you're thinking about. Is there anything you'd like to add or change here?* Even if he just shakes his head, you've acknowledged him in a positive way, and he may be ready to speak next time.
- Call on students who don't usually volunteer, and ensure their success:

  Valerie, what letter would you expect to see here? It's the same letter that your name starts with.

  Satisha, read this with me. What do you think? Should we change this word to [blank] or leave it as it is?

  Carl, we need to hear what you think. I know you have good ideas.

  Come on, Sam. I know you can add to this. I'll help you.

☐ **Stop and Reread as You Go**

- Write on large, lined chart paper. While it's slower than writing on a transparency, you'll have a permanent record that is easy to find and refer to during shared reading and independent reading. Sometimes, I have a pad that I use only for shared writing. Other times, I post completed charts on the wall.
- Pay attention to one-to-one word matching. Tell children they have to watch the pointer and listen to your voice: *When I stop, you stop.* The kids love doing this, and it works!
- Before you continue writing, have student's partner read the text-in-process. Ask, *Does it make sense? Should we change anything?*

Use Shared Writing to Teach Writing Strategies

Having a repertoire of writing strategies is a necessity for writing well. Although we may demonstrate what writers do, that does not guarantee that students will use these techniques in their own writing. *The strategies that writers use are constructed, not transmitted.* Shared writing is a terrific context in which students can practice and reinforce the strategies we model, making it more likely that they will apply those strategies when they write. (Of course, we want to make sure the writing strategies we are modeling are worth teaching.)

Shared writing is also an ideal social setting in which to get developing language learners to focus on concepts of print, words, rich language, and how stories and texts work. The atmosphere is inviting and nonthreatening. The focus is on enjoyment and making meaning. There is no pressure for the students to contribute before they feel ready, and the teacher is right there to encourage and assist them. Also, because learners, with the teacher's guidance, have a hand in creating the language of the text, the text is appealing and easier to recall and read than a commercial text. Shared writing jumpstarts students' own writing and reading while modeling and reinforcing the reading/writing process. Jointly creating an interesting story or writing on an engaging topic will keep the attention of even our youngest writers.

Keep the Major Focus on Content

Unless you have a message worth reading, editing doesn't matter very much. While, of course, you will be demonstrating correct form, capitalization, punctuation, grammar, in the act of writing, you don't need to comment much about it (for example, you needn't say, *I'm putting a capital letter here because* . . .). You can't work on everything at once, so save your energy—and the students' as well—and focus on writing a meaningful, interesting message.

Demonstrate How Shared Writing Works

- ☐ Choose a meaningful, engaging topic and narrow the focus.
- ☐ Decide what to say and how to say it—think like a writer.
- ☐ Logically organize the writing so it's easy to follow.
- ☐ Use interesting, lively language.
- ☐ Reread, rethink, and revise.
- ☐ Select a fitting title.
- ☐ Write in the correct form (letter, report, story).
- ☐ Begin with a sentence or paragraph to engage the reader.
- ☐ Be picky about word choice.
- ☐ Craft a conclusion.
- ☐ Pay attention to conventions and the mechanics of writing.
- ☐ Incorporate conversation and other literary devices authors use.
- ☐ Check to make sure the writing is clear and will engage the intended reader.

Watch Your Language

All of us need to feel supported, valued, and respected before we can learn. Therefore, it is very important to be sensitive to students' language and culture. We can compose a text collaboratively, but unless we listen to our students in the context of who they are, the activity will not help them become competent, joyful, independent learners.

If a student offers a response that is confusing or not in standard English, choose your words carefully. Shared writing is not the time to focus on students'

English or grammar. It is the time to validate students' ideas and thinking so they will *want* to write and *choose* to write. Phrase questions and comments in inclusive and encouraging language.

Use language that demonstrates respect

☐ *Thank you for sharing your thinking.*

☐ *That's an interesting idea.*

☐ *Good for you. You knew thus-and-so.*

☐ *I am glad you asked that question.*

☐ *Give it a try. I'll help you.*

☐ *Let's do it together.*

☐ *That's good thinking. Here's another way we can say that.*

☐ *You have a smart brain. I want to know what you are thinking.*

☐ *I never thought of that. Tell me more.*

☐ *Yes, you can say it like that. Here's another way to say that.*

☐ *Let's combine those two thoughts like this.*

Use language that affirms and encourages participation

☐ *How can we begin so the reader knows exactly what this is about?*

☐ *Who has a good beginning sentence?*

☐ *Does someone else have another idea?*

☐ *Okay, let's go with that.*

☐ *How many of you prefer this title? Okay, that's most of you. We'll use that one.*

☐ *Now we need to say something about such-and-such. Who has another idea?*

☐ *I won't let you fail. Give it a try.*

☐ *What's another way we could say this?*

☐ *That's a good idea. How about if we say it this way?*

☐ *What's a different word we could use here that might be clearer to the reader?*

☐ *We need to let the reader know we're changing topics. How can we do that? How about if we say it like this?*

☐ *How can we let the reader know we are ending our writing? Okay, that works, or we could say it this way. What do you think?*

☐ *Let's reread this and see if we want to change anything. Does everything make sense? Is it clear and interesting for the reader? Do we need to move anything around to make it easier to follow?*

☐ *Let's take a look at this again tomorrow to be sure it's exactly the way we want it.*

Use Shared Writing to Do Important Word Work

Shared writing texts are ideal for rereading, highlighting features of text, learning high-frequency words, and focusing on parts of words. In particular, when students are actively involved in word work, they enjoy learning and they learn quickly.

Cut Up and Reassemble Sentences

Cutting up sentences and manipulating the words is a great way for students in kindergarten and first and second grade to learn how language works. You can use sentences you have written together while studying a content area or collaboratively write some specifically for this sort of work. Have students sit together in heterogeneous groups of three or four students, so they can collaborate. Even students who don't know all their letters and sounds can put each sentence back together in order and read it, because they have helped create the language and they are working jointly with peers. Let's look at this activity as it plays out in the classroom.

Putting the sentence in order

teaching tip

Make your own copies on a transparency— one uncut to project the whole text and one for cutting, manipulating, and encouraging self-checking (see photo to right).

Reassembling the sentence and projecting it

Write the Message

In one first-grade class, we excerpted two sentences from the shared writing we had done on bats: "Bats are animals that can fly. Bats can hang upside down." In another class that was studying bats, I asked, *Tell me something that you know about bats that is very important,* and together we wrote: "Bats eat insects, and they sleep upside down."

Reading our draft, "All About Bats," and noticing features of words

<u>All About Bats</u>   a†

Bats are animals (that) can fly. Bats can

hang upside down. They fly at night and

sleep during the (day.) Bats use

echolocation at night. They make noises

[that] bounce off of objects. The sound

comes back to the bats so they don't

(crash) Some Bats are called Fruit Bats.

They eat fruit. Do you know all (about)

(Bats?)

By: Mrs. Dickens' First (Graders)

Circling words on the overhead projector

<u>All About Bats</u>

Bats are animals that can fly. Bats can

hang upside down. They fly at night ＿＿＿

sleep during the d＿＿. Bats use

echolocation at night. They make noises

th＿＿ bounce off of objects. The sound

Creating a cloze worksheet

teaching tip

Use cut-up sentences in kindergarten early in the year. Every student will grasp one-to-one matching and correctly point to words, not letters, when matching speech to print. The physical separateness of each word helps students grasp "wordness."

Demonstrate Cutting the Words Apart and Reassembling Them

Type the sentences on a word processor, with an extra space or two between words to make it easier for students to isolate each word visually. You can also draw a line underneath the sentences to make cutting them out easier. Give each student a copy. Keep two copies for yourself (along with a few extras in case students "lose" words). Demonstrate cutting out the sentences and then cutting apart the words, and have each student follow suit. Then reassemble the sentences on an overhead projector. (You could also pin them to a storyboard.) Also project on the overhead or otherwise display the second, uncut copy of the sentences so that students can see the original sequence.

Ask students to put their cut-up sentences back together, aligning the words in order (*Make sure your sentences look like mine*). They can check against the displayed original or consult their peers. Finally, have them read the sentences with you, a partner, or on their own, pointing to each word as they say it.

Helping a student arrange a sentence

Make Word Sorts

After giving students time to manipulate the words on their own, demonstrate an open sort, such as putting together all the words that contain the letter *e* or the letter sequence *at* or all the words that represent doing something (*hang, fly, eat*). Have students guess how you sorted the words and then let them try creating their own sorts. (*Now make up your own sort, and let's see if we can guess it.*) Then move on to closed sorts, directing them to find a specific pattern. (*Find all the words that have the short a sound and put them in a list. Check yourself by looking at the original sentence. Let's read those words together.*)

Work with Words

Introduce additional word-manipulation activities:

☐   *Everyone, find the word* down. *Reread the original sentence to help you. Check yourself.*

☐   *Find all the words that have the /t/ sound. Read them.*

☐   *Find the words that are the same.*

☐   *Make up a new sentence using the words you have. Read it with your partner.*

After four or five minutes, conclude the activity and give each student an envelope with his name on it in which to store the words. You can collect the envelopes and use them again on subsequent days.

Share Cut-Up Sentences with Family Members

On Friday, have students paste their words in order on a sheet of paper. Evaluate their work and let them take the sheet home to show their family members as an example of how they are working with words.

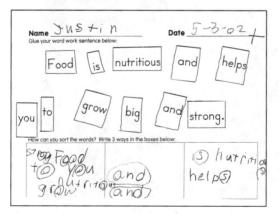

The complete cut-up sentences—with word sorts—
is read with the family at home.

Make Words with Tiles

Children's ability to transfer what they know about words to other contexts is not automatic. I often use shiny one-inch-square tiles to help students construct words, learn about onsets and rimes, work on spelling, and practice letter formation. They write letters on the tiles using dry markers. Have students work in small groups, and put a small plastic tub of thirty or forty tiles at each table.

Building on the work you have done with cut-up sentences, you can introduce activities like these:

☐ *How many tiles do you need to write the word* at? *That's right, two. Take two tiles and write* at, *lowercase letters only. Now, write* hat. *How many tiles do you need to add? At doesn't change. Keep it. Check yourself on the screen* [if you have cut up a blank transparency into small squares and projected the appropriate letters]. *Make some more words that end in* at [sat, mat, that, chat, flat].

☐ *Do the same for other rimes, such as* an: man, ran, pan, than, bran, *and so on.*

☐ *Here's a challenge word. Write* chatter.

☐ *In your group create your own challenge word. Everyone has to be able to read and write it.*

Changing "mat" to "chat;" retaining "at" and adding "ch"

Creating a challenge word and checking spelling

teaching tip

*"How Did You
Know That?"*

Help kids become
aware of the strategies
they use:

*How did you figure
that out?*

What were you thinking?

*What do you mean by
that?*

How did you decide?

*Does that make sense?
How do you know?*

Help students verbal-
ize their thinking:

*I think you probably
[looked at the chart,
word wall, knew it
from a book].*

*I saw you [sound it out,
think really hard, talk
to your partner].*

**TRY IT
APPLY IT**

Write a "Mystery Message"

Writing a short message related to content and context in front of your students is a great way to introduce word-solving techniques. In a kindergarten class one day my message was: "Today we will be illustrating our story about things we love." (See photo page 113.) I tell students their job is to be detectives and silently figure out the message: *Watch me write but don't say anything. I have to check myself. I have to make sure it makes sense.*

Then I call on students: *Who sees something they know?* I highlight with a yellow marker the letters and words students contribute so they stand out. I ask, *how did you know that?* to make students aware of their thinking. If they don't know how they knew, I say something like *I saw you look at the word wall* or *it's a letter in your name* or *it's on our calendar board* or *I think you might have done such-and-such.* If we want students to be independent problem solvers, they have to be able to articulate the skills and strategies they use.

Who knows something else? A letter, a part of a word, a word? I keep highlighting discovered parts and reading the message with only the sounds and words they've decoded. *Does it make sense yet?* Finally, the combination of decoding and context (*what would make sense here?*) will unlock the sentence. *Now it makes sense.* I often reread the message the next day and add to it.

See the mystery message example (morning message) shown on page 121.

✎ Turn your shared writing into a cloze exercise, in which you leave out some words for students to fill in (see example on page 94).

✎ Word-process a piece of shared writing and project it on a screen. Have students come up and circle frequently encountered words (see example on page 94). Teach words they don't know.

✎ Once a week, have students write five frequently used words quickly, on whiteboards. Choose words from cut-up sentences or the word wall. (Cover the words you use.)

✎ Have kindergartners write their best spelling approximations. This carries over into their journal writing and helps them become more confident risk takers.

✎ When students do word work in small groups, appoint a "checker" for each group. Kids learn to work with peers and you'll get more accomplished.

Observe Shared Writing in Action

Create a Fiction Story Through Shared Writing

LESSON FOCUS

☐ Enjoying writing a story together.

☐ Having every child participate in generating story ideas.

☐ Learning to write a fiction story.

☐ Trying out conversation in a story.

☐ Rereading to decide what to say next and what to revise.

Day 2. Rereading our draft before continuing our story, "The Magic Book"

I conducted this lesson midyear in a first-grade class in Colorado. Much of the schoolwide discussion during my weeklong residency had centered around the high-stakes writing test administered to fourth graders. Fourth-grade teachers, especially, were concerned about how much they needed to teach their students in order for them to be successful on the test. In particular, they were concerned about writing fiction, a required genre. We talked about beginning to teach writing essentials in kindergarten and building on those year by year, thus making the test requirements part of effective everyday teaching. For example, young students can easily learn how to write conversation—part of fiction writing—if we show them how. I decided to demonstrate writing conversation as an integral part of writing fiction. Our story was completed over three days in a fifteen-minute session each day. When I entered the classroom on the second day, students spontaneously got out of their seats and sat down in the reading corner in front of our story chart. It was a magical moment. I had not planned to begin our hour with our story, but they left me no choice.

We continue to reread the story *(Is there anything we want to add or change?)* and complete the story by Day 3 with attention to an ending that gives the reader a sense of closure. See complete text for how the story ended on Day 3.

Note that we did not plan the whole story before we wrote it. Part of the writing excitement is letting the story unfold. My main goal was not to craft the best story ever but rather to have fun creating a fanciful story, to see and consider many possibilities, to experiment with conversation, to model rereading as a powerful writing strategy, and to give kids confidence and joy as writers. The kids loved using their own names in our imaginative story.

Beyond the Lesson

Once the completed story was word-processed it was used:

☐   For shared reading.
☐   In a cloze exercise (some words or parts of words are whited out).
☐   To highlight high-frequency words (on a projected transparency).
☐   For word work with tiles and whiteboards: making words from common rimes like "ook"—"book" (in story) plus "took," "shook," and so on; and common phonics generalizations like "ar" ("star," "dark," and "smart" [all in story]).
☐   To teach skills (capitalization, punctuation, deleting text, using conversation).
☐   As an evaluation tool for checking reading fluency.
☐   As a take-home story to read to parents.
☐   As a springboard for free-choice writing of other stories.

THE MAGIC BOOK

Once upon time, there was classroom of smart first graders. One day they went to the library and they saw one cover shining.

Sandro said, "I want that book!"

Kevin said, "I want that book too!"

Katelin said, "You better give me that book!"

"Let's all check it out," said Sandro.

"Let's ask Mrs. Haloin if she's seen this book before," said Nicky.

All the kids gathered around the book. Everyone stared at it. The cover had glow-in-the-dark stars and a glow-in-the-dark dragon with shining, breathing fire coming out of his mouth. All of us at once opened the book and gasped.

UHHH!

The words came out of the book and put a magic spell on us. We shrunk and fell into the book. Words talked to us. The words glowed, moved around, and floated. Mrs. Vizyak shut the book and accidentally locked us in. We screamed, "Help! Help!" She didn't hear us.

Mrs. Vizyak picked up the book and took it to read to the kindergarten class. When she got to the last page, the kids in the book held up letters to spell HELP!! The kindergartners saw the kids in the book and said, "Your first grade class is in the book!"

Mrs. Vizyak shook the book up and down. Her class and a Wizard fell out of the book. Mrs. Vizyak asked the Wizard to make her class regular size. Jamie picked up the tiny Wizard and put him back in the book. We decided to never read a magic book again.

The completed and revised story: created in three 15–minute sessions

What I Do...	**What I Say...**
	DAY 1
	Setting the Purpose, Getting Started
I gather the children in front of me in the reading corner. I sit in the big comfortable chair, and there is a large lined flipchart next to me.	*You know what I was thinking, kids, I was thinking it would be great if we could write our own fiction story. We've been reading lots of fiction, and you know a lot about how stories work. Who has an idea?*
	Sandro: I know, it could be about a magic carpet.
	That's a possibility. Thank you. Who has another idea?
I solicit story ideas from students, and we list them on the chart.	Jason: I know what we could call it, *The Magic Carpet.*
I call on students who raise their hand.	*Let's get some more ideas before we decide.*
	Marie: How about a book about insects?
	Vaughn: Let's write a book on space.
	Those are all good possibilities. Does anyone else have an idea?
	How about a story about a fire department?
	We could write a story about a magic book.

I tally the results by a show of hands, and *The Magic Book* gets the most votes by far. Next, we begin to brainstorm what could happen in the book (see chart).

Okay, we have some great ideas. Let's vote and choose the one most people want. You can only vote once.

What's going to happen in this story?

Pictures could move and pop out.

Words glow in the dark.

Words go right to your brain.

Words talk to you.

Okay, you have some good ideas. Who's going to be the main character?

It could be about us!

I want to maintain kids' attention so we immediately begin to write the story. I write the title and under-line it (see page 99).

What would be a good first sentence to start our story?

Once upon a time there was a classroom of first graders.

That's a great first sentence. Watch me write it. All eyes up here.

I slowly say the words as I write them.

"Once upon a time there was a classroom of first graders."

Brainstorming ideas for our story

What do they do? Who has an idea? Make sure it goes with our magic book story.

One day they went to the library and they saw one cover shining.

I move quickly because I don't want to lose the children's attention.

That sounds great! Let's go with that.

Okay, so when the kids see this shining cover what do they say? Conversation makes a story more interesting.

I encourage written dialogue so I can demonstrate it as part of effective fiction writing.

Sandro: I want that book.

What else do they say?

Kevin: I want that book too.

Katelin: You better give me that book!

Again, I say the words as I write them.

Katelin, I love the way you said that. I'm going to put this mark here to show that.

I make an exclamation mark.

Let's reread what we have so far and see how it sounds. All eyes up here.

I keep up a fast pace as we reread

If you get some ideas for our story later, jot them down on the chart (see on p. 101).

I want them to be thinking about writing even when we're not writing

DAY 2

Affirming Their Ideas, Rereading, Continuing the Story

Wow, I can tell by the way you all came right up to our chart you're ready to continue our story. And, look at all these good ideas you have jotted down. You were thinking about our story even when we weren't writing it. That's what good writers do. They think about their writing all the time.

I point to and read aloud some of the ideas students have listed on our chart.

Okay, let's read our story so far and see how it sounds before we continue. Who wants to come up and point to each word as you read and lead the class in rereading?

Abbie leads the class in rereading.

I ask a volunteer to lead rereading so I can be sure that all students are reading and following along. (Rereading is a powerful strategy for struggling readers and writers.)

Is there anything we want to change or add? What kind of first graders were they?

Several kids: Smart!

I insert a caret and add the word "smart."

"Once upon a time there was a classroom of smart first graders." I like the way that sounds. Let's hear from a few more students. What else might someone say?

Let's all check it out.

That's good thinking.

I want students to know writers are always rereading to check how the writing sounds and looks on the page.

Watch me write it. "Let's all check it out" I'm going to add "said Sandro" so the reader knows who said it. Watch how I do it.

Let's get Mrs. Haloin, our librarian, involved. What might we ask her?

Nicky: Let's ask Mrs. Haloin if she's seen this book before.

I make a specific suggestion to shape the story and move it along.

Good idea, Nicky. Everyone, watch me write. I want to be sure I'm doing my best spelling and not leaving out any words.

I say each word as I write Nicky's sentence and add "said Nicky."

Let's read our story from the beginning and see what we want to say next. Rereading is a good way to get ideas.

I want to encourage rereading when kids do their own writing.

Now let's bring the whole class back together in the story. We need to have some girls helping to write this story too.

I want to optimize participation.

Sarah: All the kids looked at the book.

That's fine. Does someone have another way to say that?

All the kids gathered around the book.

I love that word "gathered."

I say the words as I write them.

"All the kids gathered around the book." I can picture everyone looking at the book. How can we say that so it sounds like a story? Michael, what do you think? What should we say next?

As I help shape the story, I call on volunteers and also encourage participation from those we haven't heard from.

Everyone stared at it.

I write the sentence

What do the kids see? What does the cover look like? Take a look at our chart for some ideas. Marissa, what do they see?

I point to their listing of ideas

Marissa: Glow-in-the-dark-stars.

The cover had glow-in-the-dark stars...

I supply the beginning of the sentence ("The cover had") and then write Marissa's words.

What else?

...and a glow-in-the-dark dragon ...

I add it to the sentence as I say it aloud.

I take the first response as it makes sense and I want to keep the story moving along.	*What did this dragon look like?* He had shiny, breathing fire coming out of his mouth. *". . . with shiny, breathing fire coming out of his mouth."* *That sounds great. Now what do the smart first graders do? Kelsie, give it a try. You see this glow-in-the-dark cover. Do you pick up the book?* Kelsie: All of us at once opened the book . . . *And then what?* Kelsie: . . . and gasped, "UHHH!"*
I want rereading-while-writing to become a habit.	*You said that so loud. I'm going to write it with big letters and an exclamation point to show how to read that. Okay, let's read the story from the beginning before we go on.*
I direct their attention back to some of their ideas and encourage everyone to talk. I want to be sure they stick with our story's main idea. They talk for about a minute or two.	*Look at our chart, turn and talk to your partner, what do you want to happen next? Make sure your ideas make sense. There are no witches in our story. We're writing about a magic book that glows in the dark.*
I write it as stated.	*What's going to happen now? Who came up with a good idea?* Words came out of the book and put a magic spell on us. *Interesting idea. Then what happened?* We shrunk and fell into the book. Words talked to us.
I write it.	The words were big . . . . . . and had funny faces on them.
I reread, starting with "Words came out of the book. . ."	*Let's read this part again and see how it works with our story.*
I guide students to leave out a line that may lead them off track.	*What do you think? How about if we cross out the last line. I don't think it adds to our story.* Let's cross it out. *Let's read it again and see what should come next.* The words glowed . . .
We stop here, and complete our story on Day 3.	. . . moved around, and floated. *Okay, that works. What happens now?*

Observe Shared Writing in Action

Teach Informational Writing Through Shared Writing

LESSON FOCUS

☐ Enjoying writing and feeling successful as writers.

☐ Learning how to write an informational essay.

☐ Establishing meaningful purpose and audience.

☐ Brainstorming ideas before writing.

☐ Applying criteria to writing.

☐ Writing with specificity.

☐ Including a satisfying lead and ending.

This fifteen-minute shared writing lesson took place in December during a writing residency in Sue Mikulecky's fifth-grade class (see page 221). Following the lesson framework on page 293, we had already established a

Celebrating a students writing in whole-class share

genuine purpose and audience: creating a guide to the school ("The Eagle's Eye Around Swanson School") that could be used by new students, new teachers, and visitors (see audiences chart below). Next we brainstormed the topics to be included (see topics chart [again, below]; students initialed the topic they chose). To guarantee writing success, including when to paragraph, I established criteria—a simple rubric—ahead of time (see requirements below).

So that students would remain attentive and interested and have enough time to complete their initial drafts, this shared writing, "How to Work in a Small Group" (a topic from our brainstormed list), was completed in fifteen minutes. After the draft was written, we reviewed it against our criteria and numbered each requirement we had included (see the copy of the draft below).

The next day the students and I reviewed the draft and slightly revised it. The biggest challenge was to prompt the students who were not used to writing for a real audience to see the necessity for a closing that considers the reader. It took some nudging (*Have we concluded this so that our reader feels satisfied?*) before they came to that understanding. (See last line of draft for that addition.) (The accompanying DVD includes some pages from the final publication, which was widely distributed to the audiences listed below.)

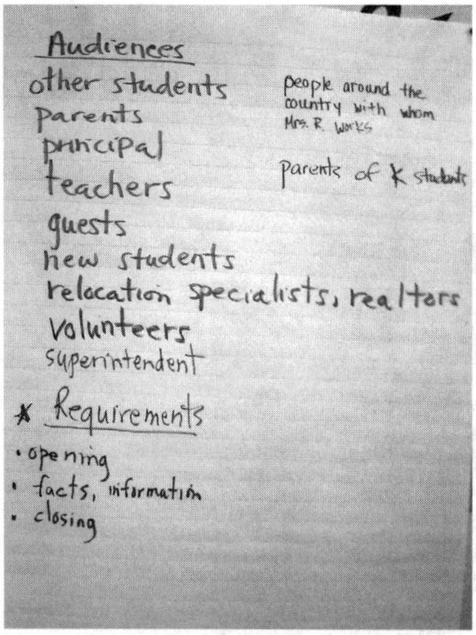

Our audience chart and our writing requirements (simple criteria)

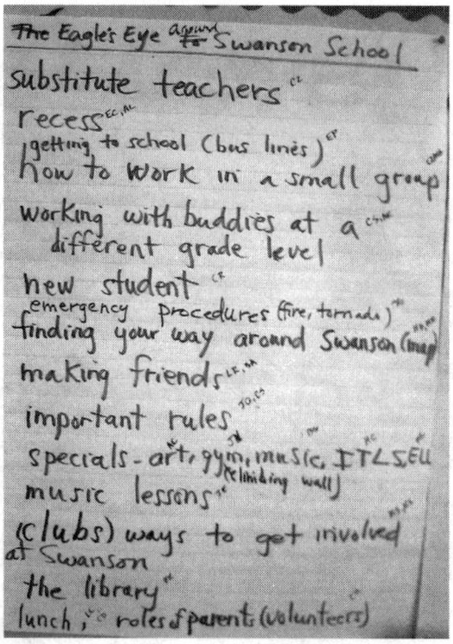

Our topics chart with students' initials (indicating their writing topic)

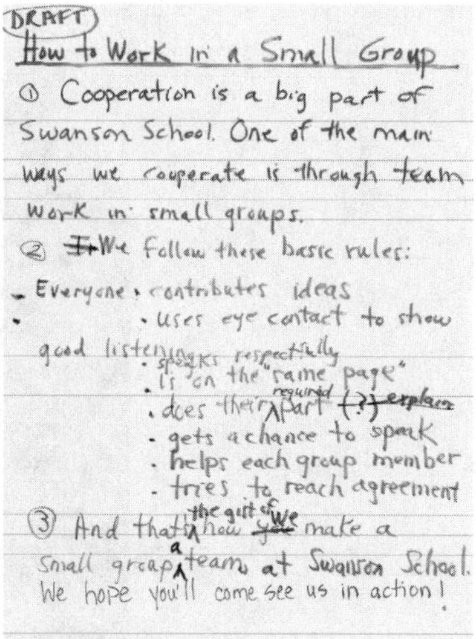

Our draft, "How to Work in a Small Group"

What I Do...	**What I Say...**
	Setting the Purpose, Getting Started
I explain why we're doing the shared writing.	*We're going to write one part of our guidebook together so when you go to write on your own, you'll know exactly what to do.*
	Take a look at the criteria we've established for our writing. Our opening needs to let the reader know what our piece is about. Who has a good first sentence?
	Colin: We work in small groups at our school.
I validate the student's response and prod with a question for more.	*That's a possibility. Colin, thank you for sharing your thinking. Kids, why is it important to be able to work in a small group?*
I call on Victoria who raises her hand.	Victoria: Cooperation is a big part of Swanson School.
	That's an interesting way to start. Let's go with that. It tells the reader right away something important about our school.
I want kids' attention focused on our writing. I say each word in the sentence as I write it.	*"Cooperation is a big part of Swanson School." All eyes up here. Make sure I'm getting it right.*
	Okay, now connect that thought to working in small groups. How do cooperation and small groups go together?
	Joe, you've got your hand up. Give us the next sentence.
	Joe: One of the main ways we cooperate is through team work in small groups.
I point to each word as we read aloud together.	*Great. Thank you, Joe. Let's read what we have so far.*
	How does that sound?
	Several students respond, "It sounds good."
	Getting the Facts Down
I want to encourage specific, detailed information.	*Let's go back to our criteria. We have our opening. Now we need the facts and information that tell how to work in a small group. If a visitor came to our school, what exactly would he see? What do you do that makes small-group work go well?*
	Kayla: Well, we have some rules.
I want to keep things moving and build on the structure Kayla has suggested.	*It would be important to include those. How about if we say it like this: "We follow these basic rules:"*

I don't worry about labeling paragraphing at this time. My focus is on getting the information down.

I'm going to write on a new line because we're done with our opening. Now we're moving to the factual part.

I write the words as I say them aloud.

"We follow these basic rules."

What are the main rules you follow? Becky? (Her hand is up.)

> Becky: Everyone contributes ideas.

Good beginning. What else?

> Clair: Everyone uses eye contact to show good listening.

Clair, that's an important one.

I write down their suggestions without commenting that I am listing items. I want to keep the focus on getting ideas down quickly.

Responses come rapidly from various students who volunteer, and I jot them down.

> Speaks respectfully.

> Is on the same page.

> Does their part.

> Gets a chance to speak.

> Helps each group member.

> Tries to reach agreement.

Wow! I can tell you've done a lot of work in small groups. You know a lot about how to participate so the group works well. Good for you.

Rereading and Rethinking

I want everyone's attention; I want to emphasize the importance of rereading.

Let's reread this part to be sure it makes sense before we move to the closing. Read it aloud with me or follow silently with your eyes.

> Ariel: I like it.

> Juliana: Me too.

Because no one has brought it up, I prod with a question.

I'm not sure about "does their part." Explain that; it feels like something is missing.

> A conversation ensues about what the phrase means.

I have the students stop talking after a minute to get back on track.

How about if we say "does their required part"? I think that makes it a little clearer.

Writing an Ending

Okay, let's wrap it up. Let's pull everything together in an interesting way without repeating our beginning.

Caitlin, we haven't heard from you. Give it a try. I'll help you. What have we told the reader in this second part?

> Caitlin: And that's how you make a small group . . ."

That's a good start. Thank you. Someone finish that thought.

Eric, how could we add on to "And that's how we make a small group. . ."

I won't let you fail. Give it a try.

> Eric: And that's how you make a small group team at Swanson School.

Thanks Eric. That works fine. Watch me write it.

Okay, anyone want to add anything else? Does it sound like it's ended for the reader? Let's read our last line: "And that's how you make a small group team at Swanson."

Something doesn't sound right.

> Chase: And that's how *we* make . . .

Thanks Chase. Good noticing. I'll cross out "you" and put "we" here.

Anything else?

> Kelsey: I think we need to add "a" after group.

"And that's how we make a small group a team . . ."

Thanks Kelsey. That makes more sense now for the reader.

You know what, I'm thinking we need to say, "And that's the gist of how we make a small group. . . ." We've told how a small group works but in general terms, so we need to let the reader know that. What do you think? Gist means the general idea.

> Lots of nods and yeses.

Okay, I'm going to add that. Let's read that together: "And that's the gist of how we make a small group work as a team at Swanson School."

Now, let's read the whole thing through and see if we want to change anything.

> Students like it as is. (See the draft on page 106.)

I am aware that our list is a bit superficial but this is our first attempt. I want students to be successful and enjoy writing.

I encourage participation from reluctant students.

I wait five seconds

I'm thinking that it's not a great last line, but it works so I take it. We read it together.

I add a caret and write *a*.

I am aware that our facts are not specific enough for the reader to "visualize" small-group work. However, I want to bring our piece to an end while excitement is high. I decide to accept what we have by adding one qualification.

I am hoping to add another line that is directed to the audience, but students are not ready for this yet.

I want everyone to have time to draft their own piece.

If I want students to end their own writing with a line that acknowledges the readers, I have to first demonstrate that. The next day I say:

What about our ending? Are we happy with it?

They are.

We'll revisit this again tomorrow. Right now, I want you to get started writing the part you signed up for. Some of you signed up for the same topic. That's fine. We can combine those together later.

Check to be sure you do all three parts of the writing that are listed on our chart. Check yourself when you're done by numbering them.

I think we need another line that invites the reader to see a small group.

Students respond: We hope you'll come see us in action.

Beyond the Lesson

After the shared writing, we establish writing criteria (see page 184), follow the five-day lesson plan on page 293, and use the procedures described on pages 194–195 to produce drafts, final copies, and a class publication (see DVD). Before students begin their drafts, I have two scaffolded public conversations to provide more support before writing (see example below).

I chart my public scaffolded conversation with Victoria (Vikki)

Victoria writes her draft on dressing for Wisconsin weather; notice how she organizes it according to the established criteria (see page 184)

WI weather

Wisconson has diffrent weather than other states. You see here in Wisconson we have hot sumers & cold winters. If your not used to that then listen otherwise go away.

Winter coats, snow pants, boots, hats & gloves for winter to stay warm Shorts & tank tops, short sleve shirts & sandals are things we're used to if the day I'm not so shure your used to it. Let me put it this way in winter unless you want to be a popsicle and a well early not early summer I'd consider dressing rite according to the time of year.

I hope this helped to make it easear for Eu to understand our goofy weather here. Just to make shure I didn't scare you I wanted to tell you that If you dress right during the correct seasons than everything going to be ao-ka. In fact I hope that some day you might get to experience Wisconsons fun and interesting weather.

LHT

Dressing for Wisconsin

It's important to dress right in Wisconsin. There are so many different types of weather like snow, rain, and sunshine. During them all it's important to have fun. You don't want to do something like dress in shorts during winter.

You need winter coats, snow pants, boots, hats, and gloves for winter to stay warm. Shorts, tank tops, short sleeve shirts, and sandals are things we're used to for summer, but I'm not so sure you're used to it. Let me put it this way, unless you want to be a popsicle in winter and salsa in summer, I'd consider dressing right according to the time of the year.

Wisconsin can be fun in winter and summer. Follow these tips and hopefully dressing yourself for Wisconsin will be easier. So come on over and experience Wisconsin's interesting weather at Swanson School. Hope to see you soon!

Nathan also chooses to write about WI weather

Victoria and Nathan collaborate on their page in "Eagle's Eye Around Swanson School"

After students finish their drafts and final copies, we brainstorm ideas for free choice writing. Now that students know how to write a straightforward informational piece, they can easily do so on their own.

Ideas for Free-Choice Writing

1. What every 5th grader needs to know
2. School etiquette
3. School rules
4. All about teachers
5. How to make friends
6. Poetry
7. Lunchroom

Tried and True Ideas for Shared Writing

Shared Writing ▶ **Shared Reading** ▶ **Independent Reading**

- [ ] Welcome letter (to a new student, to kindergartners, to a new person in the neighborhood, to a tourist in your state).
- [ ] Procedures for classroom, lunchroom, and playground activities (see page 113; pages 317–318 contain a list of procedures to follow when there is a substitute teacher).
- [ ] School alphabet book (see page 113).
- [ ] Visitor's guide (to the school, classroom, city). (See pages 105–110 and DVD.)
- [ ] "All about" books (all about our classroom, our school, our science experiment, a special person see photo, page 116).
- [ ] Class journal (daily happenings, major things learned).
- [ ] What is special about us (our school, our neighborhood); What We Love (see page 113).
- [ ] Letter to the principal requesting something or inviting her to a learning celebration (see page 289).
- [ ] A fictional story (see pages 74, 99–104).
- [ ] Poems (see pages 305–315).
- [ ] Summary of a picture book to assess understanding or share with other classrooms.

Poetry writing in kindergarten

> Dear New Student at BBC,
>   Welcome to our cool school! I think you'll have a great time at BBC.
>   The teachers at BBC are fabulous! They help kids learn to do math, spelling, writing, reading, art, science, social studies. Sometimes they give you treats such as chocolate, popcorn, jolly ranchers and suckers. At

Welcome Letter

Morning Procedures

1. Greet your teacher and friends.
2. Make your lunch choice. Put lunch boxes in the basket.
3. Put folders in cubbies.
4. Return and check-in books.
5. Hang up backpacks and jackets.
6. Put chair down.
7. Get ready. (pencils drinks restroom)
8. Sign in.
9. Enjoy choice time.
10. Clean up when the chimes ring.

Procedures

What we love

B is for Brain Boosters. You get to balance on a board.

C is for Mr. Christianson. He is the vice principal. When you have problems he helps you.

School alphabet book

- ☐ A research report (see page 114).
- ☐ Advice (to parents of new babies, to next year's students, to teachers).
- ☐ What to do if (you see a spider, bee, or wasp; when you're bored; when you've done something hurtful or wrong).
- ☐ Recipes (real or fanciful).
- ☐ Favorite foods (hobbies, places, people).
- ☐ Book reviews (see page 132).
- ☐ Profiles and biographies (of authors, neighbors, people in history).
- ☐ Predictable books (pattern books) (see page 136).
- ☐ Student survival handbook/guide (for a grade level or the whole school).
- ☐ New student handbook.

- [ ] Class newspaper, newsletter for parents, daily news.
- [ ] How to be (a big brother or sister, a friend, a good student).
- [ ] How to take care of a (pet, a plant, toys, your room).
- [ ] How to (make a meal, select a book, get ready for school).
- [ ] What to expect in second (third, fourth, etc.) grade.
- [ ] Summaries of nonfiction studies (see below "All About the Human Body;" see DVD for published book).

HOW TO MAKE A CLASS NEWSPAPER

Do you know how to make a class newspaper? We'll show you how if you read along with us.

First, we get into 4 or 5 groups, and each group has one page about a category or theme such as, soccer, science, or favorite books.

Next, we split up the jobs which are writing poems, taking photos, making drawings, writing the stories, finding games, and having interviews and surveys using a tape recorder.

Then, we take our finished writing and bring it up to Ms. Leggett. She prints it out and we reread it and revise it and make corrections on the computer.

Then, we lay out all the pieces on a medium size paper.

Last, but not least, we staple all the sheets together and add our title, *The Cougar Mountain News*. We make enough copies, 500, for everyone at our school.

Summary of content-area study   All About Our Kindergarten Classroom

- ☐ How to act on the bus, on the playground, in the lunchroom, etc.
- ☐ What to do when there's a fire drill or an emergency.
- ☐ A pamphlet explaining to younger students why they need to read.
- ☐ What We Have Learned About . . .
- ☐ Rubrics (see pages 240–242; Appendices F and I).

ALL ABOUT INSECTS

You are about to read amazing facts about insects! Did you know that they have three body parts?
The queen termite can live up to 15 years and lays one egg every 3 seconds. She must be exhausted!
Some bugs can walk on water.
The monarch butterfly eats milkweed to protect itself. Butterfly wings are made up of tiny scales. Aren't INSECTS amazing?

Grade 4 summary of study of insects

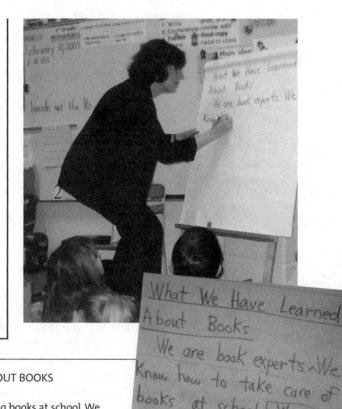

WHAT WE HAVE LEARNED ABOUT BOOKS

We are book experts. We are great at reading books at school. We find just right books to read. If we can't read five words, the book is too hard and we put it back. Sometimes we read easy books.

We know how to take care of books at school. We each take care of a couple of buckets of books. We put our names on the bucket of books. We put our names on the bucket of books we are experts on. We check the books. We look through them. We put labels on them. We also take books that are bent, ripped, or need care and put them in the books-to-fix box. We are good at our jobs.

February 12, 2003—Written by
Ms. Thompson's 1st Grade class with Mrs. Routman

What We Have Learned About Books: beginning draft and final copy

Our Pets

This is a book about our fantastic, wonderful pets. Our pets are funny, silly, and cute. They are all different shapes, sizes, colors, and kinds. Some are small; some are medium, and some are big. We have dogs, cats, birds, rabbits, fish, guinea pigs, hamsters, lizards, and snakes. Many of our pets are good thinkers.

Introductory page to class book

Thank-you letter to school librarian

☐ Classroom routines and procedures (for daily jobs, recess, independent reading). See pages 113, 316–322.

☐ Charts to assess students' knowledge (of content area, authors, reading strategies, writing strategies, spelling strategies). See charts on page 117.

☐ Letter to student council or principal (what we'd like in an assembly, school improvement) (see pages 279, 289).

☐ Thank-you notes (to volunteers, visitors, crossing guards, custodians, previous teachers, school secretaries, librarians see above).

☐ Invitations to school performances.

☐ Letters of encouragement (to students taking high-stakes tests, sick people, soldiers).

☐ A book about the teachers at our school.

☐ Keepsake memory book of school year.

☐ Appreciation writing (to custodian, parent, visitor, friend) (see gratitude letters, pages 201–203).

☐ Class books (our pets, siblings, favorite toys, hobbies, what we're experts at)

☐ Observations of class pet, plant, science experiment (science logs).

☐ Short plays.

☐ Literacy charts (when to abandon books, how to partner-read, what good readers do, what good writers do, reading tips, writing tips, editing expectations, how to "fix up" misspelled words). (See pages 129, 131, and 320.)

☐ Innovations on familiar texts. (See page 122.)

☐ Classroom job descriptions (for new and future students).

☐ Book of school records.

Ways We Choose Books

- genre
- author
- interesting cover
- reading the back
- recommend by a friend, parent, teacher
- interesting title
- award winners
- favorite series
- illustrations
- books from movies

- highlighted in book order
- reading 1st page or 2
- good length
- gift
- word choice
- size of print
- just right book
- read part of middle
- read it before

Partner Reading

Looks 👁	Sounds 👂
· Choose books you enjoy.	· Use a whisper voice (sounds like air)
· Stay in one place.	· If somebody is loud show them the quiet sign.
· The reader holds the book.	· If your partner has trouble reading tell them:
· Sit side by side. 🧑🧑	"Sound it out"
· Take turns reading each page. (You read one page your partner reads the next page).	"Chunk parts of the word"
	"look at the picture"
· Reread if you don't know what's happening.	"Skip and come back"
	"Would you like me to help you"
	· After each page turn and tell (whisper) your partner what's happening.

4th GRADE

Writing

Good Writing

My topic is easy for the reader to follow

I use ideas that tell about my topic

My ideas are easy for the reader to understand

I choose words that keep my reader interested

The reader can hear my voice

What Good Writers Do

1. Write about what they know
2. Keep their audience in mind
3. Reread what they write
4. Revise their writing to make it better for their audience to read
5. Edit their writing out of courtesy for their audience
6. Always bear in mind their Topic, Audience and Purpose (T.A.P.)
7. Explain their writing
   - back it up with examples
   - tell when, where, why, how, what happens (Description and Detail)
8. Write in an organized fashion
9. Puts a picture in the reader's head
10. Uses interesting words
11. Writes like they speak (voice)

Good Writers:

- stick to their topic
- re-read as they go
- make changes - (lassos, carrots) cross-outs
- add details
- use interesting words
- add pizzaz!
- use "snappy beginnings" (lead)
- use describing words
- say things one time
- think before they write
- their writing makes sense
- add humor to stories
- put "thoughts" in their writing
- their writing sounds like them
- name their characters
- use paragraphs to organize writing
- "explain" in their writing
- express their feelings in writing
- put their voice in writing (sounds like them)
- take out the boring stuff
- take out the run-on sentences
- write stuff that doesn't need publishing
- think about writing all the time

Literacy charts

- ☐ Rules of games
- ☐ Texts for younger readers (science, social studies, adventure).
- ☐ Retelling a story.
- ☐ Explanation of school or family traditions.
- ☐ Classroom highlights (field trips, visitors, learning experiences). See below.
- ☐ Songs, raps, chants, jump-rope rhymes.
- ☐ Persuasive letters (to businesses, teachers, community members). (See page 333.)
- ☐ What parents need to know about open house, field trip).
- ☐ Bilingual books (see below).

Organizing a bilingual book in a grade 1-2-3 classroom. (See DVD for published book)

6. Capitalize on the Reading–Writing Connection

I'm still studying writing as a reader.
—Jhumpa Lahiri

Although research strongly supports the positive impact writing has on reading comprehension and enjoyment, in reality, this connection is often ignored in classrooms. This is not surprising, given that writing is *not* routinely linked with reading in our current professional literature. In a recent popular annual survey, in which twenty-five literacy leaders examined close to thirty "key topics" that are "hot" or "not hot" in reading research and practice, neither writing nor the reading–writing connection were considered.

Yet the division between reading and writing is artificial. Research has clearly shown that reading and writing are interactive, closely connected processes that support each other and that participation in strong writing programs clearly benefits both reading and writing development. In classrooms—including those in high-poverty schools—where student achievement is high, reading and writing are routinely linked, and students have a great many writing opportunities across the curriculum.

My own experience teaching reading and writing for over thirty-five years lends strong credence to the power of writing with regard to reading and vice versa. Our best writers are usually our best readers. Popular author Stephen King notes, "If you want to be a writer, you must do two things above all others: read a lot and write a lot. There's no way around those two things that I'm aware of, no shortcut." Effective teachers who have high-achieving students (including on high-stakes tests) do more writing and reading of whole texts and spend little time on "stuff"—activities about writing and reading.

Link Writing with Reading

In many schools, reading and writing are completely separate subjects, but they should not be. Marie Clay's research with young children in New Zealand in the 1970s showed that as children write they develop many skills and writing abilities and that print awareness develops through both reading and writing. And the more experience children have in reading and writing, the more meaningful their writing becomes. Growth in reading positively impacts writing, and growth in writing positively impacts reading. Since poor readers tend to become poor writers, we need to ensure we work on reading alongside writing.

For our English language learners, who encounter much unfamiliar language even in beginning reading texts, the reading-writing integration is a necessity. When I cannot find texts students can easily read, we write our own. Students can read familiar stories that they tell and write far more easily than they can read commercial texts. Because it is easier to learn to read and write words that you already understand orally, creating original texts with familiar language and concepts makes good sense. (Ideas for the kinds of text you can create are found on page 136 and pages 112–118.)

Integrate Reading and Writing in Teaching

Integrating reading and writing leads to more authentic teaching, better reading and writing, and higher scores on tests. I have experienced these results many times. On reflection, I think I've been able to keep reading and writing together because so much of what I write with students—shared-writing of poems, stories, procedures—becomes the texts we read in shared reading, guided reading, and independent reading. Using their own writing as reading material engages all students: "When students write the literature the class reads, they bypass economically the deep split between reading and writing which afflicts classrooms from first grade forward."

Begin in Kindergarten

In a recent residency I did in a kindergarten classroom, the teacher requested I model guided reading. Because I do not see guided reading as necessary in kindergarten, I probed for more information. I discovered that this teacher really wanted to know how to cope with four daily reading groups. Not surprisingly, since these young learners were spending forty-five minutes out of the reading hour working independently, they were not as accomplished as readers and writers as I would have expected. They had spent scant time reading and writing. What I wound up modeling was how to use the same hour more efficiently and teach a whole lot more.

Here are the texts we wrote and read in one hour a day, in one week, in late March:

- ☐ Morning message (daily).
- ☐ *We Share Everything* by Robert Munsch (read-aloud).
- ☐ Book review of *We Share Everything*.
- ☐ Cut-up sentences related to what we learned about animals (daily; see pages 93–96 for procedures).

Good morning. My name is Mrs. Routman. I am happy to meet you

Today we will write more poems.

Morning Message: 2 days

We Share Everything by Robert Munsch Is a fo box oabt It's a funny book about sh— m k—. Sharing in kindergarten

We Share Everything: A book review

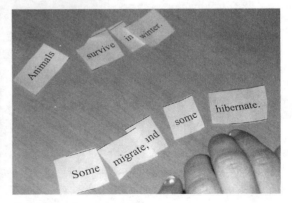

Cut-up sentences

- ☐ Poems (class shared writing).
- ☐ Poems (each student). (See one example below.)
- ☐ *Harriet, You'll Drive Me Wild* by Mem Fox (read-aloud).
- ☐ "We Drive Our Parents Wild" (shared writing innovated on Fox's text).
- ☐ Shared writing of classroom experiences (supported by photos). See similar example on page 114.

Writing and illustrating poems in kindergarten

Katie
smart
silly
loves to read
Strawberries

in my cereal
ruby red
cold and juicy
sweet and sour
Strawberries

My demonstration writing of poems before expecting kids to write

"Jellyfish. Squish. Squash. Sting. OW." Taki's poem

Elomakz

We Drive Our Parents Wild

Evan does not get dressed when he wakes up.

Vito has pillow fights with his brother, and the feathers go everywhere.

Arielle gets out of bed at night and goes into her mom's and dad's bed.

Marti watches movies

Our shared writing innovation on *Harriet, You'll Drive Me Wild* by Mem Fox

Ensure Students Read Quality Materials

Use literature as a springboard for writing. Read aloud a picture book or informational book and use the text to spur similar but original texts.

Children's writing reflects the quality of the reading they do. The complexity and literary quality—or lack thereof—of the texts children read greatly influence the quality of their narrative writing. Children who read literature—well-written folktales, narratives, and trade books—become better writers than children who primarily read basal reading texts. A lot of this is common sense. Readers of well-written material experience more language, vocabulary, and stories to apply to their writing. That is why it is critical that we continue to read aloud fiction and nonfiction to students at every age and provide rich language experiences to *all* students, not bits and pieces of decontextualized skills. For students who cannot read the texts on their own yet, hearing the rich language of literature inspires quality conversations, triggers ideas for their own writing, and motivates them to become better readers.

Don't neglect nonfiction. Expository writing develops more slowly than narrative writing, but this may be because children have less experience with and exposure to expository writing and receive fewer demonstrations of it. Most of what they hear and read is fiction—all the more reason to be sure we expose them to many informational texts and teach informational writing. Children who read nonfiction have more information with which to write, have writing models at hand, and are more aware of nonfiction features such as visual aids. (See Notes, page A–30, for nonfiction resources.)

Spend More Time Reading

Being an avid reader is the best preparation for becoming a writer. You can study the writer's craft and practice it, but there's no substitute for being immersed in literature. In his memoir *Living to Tell the Tale*, Nobel laureate Gabriel Garcia Marquez describes how he devoured books and scoured them "for clues to technique, to language, to structure, to anything that might help him learn how to write." Prolific author Gary Paulsen agrees:

> The most important part of writing is to read. I tell young people, "Read like a wolf eats, read when they tell you not to read, and read what they tell you not to read." If you read enough, ultimately when you sit down to write, that information is in your head and you can write, or it will start to work for you. The rest is learning mechanics, which you can learn from reading too.

And Kent Haruf, who wrote the acclaimed best-selling books *Plainsong* and *Eventide,* says that he reads daily from his literary heroes, such as Faulkner and Hemingway.

Do whatever you can to ensure that your students have lots of time to read and can put their hands on a variety of interesting and varied reading material. Students who read more are more confident writers "because of their superior command of the written language." And while superior writers read "good" books, the quality of what they read appears to be somewhat less important than the sheer amount of reading they do.

For our English language learners, the research is overwhelming that voluntary reading is a powerful means for developing language competence. "What the reader brings to the writing is at least as important as what the writer presents in the writing." Here, reading aloud is a necessity for developing language that students cannot yet read on their own. Teachers need to read aloud stories, poems, short books, long books, fiction, nonfiction, about topics and ideas that kids can connect to.

In *Reading Essentials*, I wrote extensively about the importance of independent reading (and the research that supports it) and how to have students organize, with our guidance, a comprehensive classroom library that includes the fiction and nonfiction materials they want to read. Don't neglect time for daily, free-choice reading. And don't underestimate the power of kids' own writing as models.

Finally, don't spend so much time studying and practicing writing craft that students lose valuable reading time. Many teachers have students apprentice themselves to an author and write in the style of that author. While that's fine, it's very time consuming. Kids can learn about the craft of writing through reading widely and noticing—with our guidance—what authors do. Prolific author Stephen King notes, "I don't read in order to study the craft; I read because I like to read."

Teach Students How to Reread Their Writing

teaching tip

Students can revise more effectively if they wait a day before rereading. That interim often makes it easier to see what changes are needed.

Rereading during the composing process improves the quality of the writing. We see this over and over again when we teach children to reread what they've written before they continue writing. My explicit modeling of writing a letter to Zach (see page 158) is one way to demonstrate for students exactly what we do when we reread.

Look for evidence of rereading. You will know students are rereading when you see them going over previously written text, crossing things out, drawing arrows to indicate repositioning, adding things in the margins. (See photo, page 319.)

Examine Written Responses to Reading

Make sure the writing children do in response to reading is worth their time. For example, research shows that when students answer teacher-originated short-answer questions, they quickly look for the needed information and copy it, with little thought or reflection. Basically, such exercises (which we have to read and assess) are not a good use of our time or the children's.

Assign writing that enhances the reading—that requires careful reexamination of the text. What we're after is a written response that deepens comprehension, causes the writer to reflect on the content, and/or fosters appreciation for the text. When children have to think about their response, meaning is likely to be extended. And be sure that before you ask students to explain, summarize, compare, evaluate, draw conclusions—all valuable activities—you first demonstrate and give adequate guided practice.

Avoid writing such as book reports and overly structured assignments that can alienate the reader. Some students lose their desire to write because we assign written work that has little relevance or we just overdo it. An upset parent of a third grader told me her son no longer likes to read because, for daily homework, he is expected to make lots of connections—in writing—to the books he is reading.

Forms of writing about reading include but are not limited to

- ☐ Book review.
- ☐ Book blurb.
- ☐ Author profile.
- ☐ Interview with an author.
- ☐ Literature response.
- ☐ Letter to an author.
- ☐ Readers Theatre script.

Be Sensible About Reading–Response Journals

Reading-response journals, also called dialogue journals, are common learning tools in many classrooms. In them, the students write an entry responding to something they have read (usually of their own choosing), and the teacher writes back a response. Teachers do not correct the student entries but, in responding, model standard language and scaffold responses. Many students, especially culturally and linguistically diverse students, substantially improve their writing—content, quantity, form, fluency—as a result of keeping these journals.

While I love the idea of this type of response and value its benefit—which for me is slowing students down to think about the text—one of the reasons I don't rely on response journals is they take lots of teacher time, sometimes up to one hour a night. Like everything else we do, balance is in order. You may want to give kids some choice. Fourth-grade teacher Sharon Sharadin, in Houston, Texas, lets her kids decide whether their response to their nightly independent reading will be written or oral (in a conference). Sharon continues to assess all students' comprehension, but for some this is now done during face-to-face conversations.

Another caution about response journals. Some students respond with lots of written details and it looks like they are getting the meaning. However, when I probe in depth, I sometimes find students have not understood after all—in fiction especially, things like character motivation, story resolution, or author's purpose. The bottom line: *Be sure that students spend more time reading than writing about reading.*

Use Writing to Improve Comprehension

teaching tip

Integrate

The only way to "find time" for daily writing is to combine writing with social studies, science, and other subjects. If kids are writing for science, that's writing time. Providing writing opportunities throughout the day leads to writing fluency.

Composing text and comprehending text are closely related processes. Students who write better get better reading comprehension and vocabulary scores. Students who receive good writing instruction also become better readers. And when students have opportunities to do a lot of writing in the content areas (learning logs, summaries, essays, writing for specific audiences), they learn the subject matter more thoroughly than students who do not do much writing.

Children develop meaning as they write. It's what we all do, especially when we're writing about something we don't fully understand or haven't figured out yet. It's what I do when I write a book. Writing makes us think harder.

Do More Informational Writing

Primary-grade students who do more writing, especially content-related writing, have higher reading achievement. Although writing connected to reading is the single best indicator of student achievement, such writing is not common. David Dickinson, a researcher who with Lori DiGisi studied mostly first-grade classrooms in very poor areas, found that students who had the highest test scores in reading and spelling came from classrooms in which writing was integrated into many activities.

We need to integrate our content-area teaching with writing instruction as a matter of course. Teaching kids how to write expository text improves their overall writing skill and their reading comprehension. Kids who write nonfiction are stimulated to read more nonfiction, so it's important to include lots of great nonfiction in the classroom and school libraries. Through reading nonfiction, students gather information, encounter writing models and ideas they can emulate, and come to understand the features of nonfiction texts (see page 196). (Be vigilante if your school takes part in the Accelerated Reader program. Accelerated Reader generally awards fewer points for nonfiction than for fiction, and kids will therefore tend to concentrate on fiction.)

There is no question that writing about reading aids comprehension and encourages readers to monitor their own reading strategies. Make writing about reading central to teaching and learning.

TRY IT APPLY IT

- Use shared writing to create informational texts (procedures, nonfiction picture books, guides, brochures, you name it—see pages 112–118 for more examples) based on content material your kids have studied or other knowledge they have.

- Have students keep journals in content areas (math, science, social studies) to explain their thinking, problem-solve, and document their observations.

- In the primary grades, use current content area information to compose sentences to use with word work (see pages 93 and 94).

- Help older students be more strategic, reflective readers: have them keep a notebook or journal in which they write predictions or summaries, copy quotations, make notes, and create informational charts. (Be sure to demonstrate first.)

Teach Summary Writing

One of the most effective ways to teach reading comprehension is by asking students to write summaries. When kids have prepared a summary, they demonstrate clearer understanding of the text, outperforming students who only read the text. Constructing a summary is not easy. It entails:

- ☐ Focusing on the purpose of the text.
- ☐ Following the sequence of information or events.
- ☐ Deciding what's most important to include (and what to leave out).
- ☐ Connecting the new information with what one already knows.
- ☐ Putting the information into one's own words.

Mostly, we've asked kids to write summaries without teaching them how, so it follows that students have great difficulty giving a summary. (Retellings, in which students recount story events in sequence, are much easier, because students don't have to delete information; they include everything.) I don't expect kids to write summaries before I've done a lot of modeling followed by shared demonstrations and guided practice. Even then, I've found written summaries are too demanding for most students before grade 4. In kindergarten through grade 3, I focus on retelling, oral summary, and shared-writing summary of texts we've read together.

Use the optimal learning model (on the inside front cover and on pages 70–73) to guide you—that is, repeatedly demonstrate your thinking aloud as you read and summarize a page or two, do it along with students as you guide their thinking, have students try it in small groups, and finally, after several months of demonstration and practice, expect them to do it on their own.

Being able to write a summary is absolutely necessary if one is to produce an efficient report. So many students write long, boring reports that go on and on. Unable to summarize, they copy copious amounts of information verbatim from the source material. When I demonstrate report writing, I always start by constructing a summary, as in the Lesson Snapshot and Framework below.

Lesson Snapshot and Framework: Summary Writing

(An example of a weeklong lesson with a class of sixth graders)

- ☐ **Set a purpose.** Talk about important people in history and how you can get information from nonfiction and make it your own. Tell students why it's important to summarize.

- ☐ **Assess what students know and do and add to that knowledge.** Share-write a chart headed "What to Do to Understand Nonfiction." (See the draft chart on page 129, which continued to evolve as students learned more and became aware of their own learning.)

- ☐ **Demonstrate how to summarize by reading a suitable book as a shared read-aloud.** (Shared read-aloud procedures are summarized in the chart on page 130.) *When Marion Sang* by Pam Munoz Ryan (Scholastic, 2002) is a terrific nonfiction picture book (the illustrations are by Brian Selznick) for students in grades 5–8.

☐ **Give guidance and feedback.** Have students, in small groups, read a short nonfiction piece and write a brief summary. Join one group.

☐ **Repeat this cycle.** Continue until students demonstrate they can summarize. Then have each student write a brief summary of a text they have read in common. Check for understanding, and reteach as necessary.

Sixth graders writing their own summaries after discussing a nonfiction article by following guidelines for "What to Do to Understand Nonfiction" (see below) and "Reading a Nonfiction Article" (see page 131).

WHAT TO DO TO UNDERSTAND NONFICTION

☐ Reread!

☐ Slow down when you don't totally understand.

☐ Go to another source if you don't understand the topic.

☐ Look at other words and sentences around the part you don't understand.

☐ Talk it over with another student.

☐ Make sure you know what you're reading about.

☐ Pay attentions to titles, chapter heads, charts, graphs, timelines, maps.

☐ Look at pictures, italics, sidebars.

☐ Look at the back cover—it tells what the book is about.

☐ Stop and think about it when you don't "get it."

☐ Try to picture it in your mind.

☐ Tie it to what you already know.

☐ Skip over some parts and try to go to the main part.

☐ Talk to yourself and peers as you're reading and after you read.

☐ Summarize.

Evolving draft, shared writing with sixth graders

PROCEDURES IN BRIEF FOR TEACHING SUMMARIZING
IN SHARED READ-ALOUDS (ALL GRADES)

*(For detailed procedures, framework, and demonstration lessons
for shared read-alouds, see Reading Essentials, pp. 130–49)*

☐ Select an excellent piece of literature. Become totally familiar with it.

☐ Gather the class in front of you.

☐ Think aloud as you read. Stop and give a summary after every few pages, so students "see" your thinking:

- *Here's what I think is most important. The main thing the author is saying is this.*

- *I'm not going to include that because it's not crucial to what's most important.*

- *I'm going to read this again to be sure I've got it right.*

- *I'm going to put that into my own words and say it like this.*

☐ Stop and have students "turn and talk" with a partner. Have them reread (on chart or a projected transparency) a paragraph or page you have read aloud. Ask for a one-sentence summary: *What's the most important thing the author says? Put it in your own words.*

☐ Go back to text to evaluate their summary. Point out that there are various ways to say what's most important:

- *Those were all good summaries, and you put things in your own words in different ways.*

- *That was hard for you. I'm going to read this page again and show you my thinking as I'm reading.*

☐ Reread and reteach as necessary.

☐ Continue reading and thinking aloud, demonstrating your construction of a summary, giving kids opportunities to "turn and talk," and rereading and reteaching as needed.

☐ When returning to a nonfiction text-in-process, ask, *What are the three most important things that have happened so far?* Accept all logical responses.

☐ Once students can summarize with some success, have them, in small groups, read and summarize a short text. (See the guidelines/rubric "Reading a Nonfiction Article," page 131.) Join one group; have student groups put their thinking in writing (see the blank form Understanding Nonfiction, in Appendix D) so you have a record and can evaluate how they did and what more you need to teach.

teaching tip

*Teach it First;
Label it Later*

When you are first teaching summarizing, it will be easier if you say something like *I'm going to show you how to decide what's most important on the page when you read,* instead of *Today we're going to work on summarizing.* Once students understand the concept, then say, *Kids, what we've been learning and practicing— deciding what's most important about what the author says and putting that into our own words—that's called summarizing.*

☐ Once students have practiced, received feedback, and been successful, evaluate what worked in creating a good summary (see "What Worked? Understanding Nonfiction," below).

**TRY IT
APPLY IT**

✎ Have students write a one-sentence summary of a story, poem, or journal entry they have previously written.

✎ Do lots of oral summarizing before doing written summaries.

✎ Use shared read-aloud to demonstrate summarizing—show how you think aloud to determine what's most important, and have students practice summarizing in a "turn and talk" (see page 183).

✎ Encourage students to spend more time talking about the text in small groups. Students who spend more time talking before writing have an easier time and write better, tighter summaries.

✎ Practice summarizing in small groups of three or four. Work with one group while the others work independently. Check for understanding by evaluating their written group work.

✎ Once students have demonstrated their understanding of summary writing, use the blank form in Appendix D to evaluate summaries done independently.

READING A NONFICTION ARTICLE
Guidelines

• **Read the entire article to get the overall meaning.**
Talk it over in your small group. Use strategies to help you understand. (You may highlight, underline, make notes in the margins.)

• **Reread the article together.**
Decide what's most important. Write 3–5 summary sentences. Put the summary into your own words.

• **Write several sentences about your own thinking.**
Read between the lines.

• **What are you wondering or still thinking about?**

Rubric for a sixth grade class, April 2003
Regie Routman

**WHAT WORKED?
UNDERSTANDING NONFICTION**

• **Finding the main points**
Summarizing
Putting it into your own words
Deciding what to leave out

• **Talking with peers**

• **Talking and writing simultaneously**

• **Rereading**
Read through the whole article first
Read it again—read and talk, skim parts, read aloud
Reread written summary

• **Writing**
Write to decide what to say next—organize your thoughts
Write short notes to self first

A shared writing with Aiyana Pendleton's sixth grade class
Rio Grande School, Santa Fe, New Mexico
April 2003, Regie Routman

Charting our procedures and expectations for reading and summarizing

Evaluating our comprehension work: Making the strategies that worked explicit and visible so students will employ them again

Write More Book Reviews

Book reviews are excellent examples of summaries. Students can also write "book blurbs," promotional summaries written by the publisher. (Examine some publishers' catalogues, and develop your own criteria.) Book reviews and blurbs are great ways to learn how to make every word count and choose those words carefully so as not to give away the surprises and conclusion. Children can start writing book reviews in kindergarten.

SHARED WRITING CRITERIA

1. **Describe the book in general.**
   (brief summary)

2. **Discuss something you like about the book.**
   (response)

3. **Recommend the book to readers.**

DUCK ON A BIKE
by David Shannon
Book Review by Mrs. Pearce's Grade 2 Class

This book is about a duck that rides a bike past all of the animals on the farm. The other animals are all thinking different thoughts about the duck. Then the other animals get so jealous of the duck that they decide to ride a bike too.

This is a funny book because you never see ducks ride bikes. The illustrations are big and colorful. The story makes you laugh out loud because the animals act silly.

If you like stories with farm animals in them, you'll be crazy for this book. People of all ages will die for this story. Kindergarten–third graders will especially enjoy this book.

A shared writing before students write on their own (see below)

Book Review   By Kylie
Skeleton Hiccups
Author Margery Cuyler

This book is about a skeleton who has the hiccups and can't get rid of them. He hiccups when he's brushing his teeth. He hiccups when he's polishing his bones. H hiccups all th time. He never stops.

I like this book because it has great pictures. It is a great book for learning about bones and skeletons.

I think third graders to adults will love this book because the pictures are funny and interesting.

Book Review   By Ronnie
Never Take a Pig to Lunch
Author Nadine Bernard Westcott

You'll laugh out loud at these silly dilly poems. They have silly titles and words! Maybe you'll think these poems are all true, maybe not Who knows? These poems may change the way you eat because they care about what food is inside of.

I think this book is just full of imagination. You will love it so much that it will make you feel all tingly inside.

I think kids and adults will like this book. It is hilariously fun. You'll love the illustrations. This book would be great to share with others.

NEVER TAKE A PIG TO LUNCH
by Nadine Bernard Westcott

You'll laugh out loud at these silly dilly poems. They have silly titles and words! Maybe you'll think these poems are all true, maybe not. Who knows? These poems may change the way you eat because they are about what food is made of.

I think this book is just full of imagination. You will love it so much that it will make you feel all tingly inside.

I think kids and adults will like this book. It is hilariously fun. You'll love the illustrations. This book would be great to share with others.

A student who now sees herself as a reader chooses to write her first book review

**TRY IT
APPLY IT**

✐ Develop criteria for a book review and a book review form with your class. If students want to, have them write reviews of their favorite books. Compile these—in a binder, in a file box, or on a bulletin board—as a reference for current and future students.

Teach and Encourage Note-Taking

When I conduct an all-day workshop on reading, I have teachers read one of three (they choose) current nonfiction articles on news of the profession. I ask teachers to pay special attention to what they do to comprehend, so they can apply what they do to their teaching and restore common sense to teaching reading comprehension. I have now done this exercise with thousands of teachers, and almost all report doing some kind of writing to aid comprehension; they write in the margins, underline, highlight, make notes, paraphrase, note a personal connection, or ask a question. Note-taking causes the reader to pay better attention to the material at hand and to process the material at a deeper level.

Observing these teachers' process and my own has convinced me that students need consumable texts—newspapers (*USA Today* is good), magazines (*National Geographic Explorer* or *Time for Kids*), response logs, summary sheets— when they are learning about comprehension. That way they can make notations as they read which, in turn, helps them focus and recall more information.

There is no question that writing about reading aids comprehension and encourages self-monitoring as a reader. Having students keep a notebook or journal where they write predictions, underline, make notes, create charts or written summaries, and ask their own questions has been found to help older students be more strategic, reflective readers.

One final point. Students who use graphic organizers remember more content than students who just underline text. Graphic organizers are useful thinking and organizing frameworks, but they can be difficult for students to do independently. They are best introduced with teacher guidance, as a whole-class or small-group shared experience.

TRY IT APPLY IT

- Use more consumable nonfiction articles. Give kids some choice as to which articles they read—this also encourages comprehension.
- Teach kids how to write notes and questions in the margins of text.
- Demonstrate how to take notes on text you are reading and how to revisit those notes. Thinking out loud, show how and when you decide to underline or otherwise highlight text, connect material with something else you know, ask a question.
- Write brief predictions; then confirm them (or find out you were wrong) as you read on.
- Draw parts of the story (beginning, middle, end; main characters; problem); illustrate facts and label the drawings.

Use Writing in Guided Reading Groups

How do you know all *your students understand what they read?* It is our job as effective teachers to know—through hard evidence—whether our students comprehend what they have read. Only then can we know how and what to teach next. When we pose a question orally, once we call on a student, the others don't have to listen. We have no idea if they "got it."

Asking a guided reading group to do a little bit of writing is a great way to monitor and improve comprehension. When I introduced little spiral notebooks in guided reading groups in grades one, two, and three, the students' comprehension greatly improved. The fact that students were required to write a very brief response to their silent reading—most often an answer to a question I posed—forced them to examine the text much more carefully. Students who had just been reading words without thinking much about the text now found they had to focus, think, figure out vocabulary, connect to what they knew, and sometimes reread in order to get the meaning of the passage. (See photo, bottom left.)

Multiage teacher Kirsten Heine noted that her first and second graders made faster gains in reading as measured by standardized Informal Reading Inventories once she held students accountable for their comprehension in writing. Using small spiral notebooks in guided reading groups enabled her to assess each student's understanding, target the problem areas, and teach what each student needed. She observes:

> Kids at all reading levels are becoming much better at giving succinct, to the point answers, often referencing the text directly either in their writing or in their verbal explanation of it. I've seen a vast improvement in my students' abilities to rephrase an idea, fact, or event in their own written words. Many students are beginning to reread independently and use it as their primary reading strategy when they lose meaning. Overall, writing is a much more integrated and independent part of their day now, and it has transformed my guided reading program.

See photos and samples of Kirsten's students' responses below.

Reading *Fly Away Home* by Eve Bunting; checking comprehension through writing in guiding reading group (and teaching as necessary, based on students' responses)

✐ Check students' comprehension through writing:

  ✐ Little notebooks in guided reading.

  ✐ Partner work.

  ✐ Journal responses.

  ✐ Understanding Nonfiction sheet (see Appendix D).

  ✐ Illustrations—posters, Venn diagrams, charts with labels, mind maps.

✎ Write your own texts. (See the "Breakfast Book," below and on DVD, written with a guided reading group of struggling first graders after they had attempted to read a poorly written and laid out commercially published "Breakfast Book.")

Ask Worthwhile Questions

Reading comprehension isn't likely to increase if the writing we ask students to do deals with low-level, literal questions. Students who grapple with higher-level questions (in the context of purposeful reading and writing) get higher scores on standardized tests. Of course, we pose such questions for students to answer on their own (and later, create on their own) *after* we've modeled and demonstrated:

☐ *What questions does the author answer?*

☐ *What did you notice about [blank]?*

☐ *What's the most important idea on this page?*

☐ *When the author says "[blank]" what does she mean?*

☐ *Why did the author use that title?*

☐ *What have you learned by reading this text?*

☐ *What's another possible solution for [blank]?*

One page of our Breakfast book: created in and for our guided reading group

Partner reading our Breakfast book after guided reading. Children reread many times for fluency.

Integrate Nonfiction Writing into All Writing

Students are fascinated with nonfiction topics. In fact, when I work in classrooms and we brainstorm topics for journal writing, most of these turn out to be nonfiction. See the list below generated in a first grade classroom.

Encourage nonfiction writing that involves visual representation and labeling. Students learn that illustrations, pictures, diagrams, and graphs can provide important information that goes beyond the written text. See the page below right from one first grader's science journal.

Prepare Students for Tests Requiring Brief Written Responses

Many students do poorly writing short-answer and short-essay responses to questions about literary selections and subject-area texts. Almost 90 percent of Texas ninth graders taking their state's high-stakes reading test in a recent year

Brainstorming topics for writing

One first grader's Milkweed Habitat

were unable to support their answers with text evidence. That is, they were unable to generate a reasonable idea from inside the text and connect it to text evidence that strongly supports that idea. We haven't taught students, at least not well enough, how to connect their ideas to text, how to think deeply about reading, and how to go back to the text to confirm their thinking.

We need to make this kind of teaching and assessing part of daily reading and writing, not a separate teaching-to-the-test focus. Remember that it's good instruction that helps students perform best on state tests, not an isolated focus on skills that will be assessed.

TRY IT APPLY IT

- ✐ Teach and encourage deep thinking.

- ✎ Teach students how to make thematic links between two texts—a story and a poem, two pieces of fiction, two nonfiction pieces with different points of view—and then go back to those texts to support their thinking. Use the optimal learning model and begin by demonstrating your own thinking.

- ✐ Use more brief writing assignments to check comprehension—in guided reading groups, with a partner, as a whole class.

- ✐ Think out loud and show how you go back to text or to notice how characters change or develop.

Accelerate Literacy

Powerful connections between reading and writing help accelerate students' knowledge and skills in both areas. Embrace writing and reading as complementary co-essentials. You will be more effective as a teacher, and your students will learn to control, monitor, and benefit from both disciplines.

Three

The Essential Writing Day

A SUCCESSFUL WRITING PROGRAM REQUIRES A KNOWLEDGEABLE, ORGANIZED TEACHER WITH EXCELLENT CLASSROOM MANAGEMENT SKILLS. MOSTLY, STUDENTS NEED LOTS OF TIME IN WHICH TO WRITE, A SAY IN WHAT THEY WRITE ABOUT, STRATEGIES THAT ALLOW THEM TO PROBLEM SOLVE INDEPENDENTLY (PLAN, REVISE, EDIT), AND HELPFUL RESPONSE.

7. Be Efficient and Integrate Basic Skills

Writers don't improve their craft unless they have a real purpose, a real audience, and a real investment in their writing.
—Mem Fox

We've made writing way too complicated by breaking it up into bits and pieces. That keeps us and the kids busy, but it's not teaching writing. We've been overfocused on standards, rubrics, a correct teaching sequence, procedures, isolated skills, and looking for the "right" program. Instead of asking *What skills should I be teaching?* we need to ask *How can I be a more effective teacher of writing?* and *How can I engage my students' hearts and minds so they want to write and do their best writing?*

When I am working in schools, teachers' initial questions and concerns often focus on the "skills"—parts of speech, sentence building, paragraph structure. Rightfully concerned about sloppy writing, with its poor grammar, spelling, and punctuation, dedicated teachers tell students, *I want complete sentences with capitals and periods* or *I want a topic sentence with supporting details.* Our students will learn to "do" all the necessary skills and a whole lot more if we shift our focus to meaningful teaching of writing and then teach the necessary skills to support that writing. I've seen it happen again and again in my residencies around the country.

Start with Meaning and Keep It Whole

Imagine having all the pieces of a large jigsaw puzzle on the floor in front of you but never seeing the picture on the lid of the box. That's what learning is like for kids when we start with the parts. They can't figure out what it all means or how the skills fit together. However, when we teach from whole to part and back to whole, when we teach the concept first and label it later, learning becomes easier and much more meaningful.

When I began teaching children to write free verse, I made writing harder for them by first teaching individual parts. I would say, *Today, we'll learn how to do line breaks [or use white space or craft endings].* Not only did that slow down the process, it took away the enjoyment. To my surprise, I found kids, even kindergartners, grasped the whole of poetry easily in one fell swoop—the title, the line breaks, the white space, the rhythm—when I started by reading and writing whole poems and noticing what poets do. After kids wrote their own heartfelt poems, we celebrated these poems and then dealt with specifics as we focused on what each writer was trying to do. (See the "heart poems" lesson, on pages 305–315 and on the accompanying DVD.)

Reduce Isolated Skills Work

I have not been able to locate any research showing that worksheets or drills carry over into students' successful application of skills in authentic reading/writing contexts. In fact, decades of research show that drills do not improve student writing. Much like passing the Friday spelling test, students can perform the skill in isolation, but they don't apply it in the course of daily writing and reading.

The National Reading Panel made the same finding with relation to phonics:

> Programs that focus too much on the teaching of letter-sounds relations and not enough on putting them to use are unlikely to be very effective. In implementing systematic phonics instruction, educators must keep the end in mind and ensure that children understand the purpose of learning letter-sounds and are able to apply their skills in their daily reading and writing activities.

I believe most of us already know that if we look closely at isolated skills work with an open mind, we'll agree that it cannot turn kids into writers (or readers).

The big problem with teaching isolated skills is that kids don't know what we're talking about and why. Our lessons should arise from what you see kids doing, or not doing, in their writing: "Skill instruction should intrude as little as possible upon students' ongoing efforts at constructing meaning from text."

Only isolate the skill if students know how and why that skill is used. For example, until a child understands that words can be broken into sounds, teaching "*p* is for paint" has no meaning for them. Most students easily gain that necessary phonological awareness through lots of read-alouds of alphabet books as well as through informal rhyming, word play, and invented spelling. Or, again, teaching paragraphing makes little sense to many kids when we say *A paragraph is a group of sentences about the same topic* and then assign them to write one. However, once you have a piece of writing then you can say something like *Let me show you how we can organize these sentences to make it easier for the reader to follow; when we put like ideas together like this, we are paragraphing.*

Focus on Quality First

If your students are doing practice exercises, take a hard look at their everyday writing. Are the skills transferring? One group of teachers wrote me: "Daily oral language exercises work; they just don't transfer." It took a while for them to realize what they had actually said about what they already recognized.

Making the shift to focusing on meaning and quality first and teaching whole-to-part-to-whole may mean changing some of your beliefs about writing and learning. In an effort to do a better job teaching writing, fifth-grade teacher Debbie Fowler and her grade-level colleagues, in Westminster, Colorado, used students' scores on the high-stakes state writing test to plan their writing program. Identifying students' weakest areas, they prioritized a list of writing skills (in isolation) and addressed them with practice sheets. Debbie had an eye-opening moment when she realized her students were doing exactly what she was asking them to do:

> I was always referring to the rubric and saying things like, "Kids, remember you need a good beginning, middle, and end. Oh, and don't forget details. You should have at least ten." I wondered why the kids had a hard time getting started or asked, "How many pages does it have to be?"

Debbie and her colleagues made four major changes to their writing program in their shift away from teaching isolated skills:

1. **Identifying writing genres that would interest students** and also fulfill district requirements.

2. **Deciding who the audience would be for each piece of writing.**

3. **Modeling their own writing process and struggle** in front of students, still the most difficult part of the new approach.

4. **Having students share their writing regularly** as a basis for celebration and great teaching moments.

(See their original Essential Writing Goals and their New Writing Goals, below.)

At the end of the school year Debbie wrote to me. She described how her kids were now "taking chances with their writing," that writing was "going great," and that "some kids were asking if they could write more than one piece and that has not happened before." Regarding the skills, she said that "skills teaching has

---

Arapahoe Ridge 5th Grade
Essential Writing Goals

Trimester I-
1. Subject/verb agreement
2. Verb tense
3. Comparative adjectives
4. Pronouns
5. Quotes/Dialogue
   • Punctuation
   • Content
   • Style, voice
   • Organization
6. Paragraph writing
   • Organization
   • Complete sentence
   • Variety of sentence structures
7. Stylistic Writing
   • Figurative language
   • Alliteration
   • Vivid verbs

We really had good intentions, just needed a little guidance— Thanks Deb

Trimester II
1. Comparative Adverbs
2. Interjections & conjunctions
3. Identification of subject, verb, pronoun, adjective
4. Style: using connecting words (however, therefore, although, as it turned out)
5. Style: choosing words for specificity (vocabulary)
6. Reference books (atlas, almanac, dictionary, thesaurus, encyclopedia)
7. Bibliography-print, electronic, encyclopedia, periodical

New Writing Goals   DRAFT

November:
   Poetry--class book
   Thank you letters (Thanksgiving)--person being thanked

December:
   Something no one knows about you--class book
   Santa letters--Buddies

January:
   Content report--books for library
            *Two sets, one for library, one for classroom. Make a big deal about the books and can advertise them to fourth grade. Other kids will use your books for information.

February:
   Hero Writing--person receiving letter

March:
   CSAP prep. work

April:
   Short stories

May:
   Memoirs, things you want to remember from fifth grade One for student and one for new fifth grader.

District requirements:
   compare/contrast
   content report
   personal narrative
   short stories

Fifth grade writing goals before and after a change in faculty's writing beliefs

become more efficient and effective." As part of the change process, she and her colleagues do refer to their original list but now it is as a check on the "parts" within the meaningful whole of a piece of writing.

What convinced these dedicated teachers to shift their teaching emphasis, to start with meaning and teach the skills in the context of meaning? It was seeing the quality of students' work and what was possible when students wrote for meaningful purposes and real audiences. (See the DVD poetry lesson and the supporting material in the Teaching in Action section. Notice in particular the list of skills we taught in the context of writing poetry.)

Include Audience in All Writing

One of the problems with skills teaching is it leaves out the audience. Yet writing for a real audience (not just the teacher) is one of the best ways to get quality writing. We adjust our language according to who our audience is (including ourselves), but kids don't know this. Too often, they are not aware that they need to think about providing information that the reader will need to have to understand the writing. When students write primarily for the teacher or for a test, they are not thinking about the reader.

When I worked with a group of fifth graders on creating a guidebook to their school (see pages 105–110), I discovered they were not used to writing for an audience. During our shared writing, it took a while for them to realize that we needed to add a personal closing—not because I said so, but so the reader would feel a sense of closure. Once they understood that, they took writing all endings more seriously.

Another example. A kindergarten teacher was having difficulty getting kids to write the letters and sounds they knew. "Teacher, teacher, I can't" many said, and they were just using dashes or marks and ignoring the resources in the room that could help them. But once the teacher added a real audience and told kids it was important to use all the letters and sounds they knew so people could read their writing, they all used some letters and sounds.

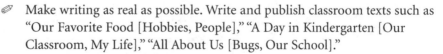

TRY IT
APPLY IT

- Make writing as real as possible. Write and publish classroom texts such as "Our Favorite Food [Hobbies, People]," "A Day in Kindergarten [Our Classroom, My Life]," "All About Us [Bugs, Our School]."

- Use shared writing to write fictional stories, books for next year's students, advice to parents, and much more. (See Chapter 5.)

- Springboard off favorite texts. One kindergarten class had read all the *Miss Nelson* books and wrote a fictional book about their teacher.

- Write patterned texts with young students and use them for guided and independent reading. One teacher and her primary-grade students wrote a "Don't Be Scared" book that began, "Don't be scared when your mom leaves. She'll come back."

Focus on Voice Through Meaningful Writing

"Voice is the single most important element in attracting and holding a reader's interest." Voice is the writer's unique personality on paper, his own melody in words, her "mark" as an individual. No two voices are alike. To write with voice, the writer has to be interested in the writing. Without that interest, students don't invest in the piece. You can't teach voice as a separate subject. Nor can you fake it, as the following story illustrates.

High school senior Andrew Thomas was a straight-A English student. He knew just how to write an essay for school and how to meet every one of the teacher's requirements, such as putting in figurative language and checking off all the parts of the accompanying rubric. So I was surprised when I read the important personal essay that was going to accompany his college applications. He knew how to apply the sophisticated skills he'd been taught, such as including detailed elaboration and clever metaphors, but his writing was bland and impersonal. When Andrew asked me to respond to his writing, he was confident that it was an "A paper." He told me his English teacher said his essay was "great." After several honest conversations that led to suggested revisions, Andrew and I talked frankly about his writing. His comments on voice are striking.

> When you're graded on putting your voice into your writing, it becomes a calculated thing. You're trying to say certain things to make it sound like your voice, but it's not your voice. It appears to work. You're rewarded with positive grades and feedback. But then, when you have to write something real, like a college essay, it doesn't work at all.

Writer Amy Tan helps explain why Andrew had such difficulty being true to his own beliefs and experiences. She writes:

> Your own voice is one that seeks a personal truth, one that only you can obtain. That truth comes from your own experiences, your own observations, and when you find it, if it really is true and specific to you, you may be surprised that others find it to be true as well. In searching for your own voice, be aware of the difference between emulation and imitation, inspiration and intimidation.

Contrived Writing Stifles Voice

A school writing program of rigid requirements and formulaic writing constrains students' real voices. When students are focused on constructing paragraphs and sentences to comply with a program or format, they may learn to write to a standard, but we often lose the voice of the writer in the process. Not only that. They often have to start all over again in learning how to compose interesting, well-written pieces. In other words, they don't automatically grow beyond the formula.

Be sure you are writing and thinking aloud in front of your students and being yourself in your writing. Kids aren't likely to write with voice if they don't hear your truthful writing voice. Don't worry about getting it "right." Close your door and write what's in your mind and heart.

Voice can be emphasized and "taught" without the teacher or students really knowing what it is. Instead of saying *Andrew has voice in his writing*, which isn't how we talk, try instead: *Doesn't that piece sound just like Andrew? I love the way he [used humor, carefully described what happened so you felt you were right there, etc.]*. Voice is in the details—but details that show the real person and story behind the words, not just details for the sake of adding more words, transitions, or sentence variety.

TRY IT APPLY IT

- Use shared writing, in which you write alongside and with students, to help individual voices develop.
- Voice and passion go together. Make every effort to ensure students are interested and invested in their writing topics and audiences.
- "Voiceless writing is like soup with no seasoning." Help students notice what authors (including their peers) do to "season" their writing. Remember, though: you can identify voice, but you can't "measure" or quantify it.

Teach Explicitly and Tell Students Why

When I asked students in a third-grade classroom why they were creating story maps, they couldn't tell me. I got the following responses: "Our teacher asked us to"; "I think they're going on that bulletin board over there"; "You learn story maps in third grade." Now, the teacher in this class was as conscientious and excellent as they come, and the quality of the story maps reflected her diligence. I have no doubt she was clear about her purpose: She wanted students to learn how stories work so they would internalize those essential features when reading stories and writing their own stories. But she never told the students that, and so, to a large extent, the activity was a waste of time. They would be unlikely to transfer skills that had no broader meaning for them.

Our students are not likely to take work seriously or feel the "need" to learn something unless they understand and value its purpose (nor do we!). And this is particularly true for our culturally and linguistically diverse learners. I always tell students why I'm doing what I'm doing—whether I'm calling them up for a guided reading group, doing a shared writing, teaching note-taking, or having a conference. I say to students, "The reason we're doing this is. . . ." And often, as a check to be sure they understand, I have them say it back me: "Tell me why we're doing this and why it's important."

Make Sure Your Demonstrations Include *Why*

A fourth-grade teacher whom I was coaching and co-teaching with was demonstrating writing. On a projected transparency, she wrote (silently) about herself, focusing on beginning with an interesting sentence and including personal facts. She stopped after she had written almost a page. Her draft looked neat and complete. Although her writing was good, unless she explained her thinking, the techniques she used were unlikely to transfer to her students' writing. She wanted her students to view drafting as making changes in thinking, but she hadn't modeled that.

So I encouraged her to:

- ☐ Reread and see if it was the way she wanted it.
- ☐ Think aloud as she wrote.
- ☐ Not to be content with the first draft, to rethink how it might go and make changes.

She went back, crossed out, moved things around, added information, and stopped to explain why she was making her changes. She reread her draft four or five times for the purpose of clarity, and each time she made improvements. The message she sent to her students changed from *Write down the page and you're done* to *writing takes time, much rereading and rethinking, and you work on your draft to make sure it says what you want it to and is clear and interesting to the reader.*

Think out loud as you write; let students in on your problem-solving, ruminating, struggling writing process.

Don't Assume Transfer Is Automatic—It's Not

Don't assume that because you have modeled writing, your students "got" your demonstration. Good teaching is more difficult than that. Here's a case in point.

A third-grade teacher wants her students to write better leads after she notices that most students begin their autobiographical writing with their names and ages. In her demonstration lesson, she shows three leads and asks students which is best. The first one is, "My name is Naomi. I am eight years old." The second one has good vocabulary and interesting "telling details." The third one is even more interesting and elaborate.

Kids easily see that the second and third leads are better than the first. However, the teacher doesn't go to the next step: *why* are these leads better? She assumes that because her students can identify the best ones, they will now write like that. When the students go to write, more than half of them choose the first, boring beginning.

So the teacher backs up. "Why is this lead better?" She names the qualities. This is what all good teachers do, evaluate, rethink as they go. Teaching is like a draft-in-process: never linear, always changing. Now when students are asked to write a better lead, they can do it.

Take Advantage of the "Efficiency of Context"

If we want all the parts of writing to make sense to kids, they need to focus first on authentic writing of whole texts for a real audience. A fourth grader says, "I don't have my lead" and can't start. I say, "Your lead and title can come later. Just start."

Shift the Focus in Teaching Writing

When I ask teachers how they teach writing, many respond as this teacher did:

> I teach it through minilessons and writing prompts. At the beginning of the year I focus on ideas, organization, and conventions. Then I add word choice, sentence fluency, and finally voice toward the end of the year.

In other words, students learn the *language* of writing (*organization, sentence fluency, voice*) but aren't helped to understand what good writing is. For example, when I ask a class of fourth graders what a draft is, they respond, "You write it before the final copy." I really have to push before the idea surfaces that a draft is our first thoughts, "getting our ideas down." When writing workshop becomes a set of procedures or isolated writing traits, our students just go through the motions.

Unfortunately, much of this fractured teaching is now being promoted in professional development programs mandated by states and school districts seeking to raise test scores. Teachers are "trained" in how to teach the individual aspects of writing, such as organization or sentence fluency, and they, in turn, teach these to their students. Students get lots of practice writing sentences and paragraphs, but their overall writing does not necessarily improve.

Here's how I respect such mandates but still teach in a way that makes sense and helps students become better writers. I tell teachers, *I will teach your students how to do all that is required, but the easiest and most efficient way to do this is to first engage students in writing about topics they care about for a reader who matters to them.*

TEACHING BEYOND THE STANDARDS

Focus on Excellent Teaching of Writing

TEACH YOUR WRITING LESSON. Now go back and look at your state standards, district objectives, checklists, and scoring guides. You can teach everything on your list faster and more effectively if you use "efficiency of context" as you teach.

HERE'S WHAT I'M TALKING ABOUT. Look at the strategies we taught in a second grade classroom in just two days (page 151), working on writing to inform for a real audience and with a valued purpose (see pp. 316–322 for complete lesson). In two days we addressed:

- ☐ effective use of language
- ☐ appropriate sentences
- ☐ transitions
- ☐ focus on main ideas
- ☐ words that connect ideas
- ☐ language that fits audience and purpose

Take a look at the highest level on the grade 4 scoring guide used by the state for content, organization, style, and conventions on the high stakes test (below). Also note the district checklist for writing to inform or explain (grades 3–5). I have deliberately skipped over grade 2 requirements to make this point: *If you focus on excellent teaching of writing, you will be teaching beyond what the standards require.*

Now look at what Brian, an average-performing second grader, has done. Compare it to our "What a Good Writer Does" (a list we developed as a shared writing in the process of drafting). You'll notice that

reflected in this simple, delightful "Cafeteria Rules" are many of the characteristics of good writing we identify on our list. (I've highlighted just a few of Brian's strengths as a writer with arrows and checked off more.) Also, notice that our young writer is already employing many of the same required elements (although at a lower level of sophistication) listed on the checklist for writing to inform or explain (grades 3–5).

Once as teachers we "see" that, we can relax and stop worrying about teaching all the little pieces of writing and keep the "big picture" in mind. More than that, we begin to realize that complex learning cannot be decontextualized or compartmentalized into discrete skills.

I laid out these pieces—state scoring guide (grade 4) and checklist for writing to inform or explain (grades 3–5)—on a table, along with copies of the district's required scoring guides/rubrics, state standards, curriculum requirements, writing continuum, and/or benchmarks—and put "What a Good Writer Does" in the center. I asked teachers working in small groups to notice how what we taught in grade 2 aligned with what is required beyond grade 2. In fact, if you notice the descriptors for grade 4 on the state rubric, we have begun to address all of these in grade 2.

▶ STATE SCORING GUIDE FOR HIGH-STAKES TEST (Grade 4, Highest Level, Level 4)

Content, Organization, and Style

- Maintains consistent focus on the topic and has ample supporting details;
- Has a logical organization pattern and conveys a sense of wholeness and completeness;
- Provides transitions that clearly serve to connect ideas;
- Uses language effectively by exhibiting word choices that are engaging and appropriate for intended audience and purpose;
- Includes sentences, or phrases where appropriate, of varied length and structure;
- Allows the reader to sense the person behind the word.

Conventions

- Consistently follows the rules of standard English for usage;
- Consistently follows the rules of standard English for spelling of commonly used words;
- Consistently follows the rules of standard English for capitalization and punctuation;
- Consistently exhibits the use of complete sentences except where purposeful phrases or clauses are used for effect.

What a Good Writer Does (Grade 2, Room 108)

- ☑ Writes for a reader
- ☑ Rereads many times
- ☑ Gets ideas and help from other writers
- ☑ Decides what to change about the writing
- ☑ Makes the writing make more sense and sound better by:
  - ☑ Crossing out words
  - ☑ Adding information
  - ☑ Using different words
  - ☐ Using more interesting words
  - ☐ Changing a word like "it" to a word that is clearer to the reader
  - ☐ Taking out information the reader doesn't need
  - ☑ Lassoing words to move them around
- ☑ Has a title that goes with the writing
- ☑ Has a "snappy" beginning
- ☑ Has an ending that completes the writing
- ☐ May use conversation
- ☑ Explains what she/he is writing about
- ☑ Writes so that the reader can get a clear "picture"
- ☐ May use humor
- ☑ Sometimes uses exciting marks like "!"
- ☑ Listens and responds to others' suggestions ("It might be helpful to the reader if...")
- ☐ Sometimes "has a little trouble"
- ☐ Helps readers understand "how to" do something by:
  - ☐ Using words like "first," "then," "next"
  - ☐ Making lists
  - ☐ Using bullets
  - ☐ Using numbers
- ☑ Rereads

Grade 2, Writing to Inform—An Example Cafeteria Rules - When you are in the cafeteria you need to eat politely by using silverware and excuse yourself when you forget something. You use a conversation voice and talk quietly with your friends and don't share food! You don't leave until you are dismissed. Make sure you follow the rules, and enjoy your food! —Brian

---

▶ DISTRICT CHECKLIST FOR WRITING TO INFORM OR EXPLAIN (Grades 3–5)

My writing will be very good if I:

Have good content and organization. That means I...

- Follow the directions in my writing task;
- Keep focused on my main ideas;
- Use specific details, reasons, and/or examples to support my ideas;
- Organize my writing so that there is an opening, a middle, and a conclusion;
- Organize my writing in paragraphs;
- Use well-chosen information that is interesting, thoughtful, and important;
- Use words that help show how my ideas are connected.

Have an interesting style. That means I...

- Show that I am interested in my topic;
- Use language that fits my audience and purpose;
- Use words that help the reader understand my ideas;
- Use different types and lengths of sentences.

Follow conventions in writing. That means I...

- Write complete sentences;
- Use correct capitalization and punctuation (for example, periods, commas, quotation marks, question marks);
- Use correct grammar;
- Have subject-verb agreement for each sentence;
- Spell words correctly;
- Show where new paragraphs begin.

teaching tip

Save Exemplary Writing

- ☐ Get students' permission. (Papers can also come from a colleague's classroom.)
- ☐ Cover students' names on papers.
- ☐ File and store examples so students can get to them.
- ☐ Share across the grade level.
- ☐ Make overhead transparencies to use in minilessons. (You can write down your points and then erase and reuse.)
- ☐ Discuss specifics— use of language, humor, voice, organization, and so on.

Teacher Talk

When teachers see the high quality of work this approach produces (which goes beyond state standards, curriculum guidelines, benchmarks, and rubrics— see Teaching Beyond the Standards, pages 150–151), plus students' engagement and enjoyment, their thinking shifts: *If I focus first on excellent teaching of writing through writing for a valued reader, I will also be teaching all the skills in the context of that writing.*

In Beth Petrie's and Jeanne Lamp's second-grade classroom, for instance, we taught students how to do procedural writing for a valued audience and in two days introduced all the skills a good writer needs. Furthermore, the students' achievements went far beyond the "standards" for second graders. It was the "efficiency of context" that made it possible. See What a Good Writer Does on pages 150–151. (The lesson on procedural writing is presented in its entirety in the Teaching in Action section, pages 316–322.)

Or again, the following lists all the techniques we covered in one hour in the second month of school as Kari Oosterveen's fourth graders wrote a short piece about something they disliked. Through Kari's and my demonstrations, our scaffolded conversations with students before they began writing, and a whole-class share afterward, we identified what made the writing memorable:

- ☐ Use leads.
- ☐ Have descriptive words and feelings.
- ☐ Use humor.
- ☐ Sound like the people we are.
- ☐ Make every sentence count.
- ☐ Give our endings some punch.

We didn't just list these things and forget about them; the kids referred to the list again and again in order to do their best writing, and Kari and her students continued to add to the list throughout the school year.

Choose your language carefully when you embed skills with younger writers for whom the terms don't yet make sense:

- ☐ *Let me show you how you can cut and paste and move these sentences around, like this, so it will be easier for your reader to follow.* (Instead of, "Today we're going to work on organization.")
- ☐ *Write a message or story about. . . .* (Instead of, "Write two sentences with. . . .")
- ☐ *You've got a lot of good ideas here. Let's put the ones that are all about the same thing together, like this. That will make it easier for your reader to understand.* (Instead of, "I'm going to teach you how to write a paragraph.") Later, when the writer is more likely to have some idea of what you're talking about, you can say, *What we worked on today was paragraphing.*
- ☐ *When you're an author you get to choose the words. Let's listen to the words this author uses.* (Instead of "We're going to learn about word choice.")

**TRY IT
APPLY IT**

✎ Have a colleague observe your teaching and record all your teaching points. Then, review and name what you did. What did you teach?

✎ Notice the language you use. Be sure it's the language of encouragement.

✎ Use a faculty meeting to develop your own criteria (and check it for "child-friendly" quality with students). See rubrics one school wrote with students, page 241.

✎ Ask kids, "What do good writers do?" Use their responses as an evaluation of what they believe and the messages they have received about "good writing." (See examples on pages 117 and 151.)

teaching tip

*Make
Paragraphing Easy*

It's not the symbol for paragraphing that's so important, it's understanding the concept:

☐ Establish simple criteria around which to organize writing. Explain that each heading represents one paragraph.

☐ Tell writers, "When you're done with one idea, skip a line [or two lines] and go onto the next idea."

☐ Frank Smith said it years ago: "Paragraph to give the eye a break." A full page of unbroken-up text is hard on the reader's eyes.

Keep Standards in Perspective

One conscientious teacher told me:

> I try to hit the standards, month by month. I spend two days doing what I have to do, for example, teaching capital letters, or verbs, or subject and predicate. I feel I have to teach these skills in isolation because they're listed that way on our standards and district curriculum. Then, the other days I focus on good writing.

Like many other teachers, she was exhausted trying to "cover" everything that was required. Let me assure you: you will be teaching subject and predicate and sentence variety and fluency and grammar in the course of teaching writing well. Even if your state or district standards and curriculum documents focus narrowly on the parts of learning, you will easily satisfy those minimum standards—and much *more*—through meaningful teaching. Believing that takes a leap of faith, along with much professional knowledge and common sense.

For example, California's K–12 language arts standards calls for students to "write clear and coherent sentences" and create "a single paragraph with a topic sentence and supporting details." If you focus only on teaching students how to write a complete sentence or paragraph, you frustrate yourself and shortchange the students, and sentence and paragraph writing in everyday writing do not improve. It's impossible to define what a sentence is in a way that helps students produce one; the best and fastest way to teach what good sentences are is to call attention to them in the context of students' good writing. Whole-class sharing and brief celebration conferences are the perfect places in which to do that. Once you have the well-expressed sentence, you can work on the conventions and correctness part.

Similarly, the more students work on writing a paragraph in isolation because writing a well-constructed paragraph is on the state test, the worse their paragraph writing usually becomes. However, once students have produced good writing (there are many examples throughout this text), I say:

> *Take a look at your informational essay [or secrets story or journal entry].*
> *Find the sentence at the beginning that tells what your writing is about.*
> *Now find all the information you added to tell about that. When the state*
> *writing test asks you to write a topic sentence and supporting details,*
> *that's what they're asking for. You already know how to do that.*

Your students learn about sentences and paragraphs not by studying about them in isolation, but through reading widely, hearing good literature read aloud, and writing for audiences and purposes that matter. Kari Oosterveen's fourth graders had been schooled in formula writing. They told Kari, "Our other teacher always wanted a topic sentence and supporting details." Kari replied, "I'm not asking you to write a paragraph. I'm asking you to write."

Teach Useful Minilessons

What minilessons should I teach and how should I teach them? There is no one right sequenced list. Listen carefully, pay attention to what your writers are trying to say, and help them say it.

Minilessons—or intentional, explicit teaching—can be presented to the whole class, a small group, or one-on-one. "In minilessons we teach *into* our students' intentions." That is, we teach what they need to know and are ready to learn so they can continue to write and polish their writing to make it clearer, easier to understand, livelier, and so on. Minilessons can and should take place any time students are writing—during whole-class share, in other kinds of conferences (see Chapter 9), as part of your demonstration teaching, during shared writing, throughout the day, across the curriculum—not just at the beginning of a writing class.

Be authentic with what you teach. Kids must internalize the reason for using descriptive words, strong verbs, leads—otherwise these lessons become writing exercises in isolation. Think about the purpose of a lesson. Ask yourself, *Is this the most important thing students need at this time to continue writing well?* Look for patterns of need during whole-class share and other conferences. Refer to the writing essentials on pages 13–14 and on the inside back cover. I teach based on what I notice kids do and need to do and make notes to myself on what I notice so I don't forget. (There are examples of minilessons in the Teaching in Action section and on the DVD.)

A SAMPLING OF COMMON MINILESSONS

teaching tip

When just several students need particular explicit teaching or guidance, form a small group to teach instead of the whole class.

Content

- ☐ Writing on a topic you care about.
- ☐ Narrowing the topic.
- ☐ Using interesting words (removing boring ones, using strong verbs).
- ☐ Rereading (before you continue, to check that it makes sense).
- ☐ Revising as you go along (as a result of rereading, rethinking, response).
- ☐ Using resources.
- ☐ Writing a beginning that grabs the reader.
- ☐ Organizing writing in a logical order (moving information around).
- ☐ Backing up statements with examples (because, why).
- ☐ Thinking about what the reader wants/needs to know.
- ☐ Taking out boring and repeated information.
- ☐ Adding information helpful to the reader.
- ☐ Adding helpful transitions for a smooth flow.
- ☐ Adding visuals to support and enhance text.
- ☐ Crafting an ending (to bring closure).
- ☐ Having the writing "sound like you."
- ☐ Knowing how and when to ask for help.

teaching tip

Watch Your Time

You can spend so much time on mini-lessons that kids never get to write. Many writing workshops are one lesson after another. Use a timer if you need to, and set it: five minutes, ten minutes, try for not more than fifteen.

Conventions

- ☐ Stretching out sounds in a word.
- ☐ Using beginning and ending sounds.
- ☐ Using best invented spelling (for example, showing that long words have more letters).
- ☐ Spelling frequently used words correctly.
- ☐ Spacing words and skipping lines.
- ☐ Using lowercase letters in words.
- ☐ Using resources.
- ☐ Editing.
- ☐ Knowing how to seek and find help.
- ☐ Capitalizing (*I*, important names and places, etc.).
- ☐ Adding ending punctuation.

teaching tip

Review

Before kids write, review key teaching points from the day before, such as how to cross out with a single line, expectations for legibility, rereading before continuing a story.

Teach Students to Care About Revision

"Revising and editing can be real torture. I'd like help in that area," an intermediate-grades teacher told me as her colleagues nodded in agreement. We've made revising more difficult than it needs to be. When we require revision as part of the writing process or a formatted writing program, kids go through the motions and cross out a few words and add other ones, but they don't put their hearts into the work or value revision. On the other hand, when kids care about their writing, revising is no big deal. It's work, but it's work they eagerly engage in. (See pages 151, 319, and 320 for examples of the work of second graders who were empowered by revision.)

Revision means, literally, to see again. Revision is when we revisit, revalue, reconsider, and look again at our writing. Revision involves rereading in order to clear up confusions, reorganize text, rewrite for clarity and interest, rethink word choices. Revision takes place even when we're not writing; it's part of our thinking process around the writing.

Help Students Develop a Revision Consciousness

I write, reread, and rewrite with a revision consciousness. That is, I value revision, strive to revise where and when doing so makes sense, and take responsibility for revision because I care about the writing. We want students to do the same and to write and revise with a mindset of *will my writing make sense to my readers? will it engage them?* Peter Elbow notes, "Of course anything must be revised if you really want it to work for an audience."

We need to teach kids to hold internal conversations so that they write with a revision consciousness (see page 48 in Chapter 3 for specifics). This is exactly what I do as a writer, and not because my editor tells me to; I do this internal thinking because my reader matters to me. Following the optimal learning model, we must show our own revision-in-process and make our thinking visible, keeping in mind that our goal for students is always independence. We want students revising on their own without our telling them to do so.

We also want students to take responsibility for the kind of feedback they want to the texts they write. Just as I guided my reader-responders to this text with questions like those above, we need to teach our students (through demonstrations and guided practice) to do the same.

Revise Your Writing in Front of Students

Students need to see what the thinking behind revision and work of actually doing it look like and sound like if they are to do that thinking and revising themselves. Much of revision is getting as close as you can to your intended message. Peter Elbow notes:

> The more you zero in on the precise meaning you have in mind, the more you can strip away unnecessary words and thereby energize your language. The key activity is crossing out words and sentences.

Getting at precise meaning is also what we teach kids to do in writing a summary (see pages 127–131). Being able to put the most important points in your own words usually involves rethinking and revision.

✄ When I wrote my get-well letter to Zach as a demonstration (before a group of fourth graders and their teacher wrote their own letters to their hospitalized classmate), I revised in front of them as I wrote and thought out loud (my draft and revisions are shown on the next page). Afterward, I asked them, "What did you notice that I did?" and we charted their responses, creating the chart below. We left the chart up for them to use as a reference while they were preparing their own letters to Zach.

<table>
<tr><td>

teaching tip

Check Yourself

When you're modeling revising, make sure you are not focusing on conventions—capital letters, punctuation, etc.—but are working on the content and coherency of the piece. A good way to check is to ask, "What did you see me do when I revised?"

</td></tr>
</table>

MY REVISION PROCESS: WHAT STUDENTS NOTICED

Go back to the text:
REREAD—constantly.
    Read whole text first.
    Read and ask questions as you go.
    ☐ Does this sound the way I want it to?
    ☐ Is it interesting?
Cross out:
    ☐ It's boring.
    ☐ It doesn't sound right.
    ☐ Repeated word (put in a better one).
Add words:
    ☐ To make it more interesting.
    ☐ To make it clearer—easier to understand.
DECIDE WHAT YOU LIKE—keep it!

Many students quickly complete writing assignments, turn them in, and never look back. When we model how to revise, we are also modeling the work ethic of effective writing. Good writing takes time and effort.

October 6, 2003

Dear Zach,

We haven't met, but I know about you because I am working in your classroom ~~teaching writing~~ this week. I'm ~~writing with~~ teaching writing with Mr. Torrens. ~~I am a teacher, and I go and your classmates into schools all over the country to work with students and teachers in reading and writing.~~ It's a great job. I love it. It's challenging, rewarding, and fun.

~~Today~~ Your classmates are writing to you, and I decided to write to you too. You see, my dad had brain surgery about a year ago. He is doing well ~~know~~ now, a I'm happy to hear you are recovering well, too. ~~quickly to~~ I think everyone in your class misses you and will be really glad when you ~~are~~ a lot return.

Maybe, when I ~~come back to BBC~~ in the spring I can meet you. I hope so. Till then, I wish you an easy, speedy recovery

Sincerely,
Regie Routman

Dear Zach,

We haven't met, but I know about you because I am working in your classroom this week. I'm teaching writing with Mr. Torrens. It's a great job. I love it. It's challenging, rewarding, and fun.

Your classmates are writing to you, and I decided to write to you too. You see, my dad had brain surgery about a year ago. He is doing well now, and I'm happy to hear you are recovering well, too. I think everyone in your class misses you a lot and will be really glad when you return.

Maybe, when I come back to BBC in the spring I can meet you. I hope so. Till then, I wish you an easy, speedy recovery.

Sincerely,
Regie Routman

(I handwrote my final copy.)

Bob Torrens writes along with his students

A student rereads and revises as she writes

Read Your Writing Out Loud

We need to demonstrate to students how to read their writing aloud "with the fresh eyes of a reader" and show them how we listen for:

- ☐ Precise language (such as lively verbs).
- ☐ Unnecessary words that we can cut.
- ☐ Confused meaning.
- ☐ Clear organization.
- ☐ Places where you stumble.
- ☐ Places where you get bored.
- ☐ Places where it doesn't sound right (grammar).

While writing this book, I read many chapters out loud to my dad. Hearing the sound of the text out loud—which is more immediate and concrete than rereading silently—helped me notice missing words, pinpoint confusions, see what and where I needed to cut, and know where I needed to reorganize. When students share in a conference and read their piece aloud, they naturally cut, add, and make changes on the spot as they hear how their piece sounds. We need to teach them to do this as a key strategy to strengthen all their writing.

Make Your Thinking About Revision Visible

A great deal of my revising happens as I am rereading and rethinking in the act of composing. I move things around, delete, add, change the direction of my thought, start again. Writing is not a sequential process, with revision neatly tucked in midway. Again, I only revise because I care about my reader. (Sometimes that reader is myself—when I write poetry, for example.)

Thinking about revision also means knowing when not to revise. Lots of stuff we write—freewrites, diaries, letters, some drafts—never gets revised. In order to learn when not to revise, students must do lots of writing: "If you want to take revising seriously . . . you need to write plenty that you don't revise." That is, students take revision seriously when they are in writing classrooms where writing happens all day long, for genuine purposes and audiences, across the curriculum.

Finally, let students know that when the writing matters to you, you are willing to do the time-consuming work of revising. Writing and rewriting these few pages on revision in this book took me two days (I reread and reworked the section at least a dozen times), because I kept rereading and rethinking what I wanted to say that would be helpful to my readers.

Much of the final revising I do is "polishing," being picky about a word here and there, after I am fairly satisfied with my writing. When I revise in front of students, they observe me reread a couple of extra times, just to be sure the wording is exactly "right."

Too many of our students from the early grades through high school only understand revision as a teacher-directed step in the writing process. Once you model the recursive, back-and-forth nature of purposeful writing, everything changes. Students become writers who willingly revise.

TRY IT
APPLY IT

- ✐ Do a shared writing with your class in which you develop (and post) a chart listing what to check for when reading a draft aloud to yourself.
- ✎ Have students write a lot of short pieces (see pages 198–199); this give them more energy to revise and write than writing that goes on and on.
- ✑ Look at students' papers. Are they revising willingly? If not, evaluate whether or not there is sufficient interest in the topic.
- ✐ Be sure students write for audiences that matter to them. An awareness of audience sensitizes writers to their readers and encourages revision.
- ✎ Make sure your students understand the difference between revising and editing. Do a shared writing on revising. Chart students' responses. Evaluate what they understand, where they are confused, and what you need to teach. Revisit the draft and revise it as students become more knowledgeable.

Focus on Editing After Students Can Produce Quality Writing

Overattention to grammar and mechanics while composing adversely impacts writing. That is, when teachers overemphasize correctness when students write, writing quality declines. Let me be clear. I am not advocating that anything goes. I expect kids to have basic conventions and spelling when they write. In fact, they must have those in order to write fluently. But I want quality writing, and I focus on that first.

When I was working with intermediate-grade students in a residency in the Southwest, their teachers requested I demonstrate how to teach grammar, editing, and spelling. We hit editing hard but not until students had content worth working with, and that took the first three days of the week. (See the "Hero Writing" lesson in the Teaching in Action section.) A fifth-grade teacher later told me, "That's the best editing work I've seen students do, and you didn't even mention editing until Thursday."

Truly, editing is the easy part, but it only matters if students have a piece of writing worth reading. It matters little if my text is perfectly edited and spelled, if what I have to say is trivial, boring, and a waste of the reader's time. Once students understand the importance of editing for making their intended message clear and easy to read (that is, after they have developed an editing consciousness), they taking editing seriously and invest their energies in it. Until then, they view editing as the teacher's job.

Make Sure Students Know Why Conventions Matter

Students won't pay attention to conventions if they don't care about the writing. When they write with a valued reader in mind, they take conventions seriously, even in a first draft. They come to understand that conventions are a necessity that make the text readable. For example, punctuation "directs you to read, in the same way musical notation directs a musician how to play."

Owen was the most struggling writer in a second-grade class. He made a breakthrough after he was celebrated for the wonderful story he told in front of the class as part of our prewriting experience (see the "Secrets of Second Graders" Teaching in Action lesson). During sustained writing, when I checked on how he was doing, I noticed he had gotten right to work on his draft. But, as usual, he wasn't spacing between words. Rather than say, "You need to space between words," I told him, "Owen, I can almost read all of what you've written. You've got a terrific start here. But, I'm having trouble reading this easily because you're not spacing much between words. You need to use spaces between words so your reader can read your great story here. Use your finger as a spacer, like this, as you write." (See Owen's draft, page 22.)

Teach Spelling Well

I ask a group of second graders what they like about writing. A few students talk about choosing their own topics and getting to use their imagination. Then a student raises her hand: "I'm worried about spelling." I tell her, "Just concentrate on what you want to say. I will help you with your spelling." It is necessary to teach spelling, but let's not lose sight of the fact that spelling only matters so the reader can make sense of the written message. Being able to spell makes writing easier, as the writer can focus on meaning and audience.

All teachers I know struggle with how to teach spelling, but spelling can't be left to chance: "the most recent research supports the need for most learners to experience words through reading, writing, and focused examination." A comprehensive literacy curriculum requires a strong spelling program that includes:

- ☐ Ongoing assessment and evaluation.
- ☐ Writing for authentic purposes and audiences.
- ☐ Developing a spelling consciousness.
- ☐ Word study and investigation.
- ☐ Effective communication with parents.

Competent spellers are almost always competent readers. They also write more and do it better and more easily. Students who struggle mightily with spelling or worry unnecessarily about perfect spelling do not write fluently or easily. You will want to have schoolwide conversations about spelling and formulate a policy on teaching spelling that also includes excellent teaching of reading and lots of time to read.

Set Up the Environment for Teaching Spelling

A classroom environment that teaches and encourages students to be good spellers provides lots of:

- ☐ Opportunities to write and talk about words.
- ☐ Opportunities to read and talk about words.
- ☐ Spelling references (wall charts, personal dictionaries, classroom dictionaries, print displayed in the classroom, word walls, classmates).
- ☐ Daily time in which to write (to include talking about spelling in an editing conference—whole class, peer, or one-on-one).
- ☐ Explicit teaching of common word patterns (which enables students to figure out related words and correct misspellings), onsets and rimes, frequently used words, prefixes and suffixes, root words, unusual features of words.
- ☐ Strategies for spelling unfamiliar words and for "fixing up" misspellings.
- ☐ Playing around with language.

Value Spelling Approximations

I choose to use the term *invented spelling* for the practice others prefer to call *temporary spelling, transitional spelling,* or *phonetic spelling.* I define invented spelling as the reasoned linguistic approximations and thoughtful strategies students use as they write, never as anything goes. In invented spelling, students make their best attempts based on what they know about words—the rules, patterns, visual configurations, and origins of language. Use the term you're most comfortable with; what's most important is that you understand invented spelling, can apply its principles to your practice, and can talk knowledgeably about spelling with other educators and parents.

Children who have the opportunity to use invented spelling to infer how the spelling system works become better spellers than students who learn to spell by rote. Since we're after fluency, invented spelling is a good thing as long as we don't overdo it. That is, students should not be inventing spellings for common words we expect them to have mastered, but we do want them to use lively vocabulary in their writing and not be limited to the words they can correctly spell.

First graders who are encouraged to use invented spellings write more words and spell more of them correctly than students who are focused on correct spelling. Such students also write more interesting text (see Kelly's story and writing sample in Chapter 4, page 64). And teaching phonics by encouraging invented spelling is faster and more effective than teaching letter sounds in isolation.

In addition, we can teach and assess phonemic awareness through writing. When we demonstrate how writing works—through writing aloud, shared writing, interactive writing, in conferences—we can stretch out the sounds in words to help students hear the individual phonemes. We can also quickly assess phonemic awareness by looking at a child's writing. "Phonemic awareness is very likely to develop as a consequence of learning phonics, learning to read, and learning to write, especially when teachers encourage children to use invented spellings."

Phonemic awareness is also easily promoted through rhyming, segmenting words, substituting sounds, omitting sounds—not as isolated activities but as part of the real reading and writing you are already doing; for example, segmenting or omitting sounds using kids' names or words from a content area.

Raise Your Expectations for Spelling

While invented spelling is great for freeing kids to use words they might not typically write, sometimes we accept invented spellings for words kids are capable of writing conventionally. It is reasonable to expect students to spell a bank of frequently used words correctly, even in drafts. Midyear in many first-grade classrooms I still find many students misspelling words such as *my, can,* and *I.* Well-intentioned teachers tell me they don't want to "interfere" with kids' writing, but invented spelling is for words we wouldn't expect students to be able to spell at their stage of development. I *do* interfere and say something like this: *Kids, in order for me to read your message easily, I expect that you will do your best job spelling. You can no longer misspell* my, can, *and* I *ever again in your writing. Check yourself on the word wall.* As long as kids are writing those words over and over again, they might as well write them correctly. (See first-grade teacher Lea Payton's letter [Appendix B] to her students' parents about raising expectations and the video clip of Derek's spelling lesson on the accompanying DVD.)

Recently I was teaching and guiding the writing of friendly letters in a second-grade classroom. A number of first-, second-, and third-grade teachers were observing. When we got to editing, I negotiated—during a shared writing of editing expectations—how much of the spelling the students should be expected to "fix up": "Should it be three words, five words, some words, most words, all words?" To my surprise, most of the teachers responded, "Some." It was midway through the school year, these letters were not more than a page or page and a half, and the words had been suggested by the children. I suggested the children could fix up most of the words, and the students agreed. This goal, in fact, turned out to be very doable. (See pages 203–204.)

Develop a Strong Spelling Consciousness

Research shows that five or six misspellings in a three-hundred word text can cause the reader to say, "I can't read this." Until students have a spelling consciousness—that is, until they value the necessity of conventional spelling and strive to produce it—they will not set high-enough expectations for themselves as writers. Specifically, having a spelling consciousness means valuing correct spelling as a courtesy to the reader. "Errors create the impression that a writer either doesn't care or doesn't know better." Stress with your students that publishing a piece means you have a contract with your reader to have correct spelling and conventions.

I had been working for months with a beginning teacher and her class of eager fourth-grade writers. The teacher skillfully taught all her writing lessons in the context of a monthly, class-published and illustrated news magazine that was directed primarily to parents but also went to every teacher and administrator. Each student was responsible for one article about such class-selected topics as a current unit of study, a field trip, a class happening, an interview with a staff member, and so on. They worked hard on their drafts, revisions, and final copies. They proudly showed off their first edition and gave me a copy.

I spoke honestly with the students after I read it:

> *Kids, I am so impressed with your writing. Wow! You have great leads, engaging writing, wonderful illustrations, lots of interesting information, and strong conclusions to your articles. Congratulations! You've done a great job. I can't recall when I've seen better writing by fourth graders. I have to tell you, though, I found nine spelling errors, and that surprised me. Instead of being able to concentrate fully on your message, I was distracted each time I came upon a misspelling. It made me stop and focus on the misspelled word.*

That's all I said, but the students "got it." Conventional spelling was necessary to fully engage the reader's concentration and interest. After that, the students tracked me down each month and challenged me to find a spelling error in their latest edition. I never did, and they were very pleased with themselves. Because they saw the necessity for correct spelling, they took it seriously. No less than eight students proofread each article. While the teacher was also one of the editors, students took the job of being the final spelling editors seriously. They not only rose to the challenge, they enjoyed becoming sticklers about spelling. They had developed a spelling consciousness that would serve them well with all their writing.

teaching tip

One-Second Rule [Spelling]

Quickly checking the spelling of words as you write and reread saves editing time.

I told that story to a class of fifth graders working on a school guidebook (see pages 105–110) and they published it with no errors (see DVD).

Use Word Walls and Other Resources Effectively

Word walls can be powerful literacy resources for students if they are accessible, manageable, and created with the children based on their needs and interests. On the other hand, when word walls are posted according to the scope and sequence of a commercial program or to fill a bulletin board, their benefit to students is limited.

Know why you are choosing to use a word wall, and explain its ongoing use to students. A word wall is only a useful literacy tool if you and your students understand and value it as a reference for finding, checking, and learning how to read and write specific words and figure out related words. Without understanding why the word wall is an important help for writing and reading, students will mostly ignore it.

I say something like the following:

On this wall we're going to display important words that you all need to know how to read and write. We'll decide many of those words together and talk about how and why they're important as we post them. Sometimes, I'll highlight part of a word in color, and that means you can use that word to help figure out other words. Let me show you what I'm talking about. . . .

As in all excellent teaching, you will need to follow the optimal learning model and first show students how to use the word wall, then try it out together, and next give them time to practice using it (with your guidance) before expecting them to use the word wall on their own.

Construct Word Walls with Students

While there are many commercial word wall packages available from publishers, I much prefer the word walls I create myself with student input. A published program can be useful as a resource or framework, but the publisher does not know your students and their needs. When you decide what words to highlight and talk about the words with students as you post them, students are more likely to refer to them and remember them. Also, by constructing the words and the word wall yourself, you give your room an inviting, unique look that you cannot get with mass-produced materials. Instead of using a commercial alphabet of upper- and lowercase letters with commercial pictures to go along with each letter, you can have your students write the letters and draw the cueing pictures.

teaching tip

Hold Students Accountable

If it's on the word wall, expect it to be spelled correctly in daily writing. When a student misspells a word wall word, I write *w.w* above it which indicates I expect students to correct the misspelling.

teaching tip

Personal Word Wall

Place a personal word wall (a blank grid with a square for each letter of the alphabet) in the child's writing notebook or folder, and write in important words the student is ready to spell. Adding words signals that misspelling them is not acceptable.

Here are some things to keep in mind that will help you make your word walls the best they can be:

- [ ] **Choose a space that is easily visible to all students and close to their eye level:**
  - Bulletin board.
  - Classroom door.
  - Chart paper.
  - Flipchart.
- [ ] **Post only those words that students will use often:**
  - Frequently encountered words (including the most important rimes). Kindergarten teachers often call these "quick and easy words": *my, and, like, to, the,* etc.
  - Students' names (for kindergarten and grade 1).
  - Words students need for their daily reading and writing.
- [ ] **Use personal word walls:**
  - Blank sheets with squares for all the letters of the alphabet, affixed to writing folders, journals, writing notebooks.
  - Personal words added to consumable spelling dictionaries.
  - Words specific to the needs/readiness of individual students
- [ ] **Create specialized word walls:**
  - Family words (*grandma, brother, cousin,* and so on).
  - Days of the week, months.
  - Content-area words.
  - Holiday words.

For older students, word walls or charts might also include common troublesome words, such as some homonyms and homophones (*there, their, they're*), multisyllable words (*beautiful, principal, audience*), and words illustrating common prefixes and suffixes (*reintroduce, precaution, preparation*).

Highlight Words and Features of Words

Keep in mind that we want students to check and evaluate their work on their own as they move toward independence. Teaching them why, how, and when to use the word wall aids their growing competency as language learners. The goal of the word wall is to empower students "to independently take words apart in reading and construct words in writing."

For example, students do not automatically grasp the fact that if they know the rimes *all* and *at*, they can figure out lots of other words (word families). Just telling them won't teach the concept. They will need lots of practice (word sorts, cut-up sentences, manipulating letters) to become expert on word families. (See pages 93–97.)

Here are some things you can do:

☐ Teach patterns of words by highlighting the pattern. (Use a different color, shape, or texture; Wikki Stix; transparent tape—anything to make the pattern stand out.)

☐ Teach exceptions by talking about the "tricky part." (Use mnemonic devices, tracing letters, talking while writing—whatever will help students think about the difficult part of the word.)

☐ Assess whether students are using word wall words:
  • Cover the word wall and then have students write specific words.
  • Verify that word wall words are being spelled correctly in daily writing and reading.

☐ Ask students to figure out new words using the rimes of highlighted words.

☐ Provide multiple ways to practice working with words.

☐ Reteach constantly and with urgency.

Capitalize on Students' Names with a Name Word wall

For developing readers and writers, a word wall that features each child's name and accompanying photo is a great aid for learning to read and write classmates' names and for teaching phonics generalizations. It can be a separate word wall just for names (see *Reading Essentials*, pages 57–62) or combined with frequently used words. Kindergarten teacher Michele Fronk now has her students use the name word wall and accompanying pictures when they pass out valentines. In earlier years, she'd had to supervise, helping three or four students at a time match their valentines to the appropriate student. She notes: "They looked at the picture and name and passed out the valentine. I did not have one single student ask me for help. They were all on task and were so proud of themselves. It was a powerful experience for all of us."

Make Your Word Wall Flexible

When you write the words in marker on heavy paper or a posted chart, you can't change your mind. They're on the wall for the school year. On the other hand, when you post words on individual cards—using Velcro or some other reusable backing—you can:

☐ Move words around.

☐ Alphabetize words.

☐ Remove words that all students know.

☐ Group words to suit needs and interests.

Monica Carrera-Wilburn, a teacher in a multiage classroom of first, second, and third graders, had been using a word wall for years, but she only recently realized how valuable it could be as a student resource.

For many years I've used a word wall in my classroom without really knowing why. Therefore, its use was limited to providing a spelling resource for my students. Now that I am beginning to understand the whys, my word wall has become a valuable literacy tool and a part of my daily literacy instruction.

Limit Dictionary and Thesaurus Use

When students write with dictionaries on their desks, taking time to look up the spelling of words, their free flow of thinking and writing is interrupted. Overconcern about correctness while composing slows writers down. Put the dictionaries away until the editing stage. Another reason to put aside resources, at first, is to encourage students to figure out spellings and choice of words on their own.

Use a thesaurus with caution, if at all. I see lots of contrived writing in classrooms because kids stick in words they would never use and don't know the meaning of. The writing no longer sounds like that particular child wrote it. Pulitzer prize–winning writer Don Murray advises, "Never use a long word where a short one will do."

Make resources in the room useful and easy to access: consumable dictionaries when editing, word walls placed at eye level, laminated cards of frequently used words on writing tables, a classroom library that supports a wide range of reading and writing, peers who have been taught how to be helpful.

Provide High-Quality Instruction to Writers Who Struggle

Writers have difficulty composing and organizing ideas for a variety of reasons. Often, they are also struggling readers or students for whom English is a second language or students who see themselves as writing failures. For these students, immediate success is necessary to break the pattern of failure and lack of writing confidence.

Our writers and readers who struggle need the same first-rate instruction, excellent resources, challenging and relevant curriculum, high expectations, and ongoing support that the rest of our students do. However, they need additional demonstrations, scaffolding, writing choices, and one-on-one conferences, all customized to fit their specific needs and interests. Unfortunately, many struggling writers receive instruction solely in basic skills and writing exercises. They rarely get to focus on the process of writing for real readers, and, consequently, they never get much better as writers or view themselves as writers. Also, don't neglect expository writing, which struggling writers often find more interesting and engaging.

Four special education students (whose label I was unaware of till later) wrote some of the best informational essays in a fifth-grade class (see pages 105–111). I did not create a different, stricter structure structure for them, but the nature of the lesson was very explicit and gave enough scaffolding and examples and conversations for them to be successful.

PROVEN STRATEGIES FOR WRITERS WHO STRUGGLE— AND *ALL* WRITERS

☐ Writing Aloud

Students:

- Listen in as you explain your thinking and planning before you write and while you write.
- Get ideas for writing and composing.

☐ Shared Writing

Students:

- Focus on meaningful message making as you do the transcription.
- Offer ideas without the pressure of having to write them down.
- Hear your and their peers' thinking and ideas.
- Observe the parts of the whole (ideas, words, grammar, spelling, editing) as you shape and write the content/message.
- Reinforce and rethink content area concepts.
- Receive needed support and more easily generate their own language.

☐ Interactive Writing

Students:

- Focus on meaningful message making as you do the transcription.
- Share the pen with you. (This is most effective one-on-one or in a small group.)
- Receive positive feedback for what they are able to write.
- See your modeling close up.
- Experience immediate success.

☐ **Guided and Scaffolded Conversations**

Before, during, and after writing.

Students:

- Explore and try out ideas with your or a peer's support.
- Hear and incorporate rich language.
- Focus, narrow the topic, and add lively detail.
- Capitalize on the fact that speaking comes before writing.

☐ **Short Writing Assignments**

Letters, book reviews, advice, procedures.

Students:

- Complete them more easily (there is less writing, revising, and editing; conferences are shorter).
- Experience more success (they are less overwhelming).

☐ **Personal Writing**

Journals, friendly letters, notes, short memoirs.

Students:

- Have their personal experiences, life stories, family, and culture valued.
- Are assured of a possible entry point, particularly if they are second language learners.
- Have their knowledge affirmed.

☐ **Free Verse**

Students:

- Play around with language and form.
- Write fewer words to create a meaningful message.
- Have fun creating the shape and style of poem.
- Experience immediate success.
- Deemphasize mechanics while writing.
- Express feelings with their personal voice.

☐ **Short Texts Created for Shared, Guided, and Independent Reading**

Predictable and pattern books, innovations on familiar stories, original text added to wordless picture books, writing modeled on an author's style, informational texts based on their interests or a curriculum focus, photo texts, bilingual texts, Readers Theatre scripts, texts for peers or younger students.

Students:

- Experience high motivation.
- Build on familiar language, experiences, and stories.
- Merge content and visual representations of that content.
- Write for a real reader.

☐ Simple Planning Techniques

Lists, charts, outlines, maps, systematic writing, patterned writing.

Students:

- Learn how to brainstorm.
- Use a temporary structure (template) to help them get started.

☐ Differentiated Instruction

Content being taught to everyone is made accessible to all learners; for example, taking the details out of a well-developed shared writing but keeping the main ideas.

Students:

- Experience the same meaningful curriculum as their peers.
- Receive support and appropriate materials to ensure success.

☐ Visuals

Illustrations, captions, comics, graphs, photos, labels, wordless picture books, timelines, use of color.

Students:

- Experience success even though writing/transcription may be difficult.
- See the interrelationship between visuals and text.
- Value another medium for composing, displaying, and arranging information.
- Can showcase their knowledge of elements of art.
- Are able to provide another perspective or point of view.

☐ Paired Writing

Students:

- Create new text with a more capable writer.
- Create familiar text with another struggling writer.
- Retell a familiar story.

☐ **Daily Sustained Time to Write**

Students:

- Keep the flow of writing going (build fluency).
- Choose their own topic.
- Try out writing forms, ideas.

☐ **Daily Sustained Time to Read**

Students:

- Experience how authors work.
- Internalize writing models, ideas, vocabulary.
- Learn to read like a writer.

☐ **Frequent Conferences and Ongoing Evaluation**

Includes whole-class share.

Students:

- Receive affirmation, encouragement, guidance, and explicit teaching.
- Set manageable goals.
- Refer to established criteria (rubric) before, during, and after a writing assignment.
- Encounter examples of good writing that will raise their standards and broaden their ideas about what quality writing is and what to write about.

☐ **Writing Celebrations**

Especially in connection with whole-class share.

Students:

- Have their efforts affirmed.
- See the reason for drafting, revising, and editing.
- Learn from their peers.
- Are encouraged to do their best work.
- Publish their writing for real readers.
- Take pride and enjoyment in writing.

8. Organize for Daily Writing

The author does not only write when he's at his desk, he writes all day long, when he is thinking, when he is reading, when he is experiencing; everything he sees and feels is significant to his purpose and, consciously or unconsciously, he is forever storing and making over his impressions.

—Somerset Maugham

"Well, what is writing workshop anyway? I've tried it but can't get it to work." Many teachers, new and experienced, share that sentiment, along with, "Nobody wants to do writing workshop any more. Preparing for the high-stakes tests takes all our time."

A successful writing program requires a knowledgeable, organized teacher with excellent classroom management skills. Mostly, students need lots of time in which to write, a say in what they write about, strategies that allow them to problem solve independently (plan, revise, edit), and helpful response. Students need to know exactly what is expected—requirements for the writing, writing routines, how to get needed supplies, when to request a conference, what to do when they finish the assignment, and so on. And, most important, we teachers need to know how to teach writing well.

Broaden Your Definition of Writing Workshop

Think of writing workshop as the time in which everything that writers do to create a meaningful piece of writing for a reader takes place. You don't have to call it writing workshop; just call it writing. It can be journal writing, assigned writing, writing in math and science. But the term *writing workshop* is widely used, so that's what I call it.

HOW I DEFINE WRITING WORKSHOP

☐ Sustained, daily writing across the curriculum of mostly self-chosen topics.

☐ Writing for purposes and audiences that the writer values and understands.

☐ Playing around with language and learning how to craft writing.

☐ Conferring with students to respond to their writing, celebrate what they have done well, and teach the next steps for moving the writing forward.

☐ Teaching students what they need to know to write fluently and accurately.

☐ Doing what writers do to make a piece engaging for the reader.

☐ Publishing for real audiences.

There are no rigid procedures or one set of best practices. In kindergarten, start with shared writing and writing aloud short messages until students know how to form some letters and apply enough phonics to begin to write (to include drawing) on their own.

Think about how you teach writing. Writing workshop is *not*:

☐ A lockstep, linear process: prewrite, draft, revise, edit, publish.
☐ Focusing on individual writing traits.
☐ Following a program or template.
☐ Writing to prompt after prompt to prepare for a high-stakes test.
☐ Practicing skills in isolation.
☐ Writing topic sentences with supporting details.
☐ Assigning a topic without teaching.
☐ Writing for purposes students don't value or understand.

Having a set of procedures in place is less important than your beliefs and philosophy about teaching writing. Rather than organizing writing class around particular skills, steps, and minilessons, shift the focus to communicating a message to an intended reader. (See the Teaching in Action lesson on procedural writing, pages 316–322, for how that happens.) Your confident, knowledgeable mind-set will guide you better than any program or series of steps. Keep the following things in mind:

- ☐ Establish a genuine purpose and audience for all writing.
- ☐ Start by demonstrating (writing aloud, shared writing, sharing exemplary writing).
- ☐ Gradually release responsibility to students (a small group or partners conversing before writing or writing together, sustained writing with your guidance).
- ☐ Celebrate, respond, evaluate, teach, and move forward (have conferences with students).

Begin by identifying an important topic for a specific reader and then teach the skills students need to write about that topic—both those you anticipate they will need and those that crop up as they write. Imagine happy and energetic students and teachers, quality writing, and high-test scores too! That's what happens when the writing program is all about excellent writing for genuine purposes and real audiences.

Find Time for Daily Writing

teaching tip

Keep the Flow

If you can't have your students write every day, at least be sure to have them write on consecutive days—it's easier to get the "flow" going. Writing regularly is more likely to lead to fluency.

Writing requires a daily commitment. Those who write every day in a regular planned writing session produce about twice the volume and twice the number of ideas as writers who write when they feel like it. Years ago Don Graves wrote that if we don't teach writing at least four days a week for at least forty-five minutes, we shouldn't bother to teach it at all. The National Commission on Writing goes further and recommends that schools double the amount of time spent writing at every grade level (some of this time is spent writing at home). The only way you will "find" time for daily writing is to highly value it and recognize the power of writing for thinking and communicating across the curriculum.

It's impossible to get a "flow" without revisiting and thinking about writing every day. Writing this book, my goal was to work for at least a few hours first thing every morning, my best writing time. Whenever life intervened and I missed even a day or two, it was always difficult to get started again. I first had to spend some time "getting back in the groove."

Value Writing and You Will Make Time for It

Teachers tell me there's no time to put writing at the center of the curriculum. There is if you value it. Recently, my husband Frank and I were preparing to move from Cleveland, Ohio, where we had lived for over thirty years, to Seattle, where our son, daughter-in-law, and two granddaughters live. I was very busy packing, trying to sell our condo, teaching, and writing *Reading Essentials*. I was trying to decide, did I have time to visit my eighty-five-year-old, independent, working-full-time dad in New York for one or two days, or (more convenient for me) should I just wait until we moved and then have him out to visit? And then my dad had a brutal stroke. I spent nearly a month at his side and was involved in every step of his care. I "found" the time to be with him because it was important. We still moved as planned and I finished my book on time. None of that was easy, but we managed it. I am humbled by that experience, and I think about it often now in relation to the choices I make: We make time for what we value.

So when teachers say to me *I don't have time to teach writing every day,* my response is *Yes, you do, if you value it; if you don't have time, you're valuing something else more* (perhaps skills in isolation or phonics drills or worksheets). Take a look at your teaching day, and decide what's really most important for helping students become independent learners. Writing is one of the best ways I know for developing deep thinking, so I make time for it.

SET UP THE ENVIRONMENT FOR SUCCESS

A successful learning environment provides:

- ☐ The rationale for what you and your students are about to undertake.
- ☐ Explicit demonstrations and explanations.
- ☐ Lots of shared experiences.
- ☐ Opportunities for negotiating the curriculum. (Students should have some say in what they'll write about and how they'll write it.)
- ☐ Support and encouragement to all learners so they experience success (may mean calling on a reticent student and "hand-holding").

☐ Many opportunities for talking, predicting, listening, thinking, asking questions, giving input. (I often tell students, *"I'm not looking for a right answer. I want your best thinking. You have something to say. Take your time."* And, *"Smart people ask questions. There are no stupid questions. If you don't know what something means, ask."*)

☐ Plenty of time for guided practice.

☐ Ongoing feedback—nudging, raising expectations, celebrating small and big successes and contributions.

Provide More Choice Within Meaningful Structure

Students need to be able to choose most of their writing topics if they are to take writing seriously, take pride in their work, and write with strong voice. But students also have to know something about the topic in order to write about it. So initially I rely on choice within structure, especially when I work in schools where students dislike writing and I want all students to experience immediate success, engagement, and enjoyment.

Tap the Potential of Choice Within Structure

Choice within structure means that students have a wide range of choices within a predetermined, engaging topic (one they often have had a hand in choosing). It does not mean writing to a rigid topic with strict requirements such as, "Begin with a topic sentence that includes who, what, and where." Rather, it is a temporary scaffold to enable students to choose their own meaningful topics and write competently and confidently. Don Graves notes, "If the teacher doesn't demonstrate choosing her own topic, kids won't understand what choice means." Kids need to see us wrestle with writing choices and then choose the topic we can write about most honestly.

Choice within structure leads to high-quality work if the topic is important to students. I always try to choose something that taps into students' passions. The topic may be very broad, such as the experience of moving, or very focused, such as a special moment spent with someone you admire. I demonstrate for students how I first come up with a broad topic and then narrow it (see page 26–27).

teaching tip

Share Your Thinking

I have several ideas jotted down on this sticky note.

I'm not sure which one I want to write about.

I'm going to briefly talk through each one. Saying the stories out loud will help me decide.

(And then) Here's the one that's pulling at me right now. I think I want to write about this.

(See also the Teaching Tip on page 184.)

teaching tip

Writing Fiction

Fiction is difficult to write well. Until you have taught students how to develop a character, setting, and problem and write dialogue that moves the story forward, tell your students in intermediate grades, "Write your fiction stories at home." Otherwise, many students write rambling, episodic pieces that take too much of our time.

The following topics, all of which were the result of choice within structure, produced well-written pieces written for meaningful purposes and valued audiences:

- ☐ Secrets of second graders (stories of our lives that no one knows).
- ☐ Heart poems (poems about things that really matter).
- ☐ A bird's-eye view of our school (informational essays in a school guidebook).
- ☐ Morning procedures (How-To writing).
- ☐ Thankful moments (personal narratives, letters).
- ☐ Heroes in our lives (informational writing, personal narratives, letters).

Teachers are always amazed that when kids really want to write about something, it's not just the content that improves. Their spelling and handwriting also improve, often dramatically (see Jon's letter, page 203). As fourth grader Ashton, after writing more freely than usual, said, "Why is it easier to write when you can write what you want instead of what the teacher has planned for you?" A wise comment indeed. Once we have shown students how to write a story, a poem, a letter, an informational essay, a "How To" book, and so on, they have the know-how to be able to create and innovate on these forms themselves.

Teach Students How to Choose Worthwhile Topics

While I do believe that kids should be able to freely choose what they write about and that "the topic is the single most important factor contributing to writer variability," I also believe we need to teach students how to make wise choices. I see teachers wasting way too much time having long conferences with students who have chosen to write, disjointedly, about things not worth reading about.

Students need guidelines for knowing when they've chosen their topic well—or poorly. Usually those guidelines are *do you care about the subject? can you tell a lot about it? can you include appropriate and interesting details?* Before students invest a lot of energy into a piece, we need to be sure they are prepared to write. Prepare your students by having them:

teaching tip

If Kids Are Truly Engaged in the Topic

☐ They stop asking *how long does it have to be?*
☐ They write fluently.
☐ They willingly revise and edit.
☐ They take pride in handwriting and spelling.
☐ They are eager to share.

- ☐ Brainstorm writing ideas (orally or in a list).
- ☐ Talk about these ideas with you or with a classmate (scaffolded conversation).
- ☐ State their intention for writing—purpose and audience (can be themselves).
- ☐ Submit a written plan (mandatory for a large project).
- ☐ Immerse themselves in the form or genre (read and study exemplars).
- ☐ Practice writing in the genre with your guidance (through a class exploration of poetry, fiction, whatever).

Teach Sensible Planning Strategies

We tend to overdo *planning*, or what is commonly called *prewriting*. Either we direct kids through a lockstep process that may not be helpful, or we put so much time and energy into planning that kids are exhausted before they begin to write.

Use professional common sense. If you are using a writing kit or program with specific steps, use it as a temporary framework or scaffold, not a recipe. Ultimately, how kids plan their writing must be up to them. Many young writers' actual planning involves talking to themselves and drawing. Always requiring kids to plan before they write thwarts many writers. Sometimes, we just have to plunge in. When I write a letter to a friend, my prewriting is my thinking as I go along.

Expand Your Definition of Prewriting

By prewriting I mean the thinking by which students generate, plan, and organize ideas with the purpose of producing effective writing. Prewriting most often occurs before writing but also goes on during writing as the writer rethinks.

Prewriting is necessary to produce effective writing but need not be time-consuming or laborious—or even written down. Much of skilled writers' planning takes place mentally, especially when the topic is very familiar (a personal experience, for example). Some types of prewriting include but are not limited to:

- ☐ Brainstorming, listing ideas.
- ☐ Discussing ideas (with teacher, peer, partner, self).
- ☐ Talking about text (literature study, debate, critique).
- ☐ Researching the subject (getting background information).
- ☐ Creating a visual organizer.
- ☐ Rereading.
- ☐ Outlining.
- ☐ Reading or viewing books, articles, movies, plays.
- ☐ Observing teacher demonstrations and think-alouds.
- ☐ Illustrating (drawing to spur writing).
- ☐ Freewriting (also called quickwriting).

Do More Freewrites

In freewriting, students write for five or ten minutes (sometimes responding to a prompt) without concern for grammar and structure. Freewriting is a great way to build endurance, confidence, and writing fluency. Don't neglect freewriting as a way to zero in on a writing topic and get the juices flowing. Often students who have no idea what they want to write about will uncover a topic through a freewrite. Freewriting is also helpful for getting students used to writing on demand, a skill necessary to complete school assignments and mandated writing tests.

Limit the Use of Graphic Organizers

Visual organizers such as flow charts and time lines do work well in the content areas for helping students think about how to organize, learn, and integrate information.

While it's helpful to teach students about graphic organizers—it gives them planning and organizing options—don't overdo it. Some students expend so much time and energy creating graphic organizers or planning for the teacher, they are too tired to write.

When I make a written plan before I write (and as I continue to write), it always involves some kind of list or outline, never a graphic organizer. And I'm not alone. Each and every time I have teachers write to a prompt or ask them to write about a learning experience, no teacher has used a visual to plan what they will say. Everyone brainstorms some sort of list. The teaching implication is clear: Real writers organize their thoughts through brainstormed lists. Take a look at your own planning for writing and guide your teaching accordingly.

One teacher told me, "Some of my students can't write without a graphic organizer." Later, she reevaluated that statement after many students wrote beautifully organized pieces without them. What took their place? Excellent teaching—demonstrating planning, thinking, and writing out loud in front of students; holding public conversations with a few students; giving kids time to talk to each other and share ideas; letting kids choose how to plan their writing; demonstrating a conference.

Do More Demonstration Writing

Start a New Page

Don't always end your demonstration writing on the last line at the bottom of the page; doing so sends kids the message that when they get to the end of the page they're done.

Don't expect high-quality writing from your kids unless you're modeling what high-quality writing looks and sounds like. This is just as critical for kindergartners as it is for older students. Many teachers find that when they do more and better modeling—writing for and with their students—everything improves: kids' engagement, abundance of ideas for writing, willingness to write and take risks, knowledge of how and what to write, and the quality and quantity of their writing. Your demonstrations can take many forms:

☐ Writing aloud.

☐ Shared writing.

☐ Sharing examples—reading aloud, celebrating students' writing, viewing a video. (*What do you notice? You could try that, too.*)

☐ Conducting scaffolded conversations before writing.

Second-grade teacher Cami Kostecki attributes the big leap her kids made in writing to her demonstration writing:

> When I took the time to effectively model my story, kids were engaged. I didn't hear, "I don't know what to write" nearly as much. Students' writing improved because they had a complete idea of what was expected of them. By the time they got to their seats, they were excited and ready to start their stories.

See the accompanying website, www.heinemann.com/writingessentials, for elaboration on "demonstrations."

Have More Conversations About Writing

A critical part of teaching writing is having students talk about their writing before they write, while they are writing, and even afterward. Scaffolded conversations with students are essential for producing excellent, coherent texts. I used to go around the room and say to each student, "What are you going to write about?" and get a few words or a one-liner in return, often followed by superficial writing. Now I have in-depth conversations with one or two students—with the whole class listening in—to ensure the students have rich ideas and language to think about as well as models of thinking to emulate. What a difference it makes in the quality and quantity of every student's writing.

These conversations take a number of forms:

☐ Teacher and student (for an example, see pages 110, 296–297) (*demonstration*).
☐ Student and student, coached by the teacher (*guided practice*).
☐ "Turn and talk" at desks or within a group (*guided practice*).
☐ Conversations initiated by students on their own (*independent practice*).

Classrooms that have more high-level talk going on have higher reading and writing achievement. When I draw students out through person-to-person dialogue, their thinking clarifies and goes deeper, and their story emerges. All students, not just the ones I am talking with, benefit and get ideas for their writing. These conversations are consistent with research showing that students make higher gains when teachers ask authentic, open-ended questions and continue with probing questions about students' responses. (See my conversation with Derek in the spelling conference on the accompanying DVD and on pages 347–349.)

A kindergarten teacher comments on the power of conversations:

Not only does conversation focus the students' writing and bring out their individual voices, it boosts their own confidence and self-esteem. Forget the dreaded show-and-tell. I'm using conversation and talk before writing! What an amazing difference this has made, and one that I was able to notice immediately. I am now laughing at the students' writing, mainly because it is so full of joy and not the typical "I like."

Keep It Simple and Direct

There is no formula for these before-during-and-after-writing conversations. I think of the process as one person (me) talking to a fascinating person (the student) and genuinely trying to learn more about the writer and what she or he is trying to say. It's a very natural kind of conversation (see the examples on pages 296–297 and on the accompanying DVD). It is never *Tell me more* just to have the student add more information to make the piece longer, but rather a genuine and sensitive listening to, questioning of, and responding to this particular student. My purposes are to:

teaching tip

Use sticky notes to jot down reminders to the child—specific language used, a goal you have set together. Be sure to demonstrate how to use these sticky notes when writing. (See the examples on page 298.)

- ☐ Convince the student he or she has a worthwhile story to tell.
- ☐ Help the student tell a meaningful story.
- ☐ Acknowledge all responses.
- ☐ Encourage lively language and interesting content.
- ☐ Scaffold the language of thinking and organization.
- ☐ Help narrow the focus: *What's the most important thing that happened or that you want to remember? Just tell about that.*
- ☐ Get students to slow down, carefully observe and remember, and fill in the details.
- ☐ Ensure that the student has enough information and confidence to begin to write or continue writing.
- ☐ Guide the "drawing" part of a child's story so that the pictures go with it.

When the student offers a "gem"—memorable language, a fascinating idea— I immediately jot it on a sticky note so I'll remember it. Doing so also signals to the student (and the other students who are listening in):

- ☐ My teacher thinks it's great.
- ☐ This is important information to include.
- ☐ There it is so I won't forget it if I choose to use it.

☐ *That is so interesting. So then what happened?* [encouraging more detail]

☐ *How did you feel about that?* [encouraging personal voice]

☐ *What did he say when you told her that?* [encouraging dialogue]

☐ *So what did that look like? Was it red like the rose on my desk or red like Jana's sweater or red like the color of your writing notebook?* [encouraging descriptive detail]

☐ *I can't wait to hear what happened after that! What did you do?* [encouraging storytelling]

☐ *Okay, slow way down so I can picture exactly what happened.* [encouraging elaboration and description]

Include Peer Talk

Especially for our English language learners and writers who struggle, talking before writing clarifies their thinking and makes writing easier. Conversation is the primary way most ethnic groups of color in the United States communicate, with the roles of speaker and listener being "fluid and interchangeable." Any "strategies that stimulate elaboration or problem solving are likely to foster better story writing."

After scaffolded conversations with one or two students, I often take a few more minutes to have students "turn and talk" and tell their story to a partner. I encourage students to use the kind of language I've been modeling. Even our youngest writers can say to a partner, *Why did you do that?* or, *That's so funny. What happened then?* Use the optimal learning model (see inside front cover and below) to show what productive peer talk looks like and sounds like:

☐ Teacher demonstration with a student (with class listening in).

☐ Two students demonstrating (with teacher guidance and class looking on).

☐ Talking explicitly about what students did well, need to work on (guided practice).

☐ Trying it out (teacher circulating to see how it's going).

☐ Independent practice.

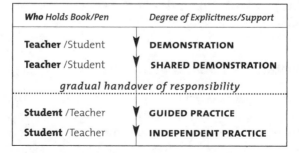

Who Holds Book/Pen	Degree of Explicitness/Support
Teacher /Student	**DEMONSTRATION**
Teacher /Student	**SHARED DEMONSTRATION**
gradual handover of responsibility	
Student /Teacher	**GUIDED PRACTICE**
Student /Teacher	**INDEPENDENT PRACTICE**

The Optimal Learning Model

Do not underestimate the power of talk on writing quality. Informal conversations among students as they write influences the amount and quality of revisions students are willing to make. Conversations with others help students express their ideas more fully and make them their own.

Establish Criteria for Writing

Often I establish criteria with students *after* they have had a chance to see me write or we've done a shared writing and/or they have studied examples of other authors' work (to include former students). Before asking, *What makes a good letter?* write one aloud yourself or as a shared-writing exercise. Then ask, *What did you notice?* and establish criteria. This is in keeping with highly literate classrooms, which tend to be inquiry and response based. Telling students the criteria without their input is likely to be less effective in promoting high achievement.

Setting reasonable criteria makes it more likely that quality writing will result, especially when students are attempting a new genre. For example, to ensure success for all fifth graders writing informational essays (see pages 110 and 111 for examples), we broke the essay into three parts (which also made paragraphing a certainty):

☐ **Opening statement**—state the topic, get the reader's attention.
☐ **Information**—provide facts and supporting details.
☐ **Summary**—restate the main points in a new way to remind the reader why the topic is important.

Make Excellent Management a Priority

I rarely have a classroom management problem. Partly it's because I teach with a sense of urgency; that is, I attempt to make every minute count and ensure that my instruction and evaluation are relevant and interesting. I teach all the skills but in service to the "big idea" of what we're working on. Because the work is engaging, I have students' attention. Better classroom managers are more likely to teach for meaning and less likely to have mastery of discrete skills as their main instructional goal. This makes perfect sense; it's easy to lose kids' attention when the work is tedious and broken into little pieces.

Maintain a Predictable Structure

The only way to "fit" writing in every day is to write all day across the curriculum. Don't separate "writing workshop" from other writing. Writing is writing—in math, reading, science, and social studies; in journals, writing folders, or notebooks; on papers, charts, the computer. Take a look at the writing schedules on pages 185–186 and notice how these teachers "find" time for daily writing.

LEA PAYTON'S SCHEDULE, GRADE 1

Previous Schedule

8:50–9:00	Calendar (includes math skills)
9:00–9:30	Shared Reading (sentence strips or big books)
9:30–10:20	Guided Reading (students worked on seatwork assignments—not reading or writing)
10:20–10:35	Recess
10:35–11:05	Journals (only basic modeling by me; no conversations to help them)
11:05–11:35	McCracken Spelling
11:35–12:20	Lunch/Recess
12:20–12:35	Read Aloud (chapter book)
12:35–1:35	Mathland (district program)
1:35–1:50	Recess
1:50–2:35	Science/Social Studies/Health/ Specialist (P. E., library, music)
2:35–2:50	Read Alouds/Sing/Class Meeting

Now we write together and read the text together—2 to 3 times a week. Also, they read Morning Message (by the teacher). These include all subject areas.

Current Schedule

8:50–9:00	Calendar (includes math skills)
9:00–9:30	Shared Reading/Writing Read Alouds
9:30–10:30	Guided Reading/Independent Reading and Writing
10:30–11:00	Math journals
11:00–11:15	Recess
11:15–12:15	Writing
	Spelling (McCracken) 10 min. (district requirement)
	Mini-lesson 10 min.
	Independent Writing/Individual Conferences (30 min.)
	Sharing/Celebrating (10 min.)
12:15–12:55	Lunch/Recess
12:55–1:10	Read Aloud–Chapter books
1:10–1:25	Mathland (district program)
1:25–2:05	Science/Social Studies/Health/ Science Journals
2:05–2:20	Recess
2:20–2:50	Specialists (P. E., library, music)

Independent writing is letters, poems, lists, stories—but not journals. Added independent work that is real reading and writing. 30 min. independent reading/ 30 min. independent writing.

Write story problems and explain how got their answers.

Shortened spelling because do more in our journals.

Previously writing time was 30 min. Now we have 20 min. more of intentional teaching/modeling, conversations, and writing.

Now include literature that relates to math too.

Added science journals—write facts, label pictures (see example, page 137) and do more expository writing.

Lea Payton

KARI OOSTERVEEN'S SCHEDULE, GRADE 4

8:35–Open Door. Kids do their jobs—coats, lunch sign in, etc.

Morning assignment: Always something little—such as read to a friend, review of a math or spelling skill.

8:50   Correct the morning assignment, if needed. Meet as a class on the floor.

9:00–10:20   Integrated Writing Time (see footnote)

Focus of our day: This could include a shared writing, a minilesson, or a continuation of a previous lesson (10–15 minutes)

Work time: This would include independent work time, me working with small groups on a focus, or writing conferences (30–45 minutes)

Sharing time: We meet, share what we wrote, and talk about our writing

10:20–10:35   Recess

10:35–11:05   Music, Physical Education, Library (rotates daily)

11:10–11:40   Independent reading choice time (30 minutes)

11:45–12:15   Lunch

12:15–12:30   Chapter book story (15 minutes)

12:30–1:30   Integrated Reading Time (see footnote)

Focus of our day: This could include a shared piece of text, a minilesson, or a continuation of a previous lesson (10–15 minutes)

Reading time: This would include an assigned piece of text, working with a book group, or conferencing with me (30–40 minutes)

Reflection time: We discuss what we notice an author has done, vocabulary that we liked or want to know about, or predictions about the text (10–15 minutes)

Recess

1:45–2:45   Math

Clean up, homework, mail

3:00   Dismissal

The biggest addition to my schedule has been the incorporation of sharing our writing. We always make time for sharing, even if it takes away time from something else. We have learned more from the sharing of our ideas and what we have written, than any other thing that we have done all year!

Footnote: I integrate many curricular areas. For example, our writing time might be used for explaining our mathematical thinking or for writing something that we learned about the state of Washington or writing a scientific study. Integrated Reading Time would include social studies text, our science stories, as well as genre or author studies.

Kari Oosterveen

Build a Climate of Trust

A successful writing classroom depends not only on clearly established routines and procedures but also on a classroom climate that encourages students to take risks without fear of failure. A foundation of respect, trust, bonding, and camaraderie underlies every successful writing classroom. Much of that trust builds from the way we talk to and confer with students. We need to bond with each child to ensure learning. It is not enough to have all the organizational pieces in place. To have successful and willing writers, we must also create a caring classroom in which students feel comfortable, secure, and appreciated. The tone of the writing classroom has to impart this message: *The writing work we do is worthwhile, enjoyable, and important; it may be hard sometimes, but I am here to help you; you can do it.*

Employ a Flexible Framework

Use the time you spend teaching writing flexibly, but allocate most of it to having students *write*—that is, let them apply what you have already demonstrated and they have been practicing. Give them control of what they want to say for a clearly understood purpose to a clearly understood reader. Think about your students' needs, not a set of required skills or procedures. Be sure to apply the optimal learning model.

SUGGESTED TIME FRAMES FOR DAILY WRITING

Writing Activity	Time Frame
Demonstration or minilesson based on students' needs and interests as well as curriculum requirements	5–30 minutes (typically 5–15 minutes)
Sustained writing • Students writing (uninterrupted, quiet) • Teacher may also be writing (on same topic as students) • Students having a one-on-one content or editing conference with the teacher • Students conversing and conferencing with each other	20–40 minutes
Whole-class share	10–15 minutes

teaching tip

Flip-Flop Time Allotments

Have a shorter mini-lesson and give more time to sharing, and vice versa.

Although occasionally a minilesson or whole-class share may take twenty minutes or more, aim for no more than ten minutes for each so students have time to write. Some days you may be tempted to skip whole-class share. Don't. It's such a valuable way to acknowledge and celebrate students' efforts, teach what students need, and give all students writing ideas (see pages 207–216 and 338–350).

Establish Daily Routines and Model Expected Behavior

Most students and teachers write best in a quiet setting. Model and make explicit what you mean by "work quietly"—what it looks and sounds like: sitting in a chair or other designated spot, using a "whisper voice" (see my writing demonstration on page 318), having your materials with you. (Of course, for kindergarten and grade 1, it can seem more like sustained noisy writing as they talk, share, and help one another!) Kindergarten teacher Karen Sher, in Shaker Heights, Ohio, uses the term *private work time* (a period of five or ten minutes) and signals its arrival by turning on little lamps on each table.

Also model all behavior you expect, such as how to get supplies, when and how to sharpen pencils, how to confer or talk with a peer, how to listen and give helpful response, how to seek help, and so on.

Apply the optimal learning model:

teaching tip

Listen for Silence

When kids are engaged in their writing, the classroom gets quiet, or there is a hum of soft conversation. A quiet room helps writers get started writing more easily. Even kindergartners can manage five or ten minutes of quiet if it is modeled and expected.

☐ Show what the targeted behavior looks like and sounds like, and perhaps create a chart with students listing the things they observe (*demonstration*). (There is an example of such a chart on page 117.)
☐ With a student, model the behavior (*shared demonstration*).
☐ Have two or more students try out the behavior with the class looking on (*guided practice*). Scaffold and teach as necessary. Ask the class, *What did you notice?*
☐ Expect students to implement the modeled behavior (*independent practice*).

Continue to monitor the behavior until it is well established and students are doing it naturally on their own. Evaluations like this (usually oral, but sometimes written) can be done with the whole class or a small group at the end of a writing session (or whenever a problem arises). Ask:

☐ *How did we do today with this?*
☐ *What went well?*
☐ *What do we still need to work on?*
☐ *How could we have done better?*
☐ *What will we do differently tomorrow?*

Go back to the learning model again, as necessary.

In Bryna Osborne's first grade in Vancouver, Washington, it took just two days to move from a whole-class share in which students constantly interrupted and talked over one another to a peaceful climate of respectful listening. It happened because we made our expectations known, modeled the desired behavior, and kept the sharing moving. Modeling desired behavior saves valuable time in the long run. Bryna comments, "I thought it would be very difficult to teach my class the importance of purposeful sharing; to my surprise the transition was fairly seamless because we had modeled our expectations."

TRY IT
APPLY IT

Model Writing Behavior

- Write on every other line (allows room for making changes).
- Write on only one side of the paper (allows for cutting and pasting and easy rearrangement of pages).
- Date everything (shows writing history and progress).
- Write legibly (makes it easier to read drafts).
- Spell high-frequency words correctly, and use your best invented spelling for other words (raises expectations for spelling, makes drafts easier to read, and saves time during editing process).
- Keep writing records (writing history, sticky notes of suggestions, writing plans).
- Model on a projected transparency using the same paper your students will be using—size, lines, spacing.

Eliminate Distractions

- Do what you can to have a peaceful writing time.
- Have all pencil sharpening done before school, and have a ready supply of sharpened pencils at hand to avoid the added noise and time wasted with students walking about instead of writing.
- Make sure students know procedures for bathroom breaks, getting supplies, requesting a conference. (Model all of these.)
- Advocate for fewer school-day interruptions, such as no, or very limited, public address announcements during the school day.

teaching tip

Quiet, Please

Conference in a private space (one-on-one or in a small group) with kids who need help getting started. Keeping the room quiet enables the other writers to get started right away. Once a student has his idea, send him back to write.

Keep Records

Don't get bogged down with lots of forms and checklists that are not useful. These days, I use as few forms as possible to keep track of students' writing. I stopped using revising and editing checklists when I noticed that students were dutifully filling them out for me but not using them for themselves. Essential records for and by teachers and students include but are not limited to:

- ☐ Minilessons taught.
- ☐ Cumulative writing history.
- ☐ Conference notes.

Having your students keep track of the minilessons you teach (see a third grader's notes on two minilessons, shown on page 191) makes your instruction explicit for students, caregivers, and teachers and makes it easy to refer back to what has been taught. I also depend on a cumulative writing record, which is similar to the daily reading record students keep. Keeping a writing history lets students, family members, and teachers know what genres students are focusing on, who the audience is for the writing, what's being completed and published (and when), and what types of writing need to be encouraged. (See the sample form in Appendix E and additional forms on the website.) You will also want to keep informal conference records (see page 217) to monitor what students are working on, what you are teaching, what goals have been set, and how the writer is progressing. Anecdotal notes can be easily organized in a notebook; use stick-on tabs with the children's names.

teaching tip

Save Everything

Keep all drafts, notes, sticky notes, and cross-outs so we, students, and parents can see their thinking process.

Organize Student Writing

Most teachers experiment with different ways to keep student writing organized. There is no single best way. Many teachers find that a spiral notebook or folder works best for young writers. For students above grade 2, I prefer a three-ring binder with sections for minilesson notes, writing forms (see Appendices E–I), drafts, specific genre writing (poetry, fiction, nonfiction), published works.

Put Genre Study in Perspective

Many districts require that certain genres—poetry, memoir, personal letters, informational essays—be taught in certain grades. Often, because of low test scores and/or a desire for more structure and consistency, the writing focus becomes learning step-by-step rules of the genre or writing form. For example, teachers focusing on friendly letters teach the language and form of the letter: heading, greeting, body, closing signature. The kids can write such a letter, but they're not much worth reading. When I write a letter, I'm not thinking "heading," I'm thinking about putting the date in so the person I'm writing to knows when I wrote it. I'm not thinking about "body" but rather the message I want to send and how I want to say it. If you focus on engaging the writer with real writing for real readers, you can teach the essentials of excellent writing, and students will be able to transfer those to any genre.

9-12-2003 Mini Lesson #4
Writing Time

Looks	Sounds	feel
• students writing at their desks	• silent	• relaxed and comfortable
• Journals open	• music in background	• safe to share ideas
Pencils writing	• teacher conferencing	
	• sharing stories	

I like writing because it seems like I'm inside my Journal.

✱ We wrote this together. I wrote on over head and students wrote in their Journals. I made a class chart as well.

Mini Lesson #5   9/15/03

What Good writers Do

1. reread

2. Stick to their topic

3. Checks to see if writeing makes sence

4. writes for the reader to get a picher in in their mind

5. Write more than One sentece.

6. Use es es intresting words

7. use humer.

8. Can use exciting marks

9. good writers think about there writing

10. Makes the writeing better by crossing out

Keeping track of minilessons: Setting up the writing classroom

Name _____		Writing Record			
Title/Topic	Audience*	Genre**	Start date	Finish date	What happened to it?***
Capture the moment	class	narative	9-9-03	9-16 03	Published
Oregon	self	narative	9-16-03		
↓	↓	↓	9-17-03		
↓	↓	↓	9-18-03		
↓	↓	↓	9-19-03	9-19-03	Publish
How to's	self class	How to	9-19-03	9-19-03	
Poetry	self class	Poems	9-19-03	↓	
↓	↓ Mom	↓	↓	↓	
Super Kid	Emily/self	comic	9-23-03		
↓	↓	↓	9-29-03		
↓	↓	↓	10-1-03		

*peers, teacher, parents, business company
**poetry, letter, narrative, directions, report, research, book review, persuasive, summary
***rough draft, computer work, shared, published

One student's writing history for September (see blank copy of form on website)

Simplify Genre Teaching

There is no research suggesting which particular genres are most effective to teach. Almost all effective writing includes description, detail, careful word choice, sentence fluency, voice, and so on. Don't go overboard on units of study or genre.

Think about adopting a broader stance for teaching genres:

☐ Narrative genres (stories, fairy tales, personal narratives).

☐ Informational genres (explanations, procedures, persuasive pieces, essays, all-about books).

☐ Other genres (poetry, biography).

Appendix L and the website list the common elements of several specific genres.

All the lessons in the Teaching in Action section have genuine audiences and purposes for the writing the kids are learning to do. We teach the genre or form (persuade, describe, explain, instruct, narrate, and so on) as a vehicle for getting our message across to the intended readers.

Make Schoolwide Decisions About Genre Study

Decide at the school and district level what genres/forms you will be teaching at each grade level—when they're introduced and practiced and expected to be mastered. Include such forms as personal narratives, descriptions, reports, letters, poetry, summaries, book reviews (not book reports), fiction, essays.

The chart on page 193 shows one school's master plan. Before the plan was created no one knew who was teaching what genres, when they were being introduced, and if and when they were revisited. It was, as one teacher noted, a free-for-all. Establishing schoolwide expectations made teaching far more intentional and consistent across grade levels.

TRY IT
APPLY IT

✐ Devote a few staff meetings to examining who's teaching what genres when. Meet first by grade levels, and list what you teach. Then, on an oversize matrix, list everything that's being taught at your grade level. Then have the entire faculty look at all the charts and establish consistency from grade to grade. Once you introduce a genre at one grade level, ensure it's revisited.

✐ Meet at your grade level and decide how you can teach the required genres using real purposes and audiences. (See the ideas in Chapter 5.)

BBC Writing forms		To	With	By
	Text form	Introduce Demonstrate	Guided practice	Independent practice
WASL	Personal letter	K-5		→
	Retelling	K-5		→
	Responses to lit.	K-5		→
	Compare/contrast	K-5		→
	Expository (explanations)	K-5		→
	Fiction/narrative	K-5		→
BBC	Summaries	2		→
	Reports	K		→
	Poetry	K		→
	Business letters	4		
	Persuasive pieces	4		→
	Journal writing	K		→
	Book related writing (reviews, short summaries)	K-5		→
	Procedural writing (steps-directions)	K-5		→

WASL (assessed on the high-stakes state test)

BBC (expected by the school)

One school's master plan outlining teaching goals for genres and writing forms

Focus First on Purposes of Writing

When the purpose of writing is to teach how to write a letter, essay, persuasive piece, or fiction, we make writing harder for kids. Focus first on meaningful purposes to real readers, such as:

- ☐ Recording findings (thinking in problem solving, observing and noting scientific changes, saying what we wonder about).
- ☐ Entertaining.
- ☐ Evaluating.
- ☐ Organizing information.
- ☐ Remembering (special events, things to do).
- ☐ Giving thanks.
- ☐ Communicating.
- ☐ Persuading.
- ☐ Informing.
- ☐ Storytelling.

"You learn to write by grappling with a real subject that truly matters to you." The purpose of writing determines the genre or form writing takes, not the other way around. Kids need familiarity with form and structure, but they need good ideas and authentic reasons to write first.

Start by Engaging Students

The hardest part of teaching a required genre is to figure out a way to present it that engages students' hearts and minds. That's where I do most of my planning: thinking about possibilities and discussing them in back-and-forth conversations with myself and with the teachers with whom I'm working. Then we negotiate the curriculum with the students.

Here's an example of how that works. I was asked to teach "multiparagraph informational essays" in fifth grade, since this type of essay was required by the district and was also an element on the state tests. However, nobody could define what an informational essay was. After much discussion and some research, we defined an essay as writing that presents important information about a subject—that is, the writer presents an opinion or information and supports it with evidence. The essay can be informational, persuasive, and/or personal.

Don Murray says, "The most effective essays, I believe, are those that find a way for the writer to reveal a process of thought that invites the reader to think alongside the writer." And the editor of the Op-Ed page of *The New York Times* offers this advice as part of his guidelines for submitting an opinion piece for the editorial page: "Make one argument thoroughly, point by point; the more detail the better. If you try to do too much you can wind up with an article that, in striving to say everything, ends up saying nothing." That good advice is exactly what we try to teach our youngest writers, even in their journal stories.

Because I wanted to get students excited about writing, I did not say, "This week I'm going to teach you how to write a multiparagraph, informational essay, because it's required by your district." If I had, I would have lost them as willing writers. Instead, I said:

> *You know what kids? I had this great idea. I was thinking how fabulous it would be if there was a guidebook to your school. It would have been a great help to me as a new person to receive such a book when I arrived—to help orient me, to find my way around, to get to know what's important here, who the teachers are, and how school operates. What do you think? Or we could do a book about what every fifth grader should know to be prepared for middle school. Let's vote on the idea we like best.*

When students chose the guidebook, I employed the optimal learning model: presenting demonstrations, setting purposes through shared writing, conducting scaffolded conversations, monitoring sustained writing by applying a simple rubric we established, holding conferences regarding content and conventions, and publishing. Highlights (the complete lesson is in the Teaching in Action section) are in the list below. Providing simple yet explicit criteria made it possible for every student to succeed on the first draft. Here are some highlights from our lesson on informational writing (see pages105–110):

☐ Established the purpose (see the topic chart on page 106) and the audience (see the chart on page 106) for writing a guide to the school.

☐ Wrote one page of the book together (see "How to Work in a Small Group," on page 106).

☐ Had scaffolded conversations before writing (see page 110 for excerpts of a conversation with Victoria about how people dress in Wisconsin) and "turn and talk" peer conversations.

☐ Drafted the individual pieces, shared them as a class, revisited the drafts, discussed them in conferences.

☐ Published the guidebook, made decisions on presentation: cover, color and design, font, style, layout, illustrations, map, headings, borders, photos. (See DVD for several published pages from "Eagle's Eye Around Swanson School.")

Teach it First, Label it Later

While you do want to teach students the parameters of each genre and how it's used in the world, use common sense; don't go overboard with rigid procedures or get hung up with terminology. For example, almost all writing involves multi-paragraphs and is expository or informational. Narrative writing is also expository writing. You can drive yourself crazy if you focus too much on the lingo. Think *less* about teaching an "expository multiparagraph essay" or any genre and *more* about teaching the student.

At the end of the week, when the fifth graders had completed their essays, I said to them:

What you wrote this week are called informational essays. Your district and the state test require you to know how to write these, and now you do. If you are asked to write an informational essay, it's no big deal. Remember the criteria you kept in mind while writing the pieces for this guidebook.

Teach Nonfiction Writing

Expository writing develops more slowly than narrative writing, but this may be because children have less experience with and exposure to expository writing and see fewer demonstrations of it. Most of what they hear and read is fiction—all the more reason to be sure we teach informational writing and include lots of interesting nonfiction in our read-alouds and classroom libraries.

At the same time, it's important not to overload students with nonfiction writing that requires a lot of research. Teaching students to do research is more challenging and requires a separate, intensive teaching focus. Too often we ask students to write reports before they know how; for example, we assign research reports but don't teach kids how to summarize (see pages 127–131), a prerequisite for writing a successful report.

Provide more time for browsing nonfiction (after you've modeled how to browse) and immersing children in the genre before expecting them to write. Starting in kindergarten introduce nonfiction text features like these:

- ☐ Table of contents
- ☐ Captions
- ☐ Labels
- ☐ Headings
- ☐ Diagrams
- ☐ Charts
- ☐ Timelines
- ☐ Photographs
- ☐ Drawings
- ☐ Highlighted text
- ☐ Glossary
- ☐ Index

Teacher Talk

- ☐ *What information does the author want the reader to know?*
- ☐ *How does the author organize it?*
- ☐ *Examine the book(s). What do you notice?*
- ☐ *Why do you think the author has a table of contents? a glossary?*
- ☐ *Look at the contents page. If you wanted to know about [blank] where would you start reading? Yes, that's right. With nonfiction, you don't always have to start at page 1. You can start with the part you're interested in.*
- ☐ *Where else could you look to find a topic of interest?*

A FRAMEWORK FOR TEACHING WRITING GENRES

- ☐ **Find out what kids know about the genre, and chart their responses.** Ask, "What do you know about [blank]?"
- ☐ **Gather lots of examples of the genre at a level appropriate for most of your students.** (Ask your school's librarian for help.)
- ☐ **Let students, in pairs or small groups, browse through these materials.** Model first. Ask students, "What did you notice, learn?" Add their responses to the chart you've begun. Notice and brainstorm any unique language. *(Immersion, demonstration.)*

☐ **Discuss and chart, "What makes a good [blank]?"** *(Determining criteria, shared demonstration.)*

☐ **With your students, choose one text to study together.** Make sure all students can see the text as you read it aloud, or have them read it in a small group or with a partner. *(Shared demonstration, guided experience.)*

☐ **Write in the genre together as a class.** Use the language of the genre. Refer to the chart you've developed. *(Shared demonstration.)*

☐ **Identify additional criteria for what to include when writing in the genre.** *(Shared demonstration.)*

☐ **Prepare to write** (have students gather resources, brainstorm ideas, talk with you and their peers, perhaps conduct interviews and generate a list of questions). *(Guided practice.)*

☐ **Write for a sustained period in the form of the genre for an authentic audience and purpose.** *(Guided and independent practice.)*

☐ **Confer with students and teach what's needed** (celebrate, assess, teach, revise, edit). *(Guided and independent practice.)*

☐ **Publish and share with intended audience.** *(Celebration and independent practice.)*

☐ **Encourage students to write more pieces in the genre.** *(Independent practice.)*

Write and Publish More Short Pieces

Length has nothing to do with quality, and it's quality we're after. We want kids to be focused, coherent writers who engage their readers with interesting, accurate writing. I love doing short pieces with students, because they take less time and are easy to publish. By the end of a week, we usually have a completed piece; we have learned and practiced everything important about writing, such as narrowing the topic, making it clear for the reader, writing an energetic lead, and so on; and no one is exhausted. I recommend that starting in second grade, at least one piece of writing be taken through to final copy each month.

Writing short pieces:

☐ Connects process with product more quickly.

☐ Makes some revision likely, without overwhelming the student.

☐ Ensures necessary practice in editing.

☐ Provides completed work for parents, students, administrators.

☐ Makes conferences more manageable.

☐ Is more enjoyable, for both students and teacher.

teaching tip
Move On
We stay too long with most writing. Make sure your students are doing a variety of writing, not just a project that goes on for weeks or months.

Short pieces can take many forms, such as brochures, booklets, posters, brief essays, vignettes, letters, poems, and cartoons. See pages 112–118 for numerous ideas for short pieces. The following lists some short writing projects, along with simple writing criteria.

Short Writing Projects with Simple Criteria

- Book of compliments (for school memory book, Valentine's Day, or birthdays):
    - Something positive about each classmate.
    - Something you admire about each classmate.
    - Why you admire that characteristic or behavior.

- Expert writing:
    - What you're an expert at and how you feel about it.
    - How you learned or how you became an expert.
    - What you do that shows you're an expert (proof).

- Letter or poem to favorite person:
    - Three positives about person.
    - How you feel about them.
    - Why person is important to you.

- Small moments:
    - Best memory (of special class, field trip, teacher).
    - Most memorable time (with family, friend, pet, classmate).

- Valentine letters, recalling a special moment (or heartfelt letters for any occasion):
    - What happened.
    - Where it took place (re-create the setting).
    - How you felt about it.

- Book reviews (with title, author, illustrator, and genre):
    - Brief overview with "grabber" lead.
    - Subject of book.
    - Memorable features to entice reader without giving away climax or conclusion.
    - Recommendation (who should read it, including appropriate age for readers). (See also page 132 for criteria for a book review.)

teaching tip

Try Another One

When a student has finished writing or doesn't like her piece, advise her, "Try writing another one." [poems—3 poems about self]

teaching tip

Show It Off

Display student work in classrooms and hallways in an attractive way that lets visitors and peers read it easily.

     ✐ Personal keepsakes (for classroom or school yearbook or special gift; can include photos):

        ✐ Best thing about me.

        ✐ What I love.

        ✐ What I want you to remember about me.

teaching tip

Let students know that we don't copy over drafts to make them neater (a waste of time). Students recopy and think it's a final copy.

Write Snapshots for Real Reasons

Fourth-grade teacher Tom Fuller had a beginning-of-the-year idea: He'd have his students write short pieces (*snapshots*) introducing themselves, which they could then post on the bulletin board. The final copies would be written on a cardboard cutout of a camera. I agreed that it was a terrific idea but knew we needed to get the kids excited about it in a way that would have meaning for them. Here's what I told them, speaking with lots of enthusiasm:

> *Kids, here's what Mr. Fuller and I were thinking. We could make a book of snapshots of each of us. When someone visits, we can share our book with them. It would have been so great to have one of you give me a copy of such a book. Then I would know something important about each of you. What do you think? Isn't that a great idea? We could make the whole book in the shape of a camera or come up with another idea.*

Then I drafted my own snapshot on large chart paper, thinking out loud (incidentally, it was also a great opportunity to model paragraphs, one paragraph per category).

My demonstration writing (before students write)

Based on what I had written, the kids and I come up with the following criteria for how their snapshots would be structured:

- ☐   Something you love.
- ☐   Things you especially like to do.
- ☐   The best thing about you.

Remember, I wrote first and set the criteria *after* we examined what I had written.

Then the kids set about writing their drafts, after I set up my expectation that they would work quickly: "I wrote this in four minutes. How long do you think it will take you?" Most kids responded *ten minutes,* and I said I thought that sounded about right.

Kids loved doing the project. The difference between compliance and engagement came about because we made the writing real and provided audience, purpose, and an interesting format; it wasn't just cookie-cutter writing for the bulletin board.

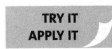

- ✐   Start the year off by writing snapshots ("little secrets," current favorite book, best friend, favorite hobby, what I'm expert at, three best things about me or a classmate, or some other easy-to-write-about topic). Set simple criteria to follow after you have written your own snapshot as a demonstration.
- ✐   Publish the snapshots along with photos of each writer. Share them with visitors, parents, administrators, and other students.

Write Lots of Letters

Call me old-fashioned but I much prefer receiving and writing handwritten letters over emails. "There is no substitute for letters, handwritten, pulsing with the vitality of the moment." I save few emails, but I have files of letters and cards I've received over the years. A handwritten letter has the special feel and sound of the person who wrote it. I enjoy writing letters on specially chosen writing paper or cards. It's a personal way of connecting in our fast-paced lives. Opportunities for letter writing are limitless. Kids can write to friends, parents, teachers, family, companies.

When I work with students, I always bring in the letters I have just written and am about to mail. I told one group of students recently, "Here are the five letters I wrote on the plane. That's one way I keep up with the people I love and appreciate."

Take a look at some fourth graders' valentine letters recalling special moments. (I first shared with students my thinking and drafting process of my own letter to my husband Frank.) The criteria for the valentine letter is included on page 198.

2-12-04

The Art Box

I remember when you first handed me that blue art box in the Art House's parking lot on my very first day of art. When you showed me what was in the box I was amazed. I was staring down at six paintbrushes, a paint spreader, and the five basic paint colors. Since the day you called me and told me you would sign me up for painting classes I had been anxious to start the classes. I was very excited, but a little bit nervous. I felt so special and loved when you hugged me and said good bye. I hope you have a fabulous Valentines' Day, Aunt Cindy!

Love,
Claire

2-14-04

Dear Dad,

Do you remember when we went to Long Island, New York to your college reunion together? Mom needed to stay home so you took me with your extra ticket. It made me feel special because we don't get to spend much time together. It wasn't like our usual vacations, because it was just you and me. I made some new friends, and you also rented a nice convertible for us to ride in.

Thank you, Dad, and have a Happy Valentine's Day!

Love,
Nicholas

My Dad and I at the Rocket's Game

I was spinning in my chair in my room crossing my fingers and hoping you would just open the door and ask me if I would like to go to the Rocket's Game with you. I was watching T.V. and overheard Mom and you talking about the Rocket's Game and trying to decide whether Lauren or I should go to the Rocket's Game with you. I raced back to my room praying and hoping you would pick me. Finally my prayers were answered. I remember when you knocked on my door and asked me,

"Ashton, would you like to go to the Rocket's Game with me?"

"YES!"

I screamed! At that moment I felt my heart rise up and burst. Happy Valentine's Day, Dad!

Love, Ashton

2-14-04

ABC Of The Rockies

Remember last Christmas when we were at your house, in the den, sitting on the chairs and couches listening to the fire crackle? Gran and Grampa you were sitting with Mommy, Daddy, Helen, and me. We were all surrounded by wrapping paper when you both got up and returned with two identical boxes. They were both wrapped in red paper, and when you handed them to Helen and me you said, "Open them at the same time." We found that inside were scrapbooks. At first I wondered why you had gotten us scrapbooks, but as I opened the book it brought back all the memories of the summer we had spent together. I felt that you had really cared about the two weeks we spent with you in the summer, and that you loved us so much that you would go to all that trouble to make a special scrapbook for us to relive all the exciting times we had together. Happy Valentine's Day Gran and Grampa and thank you.

Love,
Sydney

Letters recalling special moments are sent as valentines

Provide More Real Choice

In a third-grade classroom working on letter writing, the teacher had decided each student would write a letter to the President of the United States. In the past, these letters had gotten a response from the White House, which the students loved. However, in brainstorming possibilities with this group of students, they posed only superficial questions to ask the leader of our nation (*What is your favorite color?*). I suggested we find out who students really wanted to write to. Their responses included grandparents, cousins, friends they hadn't seen in a while. Brooke enthusiastically said, "This is a person I really want to write to. I'm already on my second page." When students are invested in the topic, they put forth their best effort.

Use Writing to Perform Acts of Kindness

Acts-of-kindness writing includes things like:

- ☐ "I appreciate you" cards and notes just to let someone (custodian, secretary, principal, parent, classmate, teacher) know she or he is appreciated. They can be sent on birthdays, Valentine's Day, any day.
- ☐ Birthday cards for classmates and teachers.
- ☐ Welcome notes to new students or school visitors.
- ☐ A special moment captured in a poem or sketch and given to the person who experienced the moment with you.
- ☐ Thank-you notes.

Such writing is not just good manners; *gratitude* has been found to be a key component of happiness and well-being.

In a second-grade class we wrote thank-you letters to someone we'd never "officially" thanked for a past kindness (see pages 203 and 204). I wrote to Jenifer Katahira, a teacher and friend who welcomed Frank and me to Seattle.

TRY IT APPLY IT

- ✐ Send a brief handwritten note to the parents/caregivers of each of your students during the first few weeks of school saying something complimentary about their child. Besides being a nice thing to do, it makes it more likely you will encounter an open mind if you need to call with a concern.
- ✎ Ask parents to donate writing paper, envelopes, and postcards to be used in the classroom.
- ✐ Ask parents to create a stationery box for their child at home.
- ✐ Set up a classroom "gratitude" message board.
- ✎ Create a classroom "good news" mailbox.

Jon's draft and final copy of his "Gratitude" letter (notice how hard he has worked on his handwriting)

Gratitude letter: Rebecca's draft and final copy

DRAFT <u>Editing</u>

<u>Spelling</u>

   Fix up <u>most</u> of them.

✱(Underline misspelled words

Reread(Read your paper at least 3 times)

  2. Try to spell the words correctly.

- Sound it out
- Look for chunks
- Look on word wall
- Look around your room.
- Use your quick word book

  Ask yourself if it makes sense

- Ask a friend

✱ • Try writing it another way

<u>Punctuation</u>

  Put ?, ! or . at end of

all Sentences

✱ Check if the words
are right <u>REREAD</u>. Check spelling

<u>Neatness</u>

handwriting.

   slow down

   look at draft

   ~~Skip lines~~

Check the format

   date

   Dear

   Love

Capitalization

Put a capital letter: at
the beginning of every sentence

- important names
- month
- Dear
- Love
- important places

• Check your ~~end~~words ∧

• check your endings
  (ing, ed)

Establishing editing expectations in grade 2 before students are expected to edit. (See also Appendix J.)

Do More Publishing

When students know their writing will be published for interested audiences, they put more effort into all aspects of their writing. Notice the multiple audiences for the school guidebook written by fifth graders (see page 105). Identifying that wide audience—and then distributing perfect, published copies to them—was instrumental in getting high-quality writing from every student and a published book with no spelling errors.

Publishing can be demanding for writers, especially those who struggle with writing's physical and cognitive demands. If they are available, parent volunteers and teacher aides can really help you out here (but make sure you model first what they are to do so they don't "take over" the child's writing). (Some helpful publishing resources are included in the Notes, on page A–38.)

Word processing is great because it makes revisions easier. While computers can make writing easier and more efficient—cutting and pasting, spelling and grammar checking—computers do not necessarily make writing better. We as knowledgeable teachers help students do that. Be sure students aren't putting more time and effort into elaborate technical presentations than into meaningful, interesting content.

Publish many short pieces for your classroom library. Make copies for other classrooms and the school library. (The accompanying DVD and five-day lesson plans include examples of such publications.)

teaching tip

For neater handwritten final copies, have students put lined paper under the piece of stationery and clip them together. The lines will show through and make it easier for students to write on the page.

9. Conference with Students

When I confer with you about your writing, you are more important than the writing.
—Don Graves

How do I fit in all those conferences? is high on the list of dilemmas associated with teaching writing. Teachers are often overwhelmed at the prospect of having conferences with twenty or thirty students, and that's just in elementary school; the number is far greater in middle and high school. Added to the huge time commitment are two other major challenges: *How do I conduct a conference anyway, and what are all the other kids doing while I'm conferencing?**

While there is no formula to ensure effective and efficient conferences, my aim is to clarify:

☐ What a conference is.

☐ When and how to have one.

☐ What a conference looks and sounds like.

☐ How to make the process useful, manageable, and enjoyable.

---

* As a point of clarification, I have chosen to use conference *as a verb. While* confer *may be grammatically correct, most writing teachers "conference" with students about their writing.*

Know What a Writing Conference Is

A writing conference is a meeting to discuss student work. Conferences can have a number of different purposes—to celebrate, validate, encourage, nudge, teach, assess, set goals—and they can take different forms. A conference can be informal or formal, short or long, public or private, teacher or student led; whole group, small group, or one-on-one. An informal conference may focus on just one of the purposes above, while a formal, one-on-one conference might focus on all of them. Effective teachers use a variety of conferences to meet students' needs.

The structure of a writing conference includes conversations about the writing work the child is doing and how the child can become a better writer. Conferences may also include teacher demonstration and guided practice. Keep the emphasis on one or two main areas per conference. Always begin with something you notice that the child has done well. Eight examples of conferences are included on the accompanying DVD; teaching points related to these video clips are included in Part 5, Teaching in Action (pages 336–350).

If you think of a conference as any time you respond, provide support, ask questions to gain understanding, and/or give feedback, you will begin to feel less pressure about having a correct set of procedures or structures in place. Third-grade teacher Millie Rable notes:

> When I realized that conferencing didn't have to be sitting down each week with every student and spending fifteen or twenty minutes talking about *my* agenda, the pressure was gone. I learned that a lot can be taught with informal conferences and they take much less time.

PURPOSES OF A WRITING CONFERENCE

Before, during, or after writing, respond to the writer by:

☐ Listening (to what writer is trying to say).

☐ Affirming (what writer has done well).

☐ Reinforcing (the writer's strengths, attempts).

☐ Assessing (confusions, strengths, next steps).

☐ Teaching (what's most important for the writer to move forward and only what the writer is ready for).

☐ Scaffolding (helping the writer say, write, and do what she can't quite do yet without help).

☐ Setting goals with students' input (for the writer to attempt to meet on his own, with minimal guidance and support).

KINDS OF WRITING CONFERENCES

☐ Whole-class shares.

☐ Quickshares.

☐ Roving, on-the-run conferences (while walking about the class-room as kids write).

☐ One-on-one formal conferences.

☐ Peer conferences.

Depend on Whole-Class Share

Whole-class share is a formal conference, conducted publicly. In other words, I do exactly what I would do in a one-on-one conference; the only difference is that all the other students are looking on, listening, and sometimes (once they have learned how to do so productively) giving feedback. Having all students "listen in" pays huge dividends, because everyone is being shown effective conference strategies and procedures. Demonstrations like this are prerequisites if students are to be able to respond helpfully to their peers and monitor and improve their own writing.

During a whole-class share, all the students gather in the reading/writing corner or class meeting area, and several students share their writing. I let the students know that our first purpose is to celebrate what the writer has done well and our second purpose is to support the writer in moving forward. I make sure students can articulate why we have whole-class share. When students know and value the purposes, they are more likely to apply the process to their own writing.

I never skip whole-class share in kindergarten and grade one. Students just learning to write need and benefit from having their efforts celebrated. They love sharing their story, journal entry, or poem. Marlene Tucker's kindergartners in Vancouver, Washington, had been writing and/or drawing about a new topic each day, so I demonstrated how to sustain a story over several days. Our sharing involved celebrating each writer's efforts and helping the writer decide what to say next, mostly by engaging him in conversation (there is a transcript of two such short conversations on pages 208–210). This is more than celebration; all students are learning what makes a good story. These conferences do not have to be long to be beneficial: in fifteen minutes, we were able to have twelve conferences.

Kindergarten teacher Marlene Tucker conducts brief conferences before and after writing each day. Here are transcripts (including Marlene's notes) from two of these conferences, one with Mikaela and one with Tristan. (The journal entries that prompted the conferences are shown after each one.)

teaching tip

In kindergarten and first grade, try small-group share. Get parents or volunteers to help you; that way every child can share and receive feedback in a short time.

Mikaela's Journal Entry

On the day we begin writing continuing journal stories, Mikaela reads me what she has written so far (on March 11). She is writing about her baby brother.

Mikaela: "My brother sat in his high chair and ate carrots."

Marlene: I like how you started your story. Tell us more about your brother. He must be a baby because he sits in a highchair.

Mikaela (*laughing*): It's so funny, because my baby brother cries at night, so my daddy buys him lots of food!

Marlene: Oh, tell us more. What happens when he eats lots of food?

Mikaela: It helps him sleep! (*Mikaela finds this funny, as do many of her classmates.*)

Marlene: Now this sounds like it will be a funny story! (*Looking over Mikaela's writing.*) I can see that you crossed off a word. Tell me about this? (*I bring this up to benefit the whole class as they listen to our miniconference. I now see less erasing and scribbling, as a result of dialogue like this. My kids know that crossing out a word is what good writers do when something doesn't make sense, and that I expect their work to be neat, an easy expectation that has paid off.*)

Mikaela: I crossed this off because I remembered that *sat* is *s-a-t*. (*She has crossed off the letters* st.)

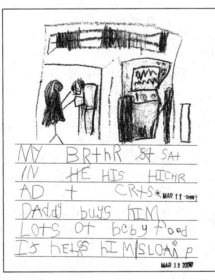

March, 2004

My brother sat in his high chair and ate carrots. Daddy buys him lots of baby food. It helps him sleep.

Mikaela

Marlene: You also know that good writers cross out what they don't need and keep going. Let's read this sentence again. (*As Mikaela reads she notices an extra word that doesn't make sense. She decides to cross out the word* he.)

Mikaela: Oh, I don't need this word. I should cross it out.

Mikaela heads off to finish her story. (She completes it on March 12.) Notice the carets she has added in her last line, evidence of rereading.

Tristan's Journal Entry

It is day 2 of writing continuing stories. During our conference Tristan reads what he had written the day before (on June 7).

Tristan: "I had fun at my birthday."

Marlene: Tell us about having fun at your birthday. What was fun about it?

Tristan: Well, my birthday was at my grandma's, and Payne was there!

Marlene: Payne? From our class? Wow! Tell us what happened. (*Tristan decides to write about Payne being at his party.*) Tristan, I also notice how well you are doing at sounding out words. You spelled *fun* and *my* correctly.

Tristan: I found *birthday* on the writing folder.

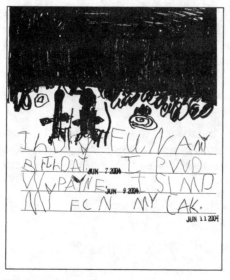

June, 2004

*I had fun at my birthday.
I played with Payne. I slammed
my face in my cake.*

Tristan

Marlene: This is wonderful! I would say the next step for you, Tristan, is to leave spaces between your words. That will make your writing easier to read. Can you try that? (Tristan says, "Okay.")

On day 3, I have another miniconference with Tristan in whole-class share. He reads his journal entries (June 7 and June 9), and we celebrate his story. I ask Tristan if he wants to add to his story today. He decides to write more and says, "I slammed my face in my cake." The class roars with laughter as Tristan tells us about his messy face. We also celebrate the spaces he has left between his words.

Notice that these conferences have focused on content first, emphasizing that writing is about meaningful communication.

BENEFITS OF WHOLE-CLASS SHARE

☐ Is an efficient and productive way to conduct a conference.

☐ Focuses on celebrating what the writer has done well.

☐ Provides teaching points and ideas to *all* writers, not just the conferee.

☐ Models the importance of rereading.

☐ Shows all students the power of language by pointing out what the writer has done—use of ideas, language, form, spelling, spacing, handwriting.

☐ Models the language of response before expecting students to try it out themselves.

☐ Gives reluctant writers confidence to write.

☐ Helps make conferences manageable (they don't all have to be one-on-one).

☐ Enables the teacher to see patterns of writing behavior and to plan lessons based on those patterns (for example, noticing that many students have difficulty with organization, leads, and so forth).

☐ Eliminates behavior problems; the whole class is right there with you.

☐ Elevates the status of writers, especially those on the fringes.

☐ Students love it!

Use Whole-Class Share as a Venue in Which to Teach

One of the greatest advantages of whole-class share is the amount of teaching that occurs in a short period (see the video teaching points related to two whole-class shares, on pages 336–350). It is through whole-class share, writing aloud, and shared writing that I do the bulk of my teaching. Minilessons can be integrated effortlessly in these public forums, and all students, not just the one in the author's chair, listen and learn.

Here's how whole-class share works:

☐ A student reads her piece aloud while the class listens for the overall sense of the piece, the whole of what the writer is trying to say. (Sometimes, to save time, with student permission, I read the piece.)

☐ The student reads the piece aloud again (see photo, page 105) as the class listens for specific language, things the writer has done well (which are always mentioned first), and things that are confusing. Sometimes I reread it and show the pages face front so I can make specific teaching and celebration points.

teaching tip

Show It

On the second reading, have the student's writing facing outwards so the class can see it (spacing, layout, spelling, words, and so on).

Whole-class share (I am looking on as he reads; usually I just listen)

☐ I and the other students celebrate what the writer has done well. For example:

- *Look how Nathan has grabbed our attention right away. Wow! I'm going to read his first line again. Let's look at what he's done.*
- *Right here, he lets the reader know what his piece is all about. That's what good writers do.*
- *And here, listen to these words. He doesn't just say [blank], which is an ordinary way to say it. These great words put us right there in the moment with him. I can picture it in my mind.*

☐ I make one or two teaching points that will help move the writer forward.

- *Let me show you how you can make this easier for the reader to follow. Is it okay if I cut this apart? Okay, I'm going to cut this part here and move it here. [A good reason to ask students to write only on one side of the paper.] Now, listen to how it sounds.*
- *I'm going to reread this part again. See if you hear a line that we could cut because you already said it somewhere else. Yes, you did say that already. Why don't you just draw one line through it. Kids, when you reread your writing today, if you have parts that are boring or repeated, you can just cross them out the way Nathan did.*

I often use students as teachers, too. When I see a student successfully doing what I've taught, I say:

- *Meredith, could you show Sam how to cut and paste?*
- *Scott was absent yesterday. Paul, would you show him what we learned about writing conversation?*

☐ I keep track of students who share. (This can be as simple as keeping a copy of your class list—with the month and days of the week—near the author's chair.)

Teach Students How to Listen

To really listen well requires full, active attention. I explain to kids what I do as I listen for the whole idea of the piece:

Kids, being able to respond helpfully to the writer means I have to listen really hard to what the writer is trying to say. I have to block out everything else and concentrate. On the first reading, I'm going to listen for the whole idea of the piece. During the second reading, I might make some notes as I listen for what the writer has done well, exact words she uses that entice the reader, and also, perhaps, some places where I might suggest a few things to help the writer.

teaching tip

Listen Up!

Don't restate children's oral responses; this compels students to listen to each other, saves time, and is respectful of students' voices.

You can meet all your state and district standards for listening through teaching writing. Teach and remind kids that active listening is hard work. They will listen if they understand and value its importance, that is, that good listeners:

☐ Respond helpfully.

☐ Learn new strategies.

☐ Get ideas from others.

☐ Connect new thoughts with their own to come to new conclusions.

Manage Whole-Class Share Effectively

teaching tip

Watch Your Time

If the conference goes on too long, you risk losing your students' attention. (I average under five minutes per conference in whole-class share.) For the student who needs more time and help, follow up with a one-on-one conference.

Whole-class share usually takes place at the end of writing workshop, but it can occasionally can take place at the beginning as a mini- or maxilesson to ensure that all students succeed in that day's writing. For example, when I have introduced a new genre or assignment and students have written a partial or complete draft, I may take the papers home and go through them so I can make specific suggestions for students before they continue writing/revising (see the discussion of Derek's "secrets" story, on pages 343–345 and on the accompanying DVD, for one example). At the same time, I am also modeling rereading from the previous day's writing and inspiring ideas for today's writing.

Some teachers find it advantageous to conference with a small group that has a similar need. My preference is almost always to include all students; the classroom is easier to manage, and more ideas are generated. More important, to raise the status of a student in the classroom, all students need to participate in the celebration and affirmation of the writer.

**TRY IT
APPLY IT**

✎ Write suggestions for students (we write faster than they do).

✎ Limit compliments (allow a few; avoid false praise; move on to suggestions).

✎ Teach and demonstrate on the spot (cut and paste, teach quotation marks, etc.; other students who are ready will also pick up the technique).

✎ Help students with where to go next (for example, say, "*So what are you going to write about next?*"; this saves time for the students at beginning of the next writing period).

✎ Most students love to share. Some days, so that all students can be heard, have everyone share with a partner.

Orchestrate Who Shares

I am always on the lookout for someone who has tried something that I demonstrated in the minilesson: reread carefully before writing, made revisions, used language in an original way, whatever it might be. Just before students start to write I say something like, *During my roving conferences today, I'll be on the lookout for kids who are trying conversation in their writing [rereading before writing again, trying a new lead to attract the reader's attention]. I'm going to invite those students to share today.* I jot those names on a pad of sticky notes I always carry with me. Several minutes before whole-class share, I approach these students and ask if they will share their accomplishment with the rest of the class. By recognizing students who have tried something I've been teaching and reinforcing, I am affirming their effort in taking a risk and trying what I've asked them to do and also encouraging others to incorporate "what good writers do."

Other students who share might include an eager volunteer proud of what he wrote, a student with whom I have a public conversation, a student who has requested a conference, or a student who shared the previous day and has followed through with the suggestions she was offered.

Sharing is always optional. When a student is reluctant, I ask whether I may read the piece aloud, and often he agrees. I still ask him to sit right next to me in the author's chair. Most students who refuse to share or sit in the author's chair lack confidence as writers. Once that confidence is instilled, refusing to share is a rare occurrence. (See the story of Max on pages 339–340.)

Prepare to Share

To ensure that no precious minutes are lost as students stumble over their words, several minutes before the end of writing workshop I say: *You have just a few minutes left. Finish up the sentence (or part) you're working on, and reread your writing. Make sure you can read it easily.* Students come to know that if they want to share their writing, they are expected to rehearse their piece by quietly reading it aloud to themselves or to a peer. Expecting students to reread also gets students in the habit of proofreading and rethinking as they write, not just after the writing is finished. Reading the writing out loud aids revision (see pages 124 and 159).

Orchestrate What Is Shared

Just as we cannot check every page a child reads, it is not necessary to "hear" every word the child has written. You don't want conferences to go on forever. Students need to have time and energy to write. Eventually, too, you want students to get good at conferencing with their peers and themselves. One of the advantages of having students write short pieces is you can listen to and talk about the entire piece. When a student has written a long piece, have her choose a short section, such as a favorite part or part she wants help with (up to two pages or whatever you decide).

At any conference, we discuss:

- ☐ What the writer did well (strengths, successes).
- ☐ What the piece is about.
- ☐ Writing for the reader.
- ☐ Memorable language.
- ☐ Organization—sequence, sense, confusions.
- ☐ Teaching points.

Who's in charge at a conference—wholly or partially—depends on how much students know about conducting a conference and improving their own writing. As with everything I teach, I rely on the optimal learning model (see inside front cover and page 221). I do not expect students to know the language and behavior of how to respond to their peers and themselves until they have seen and heard many demonstrations and had lots of practice with guided support.

TIPS FOR SUCCESSFUL WHOLE-CLASS SHARES AND CONFERENCES

- ☐ **Always focus first on what the writer has done well.** (Beginning with celebration affirms the writer and makes it more likely that she will be open to suggestions.)

- ☐ **For the first reading, try not to look at the child's paper.** (Listening without seeing the spelling errors, lack of punctuation, and messy handwriting ensures that we focus on the message.)

- ☐ **Put your pen or pencil aside.** (Sit on your hands, if necessary. Avoid the urge to write on the child's paper.)

- ☐ **Know where the child is in the learning model; that is, consider how much support the child will require.** (Will the child be able to say what he has done well, what questions he has, what response is needed, or will you need to model that?)

- ☐ **Watch your language of response.** (Whatever you say to the child, be sure it encourages her to continue writing. See pages 230–231 for examples of supportive language.)

Use a Variety of Other Conferences

While I rely on daily whole-class share, I also use other conference structures to celebrate, reinforce, and teach. There is no one best way or best type of conference. You, an informed professional teacher, need to decide what will work for you and your students. Be flexible, and above all remember you want your students to go on writing. The conference is secondary; the student as writer and confident learner is primary.

Try a Quickshare

A quickshare is a miniconference that takes a minute or less and celebrates a memorable line, an engaging lead or paragraph, rereading before continuing to write, taking a risk, or attempting something new (conversation, humor, writing a second lead). I often use quickshares when I'm pressed for time but don't want to omit celebration. In three minutes, we hear from four or five students. Often, I come up behind the student I want to celebrate and ask him to publicly:

- ☐ Read a specific part.
- ☐ Tell what he tried today.
- ☐ Read his "best" line.

Or, to save time, I pick up the piece (with the student's permission) and read aloud the memorable part or state something I noticed she did as a writer. I say something like:

- ☐ *I noticed you rereading before you went on.*
- ☐ *Wait until you hear Samantha's ending lines. Don't you love the way she [blank]. You can try that in your own writing.*
- ☐ *I saw you using your finger to space your words. Good for you. That makes it easier for the reader to read your message.*
- ☐ *Listen to this first line. I know exactly what Jared's story will be about, and I can't wait to hear more.*
- ☐ *Lara used conversation today for the first time. Listen to how these two lines move her story along. Good for you, Lara.*
- ☐ *I saw that Kevin got right to work today. Kevin, that's the most writing I've seen you do.*

Focusing on what a student has done well makes it more likely that he—and other students—will repeat or attempt the desired behavior. Students can also quickshare with each other. Peer sharing of journal entries, poems, stories, and more is a great way to validate a student's writing on a particular day.

teaching tip

Focus only on content at first. Ignore editing concerns (makes it more likely that student will work on organization and quality).

teaching tip

Decide what are the one or two most important things you can say or demonstrate that might help the writer most (keeps the conference manageable by not overwhelming student or you).

Conduct Roving Conferences

A roving conference is a conference on the run, usually very quick (a minute or two); occasionally, it may take five minutes or so. In fifteen minutes, I can circulate through the classroom and assess strengths and needs, congratulate, support, and teach. While roaming, I:

☐ Note who needs help getting started.
☐ Affirm students' efforts.
☐ Encourage students to continue writing, reread, check spelling.
☐ Teach on the spot.
☐ Assess.
☐ Offer specific guidance.
☐ Take brief notes. (One teacher's anecdotal notes from roving conferences are shown below; notice the emphasis on content.)

One teacher's anecdotal notes from roving conferences

teaching tip

Use roving conferences to teach students what they need so they can quickly move forward.

Often, I stoop down and get eye-to-eye, noting what a student is attempting to do and offering specific guidance. I have roving conferences several days a week, in conjunction with one-on-one conferences.

First-grade teacher Lea Payton uses pages in the back of each student's journal to coassess their writing and set goals together. Having children give input makes it more likely they will take responsibility for recognizing their strengths and improving their writing. (See example on page 219. For a similar blank form, see Appendix H. And see this book's website for additional forms.)

Schedule One-on-One Conferences

A one-on-one conference is exactly the same as a whole-class share, only now you are sitting right next to the child, giving her your full attention, without the class deliberately listening in. All the praising and teaching is now done privately, and it's a good idea to take anecdotal notes for future reference.

Know When Students are Ready for a Formal One-on-One Conference

It is not unusual to see kids lined up ten deep at the teacher's desk waiting for a conference or to have half a dozen or more names on the sign-up sheet. But are these students ready for a conference? You can save yourself and your students time and energy if you have realistic guidelines about conference readiness. I say something like this:

> *My editor works with twenty or more other authors, just like your teacher works with all of you. Out of respect for her busy schedule, I don't send her a batch of my writing until I think it's in pretty good shape. That means I've worked hard on it and done all the things good writers do. I don't just dash off something and expect her to give me feedback.*

It's our responsibility to know where kids are in their writing, celebrate their work-in-process, and help them move forward, but much of that work can happen through quick, informal conferences. Informal conferences are great throughout the writing process; more formal conferencing can take place when a student is stuck, needs help with organization (see the AlexSandra video clip on the DVD, and pages 345–346), and is ready to publish.

I Can . . .	I'm working on.	Date
– write about my life	– choosing topics like	3/9/04
– use interesting words	the spider + tooth	
– make a picture in the readers head	that I know a lot about	
– Write neatly	– tell stories I really care about	
– Spell many words	– try periods	
– write like I talk		
– make things funny		
	Marco	

Noting strengths and setting writing goals with a first grader (in a roving conference)

Think about doing a shared writing with your students and establishing guidelines such as the following:

I am ready for a one-on-one teacher conference when I have:

☐ Done everything I can do on my own [or perhaps with peer response] to make the writing as good as I can get it in a first draft.

☐ Reread (out loud to myself) for clarity and organization as well as practiced reading it aloud before reading it at the conference.

☐ Followed directions and completed requirements (agreed-on criteria).

Teach Peer Conferencing

In a peer conference, students take on the advisory role we have been demonstrating through whole-class share and one-on-one conferences. That is, they listen to a student's piece and give feedback, and, as we have modeled and they have practiced, their first comments are affirming.

teaching tip

Be Specific

When a student responds to another's writing with, "I liked your beginning [or the way you used detail, etc.], redirect the student to give specific feedback: "What were the actual words the author used?" General statements are not helpful to the writer.

In keeping with the optimal learning model's gradual release of responsibility (see inside front cover and page 221), before students conduct peer conferences they should:

- [ ] Observe many conferences conducted by their teacher during whole-class share (*demonstration*).
- [ ] Learn how to ask thoughtful questions that help the writer (*shared demonstration and guided practice*).
- [ ] Be invited to give feedback with teacher guidance during whole-class share (*shared demonstration*).
- [ ] Observe one or more peer conferences with the whole class looking on and the teacher giving feedback (*guided practice*).
- [ ] Try out peer conferences with the teacher nearby to give feedback (*guided practice*).
- [ ] Participate in peer conferences while the teacher is conducting one-one-one conferences (*independent practice*).

Students can give useful and specific feedback noting what the writer has done well; what language is memorable; and what parts are interesting, confusing, or boring. Such peer interaction, especially when it is spontaneous, informal, and not heavily teacher directed is likely to help writers progress.

However, I believe feedback about organization, style, craft, and structure falls primarily to us. Understandably, most students do not have the sophisticated knowledge to give the kind of feedback that we can give. On the other hand, research supports (and my experience confirms) that students can be used as peer editors to improve the mechanics and overall fluency of student writing (see page 223).

Simplify Writing Conferences

Writing conferences do not need to be long, hard, and tedious. In fact, conducting a conference is enjoyable and efficient once we and our students are clear about our writing purposes, engaged in the process, and know what is expected. By simplifying, I am referring to the structure of the conference—what happens when we meet with students—not our writing expectations for students, which remain high and rigorous.

Spend Time Frontloading

A critical piece that makes conferences more manageable and pleasurable is to do a great job of frontloading. By frontloading, I mean demonstrating—writing and thinking aloud, doing shared writing, modeling, conversing, setting realistic and clearly understood goals and expectations—in other words, doing whatever you need to do *before* students write to ensure they understand the task and expectations and are prepared to succeed. Frontloading provides the models, scaffolding, ideas, and practice so that students can write with competence and confidence.

For example, in a class of twenty-seven fifth graders learning to write informational essays, I received twenty-seven high-quality drafts, including those of the four special education students (the details of this lesson are discussed on pages 105–111). Each content conference took about five minutes, and most of that time was spent celebrating students' efforts. Classroom teacher Sue Mikulecky comments:

> Frontloading definitely assured success for all my students—including my special education students. The modeling, shared writing, thinking aloud, and clear expectations provided all the knowledge and confidence needed to succeed.

It took me many years to figure out that if I did a great job teaching and scaffolding—demonstrating, explaining, giving kids time to talk, practicing, trying things out—*before* they wrote, the quality of the writing was automatically higher, which then made my conferences easier and faster. That means that occasionally the "minilesson" may be a "maxilesson"—that is, the demonstration period may be as long as 30 minutes—but it's time well spent as the payoff is huge: quality writing, right from the start, along with efficient conferences.

Rely on the Optimal Learning Model

I used to ask students what kind of feedback they wanted in a conference, but often they didn't know. Like everything else we teach, we need to begin with explicit demonstration, then move on to shared demonstrations and guided learning experiences, before expecting students to know what they want from a conference.

In the writing classroom, before I expect students to know how to respond helpfully to one another in whole-class share and peer conferences, they will not

Who Holds Book/Pen		Degree of Explicitness/Support
Teacher /Student	▼	**DEMONSTRATION**
Teacher /Student	▼	**SHARED DEMONSTRATION**
gradual handover of responsibility		
Student /Teacher	▼	**GUIDED PRACTICE**
Student /Teacher	▼	**INDEPENDENT PRACTICE**

The Optimal Learning Model

only have seen my modeling but also have had lots of shared and guided practice over many months. Having students become "competent users" *before* they engage in a process saves lots of time and energy. Less reteaching is required. And knowledgeable students then help one another make the writing stronger rather than give comments that may not be useful.

Gradually, students take a much more prominent role via peer conferences, but initially we are in charge. This book's website and page 236 contain a number of useful teacher- and student-directed guidelines/forms to help facilitate this "handover."

Establish Routines and Procedures

teaching tip

*Listen for the
Silence*

One sure way to tell if your kids are engaged in writing is to listen. The room becomes mostly silent. Students may be talking with one another, but it's a productive hum, not a noisy free-for-all. You can "feel" the engagement and concentration.

For conferences to go well, I need to be organized and efficient, and all my students need to know exactly what's expected of them. In order to validate and help each student move forward, I need to be able to listen hard, assess what's most important to praise and teach, and make on-the-spot decisions. If the room is too noisy, or if I am interrupted by students who don't know what to do or are behaving badly, the conference is compromised. I tell students something like this:

> When I am having a conference, I cannot be interrupted. Out of respect for the writer I am talking with, my full attention needs to be on our conference. I expect you to manage your own behavior exactly as we talked about, modeled, and practiced. You will need to do all the things we have agreed on together that good writers do. When it is your turn to have a conference, you will want the same respect shown to you. Having a conference is an important and enjoyable time for celebration and teaching.

Expecting students to manage their own behavior so we can focus on conferences has to be modeled, practiced, and assessed—often repeatedly.

Do a Shared Writing

Chart exactly what students are expected to do while you are engaged in conferences with other students. Include things like:

- ☐ Expectations for the writing they are doing.
- ☐ What to do if they finish a piece of writing.
- ☐ What to do if they have questions.
- ☐ Pencil-sharpening rules.
- ☐ What kind of movement around classroom is and is not permissible.
- ☐ Acceptable noise level.
- ☐ When and where to have a peer conference.

WHAT MAKES A PRODUCTIVE CONFERENCE?

- ☐ Have visible in front of you:
  - Established criteria for the piece of writing.
  - Essentials to look and listen for:
    - ○ Organization.
    - ○ Voice (one's personal style).
    - ○ Enticing beginning.
    - ○ Satisfying closing.
    - ○ Evidence of rereading. (See also "12 Writing Essentials," pages 13–14.)
  - Language of response (see pages 227–229).
  - Conference forms.
  - Writing tools (sticky notes, pencils, flipchart or whiteboard, scissors, tape, and extra paper for cutting and pasting).
- ☐ Sit side by side.
- ☐ Have author (usually) read the piece twice.
- ☐ Listen for and focus on the writer's strengths and message.
- ☐ Focus on the overall meaning first of what the writer is trying to do (content).
- ☐ Use the language of helpful response.
- ☐ Narrow the teaching focus to one or two major points.
- ☐ Explain why editing is critical (so that the reader can understand easily).
- ☐ Don't write directly on the writer's paper. (Use sticky notes.)
- ☐ Have the writer say back what he did, said, and will do.

Put the Writer First

Focusing on the writer above everything else is like being a good counselor, one who is empathetic, nurturing, validating, gently nudging. Remember that the writer is exposed: *What does this writing say about me?* With reading, the words are already there; writing is scarier because it's just the writer and the blank page (or screen).

If we want our students to continue to write and to take risks, the conference must be an easy, confidence-building process. We have to ensure that the child leaves the conference "intact"—that is, eager to continue writing. If a child leaves the conference deflated and discouraged, we have failed.

When I coach teachers, even though they have observed me conduct several conferences, their first words when they try one on their own are often *I was confused* or *You need to do this* or *I suggest*. We are so accustomed to the "correction" mind-set that our language doesn't even register.

Always start with a compliment for something the writer has done well. We have the power to encourage the writer for the whole year or destroy his desire and energy to write with one negative comment. Even adult writers need to hear praise first:

> . . . compliments showed me what I could do and gave me confidence, criticism confirmed my fears and left me frustrated. When I confidently approached a piece to revise it, I was playful. When I went back to one in frustration, I usually made it worse.

Assume the Child Is Making Sense

Listen to what the child is saying. Try to figure out what the writer is trying to convey before you respond with suggestions. (Sometimes it helps just to listen while the child reads, without looking at the words.) Then frame your response based on the meaning the child is attempting to make, being sure to choose your words carefully (see pages 227–228). Also make sure the student understands what you're saying; this is especially important for English language learners.

Teacher Talk

☐ *Tell me what this is about.*

☐ *I know you have a story to tell.*

☐ *Tell me what happened next.*

☐ *Tell me again so I'm sure I understand what you're saying.*

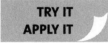
TRY IT APPLY IT

✐ Make a deliberate attempt to monitor the words you use. Adopt an accepting mind-set before you begin the conference.

✎ Accept "good enough" for first attempts.

✎ Have a colleague observe you, listening specifically for supportive language.

✐ Have students say back to you the positive comments you've made.

✎ Observe the writer after the conference. Is she confidently writing or is she discouraged? Reevaluate the messages you may have sent the writer.

Give an Overall Response First

Starting with the whole sends the message that writing is about communicating to a reader. The writer wants to know how the reader reacts, how the reader is moved by the piece. Here's an example of what I'm talking about.

In a weeklong residency in a fourth-grade classroom, each student was writing about a memorable moment with a special person, the finished piece to be given to that person as a Valentine's Day gift. (Some examples of their published pieces are on page 201.) During whole-class share, I encouraged observing teachers to practice the language of response. The first comments teachers made were along the lines of, *I really like the way you used that word.* Coaching the teachers, I said:

> *Bill [their principal] has written a valentine moment to his wife. Her first comment wouldn't be, "I really like how you used the word* beautiful *instead of* good." *She's going to comment on how touched she is, how the valentine made her feel.*

They all laughed, now seeing the comment as obviously silly. Sometimes we forget common sense when we are focused on correct procedures instead of on supporting what the writer is trying to say and do.

And again: when we comment first on mechanics (spelling, handwriting, grammar), we may give the message that students' ideas are secondary to correctness.

Be Generous with Your Praise

Note everything the writer has done well, starting with content: opening, organization, specific language used. It is not enough to say *I like your opening.* Repeat the memorable language, the actual words the child has used. Remember you are not just responding to this particular student; you are modeling the language and behavior of response for all your students. Some students will be thinking: *She thinks that's good. I can do that, too.* Praising high-quality language encourages students to use such language—or humor, or special punctuation—again.

Later on, after many more demonstrations and lots of practice, students will gradually be able to internalize your language and behavior in whole-class share and in peer conferences.

Make Important Teaching Points

Initially, ignore editing concerns (but do deal with editing marks or indications that help make the paper readable). Keep your comments to the essentials you've been stressing—an opening that brings the reader in, a closing that summarizes and ties the paper together, organizing the body of the piece.

It is easy to get distracted and try to focus on everything. *Focus first on quality content, and work on editing later.* Correct mechanics and form don't matter much if the writing is so dull that no one wants to read it.

Begin with Content Conferences

My experience has been that it takes some convincing to get teachers to focus first on content and initially ignore editing concerns. Editing is concrete. Errors in mechanics and format are more easily noticeable (and more easily fixed), so we naturally go there first. Dealing with the quality of the content requires more time and skill on our part, so we shy away from it. Because most of us have had so little professional development on how to teach writing well, many of us lack the skills and confidence to help writers hone and clarify their messages. So we go straight to the editing.

On a practical level, it's difficult to work on both content and editing at the same time. In fact, writers often experience writer's block and lose their concentration when editing concerns become a focus too early in the writing process. The exception would be kindergartners or students just learning to write. In order to focus on content, they first have to know how to form, sound out, and space at least six or more letters in order to begin to write a message.

QUESTIONS TO KEEP IN MIND DURING A CONTENT CONFERENCE

☐ What has the writer done well?

☐ What is the writer trying to say?

☐ How can I help the writer say it more clearly, succinctly, and originally?

☐ What language do I use to encourage and support the writer?

☐ What language do I use to nudge the writer to continue working on improving the quality of the writing?

☐ What options can I provide so the student is successful?

☐ What are the one or two most important things I can say and do to help this student?

Use the Language of Helpful Response

When you start by celebrating the *whole* writing piece and noting what the writer has done well, other students will want to try what that writer has done. (Make sure your praise is not overfocused on particular aspects of the craft of writing.) Use the exact words of the writer whenever possible.

Start with What the Writing *Does*
☐ *I love the way your first sentence. . . .*
☐ *Your story reminded me of. . . .*
☐ *I could picture exactly how. . . .*
☐ *When you said [blank], I felt. . . .*
☐ *Your dad is going to treasure this piece because. . . .*
☐ *I noticed that. . . .*
☐ *I really like the way you used conversation to let the reader know exactly how you felt. It seemed as if I were right there in the room with you.*

Then Move to What the Writing *Has*
☐ *You tried out conversation.*
☐ *You skipped lines so you could add in easily.*
☐ *You spaced your words, which makes it easy for the reader to read your message.*
☐ *I like the way you used the word [blank] instead of [blank].*

Encourage Your Youngest Writers and Your Developing Writers
☐ *I like how you were stretching out your sounds as you wrote.*
☐ *I saw you looking at the word wall to figure out a word. Good for you.*
☐ *You're spacing better between words. That makes it easier for the reader.*
☐ *You drew your picture first, and that got you going on your story.*
☐ *I noticed you were using your reading finger to be sure your voice and your words matched.*
☐ *I love the way your picture has lots of information in it.*
☐ *You're continuing your story from yesterday. That's great.*
☐ *Say your words slowly as you write them. That will help you hear more sounds.*

Use Language that Encourages and Clarifies
☐ *I really like how you. . . .*
☐ *So you're saying. . . .*
☐ *Perhaps you could try. . . .*
☐ *Can you say more about. . . ?*
☐ *How about if you. . . ?*
☐ *You might want to. . . .*
☐ *Think about. . . .*
☐ *Let's try this together. . . .*

However, sometimes, you will need to be more directive, and that's okay. It's our job to inform students of what's necessary to make the writing work and then to help them do it. We need to help students find the writing focus and teach whatever strategies they need to move the writing forward. That's part of our job as teachers of writing. But before making direct suggestions, we need to have first established trust with the writer by celebrating and building on his strengths.

Teacher Talk

- ☐ *I'm confused here. I'm not sure what you're trying to say. I think you need to. . . .*
- ☐ *Let me show you how to. . . .*
- ☐ *Try another lead that. . . .*
- ☐ *You've got too many "tired" words. Reread and see if you can't replace some of those with more lively language. Let's try one together.*
- ☐ *Your piece ends abruptly. Let's talk about an ending that could work.*
- ☐ *Reread your piece before you start writing again.*
- ☐ *Why don't you try. . . ?*
- ☐ *Show me where you say. . . .*
- ☐ *Explain. . . .*
- ☐ *Check the criteria we've established. Make sure you've done everything that's required.*
- ☐ *One thing writers do when they want to [blank] is. . . . Here's what I mean.*

WHAT TO FOCUS ON IN A CONTENT CONFERENCE

- ☐ Clarity and interest of topic for the reader.
- ☐ Organization and structure:
  - Clarifying ideas and thinking. (Does it make sense?)
  - Narrowing the topic.
  - Telling a story in sequence.
  - Deleting unnecessary and boring information.
  - Adding pertinent words and information (providing enough description).
  - Putting like information together (cutting and pasting).
  - Adding necessary transitions.
- ☐ Leads.
- ☐ Endings.

☐ Personal style:
- Voice. (Does it sound like the writer?)
- Dialogue.
- Humor.
- Word choice.
- Writing craft.

☐ Genre:
- Appropriately chosen.
- Appropriately executed (includes the correct qualities and features).

<table>
<tr><td>

Teacher Talk

</td><td>

What It Sounds Like to Focus on Content

☐ *Think about how you can begin your writing so your reader knows exactly what you're writing about.*

☐ *When you get stuck, read over what you've written so far. You might need to reread a few times to get ideas to get going again.*

☐ *Sometimes it's easier to hear how your writing sounds if you quietly read it out loud to yourself.*

☐ *Make sure your writing makes sense and is easy to understand.*

☐ *Always keep your reader in mind as you are writing.*

☐ *I noticed you tried . . . when you got stuck. That's what good writers do.*

☐ *I saw you reading over what you wrote yesterday before you started writing today. That helps your thinking get going and helps you decide what you want to say next. Good for you.*

☐ *Make sure your lead catches the reader's attention and makes it clear what you're writing about. You may want to try writing another lead or two and see which one works best.*

☐ *Will the reader know your piece is finished? Do you have a satisfying and interesting ending that ties everything together?*

</td></tr>
</table>

Depend on Minilessons

Minilessons—short, focused lessons in which you teach what the writer needs—are often appropriate during a conference. It might be a quick point of grammar, how to insert information, how and where to add a transition, how to cut and paste information, how to paragraph.

During your daily conferences, you will begin to notice some similar needs among your students. Use these patterns to guide your teaching and minilessons. For example, many students end their pieces abruptly, or they make the writing longer but not better, or they do not use transitions to let the reader know what's coming next. If transitions are missing, I might say something like this: *Kids, I've noticed that some of you are making it hard for your reader to follow what's happening. Let me show you how you can signal the reader that you are moving to a new idea.* (See example on pages 320–321.)

Then, with a student's permission I project the student's writing on a screen, and I explicitly show and guide the student how to make the writing clearer: *Today, before you begin writing, reread your piece, and be sure it's easy for the reader to follow.*

At this point, I am not using the word *transition*. I teach the concept first and label it later, which makes it easier for students to learn and apply. Once students understand the concept and have practiced it in their writing over weeks and months, I say something like: *Kids, what we've been working on— adding a line or two in to let the reader know that you're moving to a new idea or subject—is called adding transitions. Transitions are important. In fact, all good writing has them.*

End with Editing Conferences

Once students have done their best job with the content of their writing, you can move on to editing. An editing conference is a conversation about the final clarity and correctness of the writing; it may also include teacher demonstration and guided practice. The purpose of editing is to make the writing seamless for the reader. Shared writing is the best way I know to establish exactly what it is that students are to do in the editing process. (See Appendices J and K for examples of editing expectations. Also see pages 69–70 for "Raise Your Expectations for Editing.")

Practice the Language of Helpful Response

Teacher Talk

- ☐ *I can tell you've reread your writing over and over again.*
- ☐ *Good for you. You've circled all the misspelled words you could find and corrected most of them. I'll fix the rest of these "for free."*
- ☐ *I'm going to put the editing mark for a new paragraph here because you're changing subjects. When you do your final copy, be sure to indent here to let the reader know it's a new paragraph.*
- ☐ *I'm putting commas here because writers use commas to. . . .*
- ☐ *We capitalize words in a title, like this.*
- ☐ *I'm changing this from* be *to* is *so it sounds right.*

teaching tip

teaching tip

Stop the conference when you find two or more places in which the student has not edited work you would expect her to be able to do. (You are letting the student know she is in charge.)

teaching tip

Note the errors in a line by placing colored dots or checks in the margins. (This lets you and the student know what lines need to be reedited. Also, when the student returns for another conference, you will not need to reread the entire paper.)

Whenever you notice that a student has not done all he could do, stop and immediately give the editing responsibility back to the student. In a firm but non-punitive manner, say something like:

> *You have not done your total job as editor. You will need to read your paper carefully over and over again to fix up everything we have talked about. Check our editing expectations list. Don't take my time until you've done absolutely everything you can do.*

Then, make one or two specific comments and stop the conference:

- [ ] *There are two words in this line that are misspelled. Fix them up.*
- [ ] *I've just read three lines, and I see missing punctuation and capitalization.*
- [ ] *I see capital letters in the middle of words.*
- [ ] *You circled misspelled words, but you also need to make some attempt on correcting some of those.*
- [ ] *I need to see the work you've done. Don't erase. Cross out.*
- [ ] *What do you know about capitals in a title?*
- [ ] *I still see spelling words I know you can fix up.*
- [ ] *You have missing punctuation in this line.*
- [ ] *You're missing periods in several places.*
- [ ] *Go back to our editing expectations sheet, and make sure you've done everything that's on it.*
- [ ] *I will meet with you after you've done everything you can as an editor.*

Once students assume responsibility for their own editing, I make comments like these:

- [ ] *You've done a great job editing. Tell me some of the things you were able to do on your own* (affirms the student and encourages ongoing independence).
- [ ] *I notice you've added carets to add in information, circled all your misspelled words, fixed up most of your misspelled words, added capitals to the beginning every sentence, etc.]* (recognizes student's efforts and skills, and encourages repeated student responsibility for editing).
- [ ] *You're so close here. Let me show you. . . .* (lets student know she can count on teacher help once she's done her best work).
- [ ] *What do you think you can fix up on your own?* (lets student know you expect him to do more and have confidence he can do it).

Fourth Graders Assume More Responsibility for Editing

Even a low-performing student is able to attempt lots of editing work

Dear Mrs. Potter,

   I am so thankful because of the great education you have given me. When I was in kindergarten, first, and second grade I had a terrible education, so when I went to third here at Rio Grande School, I didn't know much. You're "my" hero because you were patient and took specific time with me, like in the first trimester you took time out of your day to teach me tricks for math and you always understand when I need help. And that's how you got me where I am today.

Love, Liana

Kristin Potter working with a student

Teach Students to Do More Editing

By fall of second grade, I expect students to do most of their own editing. Years of teaching have shown me that by second grade, students are capable of being careful editors. Some kindergartners and first graders can also edit their work, but my first priority is to get them to love writing. For many, just the physical and mental act of writing is exhausting. I want young students to choose to write and delight in writing. So I rarely expect—except for those few who demonstrate they can—these beginning writers to assume full responsibility for editing. However, I continually demonstrate and explicitly teach editing in kindergarten and first grade, through morning message, shared writing, and thinking aloud as I write and edit that writing in front of students. Students of all ages need repeated demonstrations of the editing thought process and how and why changes are made before they can take on the task at hand.

Once students know how to edit, peer editing works well for improving the mechanics and overall fluency of the writing. By having both students present and accountable at the editing conference, students eventually assume the major editing tasks. (Each student edits using a different colored pencil.)

Before I have an editing conference with students or they participate in a peer editing conference, students are expected to have:

☐ Completed every editing expectation on the list we wrote together.
☐ Reread their piece several times to check that they have done so.
☐ Fixed up most of their misspellings.

Teacher Talk

We have agreed on exactly what it is that you can do on your own as editors. In order to do your best work, you will need to read over your papers carefully at least three or four times. Once you have done everything you can (and met with a peer editor), I will have an editing conference with you. If you have truly corrected everything you can, I will do all the rest "for free." However, if you have neglected to fix up things we have agreed you know how to do, I will immediately send you back to your seat. Don't waste my time by coming up for a conference before you have checked your paper very, very carefully.

In effect I say to students, "I know you can edit on your own, and I expect you to do it." It takes a few months of having to tell and show students, often over and over, that they can do most of the editing work themselves. In general, students are so used to our doing all the work that even though we say they are now responsible for editing, they don't believe us. Stay firm. Once students see that we are serious about having them assume full responsibility for editing, they comply, and individual editing conferences go quickly, which speeds up the publication process.

My best advice on having efficient editing conferences is to be relentless in refusing to do for students what they can do for themselves. While I am very gentle with students in a content conference, carefully watching my language to be sure I am being supportive, I take a much tougher stance with editing. "Don't waste my time," I sometimes tell a student who has not done his job as editor. Content is personal; editing is not. Editing is an expected convention and courtesy for the reader. I tell students, "The writer has a contract with the reader to get it right."

WHAT TO FOCUS ON IN AN EDITING CONFERENCE

- ☐ Capitalization.
- ☐ Spelling.
- ☐ Punctuation.
- ☐ Grammar.
- ☐ Word choice (including title).
- ☐ Legibility:
  - Penmanship.
  - Spacing.
  - Capital and lowercase letters.
- ☐ Organization (final check):
  - Similar ideas grouped together.
  - Paragraphing.
  - Adding missing material and deleting unnecessary material.
- ☐ Rereading:
  - Reread piece out loud to oneself.
  - Reread with teacher (or peer).
- ☐ Presentation:
  - Form and format.
  - Possible illustrations (or visuals).

Once you establish well-defined editing expectations with the students and require them to do most of the editing work themselves (or with a peer), your editing conferences will be brief, typically about five minutes for one or two pages of writing. Only edit for the student what the student cannot do.

Hand Over More Responsibility to Students

Keep in mind that our goal is to have students monitor their own writing and problem solve independently so they can eventually draft, rewrite, revise, publish, and edit mostly on their own. When I first began writing books, my editor suggested when and where I needed leads and transitions, what the format of each chapter should be, how sections could be better organized. I didn't know what was confusing, missing, and disorganized. Now, after years of guidance, I am able to do most of that work.

Shifting the responsibility of conferences to students is a gradual process but a necessary one. One teacher noted, "Without my okay, a lot of my really terrific writers have *no* confidence." We do not want students to depend on us for their next moves. Ultimately, we want students to become their own best critics and hold internal conferences with themselves. (Such independence is necessary for students to do well on high-stakes tests.)

At first, until students "know" what they need to do to organize, revise, and craft their writing, we teachers assume most of the responsibility for the structure of the conference. Applying the optimal learning model (moving from demonstration, shared demonstration, guided practice, to independent practice), as students become more familiar with, competent at, and confident about the process and purpose of conferences, they assume increasing responsibility for leading the conference. (See the forms for teacher-directed and student-directed content conferences in grade 3 on the next two pages. For blank forms for content and editing conferences, see www.heinemann.com/writingessentials.) Initially, however, students don't know what to do when they get stuck, what parts are not clearly organized, what's confusing to the reader, how to craft the writing for a specific reader, or even what their questions are. Like all good teaching and learning, it's a process that requires explicit teaching along with ongoing support, guidance, and practice.

Use Language That Signals Students to Take More Responsibility

Our language in a conference should gradually encourage and prepare students to take increasing responsibility for determining what their needs are.

- [ ] *What are you working on?* (immediately signals the student is in charge.)
- [ ] *What parts are you pleased about? Tell me about that* (signals that you are looking to the student to recognize writing strengths).
- [ ] *I see you've added conversation [an interesting lead, more description, humor]* (affirms technique and personal style; encourages student to try it again).
- [ ] *I notice you crossed out this part [added these words, sentences, a lead, details]. Can you explain why you did that?* (recognizes students' efforts to revise for clarity and meaning; encourages repeat behavior in future writing; makes student more aware of his actions).

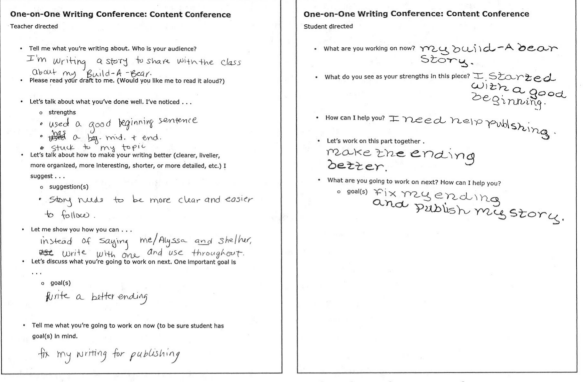

Teacher-directed writing conference   Student-directed writing conference

☐   *I like how you've organized your writing [put yourself in this piece, started with a question, used humor]. Talk about how you decided to do this* (gets at student's thinking and values and affirms her efforts).

☐   *So what do you think you want [need] to work on next?* (signals you believe the student can assume responsibility for improving his writing).

☐   *What can you do on your own?* (signals your confidence and expectation that the student already knows a lot about revising, rewriting, researching, etc.).

☐   *How can I help you?* (encourages the student to determine and ask for what she needs to move forward).

Aim for Student Independence

It's talked about very little, but independence is the goal of all excellent teaching. We want students who not only can read and write but who know how and when to adjust their rate, reread and rewrite, seek help, locate useful resources, evaluate their own literacy behavior, and improve with an eye toward excellence. Keeping student independence in mind guides all my teaching and assessing. I want students eventually to be able to have productive conferences with themselves, just as I do as a writer. I rely on the responses of others, but I am my own final reader, critic, and editor. It has to be that way. No one cares as much as I do about the content, form, quality, and accuracy of the writing. No one knows my audience as well as I do.

We need to instill that same sense of urgent caring in our students and give them the tools to become independent writers. Conducting effective conferences is one great way to achieve that goal.

One student's self-evaluation before a one-on-one conference, validating the student's self-evaluation and goal-setting

10. Make Assessment Count

If assessments of *learning provide evidence of achievement for public reporting, then assessments* for *learning serve to help students learn more.*
—Richard J. Stiggins

There is lots of writing assessment going on these days, but little of it actually improves the quality of students' writing. Assessment *of* learning includes but is not limited to standardized measures such as state and district writing tests. While this type of assessment is necessary to check whether or not students are progressing—commonly called *accountability*—it is seldom used to improve daily instruction. As clarified by NCTE:

> Furthermore, standardized tests tend to focus on readily
> accessed features of the language—on grammatical correctness
> and stylistic choice—and on error, on what is wrong rather than
> on the appropriate rhetorical choices that have been made.
> Consequently the outcome of such assessments is negative:
> students are said to demonstrate what they do "wrong" with
> language rather than what they do well.

More troubling, standardized test results are often used to make inaccurate statements about students' learning, especially minority students.

While assessment *of* learning is legitimate (we must, after all, inform the public where our students stand), it must be balanced with assessment *for* learning, which is often classroom based (we must also inform ourselves, our students, and their caregivers about their progress for the specific purpose of improving student writing). In my experience, assessment to improve instruction and learning are too often absent.

A word of caution. While the National Assessment of Educational Progress, also known as the "nation's report card," publishes claims about the status of writing in the United States, these conclusions come from impromptu writing completed in fifteen minutes. Looking at students' writing over time, for purposeful communication to real audiences, is far more valid.

Become More Knowledgeable About Assessment

Think about the last piece you read that was memorable. Was it because the writing had correct grammar, punctuation, and spelling? Certainly those elements were necessary so you could read the piece with ease and focus on the message. But wasn't it the language, the way the author used words, that gripped you? At least that's how it is for me and most readers I know. Of course we depend on correct conventions and form. That's a given. But the inspiration isn't in that; it's in the language, the way the piece flows and is organized, the impact the words have on the reader.

Good intentions around assessment can come to naught if we teachers have scant knowledge about teaching writing. For example, spending time examining students' writing—an admirable activity—does not guarantee writing improvement, even when it's done by every teacher in the school and across grade levels. If teachers sit down and look at student writing with a mind-set of correct conventions, without any concern for communicating with the reader through organization, voice, clear intention, and so on, the writing isn't going to improve much.

Likewise, placing students on a writing continuum has the potential to be helpful or a waste of time, based on teachers' knowledge. For example, knowing expected writing behavior at different developmental stages can encourage professional conversations, suggest specific language to use when talking with parents and preparing report cards, and help us choose minilessons and establish standards. But unless teachers know how to teach writing well, student writing will not improve. Take care that most of your time and effort is spent teaching effectively, not matching students with writing stages.

It is our job to ensure that assessment practices lead to targeted teaching and improved writing. "Assessment to improve instruction requires active learning communities that sustain productive conversations about teaching and learning that are based on data." As a staff, you will need to write together, study together, converse together, gather schoolwide data, analyze these data, and set goals for improving writing instruction. There is no shortcut to helping students become effective writers, and there is no program you can buy that will do it for you.

Put Rubrics in Perspective

In many schools in which I work, the teaching of writing is driven by six traits—ideas and content, organization, sentence fluency, voice, word choice, and conventions. Teaching these specific traits and judging writing on their basis is understandable, since most states' high-stakes writing tests are scored against them.

These six traits are a rubric—an evaluation tool. A rubric lists the criteria and/or the qualities expected in a piece of writing. ("Traits are the qualities—ideas, organization, voice, etc.—that define good writing. Criteria are the language we use to define how those traits look at various levels—beginning, developing, proficient—along a continuum of performance.") A rubric (see the examples on page 241) lets the writer know what is expected in order for the writing to be judged excellent (or poor). In theory, embracing the six traits is a good idea, because we know what to look for in writing to assess it; in practice, it can be constraining, because teaching the traits in isolation often becomes the writing program and approach to all writing, especially when teachers are not knowledgeable about how to teach writing effectively.

While students' test scores may be higher when their teachers adhere strictly to a set of writing traits, the writing is often "vacuous"—simplified and homogenized. Rubrics often fail to measure the development of ideas, overall coherence, and relevance of evidence presented, which sends a message to students that writing to the formula matters, not the content. Rubrics also "fail to provide a *demonstration* of the reading process that can later be internalized by the writer." For example, the writer learns he needs to improve his organization or voice or sentence fluency, but what does that mean? He may work to improve the trait because he's expected to, but he doesn't necessarily become a better writer.

Understand How Rubrics Work

Rubrics are a lot like checklists or guidelines. At its simplest, a rubric is a set of criteria for what needs to be included in a piece of writing (see pages 184 and 198). The criteria can be general, as in the six traits mentioned previously, applying to all writing, or specific to a writing genre or form (see Appendices F and I). At its most complex, a rubric can delineate many separate qualities and many levels of performance, from high to low.

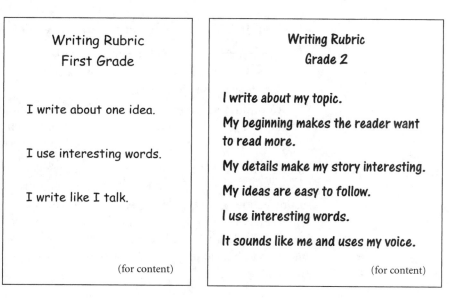

Writing Rubric
First Grade

I write about one idea.

I use interesting words.

I write like I talk.

(for content)

Writing Rubric
Grade 2

I write about my topic.

My beginning makes the reader want to read more.

My details make my story interesting.

My ideas are easy to follow.

I use interesting words.

It sounds like me and uses my voice.

(for content)

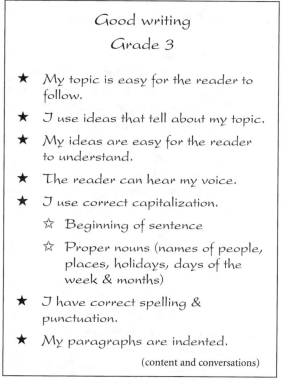

Good writing
Grade 3

★ My topic is easy for the reader to follow.

★ I use ideas that tell about my topic.

★ My ideas are easy for the reader to understand.

★ The reader can hear my voice.

★ I use correct capitalization.

  ☆ Beginning of sentence

  ☆ Proper nouns (names of people, places, holidays, days of the week & months)

★ I have correct spelling & punctuation.

★ My paragraphs are indented.

(content and conversations)

Child-friendly draft rubrics written by teachers and revised with students' input

A rubric can be used to guide text content and/or evaluate text quality:

☐ A **content rubric** provides explicit criteria to frame the writing and define the task (lets students, teachers, administrators, and parents know what is expected; helps guide the writing).

☐ An **evaluation rubric** provides criteria explaining how the writing will be rated or scored, often on a scale of numbers (such as from 1 to 4) or words (such as *limited, competent, excellent*). (See example, bottom of page 150.)

Rubrics can be *holistic* (one score for the whole piece) or *analytic* (separate scores for each trait); formal or informal; and created by state, district (see example, bottom of page 151), school, or classroom.

The rubric, like a checklist, helps teachers, students, and parents evaluate writing, decide what minilessons to teach, and what goals to set. It helps students know what to include in a writing assignment, what constitutes quality, and how they will be evaluated.

Keep Your Focus on Effective Writing

Don't overdo it. When you focus on a checklist (or rubric) instead of the child, you miss a lot of what the child is trying to do. Rubrics, like checklists, can disrupt the flow of teaching and learning. When you read a piece of writing, you lose the meaning of what the child is trying to do if, at the same time, you're trying to keep a whole list of criteria in mind. "Although rubrics promote reliability, they may simultaneously undermine validity, the more important determinant of the quality of an assessment." In other words, groups of people scoring papers can be trained to do so against a rubric in a similar, consistent manner (reliability), but whether or not those scores are an accurate representation of the skills and abilities of effective writers (validity) is another question entirely.

Assessments must be both reliable and valid. I worry that conscientious teachers will spend hours scoring papers against a rubric only to have the writing remain stagnant because they are looking primarily at word choice or skills in isolation, such as spelling or sentence fluency, and not at the big picture, at what the writer is trying to say. Teachers may agree on what they see (reliability), but if they are looking with a narrow lens focused on skills, those scores do not accurately assess effective writing (validity). The latter is a critical point; if students' writing is to improve, what we are teaching and expecting must be valid.

Use Rubrics Judiciously

In too many places students are being "rubricized": every piece of writing is scored against a rubric, sometimes even in first grade. One teacher told me, "I'm using my rubrics because I've been told I have to." Use professional common sense. It is not advisable to apply rubrics to all writing nor to score all writing. Just as our students need lots of practice reading many texts without the expectation that they will be assessed on everything they read, they need lots of practice writing without being assessed on everything they write.

Constantly having to adhere to strict guidelines can stifle our ability to write freely. Writing involves "complex subprocesses that occur interactively as writers work their way from the beginning of a writing to its culmination." *No rubric or progression of steps captures the full range of what writers actually do.* Remember Tom Newkirk's wise thought: It's not what the writing has—it's what the writing does.

Create Child-Friendly Rubrics

When I first began teaching writing in Vancouver, Washington, the teachers were rubric crazed—posting state and district rubrics in every classroom, creating rubrics for many assignments, scoring lots of papers against rubrics. Once these teachers became more knowledgeable about teaching writing, they began to use rubrics appropriately—as an evaluation tool, not as the driving instructional force. Teachers who initially relied on commercial rubrics came to prefer their own homegrown charts and criteria, almost always established with the students after the teacher and students examined and tried out a particular form of writing. Page 241 contain examples of child-friendly rubrics for grades one–three. Notice how establishing our own criteria eventually led to increased specificity about content and quality, even in grade one (see pages 58–61).

TRY IT APPLY IT

- Get together with the other teachers and students at your school (all grade levels) and develop child-friendly rubrics that align with the highest level of excellence (usually a score of 4 or 6) on your state's rubric. Make sure you do not overemphasize mechanics and grammar.

- Save examples of excellent student papers. With students' permission (or names removed), have current and future students identify exactly what the writers did to make the writing memorable (see the example on page 151). Demonstrate how to do this through your own modeling and shared experiences before you put students in small groups to work together.

*Use Rubrics
Judiciously*

- Organize examples by genre, so students can look through them for ideas, organizational approaches, etc. For example, if students are learning how to write fairy tales, have a file of excellent tales from former students.

- Study and monitor your own process as you compose a letter to parents, a research paper, a poem. Would you be comfortable with your writing being scored against a rubric such as the six traits? Could a score capture what you are trying to say? Would such a score be a valid indicator of your writing ability? (Remember, the whole is more than the sum of its parts!)

- Write together as a staff. Based on your own processes, come to some schoolwide decisions about teaching writing.

- With your colleagues, collect a set of papers at your grade level and across grade levels. Examine them and talk about what you see. Use a rubric, but make sure that your conclusions are valid as well as reliable and that your focus is on the big picture of what makes effective writing, not just on correctness. Set new goals for teaching based on what you see.

Put High-Stakes Testing in Perspective

The joy has gone out of writing. From elementary school through high school, many students are receiving extensive test preparation, much of it learning to write to a formula. They may pass the test, but they don't much like writing. More important, such "dumbing down" of curriculum does not encourage writing excellence or enjoyment. In fact, kids get a distorted view of what excellence is. We need to see high-stakes testing in writing as a challenge to teach writing well, not as a call for step-by-step, prescriptive writing.

The Best Test Preparation Is Excellent Teaching

Many teachers and administrators don't believe the above statement. I know they don't believe it, because in most of the schools in which I am invited to teach writing, an inordinate amount of time is spent on test preparation—practicing prompts, going through procedures, applying the six traits. A word of caution: Students often do worse on a test when we overemphasize its importance. Also, a narrow focus on skills does not yield high scores on state tests.

Neither does a focus on standards. According to "rigorous reviews" by the National Commission on Writing, only about 20 percent of state departments of education adequately align standards with curriculum. Furthermore, even when they do, teachers tend to overfocus on what is tested rather than the skills and strategies that underlie writing competency.

Overpreparation Is Often Detrimental

Students who spend enormous amounts of time preparing for tests and districts that invest huge amounts of dollars in test-preparation materials are often disappointed with results. Research shows that *high achievement and high test scores result when what is tested is woven into daily teaching and challenging curriculum in a relevant manner.*

So much time spent teaching to the tests exhausts teachers and students and makes everyone anxious. Fourth-grade teacher Kari Oosterveen says by the time her students took the test, they were completely worn out. Seeing the test scores drop after all the preparation she did with the students was devastating and finally convinced her that all that prep time had not worked. The following year she concentrated on excellent teaching of writing, and the scores soared. Kari comments:

> The first year I was hung up on teaching to the test. The test scores in our building were low, and there was pressure to raise them. We didn't know what else to do, so we concentrated on practicing test-taking skills throughout the year. My kids didn't do very well on the test. I think they were tired, that we wore them out before they even saw the test. After the test, they acted as if school were over for the year. We still had eight weeks to go, and they wouldn't write a thing!
>
> In the summer, I read some books and articles about standardized testing and effective teaching. This brought me back to all the reasons I went into teaching and boosted my confidence, once again, to concentrate on excellent teaching. I went into the new school year with a different strategy, which was to concentrate on developing kids as learners rather than kids as test takers.
>
> We enjoyed learning through the end of the school year—learning everything we needed to know without isolating skills. When the kids took the test, they didn't miss a beat. Their confidence level was so high. Afterward, we went right back to what we had been working on, and we continued to move forward. The result was that my kids did much better on the test.

Have Your Students Do a Lot of Writing

Extensive writing across the curriculum as part of an excellent writing program is the best preparation for doing well on these tests. Readers have to read avidly to become readers, and the same holds true for writers. Kids who write a lot develop higher-order thinking and understanding that translates to higher achievement on all types of tests.

Aim for Fluency

Expect your students (from grade one on) to be able to write a whole page of text in twenty or thirty minutes. I find when students cannot, it's most often because they are asked to write infrequently. If students are to do well on high-stakes tests, they must be fluent writers who write easily and effortlessly. They must have writing endurance, and such stamina depends on daily writing of texts (not exercises) and excellent teaching of writing, including spelling and handwriting.

**TRY IT
APPLY IT**

- Schedule writing every day. Try for 20–30 minutes of silent sustained writing.
- Time your minilessons. Limit yourself to between five and fifteen minutes.
- Don't shortchange the time for whole-class share. The celebration and teaching that take place improve the quality of students' writing.
- Announce the time frame at the start: *You will have twenty minutes to complete this piece.*
- Announce when students only have a few minutes left to write: *You have five more minutes. Finish up where you are and reread.*
- Make sure the topics students are writing about are relevant to their lives and interests.
- Do a great job of demonstrating and frontloading. The more prepared students are to write, the more easily they write.
- Use quickwrites (see page 179), also called freewrites, regularly.

Encourage Students to Do Their Best

While it's important not to overemphasize test taking, students and we teachers do need to take testing seriously—we, our administrators, our students, and our schools are judged by the outcome. It's no surprise to me that many students don't put forth their best effort on state writing tests. They don't get their papers back, so they are unable to examine their strengths and weaknesses and thus improve their writing. They don't know whom they are writing for or to, and they don't know how their writing will be used.

Nonetheless, well-constructed writing tests on which students have time to plan, draft, revise, rewrite, and proofread an extended response (often writing to a prompt) are one legitimate way of knowing how we are doing as a school or system in the teaching of writing. Students need to know this and value the assessment for that purpose. I say something like this to my students:

The state has an obligation to know how teachers are doing teaching writing and how students are developing as writers. It's important you do your very best writing on this test, because our school will be judged on how well students write. Use all the things we've worked on and talked about that good writers do, and do your best writing.

Help Your Students Visualize the Reader/Scorer

Because writing for a specific reader is of primary importance for effective writing, help your students "see" a reader, even on a high-stakes test. In Washington State, where I live, I often talk to students about Wanda WASL (so named by fourth-grade teacher Kari Oosterveen, after the Washington Assessment of Student Learning):

> *Picture the reader of your writing. Her name is Wanda WASL, and she's exhausted. She has been reading writing samples now for six hours. She is paid only eight dollars an hour to do this tedious work. She is sitting on a hard chair in front of a computer screen, about to read your writing. She is totally bored. Wake her up. She needs to be entertained. Have your lead excite her. Make sure your thoughts are organized so your writing is easy to follow. She has only ten minutes to read and evaluate your writing. Don't waste her time with poor spelling or editing errors.*

Although Wanda WASL is made up, the facts about scoring state writing tests are true. In general, scorers are poorly paid, have minimal training, are given very little time to read each sample, and are expected to read student papers for many hours at a stretch.

Kari Oosterveen puts a more positive spin on what she tells her students. She explains that they are writing to the "deciding people" who determine what should be learned and taught in our schools. "This is the only chance we get, as a class, to show off how good we are at writing. No one gets to see what we usually do, and now they want to see it. It's show time! We need to wow the crowd with all we know."

Either way, creating an audience and purpose for the state writing test will make it easier for your students to put forth their best efforts.

Prepare Students for On-Demand Writing

Writing on demand is a fact of life. Students need to be able to write essays and respond to prompts on required tests, and job seekers, including teachers, often need to fill out applications or do a writing sample for perspective employees "on the spot." So, how much preparation is sufficient and helpful?

Keep writing to a prompt in perspective. Once every six or seven weeks is fine, beginning in second grade. Use focused freewrites, which are prompts with a starter (see pages 179–180). Spend several days (to a maximum of two weeks) before the test teaching students the language and format. Be sure to emphasize following directions carefully. Sometimes, competent writers fail to test well because they are creative and inventive but fail to pay attention to key words (*describe, explain*).

Reduce Test Anxiety

If we know how to do something, we don't worry so much about being asked to do it. Just as you demonstrate writing in a particular genre or form before expecting kids to do so, use a previous year's writing test to demonstrate smart test taking. Let students observe you think aloud and strategize as you:

- ☐ Understand the language of the test.
- ☐ Figure out what the directions say and mean.
- ☐ Focus on key words in the directions.
- ☐ Think and plan before you write.
- ☐ Reread as you go along and after you write.
- ☐ Pace yourself.
- ☐ Score yourself against the state rubric.
- ☐ With your guidance, have students try out similar strategies as they take a practice test.

Lots of test anxiety also comes from students' not having been told logistical details such as:

- ☐ How much time will it take?
- ☐ How will the structure of the regular day change?
- ☐ Will we get lunch?

Share this information. Don't keep kids in the dark.

If kids have to finish within a certain time, practice that for a day so they get a feel for how much time they'll have. If the test is untimed, practice that as well, so students will experience what it feels like when everyone finishes at a different time. What will they do if they are a "quick finisher"?

Help Students Become "Test Wise"

- Have students take a practice test and score themselves against the state rubric (or an equivalent child-friendly rubric). Meet with each student. You only need to discuss areas in which you disagree with their assessment.

- Ask your state department of education for examples of papers that received the highest scores. With your students (first as a whole class, then in small groups), identify the criteria that make these papers top-rated.

- Teach any specialized vocabulary students will need to know.

- Examine previous test formats. Note what students are being asked to do. (You needn't be overly concerned about format: test performance is only slightly impacted by knowing the format in advance.)

- Practice answering multiple-choice items.

- Teach the importance of reading directions carefully.

- Discuss pacing during a test.

Put a Schoolwide Assessment Policy into Practice

Writing scores took a big leap at a school in Vancouver, Washington, where for four years we made a schoolwide professional development commitment to improve the teaching of writing (see related discussion on pages 10–12). While high test scores were always one of our goals, we needed schoolwide data that showed whether or not kids' writing was getting better over time. We also knew we couldn't rely on the test scores, primarily because they provide limited information. (Test scores can also drop for reasons beyond anyone's control.)

The teachers agreed that writing improvement and assessment are a shared responsibility across the grades and that we needed back-up data not just for accountability but as part of good teaching. Together the principal and teachers decided to take a sample of writing from all students at the beginning of every school year and at the end, a quickwrite to the same prompt. (For example, *My best school memory is . . .* or *The best thing that happened this year was. . . .*)

The quickwrites are done in a single day in the fall and spring with no teacher intervention. Students are given time to draft their pieces and can work on them again on their own later the same day, revising and editing in an effort to do their "very best work"—just as they do on the state test. Kindergartners also respond to the prompt. (An alternative would be to select a "typical" writing sample not generated by a prompt.)

Grade level and cross–grade level analyses of these writing samples are used to document improvement, note strengths and weaknesses, and provide information to teachers and children to improve instruction and learning. Samples are saved in the child's literacy file, which is passed along to each successive teacher.

Collect Useful Data to Improve the Teaching of Writing

We almost never receive feedback from a standardized test that helps us decide how to move the student forward as a writer. So it's absolutely necessary that we have reliable and valid data that will help us make writing improvement possible. Have schoolwide discussions and decide what you will do as a school, at every grade level, to assess how kids are developing as writers. Ask: *What kind of data are useful for improving the teaching of writing, and how can we collect and analyze these data?* Provide professional development on how to look at, evaluate, and use students' writing samples to improve instruction and learning and then make sure teachers have the time to collaborate on doing that work.

Showcase Students' Progress

Displays of children's writing over time help the public see growth that may be obscured by state test results. Rob Tierney suggests creating longitudinal displays of children's writing—that is, displays that show samples of one child's writing from kindergarten through grade 6 (or even grade 12), perhaps accompanied by photos showing physical development. Put these displays in the front entranceway so every visitor to the school can see them. Change the child being spotlighted once every week or two, and choose from the full range of your student body—even the child with learning disabilities will show growth.

**TRY IT
APPLY IT**

Collect Reliable Data to Share with Parents, Administrators, and the Public:

- Writing samples from year to year kept in a cumulative folder.
- Schoolwide prompts scored by teachers.
- Student-selected best pieces of writing (two or three times a year).
- A fall writing sample and a spring rewrite for content and mechanics.
- Specific anecdotal notes from writing conferences, not just catch-all phrases (see the example on page 217).
- Grade-level writing samples.
- Portfolios.
- Monthly, focused freewrites.
- Journals (celebrations/goals).
- Writing samples at grades level and across grade levels examined against both a holistic and an analytic rubric.
- Continuums. (Be aware that these are very time-consuming.)
- Student assessments of their own work (strengths, goals, weaknesses).

Rely More on Classroom-Based Assessments

State test data must be supplemented by classroom-based assessments that recognize the complexity of teaching and learning. These assessments can include but are not limited to writing folders, portfolios, rewritten work, anecdotal records from conferences, and self-assessments. Parents are able to put high-stakes testing in perspective when we teachers are rigorous about classroom assessment and clearly communicate the quality, benefits, and results of our assessments to parents and the public.

Assess Students' Writing Every Day

Assessments *for* learning have the potential to help students become more proficient writers. They include but are not limited to:

ASSESSMENTS *FOR* LEARNING: SOME POSSIBILITIES

- ☐ One-on-one roving conferences done on the run.
- ☐ Formal one-on-one sit-down conferences about content or editing.
- ☐ Whole-class shares in which students see and hear where to go next.
- ☐ Students' choices regarding content, word choice, fluency, thinking, invented spelling, mechanics, and grammar during shared writing.
- ☐ Conversations before writing.
- ☐ Type and quality of questions students ask, including their ability to ask and answer their own questions.
- ☐ Responses to literature—notes, personal responses, literature extensions.
- ☐ Summaries and other assigned writing.
- ☐ Writing as thinking.
- ☐ Planning for writing (outlines, notes, visuals).
- ☐ Evidence of revision (frequency, quality).
- ☐ Evidence of editing (self-direction, awareness of reader, spelling consciousness).

Be Realistic and Humane About Grading

When we put too much emphasis on grading, we spend our time looking to justify the grade rather than helping students learn how to become better writers. One teacher who wrote me spoke for many, "I do so many things in the classroom just to get grades and have gotten away from real reading and writing." We are grading too many papers. Eighty percent of students' writing *needn't* be graded, same with reading. Kids need lots of time to practice, experiment, and just plain "mess around" without worrying about a grade. Lots of grading should be self-assessment.

Still, grading is a requirement in most schools and many classrooms. If you are giving a grade, make sure students and parents know on what the grade is based. If need be, even a genre as personal and creative as poetry can be fairly graded. (See the draft-in-process poetry rubric being developed with students' input below, and the final blank form in Appendix F.) Balance grades with informal assessments and self-evaluations. And don't lose sight of what good writing is all about. "To become reflective writers, students must take communication, not grades, as their end goal." And finally, keep in mind that exemplary teachers rely more on effort and improvement in assigning grades than on simple achievement.

Students' work with partners further refines our shared writing rubric draft. Using the final rubric, students self-evaluate against the work they've done. There are nine areas (10 percent each); students decide to give "voice" double weight (20 percent). The teacher only intervenes if she finds the student has not graded himself fairly.

HUMANE GUIDELINES FOR GRADING

- ☐ Let parents and students know what the criteria are for determining the grade.
- ☐ When possible, have students involved in determining criteria.
- ☐ Value self-assessment.
- ☐ Leave most work ungraded.
- ☐ Recognize effort and improvement.

Work Toward Student Self-Assessment

Self-evaluation is the missing piece in writing instruction. Ultimately, we want students to internalize the qualities of good writing and to have inner conversations about their writing—in other words, to have conferences with themselves in which they notice their strengths, critique their own writing, set reasonably high goals, know how and when to seek help, and work toward accomplishing their goals. The more work the child is able to do on his own, the more learning takes place. Teach writing with self-evaluation as an end goal for all students.

- ✐ Create child-friendly rubrics that mirror those of the district and state but that are in language students can understand and use.
- ✎ Post charts—"What Good Writers Do"—as a rubric. (See examples on page 117.)
- ✑ Teach rereading as you write and after you write. Rereading and reading out loud are two things students can do easily to assess their writing. In the process of reading again, students hear what doesn't sound right, what's missing; they often will add a word or cross something out.
- ✐ Save examples—excellent ones and not-so-good-ones—with students' permission and with their names removed. Use them in your teaching and make them available to your students. (*Here's what some strong writing looks like.*) With your students, discuss:
  - ✐ *What makes this a good piece of writing?*
  - ✐ *Name what the writer has done.*
  - ✐ *What makes this not so good?*
  - ✐ *What has the writer not done?*
  - ✐ *What would the writer need to do to improve the piece?*
- ✎ Organize students in small discussion groups to evaluate writing samples (after you have modeled and practiced doing this).
- ✑ Ask students to rewrite a piece they wrote several months before. Have students assess themselves against a formal rubric as well as in relation to the characteristics of good writing posted in classroom. Have them note strengths and next steps for content, organization, style, and conventions.

**TRY IT
APPLY IT**

*Work Toward
Student Self-
Assessment*

✎ Several times a year, have students select their best or favorite everyday writing (something not done specifically for assessment)—a journal entry, poem, letter, snapshot—and assess it and set goals for improvement. (You will need to demonstrate this process first.)

✎ Involve caregivers: Have each student select three pieces of writing (from three different times of year, for example) and tell family members how he or she has grown as a writer. (Demonstrate how to do this—what to look for and the language to use to describe writing and progress.)

✎ Have students complete a written self-evaluation of their progress, the writing project just completed, or a specific piece of writing. (In the example below, Eric, an English language learner and reluctant writer, on his own initiative took the evaluation form that I give to teachers at the end of a residency and filled it out with some key insights: choice, sharing, and having enough time to write are all important to the writer.)

**EVALUATION OF WRITING RESIDENCY
February 2004
Rummel Creek Elementary School, Houston, TX**

Name (optional) _____*Eric*_____ Grade _*Fourth*_

Please write down your thoughts related to writing. Please include insights, strengths, anything you took away from demonstration lessons, conversations, things that you tried in your classroom, lingering questions, or anything that seems important to you.

I like this week because I could write so much. I think this is very important to learn how to write so much. And I think that if you write what you want, you will write betther is important. I think sharing are fun. But I don't think to rush is important.

                                              ELL student

Aim High

It can't just be up to teachers to take responsibility for quality writing. Our job is to be knowledgeable enough to have taught and assessed well enough that students can evaluate their own work, see where they need to revise for clarity and interest, and use writing throughout their lives to communicate, problem solve, and savor language.

We want students to be asking, in regard to their writing:

- ☐ Did I do enough?
- ☐ Have I done my best?
- ☐ Have I met the criteria?
- ☐ Will my writing engage my reader?
- ☐ Have I communicated clearly and accurately?

This is, after all, what we do as writers when we care about our audience. We want no less for our students.

Four

Advocacy Is Also Essential

Knowing current research gives us a voice in curriculum decisions and helps us decide whether programs really work and if cited research is valid. In fact, the main purpose of research is not to direct how we teach but to allow us to be more thoughtfully deliberate in our instruction and assessment.

11. Build on Best Practice and Research

When you choose curriculum, it is a political act. When you make decisions about who will learn what and how, you are taking political action. And even if you choose not to act, your passivity is also a political action.
—Joan Wink and Dawn Wink

Effective writing is essential, not merely to the nation's economic well-being but to its future as a vibrant, informed, and humane democratic society.
—The National Commission on Writing

Advocate for Excellence

When I began doing weeklong residencies in elementary schools in the fall of 1997 I had no idea how far reaching the effects would be. I started with a one-year commitment from one school, which led to subsequent residencies in following years. Each residency centered around a schoolwide focus on reading or writing that included demonstration teaching in at least one primary-grade classroom and one intermediate-grade classroom (the same classrooms all week). Other teachers observed the lessons and talked about what they saw and thought.

Following the optimal learning model (see inside front cover), I worked with teachers the way I work with kids—starting with modeling and then moving on to shared teaching, hand-holding, coaching, and independent practice. My demonstration teaching was a catalyst for trying things out, talking about what worked (and didn't work), and having ongoing conversations about our beliefs and practices around teaching, assessing, and learning.

I expected from the start that excellent teaching of challenging, relevant curriculum would lead to great improvement in reading and writing, including high test scores, and that has been confirmed. What I never anticipated was that the whole culture of the schools would change to include shared leadership between the principal and teachers, increased confidence and competency for students and teachers, collegial teams of grade-level and across-grade-level teachers mentoring and coaching one another, instruction driven by ongoing assessment, and a celebration of teaching and learning.

This was what education should be about, I thought—whole schools working together so that all students could succeed. I began to limit the number of one-day workshops I did, recognizing that the best I could do in a day was raise questions, confirm good teaching practices, and suggest saner approaches. Meaningful change doesn't happen in a day. It takes years of hard work, deep thought, and schoolwide collaboration. It depends on knowledgeable educators and caring relationships between teachers, students, and parents throughout a whole school.

That is why formulas, programs, and recipes don't work. Every context, school, and person is different and has different needs. Literacy is not a set of acquired or learned skills. Literacy is "a social practice that varies according to the particular use to which it is put in each context." The first day of a residency is always the hardest, because I don't know the teachers and children. I can plan lessons up to a point, but I can't finalize those plans until I meet and talk with the principal, teacher, and students.

It continues to be a thrill to see schools becoming literacy institutes in which the whole staff has a thirst for teaching, learning, and doing right by kids. Developing good readers and writers is just the beginning.

Take the Lead

Raised expectations must go hand in hand with excellent teaching and advocacy. Some principals hesitate to believe that excellent teaching of writing will lead to higher test scores. Instead of providing staff development that focuses on excellent teaching, they focus on raising test scores through formulaic, step-by-step writing and "new programs." Districts, too, often send mixed messages, confounding teachers and adding confusion to their writing practices.

• Teacher advocacy is needed to bring about change. It's a fact that teachers who employ meaning-centered approaches get results and test scores that are "significantly higher" than teachers who employ more traditional, skills-based techniques. Let your colleagues know this, and take the lead in getting professional development that will help you keep your attention on effective teaching, not test-taking.

Advocate for Saner Teaching and Assessment Practices

One primary-grade teacher told me, "We're told what to do, and mostly everyone's so stressed out that we just do it. We're worn out and discouraged." But going along with practices that are not research-based or not good for students and teachers takes more energy in the long run. "Rules made by men that restrict the realization of human potential . . . should be changed."

• Teachers can't be expected to be accountable if they are told specifically what to do. Accountability requires professional autonomy to do what's right. The best teachers are "not followers" and have an "independent spirit." Based on their professional and moral knowledge and judgment, they override directives when something else will work more effectively.

TRY IT APPLY IT

- Put energy and dollars into ongoing professional development, not into programs or "one-shot deals."

- Do not adopt any program without a thorough review of the independent research that shows results for the program.

- Become involved in ongoing professional development (staff meetings devoted to sharing professional news and research, examining children's work, focusing on literacy issues; knowledgeable collegial conversations; professional conferences; professional conversations [see Appendix N]).

- Teach reading and writing together, as co-essentials. (If you are told to teach them separately, use the research cited in Chapter 6 to state your case.)

- Trust your professional common sense and your own successful teaching experiences.

- Lobby for more time and resources. Use The National Commission on Writing's recommendation to support your request: "We recommend that the nation's leaders place writing squarely in the center of the school agenda and that policymakers at the state and local levels provide the resources required to improve writing."

- Work to make faculty meetings professional growth opportunities. Offer to be on a committee to disseminate the mundane but necessary school information another way—through email, for example.

In one school district I worked with, some of the teachers were beginning to recognize that the district curriculum guidelines for writing, with stated goals such as "varies length of sentences," "understands subject and predicate," and "knows capitalization," were constraining their teaching by forcing them to teach skills in isolation. As they became more knowledgeable during our conversations and demonstrations over a few years of weeklong residencies, they set about changing the district guidelines (which some of them had been involved in writing!) to reflect their growing knowledge.

In another district, teachers were required to administer one directed writing prompt every four weeks; tedious assessment practices like this were turning kids off to writing and killing their enthusiasm. These teachers suggested other ways their district could get the needed information and at the same time provide teachers and students helpful data with which to improve instruction and learning.

Remember that "the district" is *your* district. Someone in the central office is making decisions that affect you. You can choose to get involved, *and you should,* but you have to be knowledgeable, courageous, and willing to speak up. Suggest alternatives. Instead of saying, "I don't like such-and-such and want to get rid of it," say, "In place of such-and-such, we'd like to use thus-and-so. It will give you the data and information you want and give us more useful information as teachers."

Be Knowledgeable About Relevant Research

"Research is crystal clear: Schools that do well insist that their students write every day and that teachers provide regular and timely feedback with the support of parents." Unfortunately, many teachers, principals, and superintendents, not to mention school board members, are unfamiliar with both the research on the teaching of writing and recommended practices for teaching it. In large part, this lack of knowledge comes from lack of education. Only a few states require courses in writing for certification. Then, too, the amount of research available on the subject of writing is about half the amount of what's available for reading.

Still, taking responsibility for knowing what works in writing is particularly important: researchers and educators acknowledge that most students do not and cannot write well. We also know all too well, by virtue of the politics that continues to influence the teaching of reading, that we must know the research and be able to speak intelligently and confidently about how and when to apply it in order to have credibility as teachers, do the best job with our students, and communicate effectively with parents, district administrators and officials, policymakers, and other stakeholders. We—as highly knowledgeable practitioners— must be the ones to advocate publicly for sane, sensible, excellent practices.

Good research enhances our ability to make intelligent instructional decisions. We are not taken seriously and our voices are silenced if we cannot back up our beliefs and recommendations with solid research. Knowing current research gives us a voice in curriculum decisions and helps us decide whether programs really work and if cited research is valid. In fact, the main purpose of research is not to direct how we teach but to allow us to be more thoughtfully deliberate in our instruction and assessment.

SOME KEY RESEARCH FINDINGS

The following research principles are applicable to all students K-12—to include second language learners, students with learning difficulties, and students in high-poverty schools. See References on pages A-46–A-56 for complete citations.

The Context of Writing

☐ **Write every day.**
  - Students need to write every day for varied purposes and audiences to become fluent, competent writers. (Graves 2004; Fletcher 1993; Murray 1989)

☐ **Understand social context.**
  - Literacy learning is most effective in meaningful, social contexts. (Vygotsky 1978; Holdaway 1986; Brock, Boyd, and Moore 2003; Collins 1998; Cambourne 2000)
  - Writers who enjoy writing and are motivated to write do write more. (Holdaway 1979, Guthrie 2002, Routman 2000)
  - A community of writers who share ideas and respond helpfully to one another makes it easier and more enjoyable to write. (Calkins 1994; Routman 1994, 2000a; Harwayne 2001; Wood Ray 2004)

☐ **Provide caring teachers.**
  - Students who bond with their teachers learn more easily and take more risks. (Holdaway 1979; Cambourne 2000)

☐ **Develop professional knowledge.**
  - Teachers' knowledge of and comfort with how to teach writing greatly impacts students' writing progress, competency, and writing enjoyment. Ongoing professional conversations can help teachers become more knowledgeable. (Simmons and Carroll 2003)

☐ **Encourage both teacher and parent support.**
- Parents can effectively support their children as writers; teacher guidance plays an important role. (Wink and Wink 2004)

☐ **Create predictable writing routines.**
- Predictable routines make it easier for students to write. (Atwell 1998; Routman 2000a)

☐ **Provide support through conferences.**
- One-on-one writing conferences with students can be very effective for assisting learners to improve their writing (Graves 1994; Calkins 1994; Harwayne 2001)

☐ **Keep test prep embedded in curriculum.**
- Students do best on high-stakes testing when test preparation is skillfully integrated into daily, high-level teaching of meaningful curriculum. (Langer 2000)

☐ **Emphasize writing as a process.**
- Student achievement in writing is greater when teaching approaches emphasize writing as a process rather than as a product. (Graves 1983; Hillocks 1984; Cotton 2002)
- Writers need demonstrations (teacher writing, shared writing, student writing, published authors) along with opportunities to talk about and try out various forms with sufficient time for practice, guidance, and feedback. (Graves 1994; Atwell 1998; Calkins 1994; Holdaway 1979; Routman 1994, 2000a)

☐ **Provide choice, purpose, and audience.**
- Students are more likely to become proficient writers who enjoy writing when they have some choice of topic and audience and value the writing purpose (Graves 1994; Ball and Farr 2003; Routman 2000a)

☐ **Recognize writing's role beyond the classroom.**
- The need to write effectively is a necessity to succeed in most jobs. (The Neglected "R" 2003)

Writing as a Language Process

☐ **Provide time for extensive reading and writing.**
- Students need to read and write a lot, in all genres; this need is critical for our culturally and linguistically diverse students. (Ball and Farr 2003; Allington 2001)

☐ **Value reading and writing as mutually supportive processes.**
  - The best writers are usually the best readers. (Cunningham et al. 2002; Stotsky 1983)
  - The quantity of reading students do positively impacts the quality of writing. Writing about reading increases reading comprehension. (Cunningham et al. 2002; Bond and Dykstra 1997; Duke 2000)
  - The reading/writing connection is a powerful one: more reading leads to greater writing competency. (Stotsky 1983, Amiran and Mann 1982; Sudol and Sudol 1995; Duke and Bennett-Armistead 2003)

☐ **Recognize influence of conversation and a language-rich classroom.**
  - Oral language development and opportunities for purposeful, substantive talk are closely linked to literacy skills and writing and reading abilities. (Rice 1989; Sulzby and Teale 2003; Strickland and Feeley 2003; Chall and Curtis 2003; Tharp 1997; Hudelson et al. 2003)
  - Purposeful conversations about writing improve writing. (Routman 2000a; Strickland and Feeley 2003; Peterson 2003)
  - Talk and social interaction are necessary to support learning. (Vygotsky 1978; Tompkins and Tway 2003; Cambourne 2000; Dyson and Freedman 2003; Wells and Chang-Wells 1992)
  - A language-rich environment across the curriculum positively impacts writing motivation and achievement. (Cotton 2002; Pearson and Taylor 2004)
  - English language learners and learners who struggle are most apt to succeed when they are immersed in a challenging curriculum and given lots of opportunities for scaffolded conversations and shared experiences. (Freeman and Freeman 2002, Krashen 2003; Knapp et al. 1995)

☐ **Introduce writing as a problem-solving tool.**
  - Writing is an excellent way to problem-solve and work out confusions while learning new concepts. (Murray 1989; Graves 1994; Routman 2000a)

☐ **Invite students to tap personal experiences.**
  - Writing about personal experiences can improve the writing of young writers. (Amiran and Mann 1982; Cotton 2002)

☐ **Offer opportunities for freewriting.**
  - Freewriting (uninterrupted writing for five to ten minutes) helps writers. (Elbow 1998, Murray 1989; Ponsot and Deen 1982; Rief 2002)

The Conventions of Writing

☐ **Recognize the value of authentic writing.**
  - Students invest more energy in revising and editing when they value the topic and the reader. (Graves 1994; Routman 2000a; Atwell 2002; Calkins 1994)
  - Overreliance on formula writing is counterproductive. (Wiley 2000)

☐ **Focus on content first.**
  - Writers need to focus on their message (content) before form (editing and grammar) to achieve quality and coherence. (Romano 2004; Graves 1994; Krashen 2003)

☐ **Understand the role of grammar.**
  - Formal grammar instruction does not help students write more correctly. (Hillocks and Smith 2003; Hillocks 1986)
  - Grammar instruction "which relates to students' writing can enhance writing achievement." (Cotton 2002, p. 5)

☐ **Understand spelling development.**
  - Learning to spell a word helps learning to read it. (Gentry 2004; Templeton 2003)
  - Phonemic awareness and phonics develop from trying out invented spellings in daily writing. (Allington 2001; Weaver 1996; Wilde 1991)
  - Invented spelling expands students' writing vocabulary and is appropriate for those words we wouldn't expect students to spell automatically. (Wilde 1991; Gentry 2004; Routman and Maxim 1996)
  - Having students apply what they learn about sounds and letters to their own writing is a part of effective phonics instruction. (*Put Reading First*, developed by the Center for the Improvement of Early Reading Achievement)

☐ **Integrate skills.**
  - Teaching and practicing skills in isolation does not necessarily transfer to use in daily writing. (Knapp et al. 1995; Coles 2000; Hillocks 1986)
  - Students learn more about good writing (and in more depth) when they learn at their point of need. (Knapp et al. 1995)
  - Peer editing positively impacts students' editing ability. (Cotton 2002, p. 7)
  - Students learn more when basic skills are integrated and connected to relevant and challenging curriculum. (Knapp 1995 et al.; Langer 2002; McNeil 2000)

Revisit Recent Research on Phonics

Another look at the phonics data used by the National Reading Panel found that students who were introduced to language activities in connection with direct teaching of phonics learned more. That is, the results of the studies could not exclude contributing factors from the classroom, which means that shared reading, shared writing, morning message, reading and writing conferences, reading and writing word work embedded in the literacy context, are all valid—and may in fact be as valid as or more valid than what the panel recommended.

As teachers, we've been given the message that shared writing, teaching skills in context, and the social nature of learning are not research-based. Not true. It's just that the National Reading Panel decided not to examine those factors. They're much harder to quantify for one thing. But because they weren't looked at doesn't mean we shouldn't teach them.

Build on Best Practices in Teaching Writing

Effective teachers are constantly reevaluating and rethinking their practices in light of the students in front of them, curriculum requirements, new information and research, and the daily demands of teaching. While there is no one best program or model of how to teach writing, knowledgeable teachers make decisions based on research, teaching and learning experiences, their observations of their students, and ongoing professional conversations. While there will always be differences of opinion on how to teach writing well, we cannot go wrong by using key research findings to guide our thinking, planning, and teaching practice.

Take Responsibility for Becoming an Effective Writing Teacher

I still remember the thrilling moment over twenty years ago when I was accepted into the National Writing Project's summer institute. During those five weeks of intense writing and study, I learned that I could figure out how to teach writing if I carefully examined my own reading and writing and valued my findings. No program was involved. We read, analyzed and discussed research, wrote about issues that mattered to us, responded to one another's writing, and did lots of rewriting. Each of us also did a teaching demonstration in front of the entire group.

What surprised and impressed me was how we teachers, both experienced and inexperienced, were trusted to examine and use our own writing processes to improve our writing. We were not told how to teach writing. For the first time, I knew I could become an effective writing teacher. I felt empowered to take the lead in teaching writing.

In large part, it was our daily conversations around the writing we were each required to do—reading our pieces aloud, receiving response, celebrating others' efforts, developing trust as a community of writers—that pushed our writing forward. That experience, plus my ongoing work as a writer, convinced me that conversations with peers about writing-in-progress are a necessity and that those conversations need to be unstructured—that is, writers need to be able to talk freely with one another. That conclusion is supported by research: "the more peer interaction was spontaneous and less teacher directed, the better the outcomes in the writing progress."

Adopt Practices of Highly Effective Teachers

**TRY IT
APPLY IT**

- Engage in ongoing professional conversations with colleagues about effective writing and literacy practices.
- Read books and journal articles about writing and teaching.
- Demonstrate writing by thinking aloud and writing in front of students.
- Effectively communicate with parents, administrators, and other important stakeholders.
- Share with students the writing you do outside school; ask them to do the same.
- Examine and evaluate student writing samples at your grade level and across grade levels. Use the data to improve instruction and learning.
- Raise expectations for all students and help students meet those expectations.
- Observe other teachers' writing classrooms, at your grade level and across grade levels.
- Participate in coaching experiences.
- Advise and mentor colleagues, and have them do the same for you.
- With colleagues, examine beliefs about writing and develop a shared school vision.
- Teach authentic writing; abandon isolated writing exercises.
- Conference with all students about their writing.
- Move students toward assessing their own writing.
- Take schoolwide responsibility for students' success on high-stakes tests.
- Attend professional conferences.
- Build classroom libraries.

Most of what teachers teach is a product of the professional development they receive, which unfortunately is still often overfocused on high-stakes testing, scoring, and rubrics. The less knowledge teachers have about teaching writing, the more the "testing system tends to become the knowledge base for teaching writing," and this is particularly true in high-poverty schools. Do whatever you can, individually and with your fellow teachers, to ensure that the professional development you receive is aimed at excellent teaching at deep, lasting levels.

Make Ongoing Professional Conversations a Priority

The level of professional talk in a school impacts test scores; so does the level of teacher collegiality. Several years ago I made a decision not to go back to any school for a follow-up residency if, after two years, the school had not implemented weekly voluntary professional conversations. I found that no matter how enthusiastically teachers responded to my weeklong demonstration teaching, change was only superficial. Until the teachers and principal engaged in weekly conversations about literacy and teaching, nothing much happened of lasting consequence.

In school after school it has been the increase in teacher knowledge and collegiality across grade levels that has jumpstarted change. When second-grade teacher Linda Benedict, of Huntsville, Ohio, realized there were few professional conversations taking place in her school, she volunteered to facilitate a weekly group. (See Appendix N, "Weekly Professional Conversation Guidelines," for some suggestions about how to do this.) She has been doing so now since 2000 (about 90 percent of the staff attends each week) and says:

> By coming together weekly, we have a regular opportunity to discuss topics across grade levels and brainstorm new ideas. Some of our best ideas, such as the summer reading program we now offer our students, have come from our weekly conversations. After we had been meeting for several months, our staff members noticed a definite improvement in our school climate.

Linda's principal, Diane Gillespie, adds:

> Our weekly professional conversations have kept our staff focused on creating lasting, literacy-based school change. We share ideas, value one another's opinions, and continue to reflect on our own teaching methods. We no longer look for one-day, quick-fix seminars to attend.

TRY IT APPLY IT

- Get on the road to change and enhanced expertise by rallying a group of colleagues to read and informally discuss a professional book. Try requesting funds from your district to purchase copies of the book for any teacher willing to read it and join the discussion.

- Start your own professional conversations group, even if you begin with just a few colleagues.

You Achieve What You Believe

Exploring our beliefs about teaching and learning is a prerequisite to changing our teaching practices. A major shift in beliefs about teaching writing at Burnt Bridge Creek Elementary School, in Vancouver, Washington, led to improved practices and both high-quality writing and higher test scores. The chart below and on the next page show how teachers' beliefs and practices have changed. These teachers summarize their beliefs about why their students' test scores have gone up on page 272. Their responses demonstrate "big picture" thinking, increased

FIRST GRADE	
What We Used to Do	**What We Do Now**
No modeling of writing	Model!
Writing was "filler" time	Have conversations with kids about their writing in front of the group
Kids used to copy everything from the board	Sharing and celebrating student writing
Wasn't happening every day—writing was the first thing to go if pressed for time	Authentic sharing of self in writing
	Intentional writing time
Unintentional approach; no or low expectations (spelling and handwriting)	Higher expectations for content and conventions
Emphasis on repetitive writing "I love my dog"; "I love my mom."	Introduce "Star" words earlier in year—not just alphabet letters
No voice in writing	Focus on audience for writing
No conversations about writing	Set goals for writing with kids
No celebrations of writing	

What We Are Noticing This Year That Is Different from Past Years
- Kids came in spacing words, using ^ and cross outs
- Kids reread their writing
- More confidence as writers—no one says, "I don't know what to write."
- Not copying teacher's writing
- Not just listing—writing sentences that make sense
- Using environmental print for help in spelling
- Hearing sounds in words better

New professional understandings refine and deepen practice and improve test scores

FOURTH GRADE	
What We Used to Do	**What We Do Now**
Writing projects that were huge	Smaller assignments, quickwrites, kid choice
DOL (daily oral language exercises)	Skills are developed within kids' own writing
Focus on conventions	Focus on content with good conventions
"Success in Reading and Writing" model (some 80's thing . . .)	Model, model, model writing
Stuck to writing process	Real world writing—thinking about your writing
Formula writing	Generative
Perscriptive	Recursive/generative
Teacher dependency	Learner independence
Very few conferences	Ongoing conferences and peer conferencing
Teacher editing/revision (teacher directives)	Student revision (learner focused)
No celebration of writing	Party!
Writing to a prompt	Writing to an audience (audience awareness)
Lackadaisical commitment to writing	Committed writers workshop
No sharing (It's all about me!)	Professional conversations

What We Are Noticing This Year That Is Different from Past Years

- Kids are revising their own writing and giving helpful hints to others (specific comments, questions, suggestions)
- See themselves as writers and they like to write. They show a great deal of effort and ownership
- We see fewer reluctant writers
- They know more about what good writers do and they apply it (reread, TAP [topic, audience, purpose], revise)
- Can write in different forms—getting better at it
- Risk taking—Kids aren't afraid to try new things because they are feeling confident and OK to experiment in a "writers' community"

WHY DID THE TEST SCORES GO UP?

What are we doing better?

- More modeled writing (demonstration plus shared writing).
- Focus on audience.
- Teachers more relaxed and having more fun, has led to kids feeling less WASL (state test) pressure, kids "totally relaxed."
- Higher expectations (even though more relaxed about teaching).
- Our priorities changed, now have writing workshop daily. "We stayed the course."
- Knowledge is power. (Former student tells kindergarten teacher, "You didn't do this for our class," and teacher responds, "I didn't know. . . . ")
- Stronger community in classroom and school because of more celebrating and sharing of writing. ("When you do all this sharing, kids become a voice in the community. They are no longer invisible or overlooked.")
- Stronger community in school—focus on common language, vision, and practices.
- Knowing each student much better because of writing conferences.
- Shift of responsibility to kids. "Kids see themselves as writers rather than recipients of writing instruction."
- Teacher confidence has led to student confidence.
- Streamlining process (for example, planning for writing) has freed kids to write.
- More free choice writing and more free writing, such as quickwrites.
- Writing across the curriculum—for example, easier for kids to write in math journal, "not a big deal" because kids see themselves as writers.
- Substantial professional development—"thank you Bill and Melinda Gates"—along with support of principal and assistant principal.
- Powerful staff development model—over time, ongoing.
- A feeling of "We're all in this together." (First grade teacher says, "I see myself as part of the WASL.)
- Increase in risk taking as teachers, partly from observing peers in other grade levels. Comments of intermediate grades teachers—"I was blown away by the quality of young writers" and "I heard kindergartners talking and thought, 'They know about quotations.' That immediately raised my expectations for my fifth graders."

Reflections by treachers: a whole-school shared writing

teacher knowledge, collegiality, and growing confidence and enjoyment for both students and teachers. Without strong professional knowledge, nothing changes even though it may look like change is occurring.

Increasingly, educators are taking the time as a whole district, school, or specific grade level to sit down together and make judgments about how students are doing as writers by examining students' papers. While in theory this is excellent practice, the results are only as good as teachers' writing knowledge and beliefs. For example, if teachers believe that excellent writing is all about correctness of form and structure, then their evaluation will focus on that. So will their teaching and the goals they set for students, and the writing will continue to be substandard (although they may not realize it).

High-performing schools have many common characteristics, which are listed in the chart below. Know what those characteristics are, and get professional conversations going in your school about beliefs and practices that may be

---

CHARACTERISTICS OF HIGH-PERFORMING SCHOOLS

- ☐ **Ongoing professional conversations and study groups** (includes knowing and applying relevant research, analyzing data to improve teaching and learning, and reflecting on teaching beliefs and practices).
- ☐ **Opportunities to observe exemplary teaching.**
- ☐ **Focus on the "big picture" of purposeful learning, with skills embedded in meaningful contexts** (includes explicit teaching).
- ☐ **Massive amounts of reading and writing real texts** (and little time on "stuff" and isolated test preparation).
- ☐ **Constant assessment *for* learning.**
- ☐ **Strong leadership, especially by the principal.**
- ☐ **Continuing coaching, collaboration, collegiality.**
- ☐ **High expectations for all students.**
- ☐ **Ongoing demonstrations *for* learning.**
- ☐ **Interactive, responsive teaching styles that promote thoughtful conversations.**
- ☐ **Focus on higher level questions.**
- ☐ **Schoolwide common goals.**

Regie Routman
Based on five years of observations in week-long school residencies.

inhibiting and/or contributing to high student achievement. Outstanding teachers analyze situations, know the research, rely on their heart and spirit as well as experience and professional knowledge, and make wise instructional decisions for their students. Such teachers do not discard what they know when a new mandate or program comes along. They find ways to ensure that their students are successful.

Develop a Schoolwide Vision

It takes courage and commitment to be willing to reflect on and question your beliefs about teaching and learning. If this does not happen as a staff, in a direction that is good for all children, not much will change. In my experience, lasting change does not happen in fewer than three years, and it takes a full five years of ongoing commitment to bring about deep change that impacts achievement permanently.

For Principal Melinda Jennings, of Vancouver, Washington, her most empowering professional experience in over twenty years was hearing her teachers—now more knowledgeable and willing to take risks in front of their colleagues—speak honestly at a staff meeting about being coached by me. They openly and honestly discussed how vulnerable they felt and then received supportive, nonjudgmental feedback. Melinda said:

> I expected the teaching to improve. What I did not expect was the degree of bonding that occurred among the teachers. The energy in the room was incredible. A couple of times I actually got chills from the level of dialogue and the depth of sharing that went on. By sharing themselves as writers and through public reflections about their successes and challenges, they took their professional respect and admiration for one another to a new level. It has been a transforming experience.

Three years of working, talking, and learning together made that high level of trust possible.

As a school, you will want to make decisions about such issues as quality versus quantity of writing, genres to include (one school's plan is shown on page 193) editing, spelling, publishing, and special education students. And once those decisions have been made, the beliefs and practices behind them need to be communicated to parents and caregivers effectively.

Be Cautious About Programs

We latch on to writing programs with the best of intentions. We want to teach writing well, and we don't know how. Most of us have had little training in teaching writing, and we hope that a program or kit will show us the way. Unfortunately, writing programs can't teach writing. A program, by its very nature, breaks writing into pieces, which makes writing harder and less productive for students in the long run.

Nor is there is any research supporting a skills-first approach to teaching writing or demonstrating that adopting a writing program will improve the quality of students' writing. Frankly, I'm baffled that so many educators who have been rigorous about "scientific" approaches to teaching reading adopt expensive, unproven writing programs without a second thought. Desperate for high test scores, school districts make unwise, hasty decisions. Only a highly knowledgeable teacher, not a program, can teach writing well. ⟨

Take a lesson from the highly popularized Accelerated Reader program. Although the program is widely used (and produces exaggerated claims about its success), in fact when 70 percent of the schools in Tennessee implemented AR in the 1990s, scores across the state generally declined. During the same decade when the program's use greatly increased across the country, scores on The National Assessment of Educational Progress (the "nation's report card") went up slightly for top students but fell for low-performing students. Even the National Reading Panel weighed in on AR and other "incentive" programs and found no effect on achievement.

Be very leery of any program that breaks writing up into pieces and/or that requires large amounts of your time to read, study, and administer. Spend your time instead reading personally and professionally, having professional conversations, doing more writing yourself, and noticing what you do as a writer. Recognize that breaking writing down into specific traits can be a useful assessment guide but is ineffective as the basis for a writing program.

QUESTIONS TO ASK BEFORE ADOPTING A WRITING PROGRAM

☐ What's the research base? How current is the data?

☐ Who are the authors of the research? (Make sure they're not the program developers.)

☐ Is the research relevant for your students?

☐ Is the evidence compelling?

☐ Have districts that have used this program seen increased writing competency in everyday writing? on high-stakes tests?

☐ How is writing taught with this program?

☐ Does the program develop teacher expertise for teaching writing?

☐ Is the required time and management for program implementation realistic?

Too often districts and schools adopt programs and kits and then spend huge amounts of time and money "training" teachers (in "workshops" where teachers have little input) on how to use the program. Teacher expertise on what matters for effective teaching of writing may well remain unchanged with little resulting improvement in writing. Take an active role to ensure that your school and district are focused on excellent professional development.

Do Not Rely on Formula Writing

Step-by-step, formulaic writing is very popular and seductive because it offers an immediate, detailed writing curriculum. While such an approach may initially help struggling writers, be careful not to overdo it. Formulaic writing leads to boredom; students are stifled by the rigid format. In some cases, state evaluators do reward formulaic writing, and students pass the test. However, such "recipe" writing does not transfer to everyday, authentic writing, and students get a distorted view of what effective writing entails. They also often have a hard time breaking free from the rigid structure.

In the long run, overdependence on formulaic writing inhibits teachers and students—to include struggling students. Children fail to learn how to use their own thoughts and opinions to make judgments and choices about organization, style, and content (and all the other strategies good writers use).

Expect More from Your English Language Learners

Increasingly, English language learners make up a larger percentage of our students. I have had no formal ELL training, yet I am able to teach them successfully every time. I respect and honor students' language, cultures, stories, and backgrounds and begin there—with students' strengths and knowledge. I know that whatever I teach has to make sense or there will be no understanding. Especially, I leave nothing to chance. My teaching is deliberate and intentional.

★ When we created a bilingual text in a multiage class (grades 1 through 3) (see page 118), Spanish-speaking students were the first to volunteer. Witnessing their enthusiasm and immediate success in writing and reading reaffirmed for me the daily necessity of using or creating highly relevant texts.

Make sure your instruction is meaningful, relevant, and explicit. English language learners, like all students, do best with high expectations, interesting and challenging work, an interactive teaching style, and lots of opportunities for conversation. If students are going to acquire a second language, what they hear must make sense. Second language learners can pick up conversation pretty easily. However, academic language takes at least several years to acquire. Grammar for second language learners is best learned through revising authentic writing and reading widely.

The same **basic learning principles** I use for all students apply to English language learners:

☐ **Make learning relevant** (include children's background and cultures); when children who see how an activity they are asked to do fits into the big picture of literacy and when that activity is interesting, relevant, and challenging, they achieve more.

☐ **Explain why.** (We all invest more in an activity when we understand and value its purpose.)

☐ **Provide multiple demonstrations** through think-alouds and shared experiences. (We often don't know what our questions are till we've had time to "muck around" and get into it.)

☐ **Provide much guided practice** (shared experiences, partner work, small guided groups).

☐ **Promote and guide scaffolded conversations,** and give lots of time for peer talk and collaboration. (ELLs, particularly, need to say it before they can write it.)

☐ **Provide lots of time for attempting to apply what's been taught** (guided and independent practice).

☐ **Keep the emphasis on communicating** through reading and writing, not on mastering correct literacy forms and skills. (Students will learn the skills and correct forms because they need to communicate.)

Keep Struggling Learners in Your Classroom for Language Activities

One of the questions teachers ask most frequently is *how do I work with my struggling students and the growing number of students for whom English is a second language?* Sadly, many of these students leave the classroom for "special" help (often isolated skills instruction) during rich language activities. But until they have enough rich language experiences, the skills don't make sense. They may well learn the discrete skills but are unable to transfer them to reading and writing actual texts. Therefore, it is essential that we teachers advocate strongly that *all* our students participate in read-alouds and shared language experiences. Then, too, curriculum alignment is necessary for optimal progress. Classroom teachers have little or no knowledge about what happens in special education resource rooms. It was true years ago, and it's still true.

Make Decisions About Homework

Think about developing a schoolwide policy for homework. Homework should be limited to practicing what students can already do pretty well. We place a burden on many parents when we assign writing as homework. And, in fact, what comes back to school is often more a family member's work than it is the student's. Fourth-grade teacher Kari Oosterveen never sends writing home to be "finished," but she will ask kids to write something new (once she's taught the genre), such as a poem or letter. "That way I can tell who did the work."

Teach Kids to Be Courageous As Writers

We need to teach our students that people in a democracy can use writing to express their opinions about something they feel strongly about. They can write to a newspaper, company, legislator, school board, or any person they want to influence stating what they think and why and perhaps offering suggestions. Students learn that you can't persuade someone until you have both the facts and the conviction of your beliefs. Facts come from research and experience; conviction comes from experience and what's in your heart.

Teach Persuasive Writing

Persuasive writing can take the form of a letter, editorial, essay, request, book review, or advertisement. In Katie Schmidt's fourth grade, students wrote to the State of Wisconsin Department of Public Instruction expressing their concerns about the high-stakes writing test and were taken seriously, as the thoughtful response they received (see next page) indicates. Students were amazed at the power of language and went on to write persuasive letters to people in their lives about matters they cared about. Many of their letters brought the desired results.

A persuasive piece our son Peter wrote on his own when he was twelve (see the persuasive writing lesson in the Teaching in Action section, pages 330–335) was so convincing that Frank and I, his parents, had no choice but to accept his proposition. It is, by the way, one of the few samples of his writing I still have from his childhood. At that time, there was almost no school writing worth keeping.

TRY IT APPLY IT

For Students and Teachers:

- ✍ Write letters to the editor on the limitations of canned writing programs, the value of teaching reading and writing in tandem, the collateral damage of high-stakes testing, whatever the issues are in your school and community.
- ✍ Submit commentary to local, state, and national public radio stations on literacy issues.

✏ Urge local, state, and national professional organizations to take strong positions against formulaic writing; excessive test preparation; writing as punishment; and so on.

✏ Join other teachers, parents, and students in local and state organizations that oppose high-stakes testing and support open, constructive literacy assessment. (See *www.fairtest.org* for contact information.)

Swanson Elementary School
305 N. Calhoun Road
Brookfield, WI 53045
December 18, 2002

Wisconsin Department of Public Instruction
Attn: Elizabeth Burmeister
125 S. Webster St.
P.O. Box 7841
Madison, WI 53707-7841

Dear Ms. Burmeister:

We are smart fourth graders from Swanson School, and we have a problem with the writing prompt on the WKCE.

We would like more time to do the writing prompt. We can't brainstorm, write, revise, edit, and check over our writing in only a half hour. Other states such as WA + MA give students 2-5 hours. We can't do wonderful, quality writing in just a half hour. If you were to compare the writing we do in 30 min. to the writing we do in class when we have more time, you would notice a big improvement in the quality of the writing.

So, please give future students more time to complete the writing prompt. We would appreciate it if you would write back to us. Thank you for your consideration.

Sincerely,

Concerned 4th grade students

State of Wisconsin
Department of Public Instruction

Elizabeth Burmaster
State Superintendent

Mailing Address: P.O. Box 7841, Madison, WI 53707-7841
125 South Webster Street, Madison, WI 53702
(608) 266-3390   TDD (608) 267-2427   FAX (608) 267-1052
Internet Address: www.dpi.state.wi.us

January 22, 2003

Fourth-Grade Students
Swanson Elementary School
305 North Calhoun Road
Brookfield, WI 53005

Dear Students:

Thank you for your well-written letter telling me about your experience with the writing prompt on the Wisconsin Knowledge and Concepts Examinations (WKCE). I can tell by your letter that you have done your homework by looking at how other states do the writing part of their statewide writing tests.

It is very helpful to hear from you, the students, because you have direct experience with the test. Sometimes, we adults forget what it's like to take tests and complete writing prompts.

A committee is studying ways to change the WKCE. They need good information to make their recommendations, so I am going to give each member of that committee a copy of your letter. Information from smart and concerned fourth-graders from Swanson Elementary School will give the committee members a good idea about what it takes to do quality writing using a writing prompt.

Thank you for sharing your experience with the WKCE writing prompt with me. You are not only good students, you are also good citizens because you care about quality education.

Sincerely,

Margaret Planner

Margaret Planner, Ph.D.
Assistant State Superintendent
Division for Reading and Student Achievement

MP:sjb

Fourth graders experience the power of the pen and persuasive writing!

Include Parents as Partners

Smart teaching fosters effective writing, which translates to better test scores. Be sure you keep your students' families informed about excellent writing practices and how to keep the tests in perspective. Ongoing, effective communication with caregivers is a necessity if you are going to have their support and advocacy. Some suggestions for things parents can do to help their children's literacy development are included in Appendix C.

Use High Achievement to Promote Best Practice Teaching

I'm no fan of testing, but I'm a realist. Test scores matter, and high test scores give you power. You can say you're doing a great job at your school, but if your test scores don't support you, no one will take your success seriously.

When I first began working in one particular school, test scores had been flat for years, stuck in the lower-middle range. The principal and teachers were puzzled and frustrated. They were a dedicated, excellent staff and couldn't understand why achievement wasn't showing up in the test scores.

Together we took a hard look at their teaching practices and found that while they devoted lots of time each day to reading and writing, they did little explicit modeling and didn't offer their students much choice or feedback. They also spent very little time carefully analyzing student work for clues to how they could improve instruction and learning. As a school the faculty began ongoing professional development and collegial conversations, raising their expectations for their students and themselves. They did far more intentional teaching and modeling, involved students more in the teaching-learning process, began coaching one another, and made ongoing assessment part of daily teaching. This process took three years, but by the end of that period test scores were up—way up.

The morning that test results indicated this school was the highest performing one in the district, the principal had a call from the superintendent, a first. "What exactly are you doing over there? Can you come over this afternoon and talk to me about it?" Of course she could. And did. She told him about excellent teaching and joyful teachers and kids. Those test scores gave her the power and credibility to talk with others about excellent teaching. She now had the chance to pass on what she knew and be heard, which is part of why we do this job in the first place.

Change happens one person at a time, one school at a time, but when it's lasting change (not the fake kind that comes from a teaching-to-the-test obsession), change brought about by hearts and minds working together as knowledgeable, caring colleagues, it has a very large ripple effect. When our work gains credibility in the eyes of our colleagues and the public, excellent teaching becomes the norm rather than the exception.

12. Make Every Minute Count

Writing, like life itself, is a voyage of discovery.
–Henry Miller

Am I making the best use of children's time? Everywhere, teachers are overwhelmed with how to find time to write each day, conference with each child, meet the needs of writers who struggle, challenge the "good" writers, and incorporate more reading and writing into math, science, and social studies. Most teachers understand that extensive opportunities for sustained writing are essential if all students are to become fluent and willing writers who do well in school.

If we are to find the extended time that's necessary for sustained writing, we have to be smart about how we use and manage the time we have. Typically, we feel so pressured with the limited time we do have that we may commit to instructional activities we don't truly value. We need to stop and reflect.

I want to free you up so you have time to thoughtfully consider what's most important to teach. In this way, you will become a wiser, more efficient, and successful teacher. What's more, you will reclaim the time you need to live your life more fully.

Connect Your Home and School Lives

I enter school each day full with the anticipation of joyful learning that teaching makes possible. I know as a teacher the incredible opportunity I have to impact children's lives and influence their future. First I have to reach each child's heart, and so I have to open mine. While I do leave my problems behind once I enter the classroom and focus exclusively on children and learning, I do share with my students what I can of my life—and what is appropriate to share. If I am to be an effective teacher, our hearts have to connect as well as our minds.

The students and teachers I work with know that my dad lives nearby in a nursing home, that Frank and I are with him many hours every week, that we try to enrich his life as best we can. They know I am a good cook, that in the summer I especially love to make fruit pies, tarts, and preserves, that I love picking wild blackberries, and creating my own recipes. They know that I have two granddaughters that delight me, that I have an extensive collection of books that I have carefully organized, that I love to walk, that I like to garden and love flowers, that my most favorite thing to do is go to a farmer's market, that my friends matter to me and I make time for them, that I do little email but write lots of letters. They know I love to read because I bring in the books I have recently read and am reading. They know about my life as a writer because I show them my letters about to be mailed, poems, drafts, and I talk about how and why I write. Little by little, I share my "Secrets of Good Writers" with them (see below) and we create our own chart. Mostly, they come to know I am a person with hopes, fears, joys, hardships—just like them. Connecting our hearts and minds and lives in and out of school makes teaching and learning easier and richer. We are not just teachers of curriculum. We are also life role models, striving to make our time with students count.

teaching tip

Share the Secrets of Good Writers

Let students know that writing can be hard but that there are "secrets" that good writers know. Tell them about and model some of these secrets, and post them on a classroom chart. Keep the chart posted all year; as students "discover" their own secrets, they can add them or create their own list.

SECRETS OF GOOD WRITERS

Good writers:
- ☐ Think about their writing all the time (not just while they are writing).
- ☐ Reread as they go. It helps their thinking.
- ☐ Read the piece aloud to hear how it really sounds.
- ☐ Read a lot, read quality literature, and read like a writer, noticing what authors do.
- ☐ Get their behinds in the chair every day and write.
- ☐ Often write best in a quiet, organized space.
- ☐ Stick with it even when the going gets rough.

☐ Don't always love to write but love having written.
☐ Get feedback from other writers.
☐ Write with their reader(s) in mind.
☐ Are relentless about accuracy: facts, conventions, form.
☐ Revise as they go along, not just after they have written.
☐ Know a lot about their topic, or find out what they need to know.
☐ Write to figure out what they want to say.

Look into Their Eyes

After my dad had his stroke, he lay immobile except for a few brief moments each day when he opened his eyes. I looked into those eyes and I knew he was "in there." His spirit, his soul, his wanting to live, were in those expressive brown eyes. I saw it immediately and never doubted that his mind was mostly okay. And so I treated him as such, talking to him with dignity, with encouragement, and above all with the belief that he was an intelligent person, not just a critically ill patient. I read to him from *The New York Times* every day because that was his daily habit. I used news and sports stories to talk to him about what was happening in the world, pique his interest, and stimulate his brain.

I wrote a one-page biography about him, who he was, how he had lived and worked, what he loved to do, how dear his family was to him. I gave a copy to everyone who worked with him. "Talk to my dad," I told all the caregivers. "He is a very smart man." I knew if he was to "recover," it would happen through personal connections, through nurses and aides "seeing" the intelligent person behind the disability.

When I work in schools, I look into children's and teachers' eyes seeking to find learners who love what they do and who find energy in joyful work. I notice especially the sad, tired, defeated eyes that speak of failure, exhaustion, and heartbreak. If my time in schools is going to matter, if I'm going to help learners experience hope, risk taking, success, and enjoyment, then I have to spend time meeting those eyes and giving them reasons to smile. I have to believe I can make a difference.

One way for us to bring more joy and success into our lives in and out of school is to be picky about how we spend our time. Although there are always the non-negotiables (curriculum, standards, district requirements), we do have choices about how we spend our time teaching writing and other subjects.

Conserve Your Energy

The next time you plan a project, grade a stack of papers, create a center, ask yourself, *Is this the best use of my time? Is what I'm about to do going to help my students become more joyful and accomplished readers, writers, and thinkers?* It might be that the best use of your time is to read a professional book, see a movie, visit with a friend. Sharing that experience with your students may be a more useful way to get them to think about their writing than marks and comments on a paper.

Then, too, we sometimes tire our students before they write with all the planning, modeling, talking, and setting out of requirements. Be sure that most of your writing time is devoted to writing, not preparing for writing or doing activities about writing. Safeguard sustained writing time; it's critical for becoming a writer. (For our youngest writers, that writing time may be mostly shared writing and demonstrating, until they know enough to write on their own.)

teaching tip

Save Your Energy

One or two "big" writing projects a year that proceed to publication are plenty to manage. Usually, these are free-choice projects—a personal poetry anthology, a news magazine, a fictional story, and so on. Most often in a genre, the teacher already has demonstrated and the students already have practiced, through drafting, revising, conferencing, and publishing. (If it is an unfamiliar genre, have the student first submit a written plan.)

Reduce the Paper Load

It's hard to come to school all excited about teaching if you've spent hours the night before poring over papers. I believe we do ourselves and our students a disservice if our out-of-school time is all about paperwork.

Put more responsibility on students—for organizing the classroom library, taking over most of the editing of written work, doing classroom jobs, and setting their own goals for reading and writing. Of course, you have to show them how to do these things first and support them along the way, but once they are more independent, you are freed up to think about the profession of teaching and not the labor of teaching.

Limit the Work You Take Home

In the elementary grades, I do almost all the writing work in school. Rest assured that you are not neglecting your job as an effective teacher of writing. Teachers' comments on students' papers do little to improve writing, even if the comments are positive ones. For the most part, students ignore our written corrections and suggestions. It is far more effective to conference with students and focus on specific writing issues with the student at your side.

For teachers in grades where the student load is too great to do that, limit writing comments on papers to one issue, for example, organization or spelling. We teachers tend to comment on everything, but when comments are limited, students are more likely to pay attention and make some improvement. Writing fewer comments is a big timesaver, too.

Limit take-home work for students too, and place more emphasis on free-choice reading. Having more reading experiences positively impacts growth in writing skills.

Eliminate (or Reduce) Daily Worksheets and Isolated Exercises

My experience has been that the more knowledgeable teachers become about teaching writing, the less they rely on isolated exercises. Lots of teachers assign such work at the beginning of the day or before writing time. It's not that such work is wrong or bad; the payoff isn't big enough for the time involved, and students' attitudes about writing can be negatively affected. (See Marquita's letter, page 32.) There is no research that shows that doing isolated skills work improves writing (or reading). "Those taught well enough to complete grammatical exercises without error do not therefore write either better or more accurately."

- If you feel the need for daily oral language exercises, try composing the sentences with your students rather than using a commercial program. Your own sentences—connected to students' lives and curriculum—will be far more meaningful and engaging.
- Carefully observe whether or not your students are transferring isolated skills work to contextualized writing. If not, rethink your teaching practices.
- Take note (through observations, conferences, shared writing, district guidelines, standards) what skills you need to teach, and teach them through writing aloud, shared writing, minilessons, whole-class share.
- Evaluate how much time you spend introducing discrete skills. Teachers whose students do lots of extended writing (and have high achievement) do not spend a lot of class time teaching discrete skills.

Be Choosy About What You Read

When I am working in schools that depend on basal texts and programs for reading and writing, I am respectful of those resources and show teachers how I might use those materials with children. Usually, it takes me hours to read through the publisher's notes to teachers. Writing and reading are often broken into so many pieces that I am quickly exhausted and overwhelmed by the volume of reading required to access all the teaching points and suggestions. Even for new teachers, I recommend spending more time on professional reading that increases teacher knowledge and ability to make wise curriculum decisions and less time on directive and prescriptive materials and programs.

Ask *So What?*

So, you spent hours creating a fabulous learning center, project, assignment, bulletin board, or writing report cards. (The last one is a sticky one.) Did that effort pay off in improved learning for students? I always ask *so what?* with the teaching and assessing work I do. Just because the kids enjoyed it and everyone participated doesn't mean it was a worthwhile activity. Ask yourself, *How did what we do help students become more competent, confident, and independent as literacy learners?*

IMPORTANT TIMESAVERS

- ☐ **Schedule writing every day** or at least on consecutive days (see sample writing schedules on pages 185–186). This saves time getting back to work in progress. (If you schedule writing early in the day, you're more likely to get it in.)
- ☐ **Limit the use of prompts that have no real audience** (such as, "Write a letter to the author telling him one thing you would change about the story").
- ☐ **Provide more choice of writing topics.** Students write more easily about something they're interested in.
- ☐ **Integrate test preparation.**
- ☐ **Teach basic skills in context.**
- ☐ **Teach students to revise and edit as they go;** this saves time later on.
- ☐ **Expect high-frequency words to be correctly spelled.** This saves correction time and aids speed of writing.
- ☐ **Expect legible handwriting.** This saves time for your students and for you.
- ☐ **Encourage invented spellings within reasonable, agreed-on guidelines.** This speeds up writing and encourages broader use of words.
- ☐ **Use parents** (carefully selected and trained) as final editors in the classroom.
- ☐ **Tell students why**—make writing purpose understood. Students will invest more in their writing.

MY BEST ADVICE

Here are my top ten suggestions for fitting writing into the fabric of your classroom every day and keeping it manageable and enjoyable:

1. **Keep it short** (modeling, requirements, assignments).
2. **Keep it simple** (directions, routines, assignments).
3. **Slow it down.** (Write "small"; less is more.)
4. **Start with the whole.** (Focus first on meaningful content.)
5. **Move on.** (In shared writing, accept any reasonable response and continue.)
6. **Teach it first. Label it later.** (See pages 195, 230.)
7. **Trust yourself as a writer and as a teacher of writing.**
8. **Stop when energy is high.**
9. **Use common sense.**
10. **Enjoy writing!**

Live Your Life   Finally, don't forget to breathe. With all the time you've saved, relax and enjoy writing—and your life. One way to reduce stress and have more energy for teaching and advocacy is to have a life outside of school. I worry about teachers and principals who work twelve-hour days. I have seen no research that shows that educators who work the longest hours get the best results or that longer reading and writing projects teach more about reading and writing. Keep evaluating whether what you're staying late for—or the hours of work you take home—will help your students become more effective readers and writers.

You may be better off doing fewer elaborate projects and more thinking and reading, taking more time for conversations and outings with colleagues, family, and friends.

Take time to see the light.

Write Your Own Ending

As I was writing the final chapters of this book,
I received a letter from a very happy second-grade teacher: "I have loved every minute of writing this year! The biggest change for me is making the writing meaningful for my students." She then described how her students had just finished writing and publishing "The Game Book." Earlier in the year the school principal had asked the teachers to find ways to help students follow playground rules better. This teacher had shared that request with her second graders, who suggested, on their own, writing a book about how to play some new playground games. "There's not enough to do at recess," they reasoned, "so kids get in trouble." After the book had been drafted, a fourth-grade class, supervised by the physical education teacher, played each game with students at every grade level to test whether or not the writing made sense.

This field test produced a number of suggestions to make the writing clearer. It also revealed that the school didn't have the equipment needed to play some of the games. Undaunted, the second-grade authors researched the cost of the necessary equipment, drew up a suggested budget, and wrote a persuasive letter to the principal. They explained why the new games were necessary and broke out the cost of each piece of missing equipment. (Their letter is reproduced below.) The principal, impressed with their carefully considered argument, granted their request and arranged for the equipment to be purchased.

Dear Mrs. Jennings,

Our class decided to make a playground book for our BBC friends. Some of the students at our school can't find anything to do at recess or they are complaining about students that are not following the rules of games. We thought we could create "The Game Book" to help the students while working on our writing skills. We would like to ask for some money to pay for all the equipment needed for some of the games. We need:

1 small nerf ball	$4.00
5 hula hoops	$25.00
20 small tennis balls	$4.00
2 playground balls	$8.00
8 bean bags	$11.00
1 stuffed pig	$4.00
10 cones	$6.00
2 soccer balls	$10.00
4 bases	$8.00
1 state map	$3.00
1 toy bone	$2.00
1 large container	$8.00

Total money needed: $93.00

We know this is a lot of money! We think having a game book with organized games and equipment would make our school a better place. Students would use their lifeskills of cooperation, friendship, and common sense while having a blast at recess. We would appreciate any help you can give us with this book. Thank you for all you do!

Your friends,
The Writers of 108

Second graders do the research, price playground equipment, and write such a persuasive letter to the principal that she grants their request.

When the printed book came back from the district print shop and the new equipment arrived, the school had a big celebration. Each of these second graders, every classroom in the school, the principal, and all the playground supervisors got a copy of the book. The second graders then went on to introduce "The Game Book" to the rest of the students in person. Enlisting the help of a class of fifth graders who needed an end-of-the-year service project, they created across-grade teams, coached by the principal, and the teams made presentations in every classroom on how to play each of the games safely.

These students took the initiative to use writing to accomplish a worthwhile goal, and their teacher instilled in them the skill and confidence to carry it off. Writing as thinking and problem solving has become part of who they are as learners. Their teacher marveled, "I have never been involved in a writing project that my kids were so invested in and where they actually saw the power of the pen."

I especially love telling this story because it took place in a school in which, several years before, the teachers' greatest concern in relation to student writing had been getting high test scores. For the most part, the teachers were not knowledgeable about how to teach writing well, there was no schoolwide collaboration or vision, and writing was the first activity to go when they were pressed for time. Now writing is routinely used as a way of getting things done and is central to all teaching and learning.

Yes, the school also has high test scores now, but they have so much more. They have kids who love to write and know how to write for themselves, for genuine purposes, and for valued audiences. They have a principal and teachers who work as a team to increase their knowledge and confidence as writers and teachers of writing.

✷Writing empowers us as teachers, as students, as learners. When we have the knowledge and confidence to use our own voice to ask hard questions, examine our practices, and advocate for change, amazing things can and do happen. When we are open to possibilities and committed to excellence, kids soar as writers. As one teacher said after seeing what her students were capable of writing, "I see a lot of potential I didn't see before."

Take the lead in seeing that excellent teaching of writing is at the heart of your school's culture. Go where the excitement and the promise are. They are not in programs, scripts, drills, or story starters. They are in poetry, in the stories of our lives. They are in our collaborative thinking, the celebration of our successes, the joy we discover as writers and readers. These are the essentials. Don't settle for anything less.

Five

Teaching in Action: Lesson Essentials

Five-Day Lesson Plans

Secrets of Second Graders—*Narrative Writing Lesson*

Heart Poems—*Poetry Writing Lesson*

Procedural Writing—*Informational Writing Lesson*

Hero Writing—*Lesson*

Persuasive Writing—*Lesson*

Teaching Points: Conference Video Clips

Note: View the lessons and videoclips with a wide lens—that is, while they are specific to a grade level, they easily can be adapted to other grade levels.

Secrets of **Second Graders**

Plan at a Glance

While I have modeled a five-day lesson plan here, you will want to adapt each individual lesson to the needs and interests of your students.

Day 1 60 minutes	Day 2 55 minutes	Day 3 60 minutes	Day 4 50 minutes	Day 5 60 minutes
DEMONSTRATION			**INDEPENDENT**	**PRACTICE**

• Teaching demonstration—prewriting, thinking aloud, drafting *(20 min)*
• Getting started writing *(10 min)*
• Checking by rereading an entire story aloud *(3 min)*
• Brainstorming writing ideas *(30 min)*
	• Talking out the story before writing *(8 min)*
	• Reviewing what good writers do *(2 min)*
	• Writing the stories *(30 min)*
	• Celebrating the writing *(15 min)*
		• Whole-class share—celebrating and teaching conferences *(25 min)*
		• Continuing to write *(25 min)*
		• Acknowledging writing work *(10 min)*
			• Editing *(50 min)*
			  • Shared writing *(25 min)*
			  • Demonstrating how to fix up spelling *(10 min)*
			  • Beginning to edit *(25 min)*
				• Continuing to edit *(60 min)*
				  • Beginning to publish
				  • Completing the anthology

DEPENDENCE	**HANDOVER OF RESPONSIBILITY**			**INDEPENDENCE**

Introduction

My purpose is to get kids who expressed a dislike for writing to enjoy writing. I have deliberately chosen short, "snapshot" writing to hook them. (See pages 199–200 for more "snapshot" ideas.) Our "secrets" writing is structured, yet kids have wide latitude for choice (choice within structure). These writing lessons take place when students have been in second grade for almost three months. My goal is also to get quality writing right from the start. (Lessons for days 1–3 are easily applied to journal writing and other forms of narrative writing.)

Lesson Framework

Not every action in the following list is included with every piece of writing or in a prescribed order, but every step in the optimal learning model is always incorporated. Gradually releasing responsibility to students after showing them how (demonstration, shared demonstration, guided practice, independent practice) makes it likely they will be successful.

- ☐ *Select a real audience and purpose for the writing.*
- ☐ *Read, examine, and discuss examples and characteristics of the genre or form (immersion, demonstration).*
  What do you notice? (shared demonstration).
- ☐ *Write a piece in front of students (demonstration) and/or*
  Write a piece together (shared demonstration).
- ☐ *Talk before writing (shared and guided practice).*
- ☐ *Provide sustained writing time with feedback (guided and independent practice).*
- ☐ *Conference with students (guided and independent practice).*
- ☐ *Share, celebrate, and reflect.*
- ☐ *Revisit drafts (guided and independent practice).*
- ☐ *Conference with students.*
- ☐ *Share, celebrate, and reflect.*
- ☐ *Proofread and edit.*
- ☐ *Publish.*

Think of this framework as a self-perpetuating loop of ongoing writing, demonstration, teaching, sharing, celebrating, and setting new goals—not as a linear model. With short pieces of writing, you can go from inception to publication in one week.

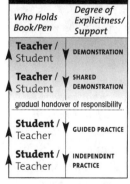

Day 1	
Who Holds Book/Pen	*Degree of Explicitness/ Support*
Teacher / Student	DEMONSTRATION
Teacher / Student	SHARED DEMONSTRATION
gradual handover of responsibility	
Student / Teacher	GUIDED PRACTICE
Student / Teacher	INDEPENDENT PRACTICE

Lesson Plan Summary

Day 1 (60 minutes)

▶ **TEACHING DEMONSTRATION—PREWRITING, THINKING ALOUD, DRAFTING** (20 minutes)

My planning includes thinking ahead the night before and jotting on a sticky note (to jog my memory) three possible story ideas from when I was about the same age as the students: hiding under the bed, reading under the covers with a flashlight, and eating stuffed celery. I have deliberately chosen a secret to share that is a mischievous, "naughty" story, not a dreadful one or one so private it shouldn't be told. The students are gathered on the floor in front of me and I compose on an easel holding large, lined paper.

I briefly tell each of my three stories to see which one they react most to and, mostly, to help me decide which one I want to write about. While sometimes I ask kids to choose which story they want me to write in detail, usually I make that decision.

> **Teacher Talk**
>
> **Creating purpose and audience** *Mrs. Kostecki* [their teacher] *and I talked for a long time yesterday and came up with something I think you're going to love, "Secrets of Second Graders," fun secrets about you that nobody else knows. It has to be a secret that you don't mind other people knowing. This is going to be great. We'll turn our stories into a book, and each one of you will have a page. Everyone in our class will get a copy, Mrs. Jerde* [the principal] *will get one. Visitors to the classroom can read it. Your parents will read it. We can also make copies for the other second grades, and, perhaps, the first grades.*

Choosing my topic and giving students writing ideas (5 minutes) *I haven't decided yet what I will write about. Here are three secrets about me. After I tell them to you, I'll decide which one to write about. While I'm talking, listen carefully and see if you get any ideas for your own writing.*

1. *My mom used to make this wonderful stuffed celery for dinner parties, and I would sneak it from the refrigerator when she wasn't looking. . . .*

2. *My sisters and I would "outsmart" an elderly babysitter by hiding under her bed and watching television while she watched, and she never knew we were there. . . .*

3. *I used to read comic books under the covers with a flashlight when it was way past my bedtime, listen for my mom's footsteps and pretend to be asleep when she checked on me. . . .*

You know what, after telling a little about each story, I think I want to write the stuffed celery story. I'd forgotten how many times I sneaked that celery over many years of my childhood (see completed draft, page 73).

▶ **GETTING STARTED WRITING** (10 minutes)
Okay, let me think about how I want to start. The reason I'm going to be writing in front of you is that writers do not always have all their ideas in their head before they start. One of the secrets of good writers is that they are thinking before they write, as they write, and after they write. I want you to see what I do as a writer so when you write you'll have lots of ideas and know just what to do.

Sometimes when I'm writing, I put my title down right away. This time I'm going to leave a blank for my title and add it later. I don't know what my title is yet.

My first sentence has to be interesting 'cause I'm not writing just for myself. I'm writing for Mrs. Jerde, you, parents, other students. Hmm. How can I start? My mom used to have big dinner parties. [I say words as I write them, and then I reread.]

Adding a new beginning *You know what, that sounds pretty boring* [I cross out first line]. *Let's see. I want to get my readers interested.* [I say words aloud as I write them]: *"Wait until you hear about what I did when I was little. My mom was a great cook and we were always having dinner parties. One of the hors d'ouvres she often made was stuffed celery. Here's what she did. She would mix cream cheese with olives, pimentos, and seasoning."*

Explaining writing process *The reason I need to skip lines as I write, kids, is I need space to add things like when I change things and cross out. I'm just worrying about my ideas now. I'll deal with spelling later.* [I deliberately comment on spelling because several students expressed worry about spelling in connection with writing.]

Rereading before continuing *You always have to read your story again. Watch what I'm doing. I'm changing my story as I go along to make it more interesting. Rereading helps my thinking and helps me know what I want to say.* [I make changes so it makes sense and sounds better. See draft on page 73 for specific changes—includes grammar, adding and changing words for clarity and interest. Note I do not name what I'm doing; I just do it. I keep my focus on telling the story.] [Continuing to say words aloud as I write them]: *"She would pipe the mixture through a pastry bag so that the* [I cross out last three words] *into the ridges of the several celery stalks. Then she would cut each stalk into small pieces and arrange them on a beautiful plate. When she wasn't looking I opened the refrigerator, lifted the aluminum foil, and sneaked three or four celery pieces. They tasted fabulous."* [Checking to be sure story makes sense before I go on]: *I have to read it again to make sure it makes sense.*

[Again, as I reread I make small changes—cross out and add words for a clearer picture, without naming what I'm doing, which would slow down the storytelling and take attention away from the story. See draft for changes I make.]

I think I want to end this now. Let me see. "I don't know why I loved that stuffed celery so much but I did. My mom never found out that pieces were missing." [I say the sentences out loud and then write them.] *That sounds like an okay ending for my story.*

Adding a title *Something's missing. I left something out. I think I'm just gonna call this "Stealing Celery."* [I write it on draft.] *"Stealing Stuffed Celery" sounds better.* [I add "stuffed"]. *I don't know if I'm going to stick with this title.*

▶ **CHECKING BY REREADING ENTIRE STORY ALOUD** (3 minutes)

I need to read this again and see if I want to change anything. I want my story interesting and clear for my readers. [I reread and revise. See draft for changes.] *I'm going to stop here 'cause I'm pretty happy with it. I might read it over one more time.*

▶ **BRAINSTORMING WRITING IDEAS WITH STUDENTS** (30 minutes)

Scaffolded (public) conversations (10 minutes) Every student has a story to tell, and it's our job to help them "find" their story. I converse with two students in depth. Students listen in, which gives them ideas for their own writing and a model for conversing with peers. (See page 77 for more on scaffolded conversations.)

Modeling a conversation with a strong writer *Okay, who has an idea you could write about?* [Madison raises her hand, and I call on her. Notice how my demonstration writing influences Madison's story.]

> *What's your story about?*
>
> Sneaking food.
>
> *Tell us what happened. Use words that put us right there with you. Kids, listen carefully because you may get good ideas for your own story.* [Stating purpose for why it's important to listen to peers.]
>
> One night when my mom wasn't looking and my dad was on the computer, I went to the refrigerator and opened it.
>
> [I immediately write her opening on a sticky note so it's not "lost" and can be retrieved, if she chooses to do so, when she writes. I write just enough to jog her memory: "One night when my mom wasn't looking and my dad was on the computer. . ."] *Listen to her beginning, kids. It sounds like a story already.*
>
> I saw chocolate.
>
> *What kind of chocolate was it? What did it look like?* [Encouraging description.]
>
> It was a medium-sized bar with Hershey's on it.
>
> [I write her words on a sticky note.] *Now, I can picture that chocolate. Why did you have to sneak it?* [Because I don't know and am curious.]
>
> I heard Mom coming down the steps. . .
>
> [I capture her words on a sticky note as I respond at the same time.] *Sounds like an adventure. Then what happened?*
>
> Mom came in and said, "Whatcha doing?"
>
> *I love that "Whatcha doing?"* [I write "Whatcha doing?" on a sticky note.] *What did you say?*
>
> "Watching TV."
>
> *Did she believe you?*
>
> She said, "Okay," and left.
>
> *Let's clap for Madison. She's got a great story.*

I publicly review with Madison and the whole class what I wrote on the sticky notes so we can hear and remember the language. I also explain that the three dots ". . ." on a sticky note mean "there are more words coming," that I don't need to write everything Madison said, just enough to jog her memory. I also show on chart paper how to include conversation in stories, as Madison did.

Kids, writers often use conversation—what people say—to make their stories come alive. Think about doing that in your story, like this. . . . Madison, the sticky notes are for you. Keep them because we save everything so we have a record of all parts of your thinking and writing. (For Madison's completed draft, see page 302.)

Modeling another conversation with a reluctant, struggling writer *How many of you got ideas from Madison's story?* [Lots of hands go up.] *That's why it's so important to listen. Who else would like to tell their story? Who has a good idea?* [Owen has his hand up, and I call on him.] *Tell us your story Owen. How do you want to start? Start it so it sounds like a story* [see page 22 for more about Owen].

Once when I was five I was watching TV.

Owen, that's a great beginning, sounds like the start of a good story. [I write his words on a sticky note as I am talking to him.] *Keep going. What happened?*

I heard Mom in the kitchen. [I write the words on a sticky note.]

Okay, back up. Take us to where you were so we can picture it. "Once when I was five I was watching TV." [Repeating his opening line.] *Where were you? What time of day was it?* [Encouraging more detail because I want to know the whole story.]

One night when I was five I was watching TV in bed with the lights off. It was past my bedtime.

Owen, that sounds great. I love the words you added. It sounds like a story. You said before, "I heard Mom in the kitchen." How did you know she was there?

I heard her footsteps. [I write words on sticky notes as he says them.]

What happened then?

I jumped out of bed and turned the TV off.

What else happened? [Encouraging him to tell the full story.]

She was checking on me. I pretended to be asleep. [I put words on a sticky note.]

Deciding how to guide Owen I reread from the sticky notes and number them in order. I am worried that this may be too much for Owen to write as he has complained writing gives him a "handache." He is also the writer who struggles the most.

Owen, if this is too much to write you can keep it short 'cause I don't want you to get a handache.

I can do five. [Referring to the number of sticky notes I've written.] See, if my hand gets tired, I'll just pull it in under my sleeve, like this [giving us a demonstration], give it a rest, and keep on writing. [Owen is clearly enjoying his storytelling and the attention he is getting.]

teaching tip

Don't Overdo Sticky Notes

They're not necessary for a student who has the story in her head. Then, I only use them to jot down language I want to encourage and remind the student to use, which is what I did with Madison.

Talking out their stories before writing.

Okay, that's great, Owen. The sticky notes are to help you remember all the smart things you said. I'm numbering them so you'll know what order to go in. Use them to help jog your memory and get ideas when you go to write.

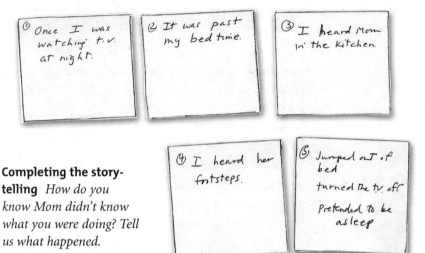

① Once I was watching t.v. at night.

② It was past my bed time.

③ I heard Mom in the kitchen.

④ I heard her fntsteps.

⑤ Jumped out of bed
turned the tv. off
Pretended to be asleep

Completing the story-telling *How do you know Mom didn't know what you were doing? Tell us what happened.*

She said, "Owen, were you watching TV?" I kept pretending to be asleep. [Class laughs.]

Kids, you laughed, and we call that humor. Owen, how will you end it? How will we know your story is over? After you write your story, reread it a few times, and think about how you can end it for your readers. [I am reluctant to write any more on sticky notes and also want to see what Owen can do on his own.]

How many of you got some ideas for your story by listening to Owen? [Affirming the importance of good listening.] *Good, that's why it's so important to listen to each other.*

Kids, your homework tonight is to think about your story and come in ready to write. Good writers think before they write. If you're not sure about what you're going to write, you may want to talk with someone in your family or your friend at lunch or on the bus. [Even though we have done no writing today, all this front-loading (pages 220–221) will pay off.]

▶ STRATEGIES TAUGHT ON DAY 1

The "Secrets of Second Graders" took place during a weeklong residency in which teachers at the grade level and adjacent grade levels observed. Before and after each lesson, teachers met and talked about what they noticed, what they were trying out in their own classrooms, questions they had, and so on. After day 1, we generated the following chart of what we had already taught—"efficiency of context" (pages 149, 152–154)—through teacher demonstration and conversations with two students.

Principal Marilyn Jerdy observing and supporting Owen.

Owen referring to his sticky notes as he writes.

Writers:

- ☐ **Write for readers.**
- ☐ **Change their mind.**
- ☐ **Talk and think about their writing before they write.** (Sometimes this talk is in their head.)
- ☐ **Revise while writing.** (Is the writing clear to the reader?)
- ☐ **Reread for different purposes.**
- ☐ **Think about their beginning and ending.**
- ☐ **Change some of their words.**
- ☐ **Don't overfocus on spelling when writing a draft.** (Save major spelling checks for final draft.)
- ☐ **Use transitions** (without labeling that word, such as, "This is what she did" and, "Here's what happened").
- ☐ **Write with detail.**
- ☐ **Put themselves in the story** (voice).
- ☐ **Use interesting words.**
- ☐ **Craft a title that captures the story.**
- ☐ **Make sure their writing makes sense.**
- ☐ **Use humor as appropriate.**
- ☐ **Get ideas by listening to other writers.**

Many additional writing strategies are taught through whole-class share (public conferencing) for both content and conventions. See DVD and accompanying notes and pages 207–215.

Day 2 (55 minutes)

▶ **TALKING OUT THE STORY BEFORE WRITING** (8 minutes)

Talking before writing ensures greater writing success for all learners and is essential for our English language learners. I say to students, *Talking about your story will help you write a better story. That's why we're doing this. Turn to your partner [the person next to you] and tell your partner your story. Then listen to your partner's story, and make sure it makes sense. If something is confusing, ask questions—just like you saw me do.* (See page 77 and the photo on page 298.)

Day 2	
Who Holds Book/Pen	*Degree of Explicitness/ Support*
Teacher / Student	▼ DEMONSTRATION
Teacher / Student	▼ SHARED DEMONSTRATION
gradual handover of responsibility	
Student / Teacher	▼ GUIDED PRACTICE
Student / Teacher	▼ INDEPENDENT PRACTICE

While students talk out their stories, their teacher and I circulate from table to table. We help students get their ideas out, guide their thinking, and ask questions to spur their thinking.

▶ REVIEWING WHAT GOOD WRITERS DO (2 minutes)

Before we begin writing, I reinforce what I demonstrated yesterday when I wrote my draft.

Kids, as you write today, think about what good writers do and some of the things I did to make my writing more interesting for the reader. Yesterday, you saw me:

- ☐ *Reread constantly to help my thinking and make sure it makes sense.*
- ☐ *Cross out boring words.*
- ☐ *Cross out my beginning and write a better one.*
- ☐ *Add words to make it sound better and make more sense.*
- ☐ *Cross out things that didn't work.*
- ☐ *Skip lines so I have room to add in.*
- ☐ *Check that my ending wraps things up.*

Most of all, have fun writing your story. Have a good time with it. Think about making it clear and interesting for your readers.

I do not establish any criteria for writing. My number one goal is for students to enjoy telling their "secrets" story and to have fun and success as writers.

▶ WRITING THE STORIES (30 minutes)

While the class gets started writing, I meet in a small group with those students still having difficulty "finding" their story. During partner sharing, I jotted down the names of those few students who were having trouble getting their story out. It takes just a few more scaffolded conversations to get everyone ready to write.

As students write, classroom teacher Cami Kostecki and I have brief roving conferences with students. Occasionally, we interrupt the writing and celebrate:

You have to hear Keely's beginning. Keely, would you stand up and read it?

Dimitri, read your first line. Listen to how he's used conversation.

Owen gets right to work, writes without interruption for thirty minutes, and completes his draft without further assistance. See evidence of rereading where he has used a caret and added information and also crossed out a word. Notice that Owen does not simply copy from the sticky notes but uses them as a scaffold for ideas and then freely elaborates at the end. (See his draft on page 22.) This is the most writing he has ever done.

Signaling the end of writing time *Kids, you have about three more minutes before we begin our whole-class share and celebration of what you've done. Reread,* *make the changes you want, finish up the sentence you're writing.*

Letting kids know writing time for the day is about over encourages them to:

- ☐ **Reread for clarity.**
- ☐ **Pull their last thoughts together.**
- ☐ **Prepare to share.** (Practicing reading the text before sharing saves time, as students are less likely to stumble over their words.)

▶ **CELEBRATING THE WRITING** (15 minutes)

I want kids to feel great about themselves as writers so they want to go on writing. Observing teachers comment that students are "exhilarated rather than exhausted."

Reinforcing what helped produce "good" writing *Raise your hand if you're proud of your writing.* [Just about every hand goes up.] *Why do you think your writing was so good?*

Owen: I used my own ideas, not just on the sticky notes.

Madison: It was silent.

Good for you, Madison. You discovered one of the secrets of a good writer. Yes, having it absolutely quiet—some call it "sacred" writing time—helps a lot.

Rue: You inspired me.

How did I do that?

Rue: When I usually start to write, I think my story will be boring. But I saw how you did your story, all your talking and thinking, and that helped me.

What else helped?

Ervin: Talking with my partner and saying my story out loud.

Justin: Listening to Madison and Owen.

Eric: All the secrets we did, nobody ever knew.

▶ **CONDUCTING PUBLIC CONFERENCES**

Affirming, celebrating, and teaching the writers Students bring their papers to whole-class share (a public conference) and are invited to read their stories. Everyone is excited and wants to share. I begin with Madison. In fifteen minutes we have seven conferences with the emphasis on celebration.

Madison's personal "secrets" story, grade 2 I want to see if Madison has written the complete story we talked about (and that all students listened to her tell). She has, and her writing is engaging, well organized, and mostly complete. (See her draft on the following page.)

I find teachers are often surprised to hear me tell a student in a conference, "Great job. Your writing is fine as it is." We don't always have to find things for a student to work on. Of course, writing can always be improved, but deciding

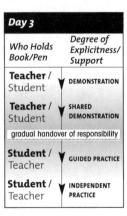

Notice how Madison reconsiders her ending in her draft. See DVD for final copy.

that a piece is "good enough" is important, because we want students to continue writing—and to do so with motivation and enjoyment. Not only that, much time is saved that can be spent with another student who truly needs specific help.

In this one-and-a-half-minute conference, I celebrate Madison's efforts and help her with one confusing sentence. The following teaching points are made:

- ☐ **Affirming first sentence** ("You have a great beginning.")
- ☐ **Celebrating completeness of story** ("You've told your story carefully.")
- ☐ **Celebrating ending** ("I love your ending!")
- ☐ **Noting use of exclamation mark** ("Look at her mark here," pointing to exclamation mark in ending line, "I love chocolate!")
- ☐ **Clarifying for the reader** ("Where did the pillow come from?... You need to make that clearer for the reader.")
- ☐ **Directing the writer** ("I have one tiny suggestion.... You might want to put that in.")
- ☐ **Expressing confidence that the writer can make the minor revision on her own** ("I think you'll be able to do that yourself.")
- ☐ **Modeling for all students what a complete, sequenced, detailed story sounds like.** (Reading entire story all the way through and applauding writer.)

See DVD and accompanying notes for conference with Derek (photo, page 344), a writer who needs support to tell and sequence his story.

Day 3 (60 minutes)

▶ WHOLE-CLASS SHARE—CELEBRATION AND TEACHING CONFERENCES
(25 minutes)

At the end of day 2, I took all the drafts back to my hotel and read them in order to help move everyone's writing forward. I made brief notes to myself on sticky notes and placed them on top of each paper I wanted to comment on. I wanted to be sure that when students resumed writing, everyone would be prepared to write independently.

We're going to be celebrating everyone's writing. You're going to learn from all the writing and get ideas from each other for your own writing. Usually, I like you to read your own stories, like we did yesterday, but to save time so we can hear all

Day 3	
Who Holds Book/Pen	Degree of Explicitness/ Support
Teacher / Student	DEMONSTRATION
Teacher / Student	SHARED DEMONSTRATION
gradual handover of responsibility	
Student / Teacher	GUIDED PRACTICE
Student / Teacher	INDEPENDENT PRACTICE

of the stories, I'm going to read them. I'm going to tell you all the things I love about your writing and make a few suggestions, too. Remember to listen, because that is how you can get some good ideas for your own writing.

See DVD and accompanying notes for conference with Ervin, who needed support to tell his story.

In twenty-five minutes, I read, celebrate, and comment on fifteen papers. I tell several students who need a lot of help that I will also have a one-on-one conference with them.

▶ **CONTINUING TO WRITE** (25 minutes)

Students continue writing, revising, and finishing up their drafts. During that time, Cami Kostecki and I conduct roving and one-on-one conferences. See DVD and notes for an excerpt from my ten-minute one-on-one conference with AlexSandra (see pags 345–346), who needed much scaffolding to have her story make sense.

Principal Marilyn Jerde noted: "I ran into Owen on his way to lunch today and he told me he finished his story and he can't wait to get started on the next one. He was so proud!"

▶ **ACKNOWLEDGING WRITING WORK** (10 minutes)

How many of you changed your writing or tried something new because you got ideas from other writers? [Many hands go up.] *Turn to your partner, read your story, and tell your partner what you did. Check to be sure your story sounds like it's ended and that it has an ending that works well for the reader.*

Day 4 (50 minutes)

▶ **EDITING**

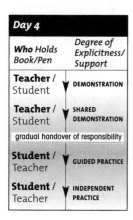

Day 4	
Who Holds Book/Pen	Degree of Explicitness/ Support
Teacher / Student	▼ DEMONSTRATION
Teacher / Student	▼ SHARED DEMONSTRATION
gradual handover of responsibility	
Student / Teacher	▼ GUIDED PRACTICE
Student / Teacher	▼ INDEPENDENT PRACTICE

Shared writing (20 minutes) *Today we're going to work on editing—capitals, periods, spelling—so the reader can read easily all the great things you write about. We're going to decide together what you can fix up and find on your own.*

On a large chart, we do a shared writing of editing expectations. Eventually this draft is revised and everyone, including parents, gets a copy. (See page 204 and Appendices J and K for samples of editing expectations.)

Demonstrating how to fix up spelling (10 minutes) Because fixing up spelling is such a big part of editing, with a student's permission, I use a projected transparency of his draft to guide him through fixing up misspelled words. See video clip and accompanying notes of teaching Derek how to edit for spelling.

Beginning to edit (20 minutes) Using a colored pencil, students begin editing.

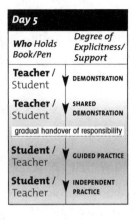

Day 5	
Who *Holds Book/Pen*	*Degree of Explicitness/ Support*
Teacher / Student	▼ DEMONSTRATION
Teacher / Student	▼ SHARED DEMONSTRATION
gradual handover of responsibility	
Student / Teacher	▼ GUIDED PRACTICE
Student / Teacher	▼ INDEPENDENT PRACTICE

Day 5 (60 minutes)

▶ **CONTINUING TO EDIT**

Kids, it's your responsibility to do most of the editing work. You are only ready for an editing conference with me when you've done everything you can on your own.

Students are reminded to:

☐ **Refer to editing chart.**

☐ **Edit for spelling, punctuation, capitalization.**

☐ **Reread at least five times.**

☐ **Do your best.**

☐ **Have an editing conference.**

☐ **Get the rest "for free" once you've done your best.**

Students are expected to do all the editing work we have agreed on (see a similar shared writing expectations chart on page 204). Once they have done that, and we verify it during an editing conference, their teacher or I will fix up the rest "for free" at that same editing conference. (See pages 230–234 and 346–349 for information on editing and editing conferences.)

Because this is the first time students are assuming responsibility for editing, we are not including peer editing. I want to see what they can do on their own and what I need to teach and demonstrate.

Students who are done early begin a new secrets story or free-choice writing.

Begin publishing The class decides they want the stories word-processed. Cami enlists a school volunteer to type them, after showing the volunteer a model of how they are to be done. However, she says, "Later in the year, on other writing projects, I had the students publish their final copies in their own handwriting. I didn't want them to think someone would always type their final copies for them."

Completing the anthology Instead of illustrating their stories, the class decides to take pictures and put their photos on the page with their story. Cami uses a school digital camera and adds each student's photo to his/her story page. She has the classroom book printed in color and bound with a cover that is made by a student. (See DVD for sample pages.)

Each student receives an individual black-and-white copy, as does the principal and other classes. The class receives "many great comments" from other students and teachers and especially from parents. Other classes at various grade levels are motivated to write similar "secrets" stories.

Heart **Poems**

Plan at a Glance

While I have modeled a five-day lesson plan here, you will want to adapt each individual lesson to the needs and interests of your students.

Day 1 60 minutes	Day 2 50 minutes	Day 3 50 minutes	Day 4 60 minutes	Day 5 60 minutes
DEMONSTRATION			INDEPENDENT PRACTICE	
• Sharing poems by others *(10 min)* • Teaching demonstration *(8 min)* • Talking before writing *(5 min)* • Writing the first poems *(20 min)* • Acknowledging efforts *(2 min)* • Celebrating— whole-class share *(15 min)*	• Continuing to celebrate, teach, and write poems • *Affirming the power of sharing (2 min)*	• Writing poems	• Selecting a favorite poem • Editing poems • Creating a rubric *(20 min)*	• Publishing a poetry anthology • Writing about the author *(50 min)*
DEPENDENCE		HANDOVER OF RESPONSIBILITY		INDEPENDENCE

Introduction

Free verse is the easiest and best way I know to turn all kids into successful, joyful writers. The unstructured form of free verse (nonrhyming poetry), with its accompanying possibilities for using phrases and words instead of full sentences, seems to make writing easier for kids than more traditional forms. Additionally, kids love the choices poetry encourages for the shape, length, sound, and look of the poem on the page. Strict rules that apply to other genres can be relaxed with poetry.

While poems can be about anything—family, friends, sports, small objects, nonfiction interests—I have found that when we write about what's deep in our hearts and what really matters to us—what students have named "heart poems"—student engagement and the quality of writing are high.

teaching tip

Get Ready to Write Poetry

Read lots of free verse aloud (see "Some Favorite Poetry Books," in Appendix M), notice what poets do, examine poetry anthologies, establish a poetry corner. Share lots of kids' poems before students write and throughout the poetry writing lesson.

These lessons take place in a grade 4 class three months into the school year. Students have already done some poetry writing, but many are not enthusiastic about it. What seems to make them passionate the second time around is:

- ☐ **Teacher modeling "heart" poems.**
- ☐ **Sharing many "heart" poems by other students.**
- ☐ **Conversations before writing.**
- ☐ **Celebrating students' efforts.**
- ☐ **Publishing an anthology.**

Lesson Framework

Not every action listed below is included with every piece of writing or in a prescribed order, but every step in the optimal learning model is always incorporated. Gradually releasing responsibility to students after showing them how (demonstration, shared demonstration, guided practice, independent practice) makes it likely they will be successful.

- ☐ *Select a real audience and purpose for the writing.*
- ☐ *Read, examine, and discuss examples and characteristics of the genre or form (immersion, demonstration).*
  What do you notice? (shared demonstration).
- ☐ *Write a piece in front of students (demonstration) and/or*
  Write a piece together (shared demonstration).
- ☐ *Talk before writing (shared and guided practice).*
- ☐ *Provide sustained writing time with feedback (guided and independent practice).*
- ☐ *Conference with students (guided and independent practice).*
- ☐ *Share, celebrate, and reflect.*
- ☐ *Revisit drafts (guided and independent practice).*
- ☐ *Conference with students.*
- ☐ *Share, celebrate, and reflect.*
- ☐ *Proofread and edit.*
- ☐ *Publish.*

Framework Summary

- ☐ *Demonstrations (5–15 minutes) includes one or more of the following:*
  - ☐ Sharing poems by others, such as discussing kids' poems—includes minilessons woven in on aspects/elements of poetry.

☐   Teacher thinking aloud and writing a poem.

☐   Scaffolded conversations before writing.

☐   ***Sustained writing time and conferencing*** *(20–30 minutes)*

☐   ***Sharing and celebrating*** *(10–15 minutes)*

Think of this framework as a self-perpetuating loop of ongoing writing, demonstrating, teaching, sharing, celebrating, and setting new goals—not as a linear model. With short pieces of writing, you can go from inception to publication in one week.

Day 1	
Who Holds Book/Pen	*Degree of Explicitness/ Support*
Teacher / Student	DEMONSTRATION
Teacher / Student	SHARED DEMONSTRATION
gradual handover of responsibility	
Student / Teacher	GUIDED PRACTICE
Student / Teacher	INDEPENDENT PRACTICE

Lesson Plan Summary
Day 1 (60 minutes)

Teacher Talk

We're going to be writing poems this week because poetry writing is one of the best ways I know to have fun with writing and say things that are important, playful, serious, or on your mind. Afterward, we'll put together an anthology, a collection of our favorite poems for other readers—ourselves, our teacher, all the teachers in the school, other classrooms, our parents. [Establishing purpose and audience.]

The poems we'll be writing are free-verse poems, poems that don't rhyme but still have rhythm and a beat. Rhyming poems that make sense are hard to write, unless you're someone like Shel Silverstein or Doug Florian.

▶ **SHARING POEMS BY OTHERS** (10 minutes)

I want you to really put yourself in your poems. Let me show you a poem I wrote in another class about how I felt being overweight when I was your age. [Read and show "Being Fat!"] *We all have things that are hard for us, and that was really hard for me. Listen to my poem. Look at how I set it up on the page.* [I show the poem.] *Notice, kids, how I tell exactly how I felt. Look at the end. See how I changed my mind about the way I wanted my poem to sound. I just lassoed my words and moved them where I wanted them. It sounds better like this. Listen, I'll read it again.*

Noticing a student's first effort *Now, let's take a look at some poems by other kids just like you. See what you notice. Here's Bradley's first attempt at writing a poem. He's a fourth grader in another school.* [Read Bradley's

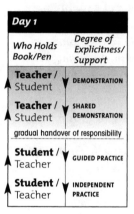

Being Fat!

When I was nine
I weighed a lot.
Kids called me
"Fat face"
"Blubber"
"Big one."
I felt horrible.
My mom said,
"Ignore those names"
But I couldn't.
In my mind
I heard them

over and over again.
Today
All grown up
I'm just right
But
I still remember
Being fat.

Bradley narrows his broad topic (page 1), and carefully considers word choice, line breaks, white space, and more (page 2).

> ① Hi! My name is Bradley and I love science! Well I like learning about water and magnetism stuff. I also like math, like hard equations but I especially like frogs. and parakeets. I can also make you laugh when you feel sad. Also I'm really smart at math and science. When I Frist got my glasses I felt shy, I've been wearing glasses since I was 2 years old because I'm lazy eye. Well thats how I can tell about myself.

> ② Wearing Glasses
> Hi!
> My name is Bradley.
> And I was 2 when I had to wear
> glasses.
> When I frist got my
> glasses.
> I felt very shy.
> Because I know people will call me
> four eyes
> bug face
> spider boy
> My mom said
> "Ignore those names"
> But deep down in my heart I still
> Now that I'm older I stand up for
> those mean
> bullys
> that call me names.
> I say.
> "leave me alone"
> and I walk away.
> Now I also have friends that
> stick up for
> me
> when I need it.

poem aloud, and show his draft.] *Notice how he wrote about lots of things and that his poem looks like a journal entry. Here's how I showed him to make choices in having it look and sound like a poem.*

I said to him, "Bradley, do you want it to look and sound like this:" [I write on a projected transparency and read aloud]:

> "Hi! my name is Bradley"

or

> "Hi!
> My name is Bradley."

[I do a few more demonstrations of the choices I gave Bradley and tell the class]: *When you're deciding how you want your poem to look on a page you need to say it out loud to yourself and decide where you want your line breaks to be. One of the fun things about writing poetry is you get to decide how the poem looks and sounds.*

Getting to the heart of the matter *Now take a look at Bradley's poem "Wearing Glasses." His first poem was about everything. Here he chooses what's closest to his heart and just writes about that.* [I read aloud his poem twice and show his draft of "Wearing Glasses."] *What do you notice?*

Maelina: He narrowed it down to one thing.

Alex: He told a lot about wearing glasses.

What makes it a heart poem?

Paige: He told his feelings.

Jessi: He wrote about something that really mattered to him.

[If these responses had not been forthcoming, I would have said, "Here's what I noticed. . . ."]

What did he do that makes it a good poem?

Aaron: He's got line breaks.

What else did he do that shows he's fooling around with how his poem looks, how it sounds?

Katie: He told us exactly what he's worried about.

Megan: He tells us the names people call him like "four eyes" and "bug face"; he doesn't just say, "People call me names."

He has conversation in here, too. That helps his poem in the same way. He's very specific. He also has thought about ending his poem so his reader feels a sense of closure.

Listen to this poem by Catherine. [See Catherine's poem, "Middle."] *It was inspired by a poem her teacher wrote about being a middle child.* [I read the poem twice and show how it looks on the page.] *What did you notice?* [We notice that she has thought about her white space (blank space around the words) and line breaks and that she changes the rhythm of the poem in her last two lines.] *What makes it a heart poem?* [She really tells us what's in her heart.]

▶ TEACHING DEMONSTRATION—THINKING ALOUD, WRITING

Choosing my topic (3 minutes)   If I want students and teachers to be risk takers and write from their hearts, I have to model that. I write about things that were important to me when I was the students' age, things that pulled at my heart. My only planning is jotting down the topics I might write about: having my best friend move away, fighting with my sister, being a nervous test taker, being afraid of my father (until I was older).

I'm going to write a poem in front of you because I want you to hear and see my thinking so you'll get ideas for what to do when you write. While I'm writing I hope you'll be thinking of possibilities for your own poems. One of the things I love about writing poems is I get to decide how it looks and sounds on the page, if I want to skip lines, how I use punctuation, and so on.

Here are some things that pulled at my heart when I was your age. [I briefly talk about each of my topics named above.] *I think I'm going to write about my dad. I'll never forget how mad he was at me and my sisters for letting my mom wash the kitchen floor.*

Writing the poem (5 minutes)   *Hmm, how should I start? Beginnings are important for getting the reader's attention. I think I'll call my poem, "Being Afraid of Dad."* [I write title.] *I'm going to start the poem when Dad came home from work. I want to capture just that moment. Let's see. . .*

"~~Why is your~~ [I write it as I say it, then cross it out.]
"WHY IS YOUR MOTHER
WASHING THE FLOOR" It has to be all capitals because his voice was so loud.
YOU SHOULD BE DOING IT!" I'm underlining "you" because of the way he said it.

Let me see if I like the way that sounds. [I reread first lines.] *I'm going to read it again 'cause I don't know what I want to say next.*

I froze. [I continue speaking aloud as I write.]
Dad's booming voice
TERRIFIED me.

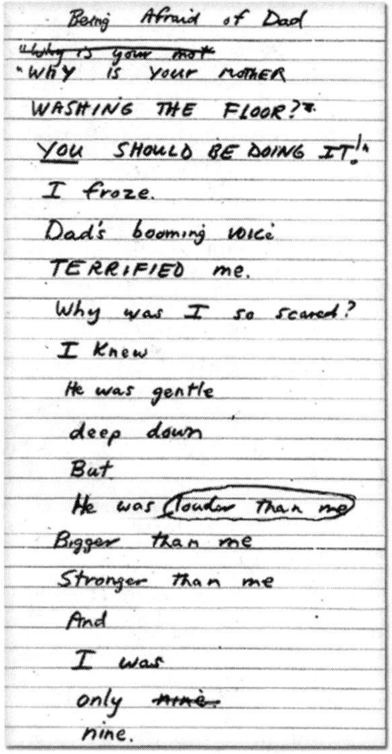

The handwritten draft reads:

Being Afraid of Dad

"Why is your mot—
"WHY IS YOUR MOTHER
WASHING THE FLOOR?"
YOU SHOULD BE DOING IT!
I froze.
Dad's booming voice
TERRIFIED me.
Why was I so scared?
I Knew
He was gentle
deep down
But
He was (louder than me)
Bigger than me
Stronger than me
And
I was
only nine.

Why was I so scared? [I stop and think for a moment.]
I knew
He was gentle
deep down.
But
He was louder than me
Bigger than me
Stronger than me

   I need to read it again to see how it sounds. [I reread.] *I think I want "He was" on a line by itself.* [I lasso it, reread from beginning.] *I need to end it now.*

And
I was
only nine

   I think it sounds better if I say it like this, with "only" by itself.

And
I was
only
nine

See poem draft.

How long did it take me to write my poem? [Kids respond, "five minutes."] *I'm going to give you three times that, fifteen, maybe even twenty minutes. You'll be surprised how much writing you can get done.* [Almost everyone completes at least one poem, and many write two or three.] *Kids, this week, we expect you to write five or six poems. Then, you'll get to choose your favorite one for our anthology.*

What did you notice about my poem?

Danny: You didn't write it out like a story.

Megan: You stuck to the subject.

Alec: You used voice.

What do you mean by that?

Alec: It sounded like you were talking to us.

I put myself into the poem.

▶ **TALKING BEFORE WRITING** (5 minutes)

I have scaffolded conversations with two students, one at a time, with the class looking on. Mostly, I help them narrow their focus and remind them of Bradley's poem, how at first he wrote about lots of things but then zeroed in on the part that was closest to his heart, "getting glasses" (see page 308). I write each student's words on a projected transparency and guide them in thinking about their beginning, ending, how they want their words to sound and look on the page, and so on.

Teacher Talk	☐ *What do you want to say next?*
	☐ *It sounds like a story. Let's make it sound like a poem. You could. . . .*

☐ *Let's read it again and hear how it sounds so far.*

☐ *Do you want these words on one line, like this, or on two lines, like this?*

☐ *I'm going to suggest that you stick to the part about. . . .*

☐ *Why is this a heart poem? Really put yourself into it.*

☐ *You may want to think about ending it now.*

Neither student who volunteers seems to "get" the idea of heart poems. Michael talks about making chili and Katherine talks about getting candy on Halloween. So, later, I am surprised by the heartfelt writing of most of the students, in spite of what felt like inadequate examples.

Although we didn't do it for this lesson, sometimes I move from teacher-scaffolded conversations to student-to-student conversation. (*Turn and talk to your partner about what you're thinking of writing about.*) In this case, because the lesson had already gone on so long, I did not. However, if we had not gotten quality poems the first day, then on day 2, I would have had additional scaffolded conversations followed by partner talk.

▶ **WRITING THE FIRST POEMS** (20 minutes)

Kids, really put yourself into your poem the way Bradley did and I did. If you're sitting there with nothing to say, you probably don't have the right topic.

Everyone gets right to work as teacher Darcy Ballentine and I walk about and have brief roving conferences, which mostly involve affirmation:

☐ *I love your title*

☐ *I like the way you're setting that up on the page.*

☐ *Your first line is a grabber.*

For the couple of students having trouble getting started, Darcy or I have a quick conference and conversation to help them get going. For example, Garrett had copied another student's words from one of the scaffolded conversations. When Garrett said he didn't know what to write about, I looked at his red hair and asked, "What about your red hair? I bet you have some interesting stories about that," and that was enough to get him going. (See his poem and video clip with accompanying notes.)

Notice how Paige has been influenced by my poem "Being Fat." She has taken my line in which my mom says "Ignore those names," and included it in her poignant poem, "Getting Braces," as "If they do, ignore them." She may also have been influenced in her topic by Bradley's poem, "Getting Glasses." (See DVD for her poem and video clip with accompanying notes.)

► **ACKNOWLEDGING WRITING EFFORTS** (2 minutes)

Students bring their poems up to the area where the whole class gathers.

> *How many of you think you did a good job with your poems?* [Almost all hands go up.] *What made it easier for you to write poems this time?*

Max: It's easy to write about something that's really important to you.

Tina: You were leading us through how to do it.

Catherine: Actually expressing from your heart.

Paige: Hearing other poems helped a lot.

Samantha: We didn't really get deep into it until you showed us. Then it was kinda easy. You gave us examples. You made us think.

Danny: We piggybacked off others' ideas.

Garrett: We knew what to do. We knew what heart poems were.

Alec: After our first poem, we found out it was easy and fun, and we thought "Wow! This is fun. We want to write more!"

Paige reads her poem aloud. (See poem, page 341.)

► **CELEBRATING POEMS IN WHOLE-CLASS SHARE** (15 minutes)

There are two chairs in our sharing area, one for the teacher and an "author's chair" for the writer. Students read their poems aloud, and mostly, we just celebrate—their efforts, language, risk taking. After the author has read the poem, I read it again (holding the poem so students can see it), point out all the things the student has done well, and may make some teaching points. In fifteen minutes, five students share. (See video clips for Max's, Lahana's, Paige's, and Garrett's conferences and accompanying notes.)

► **TEACHING POINTS FROM DEMONSTRATIONS AND SHARING**

Had I planned to teach all the following strategies in one lesson, I would have exhausted myself planning and thinking about it all. The "efficiency of context" (pages 149, 152–154) makes lots of meaningful teaching possible. These teaching points were made on the first day and retaught and reinforced on subsequent days. (See, also, video clips with notes.)

Writers:

- ☐ **Think about their audience when they write.**
- ☐ **Reread for:** ☐ **Word choice.** ☐ **Line breaks.** ☐ **Meaning.**
    ☐ **Rhythm.** ☐ **What to say next.**
- ☐ **Use conventions of print for emphasis:**
    ☐ **Capital letters.** ☐ **Bold print.**
    ☐ **Punctuation.** ☐ **Underline words.**

- ☐ **Have a good title.**
- ☐ **Read with expression.**
- ☐ **Think about opening lines.**
- ☐ **Think about white space.**
- ☐ **Use humor** (to entertain).
- ☐ **Put themselves into a poem** (voice).
- ☐ **Craft an ending** (so the poem feels and sounds like it's over).
- ☐ **Get ideas from sharing and listening to peers.**
- ☐ **Clarify their ideas through talking with peers.**
- ☐ **Move things around** (lasso, cut-and-paste).
- ☐ **Read poem aloud to hear how it sounds and where to put line breaks.**

- ☐ **Think about line breaks.**
- ☐ **May use conversation.**
- ☐ **Can repeat a line or phrase.**
- ☐ **Use imagery.**
- ☐ **May play around with sounds.**

Day 2 (50 minutes)

▶ **CONTINUING TO CELEBRATE, TEACH, AND WRITE POEMS**

To ensure we celebrate everyone's efforts, we begin with whole-class share—affirming, celebrating, and teaching. Although sharing is time consuming, the power of sharing kids' poems is electric. When students write, the influence of hearing classmates' "heart poems" is evident.

Katherine, a struggling reader and writer who is not a risk taker, writes "My Lovable Sister," remarkable for its honesty and grit, and quite a leap from her first poem on Halloween candy.

During whole-class share, in addition to celebrating, I model some of the teaching points just listed: line breaks, precise language, titles that fit the poems, endings with satisfying closure, inserting humor, and so on.

Day 2	
Who Holds Book/Pen	Degree of Explicitness/ Support
Teacher / Student	DEMONSTRATION
Teacher / Student	SHARED DEMONSTRATION
gradual handover of responsibility	
Student / Teacher	GUIDED PRACTICE
Student / Teacher	INDEPENDENT PRACTICE

Katherine's draft and final of "My Lovable Sister." Her teacher, Darcy Ballentine, listens and celebrates.

Classroom teacher Darcy Ballantine comments on the power of extensive whole-class share: "Taking the time up front is key. This time spent really makes the actual writing so easy! Otherwise you spend hours conferencing, not to mention frustrated."

Affirming the power of sharing (2 minutes)

What was it like for you when you shared your poetry?

Alec: Scared 'cause there were so many people listening [other teachers were observing the lesson] but I could see they enjoyed what I wrote, and I liked that.

Danny: I was embarrassed at first, but then everyone clapped, and I felt great.

Casie: It felt good when I realized people liked my work.

Cayce: I wanted to write more.

Classroom teacher Darcy Ballantine says that after her kids wrote heart poems, they were more confident as writers and learners, spoke out more in class, and were always eager to share their work. "It gave those kids who never volunteered a voice. After this experience, they wanted their writing to be heard."

Day 3 (50 minutes)

▶ **WRITING POEMS**

Students continue writing poems and rereading their poems. Revision is minimal. Our focus remains on the joy and freedom of writing from our hearts.

I affirm students for getting ideas from each other's poems and making a new poem of their own. Inspired by Bradley's poem, Alex writes her own heartfelt poem about being afraid kids will make fun of her with her new glasses. Cody writes longingly about losing his puppy. Cassie writes about her invisible friend. Tina writes how she hates being short. (See part of published anthology on DVD.)

Day 4 (60 minutes)

▶ **SELECTING A FAVORITE POEM**

By now, everyone has written at least five poems. Darcy reminds her class it's time to pick a poem to publish for our anthology. Each student carefully reads through each draft and chooses her or his favorite.

▶ **EDITING POEMS**

As described on pages 160–165, we establish editing/spelling expectations and go through the editing process. Students willingly take on this task, and editing conferences go quickly, averaging just a few minutes each. Poems are short, students only have to edit one, and they know their final copy will go into a beautiful anthology that will be read by many.

▶ **CREATING A RUBRIC** (20 minutes)

Teachers say, "It always comes down to this. We have to give a grade for the report card." Although I am not a fan of grades, especially for poetry, it is pos-

Days 3 & 4	
Who Holds Book/Pen	**Degree of Explicitness/ Support**
Teacher / Student	DEMONSTRATION
Teacher / Student	SHARED DEMONSTRATION
gradual handover of responsibility	
Student / Teacher	GUIDED PRACTICE
Student / Teacher	INDEPENDENT PRACTICE

sible to fairly grade poetry writing if you use an accurate, child-friendly rubric. See page 252 and Appendix F for how we created such a rubric with much input from students.

Day 5 (60 minutes)

▶ PUBLISHING A POETRY ANTHOLOGY

Day 5	
Who Holds Book/Pen	**Degree of Explicitness/ Support**
Teacher / Student	▼ DEMONSTRATION
Teacher / Student	▼ SHARED DEMONSTRATION
gradual handover of responsibility	
Student / Teacher	▼ GUIDED PRACTICE
Student / Teacher	▼ INDEPENDENT PRACTICE

Examine anthologies This can be done at any time in the poetry writing process. Have students examine a variety of anthologies. Until you have samples of student anthologies, look at commercially published anthologies. As a class, make decisions about organization, title page, table of contents, dedication, acknowledgments, author information, index, illustrations. (See *Kids' Poems: Teaching Third and Fourth Graders to Love Writing Poetry*, Scholastic, 2000, for more specifics.) See DVD for excerpts from their published anthology, which included a table of contents, a page for each poet, and their favorite poem.

▶ WRITING ABOUT THE AUTHOR (50 minutes)

Writing the author profiles (which accompanied each child's photo) followed the optimal learning model, including demonstrations and scaffolded conversations. Darcy first showed examples written by other fourth graders and wrote her own profile while thinking aloud in front of her students.

The whole process went fairly quickly. Taking the pictures and revising and editing the rough drafts required two days (two fifty-minute sessions) to complete.

Start publishing Students peer edited their poems, had editing conferences with Darcy, and word-processed and illustrated their final copies. It took an additional day (fifty minutes) to complete the poems.

Putting the anthology together (one week, 50-minute periods)

Students finished up all the pieces including finalizing author profiles. Darcy listed each of the parts of the anthology the class had decided to include, and students signed up in groups for the section they wanted to work on, such as title page, cover, dedication, table of contents, and index. Students designed each of these pages using other anthologies as models.

Celebrating Students were thrilled with their efforts and at being able to read and have a copy of everyone's poems. Each student received a bound black-and-white copy of the anthology and proudly shared it with their family. The school library and other fourth grades received copies as well. The original was proudly displayed in the classroom library, where it became a favorite for independent reading throughout the school year.

See DVD and pages 338–342. Students worked hard to publish the anthology error-free.

Procedural **Writing**

Plan at a Glance

While I have modeled a five-day lesson plan here, you will want to adapt each individual lesson to the needs and interests of your students.

Day 1 60 minutes	Day 2 60 minutes	Day 3 60 minutes	Day 4 60 minutes	Day 5 60 minutes
DEMONSTRATION			**INDEPENDENT PRACTICE**	
• **Select a real audience and purpose for the writing** *(20 min)* • **Write a piece together** *(15 min)* • **Write a piece in front of students** *(10 min)* • **Talk before writing** *(15 min)*	• **Provide sustained writing time with feedback** • *Sustained writing and roving conferences (30 min)* • **Conference with students** *(30 min)*	• **Continue whole-class share** *(20 min)* • **Revisit drafts** • *Teacher demonstration (10 min)* • *Shared demonstration (10 min)* • Sustained writing time and conferences *(20 min)*	• **Proofread and edit** *(60 min)*	• **Publish** *(60 min)*
DEPENDENCE		**HANDOVER OF RESPONSIBILITY**		**INDEPENDENCE**

Introduction

These lessons take place in a second-grade class in March. Teachers wanted to "see" how to teach procedural writing, a district requirement, with a focus on revising, editing, and publishing. As always, we start with getting the students excited about writing on a genuine topic for a real audience: *Wait till you hear this great idea!* not, *This week we're going to learn how to do procedural writing.* (Teach it first; label it later.)

Lesson Framework

Not every action in the following list is included with every piece of writing or in a prescribed order, but every step in the optimal learning model is always incorporated. Gradually releasing responsibility to students after showing them how (demonstration, shared demonstration, guided practice, independent practice) makes it likely they will be successful.

- [ ] *Select a real audience and purpose for the writing.*
- [ ] *Read, examine, and discuss examples and characteristics of the genre or form (immersion, demonstration).*
      What do you notice? (shared demonstration).
- [ ] *Write a piece in front of students (demonstration) and/or*
      Write a piece together (shared demonstration).
- [ ] *Talk before writing (shared and guided practice).*
- [ ] *Provide sustained writing time with feedback (guided and independent practice).*
- [ ] *Conference with students (guided and independent practice).*
- [ ] *Share, celebrate, and reflect.*
- [ ] *Revisit drafts (guided and independent practice).*
- [ ] *Conference with students.*
- [ ] *Share, celebrate, and reflect.*
- [ ] *Proofread and edit.*
- [ ] *Publish.*

Think of this framework as a self-perpetuating loop of ongoing writing, demonstrating, teaching, sharing, celebrating, and setting new goals—not as a linear model. With short pieces of writing, you can go from inception to publication in one week.

Days 1 & 2	
Who Holds Book/Pen	*Degree of Explicitness/ Support*
Teacher / Student	DEMONSTRATION
Teacher / Student	SHARED DEMONSTRATION
gradual handover of responsibility	
Student / Teacher	GUIDED PRACTICE
Student / Teacher	INDEPENDENT PRACTICE

Lesson Plan Summary
Day 1 (60 minutes)

▶ **SELECT A REAL AUDIENCE AND PURPOSE FOR THE WRITING** (20 minutes)

Teacher Talk

Your teacher and I were talking and thought it would be a great idea to write a book for substitute teachers. You've had a lot of subs this year, and they always need to know how the classroom works. Well, you're experts at that. Here's what I was thinking. We could write how the morning procedures work, and then they'd know exactly what to do when they enter your classroom. Isn't that a terrific idea?

▶ **WRITE A PIECE TOGETHER** (15 minutes)

We write "Morning Procedures for a Sub" (see final draft and published brochure on following page and DVD). (See Chapter 5 for shared writing framework, typical demonstrations, teaching tips, teacher talk.) Finished copy was published as a full-color brochure with copies available to subs in a guest-teacher folder provided by the school office.

▶ **WRITE A PIECE IN FRONT OF STUDENTS** (10 minutes)

Sometimes, shared writing is enough of a demonstration. Other times, you need both teacher modeling and shared writing before students are ready to write. Teacher judgment on how much scaffolding kids need before they write is key here. Since these are second graders and they have not done procedural writing before, more frontloading is needed.

Now that we've written "Morning Procedures for a Sub," think about something we do in the classroom that everyone needs to know. There are lots of things you do, like lining up and putting books back in the classroom library, that we could write about. Here's what I was thinking. Each of you could write about one of those things that interest you, and we could publish a classroom book, not just for us but for all the second grades and other classrooms too. That would be so great!

I'm going to write about how to do something, too. I was thinking I would write "How to Whisper." I'll be having guided reading groups with you later, and I want to be sure everyone understands what I mean by "whisper" if you're working at your seats.

I'm going to write in front of you so you'll know exactly how good writers work —what they do, how they think. It's important you all listen so you get good ideas for your own writing. Okay, let's see how I want to start. I always think about my beginning because I want it to be interesting for my reader. . . .

I think aloud and write "How to Whisper." (See draft. I use the same kind of language as previously.) Students see me reread as I go along to help me decide what to say next, move things around that don't sound right where they are (use arrows, lassoes, carets), cross out, add information, reread several times for clarity. Notice how my modeling influences students to do similar rereading and revising on their own.

▶ **TALK BEFORE WRITING** (15 minutes)

Brainstorming topics (5 minutes) We make a list of possible procedures we can write about (see chart at top on facing page). I want to be sure everyone has an idea before they write.

Having scaffolded conversations (10 minutes) I talk with a few students and chart their thinking so they and other students can refer back to the chart for

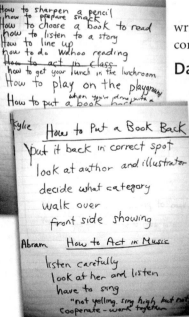

(above, top) Brainstorming topics through shared writing.

(above, bottom) Public scaffolded conversations with two students before all students write.

(right) Drafts of "Cafeteria Rules" by Brian (see also pages 320 and 151) and "How to Put a Book Back" by Andrew.

writing ideas. (See chart, below left. See also the language of scaffolded conversations, page 77.)

Day 2 (60 minutes)

▶ **PROVIDE SUSTAINED WRITING TIME WITH FEEDBACK** (60 minutes)
Look at our chart for all the terrific ideas you came up with yesterday. Pick one you want to write about. Look at the chart, too, that we did when Kylie and Abram were talking with me and you were all listening. Take a few minutes to think about what you want to say before you write. You can talk to your partner if you want to. Then, we'll have our usual quiet for writing time.

Sustained writing and roving conferences (30 minutes) *When you're done writing, read it to a friend to see if it's clear.*

Another way students checked whether the writing was clear to the reader was by acting out the procedure as the draft was read aloud.

Notice the amount of revising students did on their drafts—and we never mentioned revision (see photos below). They revised in the process of writing because they cared about the writing and valued the audience and purpose.

▶ **CONFERENCE WITH STUDENTS** (30 minutes)
Whole-class share is a combined celebration and teaching time. One of the things we celebrate is all the revising you did. Tell us why you made these changes. . . . Good for you. You were rereading and checking to be sure it made sense and would be interesting for the reader. That's what good writers do. How many others of you made changes? (We are talking only about content.)

Notice what good writers do We use whole-class share to document all we are teaching. (When I began to notice how much we were teaching in response to students' writing, we began to chart our teaching points, including the language of "how to" writing: "first," "next," "then," "usually," "finally." See page 151.)

Note: I did not say, *Now I'm going to teach you the words you use for procedural writing.* I did say, *Notice how Andrew used "first" and "then" in his writing. That really helps the reader see the sequence of events. Let's write those words down and others like them. I'm putting them right here on our chart in case you want to use them.*

See chart excerpt (at left) of all we taught in two days (the efficiency of context): "What Good Writers Do," in addition to "Teaching Beyond the Standards," pages 150–151. Notice that we taught "transitions" (without labeling it) because writers needed to know how to move smoothly from one part to another. (See examples of both the drafts and finished pieces below.) In whole-class share, here's what I said to Andrew, who was missing a transition in his "Walking in the Halls" draft.

Here you have a humorous introduction. Then you go right into telling how to walk in the hall. How can you let the reader know you're moving to a new idea? What could you say to make that clear to the reader?

"This is what we do."

A partial draft of our shared writing chart.

What a Good Writer Does

Teaching

~~transitions~~ lets the reader know when
you're changing ideas
leads
procedural words
writing has to make sense +
use the language of responding to writing
making a list
writers "have a little trouble"
title
"Maybe, it might be helpful".
the writer decides what to change
Narrowing the topic

Also see photo on page 319.

Cafeteria Rules
When you are in the cafeteria you need to eat politely by using silverware and excuse yourself when you forget something. You use a conversation voice and talk quietly with your friends and don't share food! You don't leave until you are dismissed. Make sure you follow the rules and enjoy your food!

Brian

Walking in the Halls of BBC
Walking in the hall is sort of easy but some people can't help themselves. Because some people yak, yak, yak, all the time. But most people can be quiet. This is what we do. You whisper and look ahead and follow the line at all times. We also walk in the hall because if you run, you will get in so much trouble or you will just hurt someone or you will trip. Walking in the hall is important. And that is how we walk in the hall.

Andrew

And I said *"Great, put that in."*

After I showed Andrew how to do that, I said to the class, *Look at how adding this one sentence helps the reader know what's coming next. Now the reader won't be confused. When you reread your writing, make sure you've done that.* Several students independently add in transition sentences.

While I didn't label "transitions" for this group of students, I could have. For example, later on, once students understood the concept (through guided and independent practice,) I could have said, *What we've been doing, adding in words to let the reader know what's coming next, that's called using transitions. All good writers use transitions to make the writing smooth and easy for the reader to follow.* You can teach transitions this way, even in kindergarten, in a shared writing.

Days 3 & 4	
Who Holds Book/Pen	*Degree of Explicitness/ Support*
Teacher / Student	DEMONSTRATION
Teacher / Student	SHARED DEMONSTRATION
gradual handover of responsibility	
Student / Teacher	GUIDED PRACTICE
Student / Teacher	INDEPENDENT PRACTICE

Day 3 (60 minutes)

▶ CONTINUE WHOLE-CLASS SHARE (20 minutes)

We begin with sharing to ensure that all students are celebrated, and that necessary teaching points are made. We continue to add to our chart, "What Good Writers Do." (See page 151 for the completed chart.)

▶ REVISIT DRAFTS

Teacher demonstration (10 minutes) *The reason it's necessary to reread your piece two or three times is to be sure it's clear for your reader. I'm going to reread my draft and see if I need to change anything.* [I reread and change some words.] *I'm missing an ending. I haven't said yet why whispering is important. Let's see.* [I write the words as I say them aloud]: *"When everyone whispers, it's a quiet room, and it's easy to get work done." Let me read that again, and see if I like how it sounds.* [I reread.] *Okay, I like it. I'm going to reread two more times, just to be sure my writing is exactly as I want it and that it's clear for my reader.*

Shared demonstration (10 minutes) With permission, I make a projected transparency of a student's draft. I model in front of the whole class how to reread two or three times for the following:

☐ **Does it make sense to reader all the way through?**

☐ **Do you need to add more detail to make it clear?**

☐ **Do you need to cross out anything that doesn't work?**

☐ **Do you need to add anything?**

☐ **Do you have a good beginning and ending?**

I have a back-and-forth conversation with one student as we go through the revising process.

Sustained writing time and conferences (20 minutes) Students complete their drafts, read them to peers, and some choose to start a second piece (if first is completed). At the same time, roving and one-on-one conferences are taking place.

Day 4 (60 minutes)

▶ PROOFREAD AND EDIT

Because our focus is on content and students have worked so hard drafting and revising, we want to make the editing easy for them. We also want to finish up quickly while interest is high. (Typically I do an "editing expectations" as a shared writing and hold students accountable [see page 204 and Appendices J and K for examples] through editing conferences. But for the reasons stated, we skip this stage.)

I do a quick minilesson of what to check for now that our pieces sound just right. That list includes capital letters, punctuation, and word wall words spelled correctly. I tell students: *Since you've worked so hard on your writing, our gift to you is we will edit the spelling (not including word wall words) "for free."*

Day 5 (60 minutes)

▶ PUBLISH (60 minutes)

Students are given the choice of copying over their final draft or word-processing it. The classroom teacher uses a digital camera to photograph each child engaged in the procedure and then inserts the picture onto the document. The students "design" the concept of the picture on their own and ask fellow students to be in the picture to help model the "action." The whole publishing process takes three days (an additional sixty minutes on two more days) and goes quickly, since the pieces are short.

See pages of completed book of procedures on DVD.

Day 5	
Who Holds Book/Pen	Degree of Explicitness/ Support
Teacher / Student	▼ DEMONSTRATION
Teacher / Student	▼ SHARED DEMONSTRATION
gradual handover of responsibility	
Student / Teacher	▼ GUIDED PRACTICE
Student / Teacher	▼ INDEPENDENT PRACTICE

Hero **Writing**

Plan at a Glance

While I have modeled a five-day lesson plan here, you will want to adapt each individual lesson to the needs and interests of your students.

Day 1 60 minutes	**Day 2** 60 minutes	**Day 3** 60 minutes	**Day 4** 60 minutes	**Day 5** 60 minutes
DEMONSTRATION			**INDEPENDENT PRACTICE**	
• Select a real audience and purpose for the writing *(10 min)* • Read, examine, and discuss examples and characteristics of the genre or form *(30 min)* • Define a hero *(10 min)* • Write a piece in front of students *(10 min)*	• Talk before writing *(15 min)* • Provide sustained writing time with feedback *(30 min)* • Conference with students • Celebrate *(15 min)*	• Revisit drafts and conference with students *(45 min)* • Share, celebrate, and reflect *(15 min)*	• Proofread and edit • Establish editing expectations • Demonstrate editing • Provide sustained time for editing • Conference with students • Reflect on editing	• Publish • Provide sustained time for publishing
DEPENDENCE	▷ **HANDOVER OF RESPONSIBILITY**		▷ **INDEPENDENCE**	

Introduction

This lesson is adaptable for biography writing or personal narrative. Although this lesson takes place in a grade 4 class, it can be reworked for any grade level.

Lesson Framework

Not every action below is included with every piece of writing or in a prescribed order, but every step in the optimal learning model is always incorporated. Gradually releasing responsibility to students after showing them how (demonstration, shared demonstration, guided practice, independent practice) makes it likely they will be successful.

☐ *Select a real audience and purpose for the writing.*

☐ *Read, examine, and discuss examples and characteristics of the genre or form (immersion, demonstration).*
What do you notice? (shared demonstration).

☐ ***Write a piece in front of students*** *(demonstration)* ***and/or***
Write a piece together *(shared demonstration).*

☐ ***Talk before writing*** *(shared and guided practice).*

☐ ***Provide sustained writing time with feedback*** *(guided and independent practice).*

☐ ***Conference with students*** *(guided and independent practice).*

☐ ***Share, celebrate, and reflect.***

☐ ***Revisit drafts*** *(guided and independent practice).*

☐ ***Conference with students.***

☐ ***Share, celebrate, and reflect.***

☐ ***Proofread and edit.***

☐ ***Publish.***

Think of this framework as a self-perpetuating loop of ongoing writing, demonstrating, teaching, sharing, celebrating, and setting new goals—not as a linear model. With short pieces of writing, you can go from inception to publication in one week.

Lesson Plan Summary

Day 1 (60 minutes)

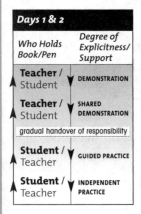

▶ **SELECT A REAL AUDIENCE AND PURPOSE FOR THE WRITING** (10 minutes)

> *Teacher Talk*

Kids, I want you to think about someone in your life who is a hero, someone you admire because of how they have conducted their lives. I want to tell you about a hero in my life. My husband Frank is a hero to me, and I've never told him that. Since my dad had his stroke, Frank has spent an enormous amount of time with him. I knew he would be supportive, but I never expected that he would do all of what he has done for my dad. I never asked him to do it. Now I'm going to write and thank him and tell him how I feel about what he's done.

I want you to think of someone who is a hero to you but you've never told that person. It could be a classmate or teacher or relative. Now you'll have the opportunity to tell that person why she or he is a hero to you. We're going to write letters and send them. Your reader will feel great getting your letter.

Let's talk about what a hero is. [I chart their responses.] That's a good start. Now, I want to read to you about some amazing heroes. Some of them are kids, just like you. Think about what a hero is and does as I read aloud. Then we'll add to our chart.

▶ **READ, EXAMINE, AND DISCUSS EXAMPLES AND CHARACTERISTICS OF THE GENRE OR FORM** (30 minutes)

I read aloud excerpts from *The Hero's Trail: A Guide for a Heroic Life*, by T. A. Baron (Penguin Putnam Books for Young Readers, 2002), which has stories of heroes, some of whom are children. (Baron has created a prize to celebrate young heroes —see www.barronprize.org.) A few other recommended books for reading and writing about heroes are *We Were There, Too! Young People in U.S. History*, by Phillip Hoose (Farrar, Straus & Giroux, 2001); *Rabble Rousers: 20 Women Who Made a Difference*, by Cheryl Harness (Dutton Children's Books, 2003); *Coming to America: The Story of Immigration*, by Betsy Maestro (Scholastic, 1996); *Through My Eyes*, by Ruby Bridges (Scholastic, 1999); *It's Our World, Too! Young People Who Are Making a Difference: How They Do It—How YOU Can, Too!* (Farrar, Straus & Giroux, 2002).

Using *The Hero's Trail* as a guide, we add to our chart.

▶ **DEFINE A HERO** (10 minutes)

"A hero is someone who, faced with a tough challenge, reaches down inside and finds the courage, strength, and wisdom to triumph. . . . In every case, it's someone whose special qualities of character make a real difference. . . . A celebrity, by contrast, is just someone who has won our attention. . . . For a hero, what counts is character. For a celebrity, what counts is fame." (*The Hero's Trail*, pp. 2–3)

We discuss that a hero can be a friend, family member, prominent person, or neighbor. A hero can be found in real life, fiction, and history. It's all about the exemplary character of the person.

Discuss different kinds of heroes A hero can be someone with a strong will to live (survivor hero), positive spirit (hero within), one who consciously sets out to make an important difference (hero to others), or a hero for all time.

Discuss the character of a hero Baron names seven qualities heroes have: courage, faith, perseverance, hope, humor, adaptability, moral direction (pages 98–102).

Our final chart looked like this:

Character of a Hero

☐	**Is unselfish**	☐	**Does what's right**
☐	**Has confidence**	☐	**Has courage**
☐	**Is caring**	☐	**Acts like a good friend**
☐	**Sticks with it a long time** (perseverance)		

▶ **WRITE A PIECE IN FRONT OF STUDENTS** (10 minutes)

Thinking and writing aloud, I compose my draft to Frank. (See excerpt on following page.) I reread and make changes as I go along and explain why I am

Dear Frank,

I've told you many times how much I appreciate what you've done for Dad- and continue to do for him- but I ~~have~~ ^{have never} told you that you're ^{number one} my hero.

For almost a while year you have put your own life and ~~daily painting~~ ^{work as an artist} on hold. ~~to you~~ _{Visit} Dad for many hours several days a week, ^{you} read to him, bring him flowers, magazines and videos, and try to cheer him up when he's sad. ~~Just brighten up his day.~~

Beginning of my draft.

making each change (didn't sound right, boring word, missing words, uninteresting lead, and so on). I complete the first draft in fifteen minutes.

Day 2 (60 minutes)

▶ **TALK BEFORE WRITING** (15 minutes)

Establish writing expectations Through shared writing, we examine my draft and create a rubric for student writing.

Criteria/rubric

☐   Keep the reader in mind!

☐   What happened?

☐   What makes this person a hero? (Prove it. Give several reasons.)

☐   How do you feel about this person?

Have one or more scaffolded conversations.

Encourage partner talk before writing.

Meet in a small group with anyone having trouble coming up with a topic.

▶ **PROVIDE SUSTAINED WRITING TIME WITH FEEDBACK** (30 minutes)

Students eagerly begin their drafts. Gracie writes to a cousin who saved her life. Rebecca writes to her mom. Kaira writes to a friend who stood by her. Liana writes to her teacher.

▶ **CONFERENCE WITH STUDENTS**

Roving conferences take place as students begin to write. Once everyone is writing, one-on-one content conferences begin. Students also share their writing with each other (see photo).

▶ **CELEBRATE** (15 minutes)

In whole-class share we celebrate and teach. As students listen, they get ideas to strengthen their own writing.

Day 3 (60 minutes)

▶ **REVISIT DRAFTS** (45 minutes)

In front of students, using a projected transparency (you can also go back to a draft written on chart paper), I reread several times, think aloud about changes I might make and why, make revisions, and get my draft as close to final form as I can.

Students go back to their writing, reread before going on, continue writing, and revise for clarity and interest.

Days 3 & 4

Who Holds Book/Pen	Degree of Explicitness/ Support
Teacher / Student	DEMONSTRATION
Teacher / Student	SHARED DEMONSTRATION
gradual handover of responsibility	
Student / Teacher	GUIDED PRACTICE
Student / Teacher	INDEPENDENT PRACTICE

4th grade teacher Kristin
Potter conducts a conference.

Students assume responsi-

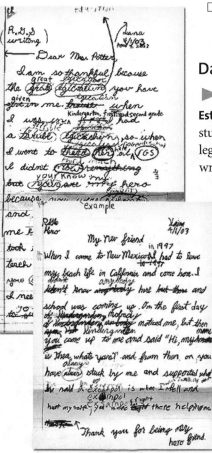

▶ **CONFERENCE WITH STUDENTS**

Continue one-on-one content conferences. (See pages 218–219.)

▶ **SHARE, CELEBRATE, AND REFLECT** (15 minutes)

Students continue to share. Afterward we reflect. *Reflect on your draft writing. How did it go? Why was writing easier/better (than previous projects)?*

☐ "Talked about it ahead of time."

☐ "Had notes from conversation." *(conference)*

☐ "Writing to someone special."

☐ "Wrote about something important to me."

☐ "The room was quiet."

☐ "Listened to others to get good ideas."

☐ "Saw how to cut and paste and move things around." *(observing teaching in whole class share)*

☐ "Heard positive comments and suggestions." *(to ourselves and others)*

Day 4 (60 minutes)

▶ **PROOFREAD AND EDIT**

Establish editing expectations Have in mind the big areas you expect students to handle: spelling, grammar, capitalization, punctuation, legibility, and so on. Then, negotiate with the students in a shared writing. (See final version by this class in Appendix K.)

Say, *What can you do on your own, without any help from a teacher? If you do all you can, I'll do the rest "for free."*

See Chapter 5 on shared writing for teacher talk for setting editing expectations. See pages 69–70 for Raise Your Expectations for Editing.

Demonstrate editing Demonstrate proofreading (noticing the errors) and editing (fixing them up). With permission, make a projected transparency of one or more students' drafts. With the student beside you, think aloud, scaffold, teach, encourage the student to problem-solve. (As an example, see Derek's spelling conference on the DVD with accompanying notes.)

Provide sustained time for editing Expect students to reread at least four or five times, refer to editing expectations list, and use a colored pencil to make changes so they are evident

A student works hard on editing.

Edited and final draft of "My Hero Friend." (My initials, "RR," at upper left, indicate that the student has successfully completed editing and is ready to do the final copy.) See also final draft of Jennifer's letter, page 329.

(no erasing). Also, consider using peer editing (see page 233) before a one-on-one conference with the teacher.

Conference with students If students have done all they can, which means most have found almost all editing problems, do the rest "for free." A typical conference on a short piece of one to two pages, such as a letter, averages two minutes.

Reflect on editing This particular group of students had never done almost all the editing themselves. Their teacher, Kristen Potter, in Santa Fe, New Mexico said: "I was amazed at how much they could fix up themselves and, then, how quickly the conferences went!"

Ask students, *How did it go? What did you learn?*

- ☐ "It takes a lot of rereading."
- ☐ "It takes a lot of hard work."
- ☐ "You have to work really hard on spelling."
- ☐ "You have to look carefully at the format."
- ☐ "You may not 'get it' on the first try."
- ☐ "Getting spelling hints helps."
- ☐ "Editing is fun—reading, correcting, fun to try to find the correct spelling."

Don't skip reflection. Remember, students are used to us doing most of the editing work, usually out of their sight, and now we are shifting responsibility to them, so we need to heighten their editing awareness.

On the facing page are the draft and final revisions of Kelsey's hero piece, and on this page the final version of Jennifer's. (See also page 232 for Liana's editing work.)

Day 5 (60 minutes)

▶ **PUBLISH**

Demonstrate exactly what you expect students to do. Using beautiful writing paper (and having the template for a friendly letter format in front of me), I carefully and slowly handwrite the beginning of my letter as I check back and forth with my draft so I get it right. I think aloud as I write.

▶ **PROVIDE SUSTAINED TIME FOR PUBLISHING**

As some students are ready to go ahead with final copies, continue editing conferences with others.

Day 5	
Who Holds Book/Pen	**Degree of Explicitness/ Support**
Teacher / Student	DEMONSTRATION
Teacher / Student	SHARED DEMONSTRATION
gradual handover of responsibility	
Student / Teacher	GUIDED PRACTICE
Student / Teacher	INDEPENDENT PRACTICE

♥ Mom and Dad,
you know that I love you very very much, but did you know that you're my heroes? Since my birth mother couldn't take care of me and I had to be adopted anyone could've taken me home, but I'm very glad it was you. If you hadn't come along, I might not be living with such great parents!!! You're funny, you've taught me so much, you're loving and very very caring. I feel very grateful that I'm in such great hands. Thanks for being such terrific parents!!
Love,
Jennifer ♥

Happy Family

Format for a Friendly Letter

(Heading) 146 Grove Avenue
Marbletown, KY 02891
April 6, 2004

Dear Joe Hiller, (Salutation)

Begin your letter here. Remember to indent ONLY the first line of each paragraph. The other sentences can go all the way from the left margin to the right margin. Use your neatest *cursive handwriting*. (Body of letter)

(Closing) Sincerely,
(Signature) Susan Chester

Providing a model of the correct format for a friendly letter.

Persuasive **Writing**

Plan at a Glance

While I have modeled a five-day lesson plan here, you will want to adapt each individual lesson to the needs and interests of your students.

Day 1 60 minutes	Day 2 60 minutes	Day 3 60 minutes	Day 4 60 minutes	Day 5 60 minutes
DEMONSTRATION			**INDEPENDENT PRACTICE**	
• **Read-aloud** (20 min) • **Demonstration: sharing exemplars** (20 min) • **Shared writing** (15 min) • **Preplanning for Day 2** (5 min)	• **Revisit shared writing** (10 min) • **Establish criteria** (10 min) • **Talk before writing** (10 min) • **Sustained silent writing** (20 min) • **Whole-class share** (10 min)	• **Whole-class share** (30 min) • **Sustained silent writing** (30 min)	• **Minilesson** (10 min) • **Establishing editing expectations** (20 min) • **Writing, revising, editing, and editing conferences** (30 min)	• **Publishing and conferencing** (60 min) • *Set expectations for final copy* (20 min) • *Writing final copies* (40 min)
DEPENDENCE		**HANDOVER OF RESPONSIBILITY**		**INDEPENDENCE**

Introduction

Writing (and speaking) persuasively is a necessary life skill for advocating for change, obtaining a desired goal, and stating an opinion when you hope to influence the reader (or listener). In persuasive writing, the main goal is to convince someone to take some action or to bring about change.

In the following lesson, fourth graders wrote a class letter to the state department of education (see pages 278–279). Then they selected a person or company to write to for the purpose of persuasion on some issue. Michaela wrote to her uncle urging him to stop smoking. Sasha wrote to a game company requesting that a video game that had been discontinued be reissued. Aaron wrote to his parents requesting a desk for his room. Ebony wrote to her mom requesting an increase in her allowance. Almost every student received a reply, and some got what they asked for. (Aaron got his desk, and Ebony got her increase.) Students learned how powerful persuasive writing can be.

Notice that the following lesson plan follows the optimal learning model and can be adapted for any writing genre. If students can successfully write a persuasive piece, more than likely they have met (and probably exceeded) the requirements posed by required standards and rubrics.

Extended Lesson Framework

Not every action listed below is included with every piece of writing or in a prescribed order, but every step in the optimal learning model is always incorporated. Gradually releasing responsibility to students after showing them how (demonstration, shared demonstration, guided practice, independent practice) makes it likely they will be successful.

☐ **Select a real audience and purpose.**
Students had just completed the high-stakes test and felt frustrated. We decided to write to the State Department of Education and offer some suggestions.

☐ **Read, examine, and discuss examples of persuasive pieces** (demonstration).
We read and reviewed some examples of persuasive writing. I asked:

☐ *What do you notice?*   ☐ *What struck you?*

☐ *What makes this a persuasive piece?*

☐ *What impact did the writing have on the reader(s)?*

We could also have created a chart, "What We Notice About Persuasive Writing."

☐ **Write a piece together** (shared demonstration).
Following procedures for shared writing (see page 88) as a whole class, we drafted a letter to the state department. (See page 333.)

☐ **Talk before writing** (shared and guided practice).
☐ Students chose to write to someone about an important matter and to try and persuade that person to do what the writer deemed important.

☐ Talk included scaffolded conversations and partner talk.

☐ We created a simple rubric based on the class letter we wrote.

☐ **Sustained writing time with feedback** (guided and independent practice.)
Students wrote while their teacher and I had roving and one-on-one conferences. Students were reminded to refer to the criteria we had established.

☐ **Conference with students** (guided and independent practice).
After students had content conferences and made revisions, we moved to editing.

☐   *Celebrating, publishing, and reflecting.*

We mailed the letters and almost everyone received a response.

Think of this framework as a self-perpetuating loop of ongoing writing, demonstrating, teaching, sharing, celebrating, and setting new goals—not as a linear model. With short pieces of writing, you can go from inception to publication in one week.

Lesson Plan Summary

Day 1 (60 minutes)

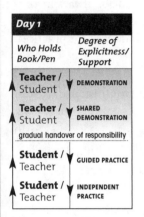

This lesson takes place in late November, the week before Thanksgiving, in a grade 4 class. Briefly, we first discuss what persuasion is and how and why it's important in life. To persuade is to try to convince someone to do something you want them to do.

▶ **READ-ALOUD** (20 minutes)

To set the stage for the power of persuasion, I read aloud *Thank You, Sarah: The Woman Who Saved Thanksgiving,* by Laurie Alse Anderson, the story of a young woman who was very influential in making Thanksgiving a national holiday.

I also read aloud a newspaper article describing how a group of outraged seventh and eighth graders convinced Senator Hilary Clinton to recognize Harriet Tubman's service to our country by finally creating a pension for her descendants (Slackman 2003).

We discussed the power of persuasion and how it brought about positive changes.

▶ **DEMONSTRATION: SHARING EXAMPLES** (20 minutes)

On projected transparencies, I show two persuasive pieces of writing to the class. One is a letter I sent to former workshop participants urging them to search for my missing reading log—my record of monthly reading (which I discovered missing a few weeks later)—and explaining why it was so important it be returned to me. (It was.)

The second piece was "Why I Should Have ColecoVision" (see facing page, and DVD for color version), written by our son Peter to Frank and me when he was twelve. Peter had been begging us to allow him to buy, with his own money, an expensive computer game. We steadfastly refused until we received his impressive, five-page persuasive piece.

We discuss what Peter did that finally made his parents give in to his request. He:

☐   **Had all the facts and accurately presented them.**

☐   **Backed up statements with additional pertinent information.**

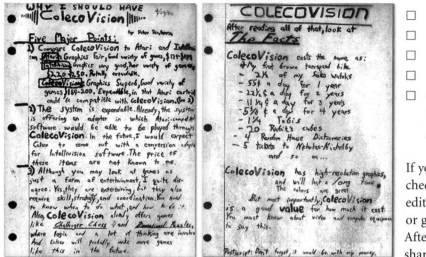

Pages one and five of "Why I Should have ColecoVision."

- ☐ **Used convincing language.**
- ☐ **Used humor.**
- ☐ **Included a detailed visual.**
- ☐ **Summarized his major points.**
- ☐ **Made a beautiful presentation** (easy to read, full color, well organized, correct spelling and conventions).

If you have no examples handy, check your local newspaper for editorials or letters to the editor, or go directly to shared writing. Afterwards, save exemplars to share with future classes.

▶ **SHARED WRITING** (15 minutes)

See guidelines for shared writing (page 88) for procedures. See beginning of draft we wrote (shown at right).

▶ **PREPLANNING**

Students' homework is to think ahead and come prepared to persuade someone about something important to the student (and bring the recipient's address if they have it).

Day 2 (60 minutes)

▶ **REVISIT SHARED WRITING** (10 minutes)

We reread our draft several times, make some changes, and finalize our letter. We discuss the format of a business letter and ask for a volunteer who has good handwriting to put it in final form. (We deliberately handwrite it for personal appeal.)

▶ **ESTABLISH CRITERIA** (10 minutes)

Based on what we've done and discussed, I guide the students in setting up requirements for their persuasive piece. Our simple rubric includes:

- ☐ **Opening lead that states purpose.**
- ☐ **Position statement with supporting arguments.**
- ☐ **Closing/summary.**

Day 2	
Who Holds Book/Pen	**Degree of Explicitness/ Support**
Teacher / Student	DEMONSTRATION
Teacher / Student	SHARED DEMONSTRATION
gradual handover of responsibility	
Student / Teacher	GUIDED PRACTICE
Student / Teacher	INDEPENDENT PRACTICE

We also note and record some of the vocabulary we noticed in other persuasive pieces:

- ☐ **because of**
- ☐ **that is why**
- ☐ **first of all**
- ☐ **therefore**
- ☐ **lastly**
- ☐ **I hope to convince you**

▶ **TALK BEFORE WRITING** (10 minutes)

As usual, before writing, we have scaffolded conversations (see example below) followed by partner talk.

▶ **SUSTAINED SILENT WRITING** (20 min)

Students begin their drafts. I asked students, many of who were not previously enthusiastic about writing, to talk about their process after they wrote their drafts.

Why was this writing easier for you?

- ☐ "We saw examples."
- ☐ "We got to talk before we wrote."
- ☐ "We brainstormed ideas."   ☐ "We listened to others' ideas."
- ☐ "We learned how to do it before   ☐ "We had a lot of time."
  we wrote."

Why was this fun?

- ☐ "I got to make a point."   ☐ "I might get what I asked for."
- ☐ "Knowing we're really going to send our letters."

▶ **WHOLE-CLASS SHARE** (10 minutes)

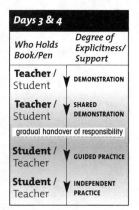

Days 3 & 4	
Who Holds Book/Pen	**Degree of Explicitness/ Support**
Teacher / Student	DEMONSTRATION
Teacher / Student	SHARED DEMONSTRATION
gradual handover of responsibility	
Student / Teacher	GUIDED PRACTICE
Student / Teacher	INDEPENDENT PRACTICE

Day 3 (60 minutes)

▶ **WHOLE-CLASS SHARE** (30 minutes)

Beginning with sharing celebrates everyone's efforts and allows me to see who will need a one-on-one conference before continuing to write. I also look for patterns, areas where several or many students need explicit teaching. Then I may pull them into a small group or do a whole-class minilesson.

▶ **SUSTAINED SILENT WRITING** (30 minutes)

Students complete their drafts. Content conferences occur as students write.

Day 4 (60 minutes)

▶ **MINILESSON** (10 minutes)

Determined from what you observe students need (see pages 154–155 and 229–230 for more information on minilessons).

Carefully rereading her draft.

Coaching Katie Schmidt in a one-on-one conference.

▶ **ESTABLISH EDITING EXPECTATIONS** (20 minutes)
See shared writing, pages 88 and 327, for procedures, and page 204 and the appendix for examples.

▶ **WRITING, REVISING, EDITING, AND EDITING CONFERENCES** (30 minutes)
Students who have completed drafts with revisions (after a content conference) begin editing. Student editing, peer editing (page 233), and one-on-one conferences (see pages 218–219 for procedures) take place.

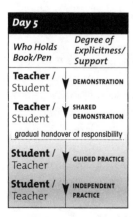

Day 5	
Who Holds Book/Pen	**Degree of Explicitness/ Support**
Teacher / Student	DEMONSTRATION
Teacher / Student	SHARED DEMONSTRATION
gradual handover of responsibility	
Student / Teacher	GUIDED PRACTICE
Student / Teacher	INDEPENDENT PRACTICE

Day 5 (60 minutes)
▶ **PUBLISHING AND CONFERENCING**
Some students will be ready for publishing. Others will be revising, editing, or conferencing with a peer or teacher.

Set expectations for final copy (20 minutes) Give each student a blank template for the form of a business letter or friendly letter. (See page 329 for example.) Review/teach format of writing a letter and addressing an envelope. Provide paper for final copies.

Writing final copies (40 minutes) Some students may word-process their letters. If students are done early, they may write another letter or work on another writing project, usually free choice.

Teaching **Points**
Conference Video Clips

These conferences took place the first week in November in a K–5 public school outside a large urban area. These clips are raw footage and videotaped by a teacher during a regular teaching day. Because I was demonstration teaching in a weeklong residency, many teachers were observing; occasionally, I am heard making remarks to them.

PURPOSE OF THE WRITING

Because many students expressed a dislike for writing, my main purpose was to have all students experience joy and success in writing, and that purpose was realized. In fourth grade we wrote "heart poems"; in second grade we told "secrets that no one knew."

The writing focus was on authentic writing for real readers. Poems written by fourth graders became part of a beautiful anthology. "Secrets of Second Graders" became a favorite class book. Both publications were shared and celebrated schoolwide, with additional copies printed for other classrooms, parents, administrators, and the school library. Daily writing that included demonstrations (teacher modeling and sharing student writing), teacher and peer conversations, and brief, productive conferences with every student made it possible to publish student writing formally within two weeks. See excerpts from the publications "Heart Poems" and "Secrets of Second Graders" also on this DVD. (Also see five-day lesson plans for teacher demonstrations, student drafts, and procedures.)

OVERVIEW

The average length of a student conference was three to four minutes. Efficient, productive conferences were possible because students were engaged in the topic, they were ready and prepared to write, and the pieces were manageable—one to two pages, maximum length.

The celebrating and teaching points during the content conferences are not preplanned. My comments, support, and suggestions arise from what I see and hear these writers trying to do. I trust each writer has something meaningful to say, and I try to help the writer convey his/her message more clearly to the reader.

During each conference, the writer sits in the "author's chair" next to me. The piece is read twice, first to get the overall meaning and second to listen for specific words and ideas to celebrate the writer and help him move forward. While normally the student always does the first reading, to save time and with the student's permission, I occasionally do it. I often do the second reading (again with the student's permission) holding the text so it faces the other students and they can see it as I read aloud, celebrate, affirm, and make teaching points.

STANCE TAKEN

As it is early in the school year and students and teachers are just learning about conferencing, I am in charge, and the notes describe the conference from my perspective. However, in Derek's editing conference, he is in charge, as my aim is to scaffold, teach, and nudge him to assume more editing responsibility. Those notes are written from the perspective of what Derek does and is expected to do.

VIEWING THE CONFERENCES

To make it easier to note the specific focus of each one, I have organized the conferences as follows:

- ☐ **whole-class share/celebration conferences**
- ☐ **whole-class share/teaching conferences**
- ☐ **one-on-one teaching conference**
- ☐ **whole-class editing conference and minilesson on spelling**

Of course, each conference involves celebrating, direct teaching, scaffolding, responding, nudging, and coaching to greater or lesser degrees.

First, watch the DVD Don't read any further. If you have a DVD player, stop and view the conference(s). This is in keeping with whole-to-part-to-whole learning. If you try to watch with the teaching notes in front of you, you will miss what the students and I are trying to do. Enjoy the conference. What do you notice about the conference as a whole?

Next, read the notes Now take a look at the conference notes for an analytic view of what you just saw.

Now, watch the conference again You can re-view the conference as you just did. Alternatively or in addition, you can include my commentary—general introductory comments not in the notes—just skip to that part of the DVD.

Before viewing again, look first at the framework below for thinking about teaching decisions. Try to watch the students with a new perspective.

> ### VIEWING FRAMEWORK: WHAT TO LOOK FOR
> ☐ **What has the student done well?**
> ☐ **How is the student validated and helped as a writer?**
> ☐ **What are the teaching points?**
> ☐ **What else might have been done?**
> ☐ **What did you learn that might help your teaching?**

Whole-Class Share:
Celebration Conferences

See pages 207–215 for information and procedures on whole-class share.

One of the great benefits of whole-class share is that not only do students hear the language of response (which they will later try to apply with peers), they also are encouraged and supported to apply the content and suggestions from the public conference to their own writing.

However, all celebration points become teaching points for the other students listening in. At the same time that we celebrate and specifically show what good writers do, we are also teaching and encouraging other students to do similar things in their own writing. As students hear the writer celebrated, they are also getting this message: "My teacher thinks that . . . makes good writing. I can try that too." Notice how much celebrating and teaching occur in a short time.

▶ **LAHANA'S POEM, GRADE 4**
While walking around the classroom (and having some roving conferences, see page 217) as students were writing their "heart poems," I was struck by Lahana's use of language in "Eating Chocolate Is a Glory" (see DVD for her published poem). I jotted her name on a sticky note so I would remember to invite her to share. I wanted to celebrate what she had done and, also, I wanted other students to hear her memorable choice of words so they would think about carefully choosing words in their own poems.

While Lahana does the first reading of her poem, I do the subsequent readings so that I can show students how her poem is positioned on the page and point out all the great things she has done with language. I also read it

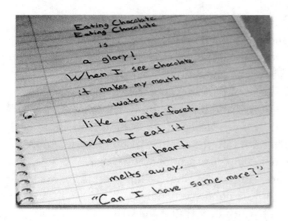

to demonstrate the language of response, as students are just learning how to respond in a conference.

Lahana, a Native American, is an average-performing student. Teachers describe her as "reserved and quiet" so peers seldom get to hear her thinking. Celebrating her poem makes us all appreciate her unique voice.

The following celebrating/teaching points are made in this two and one-half minute conference:

- ☐ **establishing the purposes of whole-class share** *("The main reason we're sharing is to celebrate all the good work you've done.")*

- ☐ **checking for understanding** *("So what's the main reason you're going to be sharing your poem? Everybody."* [Students respond, *"to celebrate…."*])

- ☐ **inviting students to share** (Students *"who have done something wonderful"* and all students who want to share are invited to read their poems.)

- ☐ **celebrating the writer** *("Let's give her a round of applause.")*

- ☐ **reading the poem again** *("Can I read it again? Here are some things I noticed."* And, later, *"I'm going to read it one more time. Poetry has to be heard."* I read it a third time to savor the language once more.)

- ☐ **highlighting the first line** *("I wouldn't have thought to say it like that. . . . Wonderful words.")*

- ☐ **appreciating the writer's use of poetic language** (Restating the line, 'When I see chocolate it makes my mouth water like a waterfall.' *"I'm picturing her mouth is really watering."* And, later, *"I really like what you did here . . . chocolate melting, your heart melting away.")*

- ☐ **focusing on the ending** *("Look at her last line. She doesn't just end it with. . . . She says, "Can I have some more?")*

▶ MAX'S POEM, GRADE 4

Max was a new student who, three months into the school year, was not yet part of the fabric of the classroom. He was, in fact, a social isolate and rarely volunteered in class. When I asked him if he would share his poem, he refused. It was only when I said I would read it for him that he agreed to share it. Then, when he sat in the author's chair and I looked at all the sound effects and conversation in his poem, I realized I couldn't read it the way it needed to be read. The poem needed Max's voice to do it justice. Max's initial reluctance and reserve gave way to exuberance once he and his poem were celebrated. When Max's peers appreciated his wry sense of humor, Max visibly relaxed, and his facial expression changed to one of happiness. He followed up his poem "Pet Monkey," about his

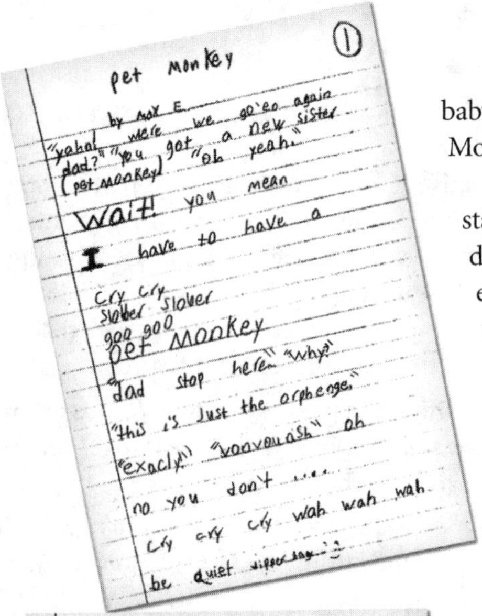

[Handwritten draft, page ①]

> pet Monkey
> by Max E.
> "yabal" where we go'eo again
> dad? "you got a new sister"
> (pet monkey)
> Wait! you mean
> I have to have a
> cry cry
> slower slower
> goo goo pet Monkey
> dad stop here "why?"
> "this is just the orphenge"
> "exacly" "vonvonosh" oh
> no you don't ...
> cry cry cry wah wah wah
> be quiet ...

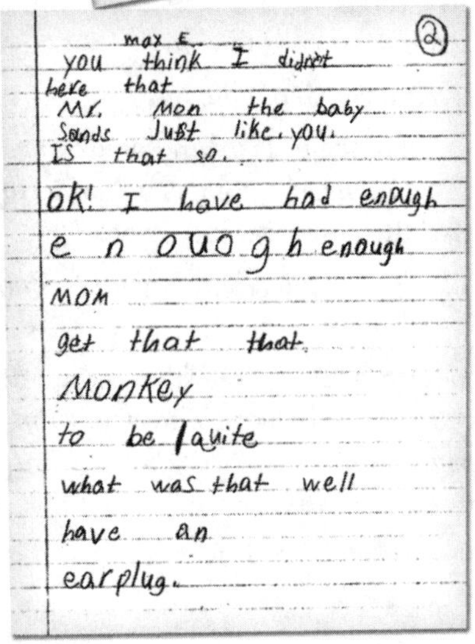

[Handwritten draft, page ②]

> max E.
> you think I didnt
> here that
> Mr. Mon the baby
> sonds just like you.
> Is that so.
> OK! I have had enough
> e n o u o g h enough
> MOM
> get that that
> Monkey
> to be quite
> what was that well
> have an
> earplug.

baby sister (see published poem on DVD), with "Return of the Pet Monkey: The Sequel" to hilarious peer approval.

That one celebration conference forever changed Max's standing in the classroom. Feeling appreciated, his shy demeanor disappeared and his true, funny, outgoing self emerged. His mother confirmed that the celebration of his writing brought him into the classroom community, and that "Max is so much happier in school now."

The following celebrating/teaching points are made in this four-minute public conference:

- ☐ **celebrating and affirming the writer** (*"It's a great poem. I wouldn't change anything here."*)

- ☐ **having the writer read own writing** (*"Only you can read it...."*)

- ☐ **reading the poem twice, to appreciate it and make sure it's clear to readers** (*"We need to hear it again. Did everyone understand?..."*)

- ☐ **paying attention to line breaks when reading a poem** (*"Read it where you have your line breaks."*)

- ☐ **using sound effects**

- ☐ **making conversation integral to the poem**

- ☐ **deliberately putting in humor** (*"He made the audience laugh."* And, *"He was trying to do that because he knows other people will be reading it."*)

- ☐ **reading with expression** (*"I want to hear that 'wah' 'wah'* [baby crying] *really like you put it in there."*)

- ☐ **using a catchy title to get reader's attention** (*"I was very intrigued with the title. I love your title.... Titles are very important."*)

- ☐ **crafting an ending** (*"Your last line is great."*)

- ☐ **getting writing ideas by listening to a peer** (*"You're, I think, the first person who put sound effects in, which might be a good idea for some of you."*)

- ☐ **enjoying the sharing process** (*"It sounded like you had a good time reading it. Did you?"* [Max shakes his head yes.])

- ☐ **writing for a reader and having fun with language** (Listeners are attentive and smile and laugh at the language, message, and expressive reading.)

- ☐ **appreciating the writer's language** (Applauding the writer.)

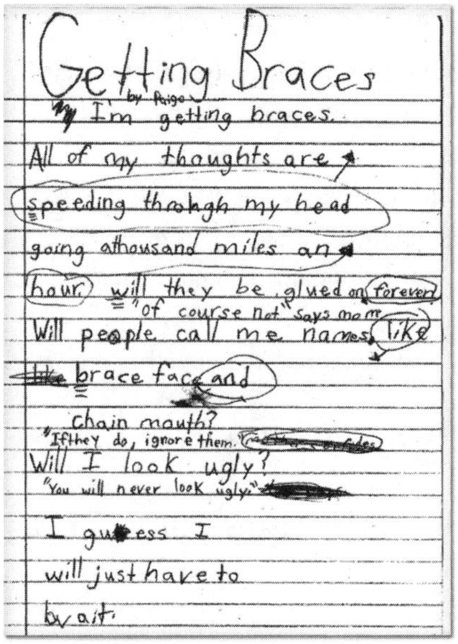

The handwritten poem (as transcribed in the box):

Getting Braces
by Paige B.

I'm getting braces.
All of my thoughts are speeding
through my head
going a thousand miles an hour.
"Will they be glued on
forever?"
"Of course not," says Mom.
"Will people call me names
like brace face
and
chain mouth?"
"If they do, ignore them."
"Will I look ugly?"
"You will never look ugly."
I guess I
will just have to
wait.

▶ **PAIGE'S POEM, GRADE 4**

Paige is a high-achieving student and a strong writer. She has done a lot of writing on her own, including a book review of *Frindle*, by Andrew Clements, which was published in the local newspaper. She is highly regarded by her peers and sought out by them for her writing advice.

Notice how part of Paige's poem, "Getting Braces," piggybacks on my demonstration writing (see pages 307–308). She was probably also influenced in her topic by hearing and seeing Bradley's poem, "Wearing Glasses" (see page 308).

In this two-minute conference, I am celebrating her lovely poem and encouraging students to try out some of the things Paige has done so well:

☐ **reminding her to read with her line breaks** (*"We want to hear them the way your wrote it."*)

☐ **celebrating the whole poem** (*"It's a beautiful poem."*)

☐ **noting how her personal voice affects the reader** (*"It almost made me want to cry." "I got kind of teary." "I'm really feeling what she's feeling."*)

☐ **encouraging other students to use personal voice** (*"She did something I'm going to ask some of you to try tomorrow. She really put herself into it, didn't she?"*)

☐ **celebrating use of conversation** (*"Sounds like Mom, doesn't it? I love the way she has conversation in there."*)

☐ **explaining how to write dialogue** (*"She doesn't have to say, 'said Mom' because we know, don't we? She has quotation marks."*)

☐ **celebrating her ending** (*"Don't you love her ending? It pulls it all together."*)

▶ **GARRETT'S POEM, GRADE 4**

According to his teacher, Garrett is "a very average writer." He can pick a topic and stick to it, but there's not a lot of description or emotion. His stories are almost always about soccer. He has trouble focusing on the important ideas. Still, his teacher notes that he does have a strong voice—his personality comes through—and that he likes to make people laugh.

His poem about his red hair resulted from a brief conversation I had with him because he was having difficulty finding an original topic for his poem. In this two-and-one-half minute conference, I am celebrating and enjoying his humorous, honest poem:

☐ **acknowledging his risk taking for "putting self into it"** (*". . . had copied Catherine's poem. . . written her exact four lines. . . . That wasn't really you, was it?"*)

It's hard to have
<u>Red Hair!</u>
Some-times when we
go
places
little grandma's come up and
say
"I wish I had red hair.
It just gets crepy because
love to they feel my Red hair.
Also
When we go to the
barber shop they say
people would spend alot
of
<u>Money</u> just for my
<u>Hair!</u>
mybe my red hair
isn't that bad

☐ **reinforcing (for teachers) the power of talk to help get the writer going** (*". . . I looked at him and I said, 'You've got red hair and freckles.' Maybe there's something there."*)

☐ **noticing his line breaks** (*"You did not read it the way you wrote it."*)

☐ **celebrating his line breaks and spacing** (*"I want you to see his line breaks and spacing. Some of you are having a little trouble with that. He's done a beautiful job."*)

☐ **savoring a memorable line** (*" 'I wish I had red hair.' Don't you love that?"*)

☐ **celebrating his use of humor** (*"Everyone laughed. That's wonderful. You entertained us. Great."*)

☐ **commenting on actions for deliberate emphasis** (*"'Also' on a line by itself. That's great."* And, earlier, noting when he underlined and used an exclamation point.)

☐ **affirming "show off" ending** (*"Listen to his ending. . . . That last line is kind of a surprise. Great job."*)

🔘 **Whole-Class Share:**
Teaching Conferences

▶ **ERVIN'S PERSONAL "SECRETS" STORY, GRADE 2**

Students in Ervin's classroom had already had a chance to read their story to a peer or whole group and receive affirmation. To make sure no one "slipped through the cracks," I took home and read all the beginning drafts so I could make specific teaching points—to move the writing forward—before students wrote again. Ervin's conference was one of about seven that took place during whole-class share as a "maxi-lesson" at the start of writing workshop. While each student sat in the author's chair right next to me, I read the pieces aloud to save time.

Ervin is a second language learner, and English is not spoken in his home. In grade 1 he received intervention reading instruction. As a second grader, Ervin was a reluctant writer who rarely volunteered in class. Telling a story

in sequence was difficult for him. With teacher support, he was encouraged to tell his story to make it clear for readers. Much scaffolding and teaching occurs in just a three-minute conference.

- ☐ **telling a story so it is complete and makes sense** *("Then what happened?" and, then, "Tell us what happened after that.")*
- ☐ **clearing up confusions** *("I got confused here. What happens . . . ?")*
- ☐ **crossing out repeated information** *("You've already told us that. You don't want to bore your reader."* While it appears I am doing the initial crossing out, I am not. I am modeling what might be crossed out by moving my pencil above those lines.)
- ☐ **directly suggesting changes to writer** *("I'm going to suggest . . ."* and *"Here's what I think.")*
- ☐ **leaving changes to the writer** *("What do you think about that?")*
- ☐ **adjusting language (grammar) to help the reader** *("It sounds easier for the reader if you say it like this. . . .")*
- ☐ **celebrating the title** *("Let's all clap for Ervin's title"* ["Getting in Trouble"].)
- ☐ **affirming student's language for story ending** *("That would be a great ending.")*
- ☐ **importance of rereading** *("Be sure you reread before you start writing today"* [directed to all students].)
- ☐ **writing on sticky notes to "save" student's language** (He can access it while rewriting.)
- ☐ **focusing revision on making it easier and clearer for the reader** *("What would help the reader. . . .")*

▶ DEREK'S PERSONAL "SECRETS" STORY, GRADE 2

Derek is a willing writer but one who struggles. In grade 1, he was one of the lowest-performing students and had great difficulty telling a story in sequence. When he retold a story, he spoke mostly in short phrases. Oral language development continues to be a goal.

After talking through the beginning of his story with his teacher, Derek began to write but had not gotten past the opening lines. Derek is a good example of a student who has a story to tell (all students do!) but has difficulty doing so on his own. In this conference I encourage his fine start and focus on getting him to tell the complete story in sequence so it is organized and makes sense. In his story, he gets mud on his pants and turns them inside out so his parents don't notice. (See draft at left).

By the time I get to Derek's draft, whole-class share (which is taking place before students resume writing) has gone on for over fifteen minutes. I am now speeding things up by reading the remaining papers while students stay seated on the carpet in the reading area. Note that I am not writing on Derek's paper. I am recording his memorable language on sticky notes so he (and I) can remember and go back to his own words when writing.

Notice how much celebrating and scaffolding can take place in a three-and-one-half minute conference:

- ☐ **alerting the writer, in a relaxed way, that a title will be needed** (*"I don't know if you know what your title is yet, but you can add it later. Don't worry about it."*)
- ☐ **congratulating the writer on his beginning** (*"You have a really nice beginning,"* after reading first line, and, again, after reading next two lines, *"It's a great beginning. Let's clap for Derek for what he has so far."*)
- ☐ **letting the writer know his words give a clear picture** (*"I can just picture that."*)
- ☐ **helping the writer tell and sequence his story from beginning to end**
    - ☐ **repeating what's happened** (Restating the events in order as the writer has them, so far.)
    - ☐ **cueing the writer from his own words** (*"You were jumping in mud." "What happened?" "Then what happened?"*)
    - ☐ **leaving student's language intact** (*"Me and my friend"* keeps the flow and can be changed later.)
    - ☐ **encouraging the story to unfold in sequence by asking questions and responding to his evolving story**
        - ☐ *"Tell us what happened."*
        - ☐ *"Then what happened?"*
        - ☐ *"So did you. . . ?"*
        - ☐ *"Tell us how you. . . ."*
        - ☐ *"You mean you. . . ."*
        - ☐ *"You have to put that in."*
        - ☐ *"So then what happened?"*
        - ☐ *"Then what?"*
    - ☐ **clearing up confusions** (*"I didn't know what you were talking about. . . ." "Who was home with you?" "Did your parents notice?" "Then what did she* [your mom] *say?"*)
    - ☐ **expecting a story** (Building on his story beginning, naming the happenings, supporting him to tell the full story, showing confidence in him. *"Put this in your own words. Make it sound like a story."*)
- ☐ **jotting the writer's language on sticky notes for later referral**

☐ **scaffolding and directing the ending** (*"How are you going to end this?" "You don't want it to go on and on." "You could just end it there. . . ." "I'm going to give you a suggestion. You could say. . . ."*)

☐ **expecting the writer to compose the ending on his own** (Modeling possibilities first, and, then, *"I'm not going to write that down because I want it to be your words."*)

☐ **celebrating the complete story** (*"Everyone's laughing, so you know you have a good story."*)

One on One
Teaching Conferences

See pages 218–219 for information and procedures on one-on-one conferences.

▶ **ALEXSANDRA'S PERSONAL "SECRETS" STORY, GRADE 2** Alex (the student on the cover of this book), is a shy student who experiences difficulties with language and, especially, with all aspects of written language. She continued to need lots of support to build her language skills and her confidence.

Alex's piece had already been celebrated in whole-class share, where I determined she needed a one-on-one conference with specific direction to clear up the many confusions in her story. While we were conferencing, the rest of the students were reworking their drafts. Some were writing; some were sharing their writing with peers to get ideas; others were conferencing one-on-one with other teachers. (As part of how school residency works, other teachers were observing in the classroom, and many were trying out conferences with students. Therefore, the classroom is unusually noisy. Typically, it would be fairly quiet.)

The following teaching points are made in this four-and-a half minute conference, an excerpt from a ten minute conference.

☐ **affirming the writer** (*"You have a really interesting story"* and, later, *"This is a great first sentence now."* And, also, leaving her language intact for now and not focusing on grammar [*"my friend and I"*] till the editing stage.)

☐ **revising for a reader** (*"This is hard for the reader to understand."* And, later, *"What do you need to do so it's clear to the reader?"*)

☐ **noting confusions** *("Here's where I got confused." And, later, "What do you mean by that? I don't understand that.")*

☐ **helping the writer "see" her story** *("Really this is about. . . .")*

☐ **crossing out what doesn't belong** *("How about if you leave out. . . ?")*

☐ **adding information** *("What do you need to put here so it's clear to the reader?")*

☐ **helping select a better title based on what story is about** *("What would be a better title?" "I agree." "You could just call it. . . .")*

☐ **showing that the title lets the reader know what the story will be about** *("This is why titles are important. Now I'm not confused anymore.")*

☐ **jotting ideas and writer's words on sticky notes so she can use them later, when writing on her own** *("I'm going to write that here to save time.")*

☐ **explaining how and when to use a caret to add information** *("The caret tells the reader where to move your eyes.")*

☐ **clearing up confusions** *("This is a great first sentence now.")*

☐ **encouraging independent problem solving by revisiting what was just taught** *("What did we do right here?")*

☐ **demonstrating how to** *("Let me show you how to add a caret.")*

☐ **directing the writer** *("How about if you say. . . ?" "Put 'around' right there." "You're going to be adding. . . ." "Cross out. Put a caret in there.")*

☐ **assisting with spelling** *("Here's the spelling* [on sticky note] *if you're not sure.")*

☐ **repeated rereading for clarity and to help the writer "hear" the story and talk it through** *("Let's see how it sounds so far.")*

Alex's teacher continued with this kind of in-depth conferencing with her and reported that by the end of the school year Alex had made major gains in spoken and written language and, in particular, sequencing her stories.

Spelling
Editing Conference and Minilesson

All of the students in Derek's class have completed content conferences with a teacher and have satisfactory drafts for "Secrets of Second Graders." After we do a whole-class shared writing on editing expectations (see page 204) and before students begin their own editing, I model how to "fix up" spelling errors. With Derek's permission, we use a projected transparency of his draft (see page 347).

A big goal for all students in this classroom is to raise expectations for spelling. Derek and many of his peers are misspelling high-frequency words. Following the optimal learning model, Derek cannot independently edit until I show him what I expect, and, then, scaffold, coach, teach, and problem-solve with him.

▶ DEREK'S PERSONAL "SECRETS" STORY, EDITING FIRST LINES FOR SPELLING

The teaching is directed to have Derek do most of the "fix up" work himself. Our goal is always independence; that is, we want writers who are able to self-monitor and self-edit throughout the writing process. With that goal in mind, I am directing, co-problem solving, expecting specific behavior, putting increasing responsibility on the learner, finding out what the speller knows, scaffolding, teaching, questioning, assessing, encouraging, affirming— all, interactively, during the short conference.

Notice that I do not tell Derek "the answers" but rather "guide" him to "fix up" the spellings himself. (This is consistent with research that tells us that students achieve more through a responsive, interactive teaching style—that makes them think— than when teachers rely on telling.)

Although this nine-minute conference is much longer than average, it serves as an important minilesson for the whole class as editing expectations are being explained and demonstrated for the first time.

With teacher direction and support, Derek is expected to:

☐ **inspect the words and find those that are misspelled** (*"Look at this line. Do you see any words that are not spelled correctly?"* [Derek replies, "Yes."] *"Circle them."*)

☐ **find all misspelled, high-frequency words** (*"Let's look at the next line. There are a couple of words there."* [Derek circles two.] *"There's one more there."*)

☐ **"know" what he knows** (*"Some of these I know that you know."*)

☐ **use what he knows** (*"Check the letters you know are right."* [Derek puts a check over the letters *c-m-e*.])

☐ **apply what he knows** (*"You know how to spell 'came'. Write it up here."*)

☐ **remember what he knows for all future spelling** (*"Forevermore, you are never allowed to misspell 'came'."* And, again, later, *"You may never in your whole life ever misspell 'over' again."*)

- [ ] **try an alternative spelling** (*"You've got all the right letters but in the wrong order. ['ovre'] Try writing it another way."*)

- [ ] **self-check** (*"Does that look right?"* And, later, for 'house,' *"Try it. See how it looks."*)

- [ ] **apply the known to the unknown** (*"What do you know about words that end in 'er'?"* [for spelling 'over'] And, later, *"What do you know about words that have 'ou' in them?"* [for spelling 'house'])

- [ ] **self-monitor and self-evaluate** (*"Write 'over' without looking. Check yourself. Is it right?"* [Derek says, 'No.'] *"Cross it off. Write it again. Is it right now?"* ['Yes.'])

- [ ] **focus on what's right and notice what's missing** (*"All those letters are right so check them off,* [Derek has written 'hose'], *but something's missing so try it another way. I want you to think about what you already know."*)

- [ ] **think and problem solve** (*"What do you know about words that have /ow/ in them?"* [I exaggerate the /ow/ sound.] *"Think about that; write 'house' again. Try it another way."* And, again, later, *"Do you know the word 'out'?* [Derek says, 'Yes.'] *How do you spell it?* [Derek says 'o-u-t.'] *Well, that's what I want you to be thinking about."*)

- [ ] **stretch out the sounds** (*"I like what you're doing with your mouth"* [as he sounds out /ow/ (the sound, as in 'now') while thinking about how to spell it.])

- [ ] **attempt an alternative spelling** (*"Think about words you know that have the /ow/ sound. Now, how are you going to make it say 'house'?"* [I stretch out the sounds as I say 'house'.] *"How are you going to make that 'ou' sound?"* [Derek says the letters, 'o-a'.] *"Try it. See how it looks."*)

- [ ] **examine the attempted spelling** (After he writes 'hoase' for 'house', *"Does that look right?"* [Derek says, 'No.'] *"No, it doesn't, try it again."*)

- [ ] **connect the known to unknown** (*"Do you know the word 'out'?"* [Derek orally spells o-u-t.])

- [ ] **try an alternative spelling that makes sense** (Speaking to teachers who are observing the lesson: *"We have to get them to use what they know. We should be seeing one form of /ow/ or another [either 'ow' or 'ou'], no excuses."*)

- [ ] **confirm the spelling** (*"Is that it?"* Derek asks after he writes 'house.' *"Is that it? Does it look right?"* ['Yes.'] *"I think it does look right."*)

- [ ] **practice the spelling** (*"Write the word 'house' without looking. Think about the tricky part."*)

- [ ] **attempt to self-correct** (*"Check yourself. Cross it out if you think it's not right, and start again."*)

☐ **check back to the correct spelling** (After he doesn't spell it correctly, *"Take another look at it. Where's the tricky part for you? Let's look at where you wrote 'house.' You wrote it [correctly] right here."*)

☐ **work through the tricky part** (*"And the tricky part was. . .? You had h-o-s-e. What letter were you missing?"* [The 'u.'] *"This is the part that gave you trouble* [and circling the specific letters—*o-u*—as Derek looks on], *the 'ou' sound. Got it?"*)

☐ **learn the spelling** (*"What are the two letters you need to remember?"* [Derek says *"o-u."*] *"O-u."* [I say the letters.] *"Now write it quickly."* [As he writes,] *"I'm glad you're thinking."* [He spells 'house' correctly.])

☐ **master the spelling** (*"Write it one more time as fast as you can."*)

☐ **expect correct spelling for all writing** (*"That's another word you can never misspell."*)

☐ **apply the learned spelling pattern to other words** (*"Would you write 'mouse'? It's going to be the same except for the first letter. Write it right underneath 'house.' Do it quickly."* [He writes 'mouse.'] *"Got it? Good for you."*)

▶ **EXPECTATIONS FOR THE WHOLE CLASS**

As in other whole-class share conferences, students are expected to apply the teaching points to their own editing. While I have explicitly conferenced with one student, all students are expected to attempt similar strategies as they edit their spelling. For example, one important message students receive during this lesson is that it is not permissible to misspell common, frequently used words.

Other expectations are specifically stated to the whole class during the conference:

| *Teacher Talk* | *This is what I would expect to see from second graders. There are two main ways to spell /ow/. There's this [writing "ow"] like in the word "how," "now," or "owl,"* |

or there's "ou" as in "out," "shout," "loud." . . . *Use the sounds you already know.*

And again,

I don't want to see any erasing. We're going to be doing this [editing] with colored pencils so we can see your work. No erasing because then we can't see what your thinking is, and we can't help you.

And to the teachers who are observing:

We do need to be teaching spelling.

▶ **SUMMARY OF EXPECTATIONS FOR ALL STUDENTS: EDITING FOR SPELLING**

Strategies to apply Taken from Derek's spelling conference during whole-class share:

- ☐ **carefully reread draft, line by line**
- ☐ **check to see if words look right**
- ☐ **circle misspelled words**
- ☐ **put a check mark over the letters in a word you know are correct**
- ☐ **think about what you already know**
- ☐ **connect what you know to the misspelled word**
- ☐ **now try writing that word another way**
- ☐ **say the word and stretch out sounds as you write it**
- ☐ **check to see if word looks right now**
- ☐ **if not, try writing it again**
- ☐ **check a resource for correct spelling** (but do set resources aside during writing; see page 168)
- ☐ **to keep a record of your thinking process, cross out your changes** (do not erase)

See pages 161–165 for additional spelling strategies we teach students.

Appendices

A. **Examining Beliefs About Writing**

Communications to Parents

B. Letter to Parents About Raising Expectations (Grade 1)
C. Suggestions to Parents

Writing Forms

D. Understanding Nonfiction
E. Writing History
F. Poetry Writing Rubric
G. Word Work Sentence Worksheet
H. Writing Strengths/Next Steps
I. Writing Rubric

Editing Expectations

J. Grade 2, Editing Expectations
K. Grade 4, Editing Expectations

L. **Genre Characteristics**

M. **Favorite Poetry Books**

N. **Weekly Professional Conversation Guidelines**

(See this book's website to print out most of these pages and find additional forms.)

Examining Beliefs About Writing

Writing Process

Agree or Disagree?

Read, think about, and discuss the following statements with your colleagues. (There are no right or wrong answers.) Use these beliefs to get conversations going in your school and to begin to develop a common belief system about writing.

- Teachers need to read everything that kids are writing.
- Students should write only if they can publish their writing.
- In a writing conference, the student decides what kind of response he/she wants.
- Spelling doesn't matter in a first draft.
- Students should choose most of their own writing topics.
- Prewriting needs to be separate from other writing activities.
- Students can write fiction without much teacher guidance.
- Students need to see their teachers as writers.
- Revising and editing are really the same thing.
- Students can write well without writing models.
- Peer conferences are mostly a waste of time.
- A lot of writing never gets revised.
- If students write every day, their writing automatically improves.
- Revision takes place after the first draft is written.
- Direct teaching of skills is not part of writers workshop.
- Good sharing of writing is really a public conference.
- The teacher usually corrects students' spelling errors.
- The room needs to be quiet when students are writing.

- The teacher makes the final decision about what gets published.
- Once a piece is published, conventions and spelling must be perfect.
- Having kids talk about what they are going to write about makes the writing easier for students.
- Spelling and handwriting are part of writers workshop.
- Journal writing is separate from writers workshop.
- Invented spelling is always encouraged.
- It is okay for a student to write about the same topic for many weeks.
- If students write to a formula, their voices are constrained.
- For students to take writing seriously, they need to write every day for a sustained period.
- Students learn skills and grammar best when they are directly taught as isolated writing activities.
- Young children cannot be expected to edit their own work.
- Writing rubrics are a proven way to improve writing quality.
- Six Traits is an evaluation tool, not a writing program.
- More nonfiction writing needs to be taught and engaged in.
- Students who read more are better writers.

Adapted from a list originally created with Andrea Butler

Writing Essentials by Regie Routman (Heinemann: Portsmouth, NH); © 2005

Letter to Parents About Raising Expectations

Dear Families,

Did you see the wonderful class book "What Is Special About Us?"
I hope your child reads it to you and several others. Please read
the rest of this newsletter that explains all the wonderful things
Mrs. Regie Routman worked with the children on. I wanted to tell you what a terrific
job your child did and include what the children said they learned from her this week:

"To put spaces between our words." (Jacob)
"To use the lines." (Nicole)
"To make a list of stuff you're going to write about . . . brainstorming."
    (Lindsey)
"How to use carets ^." (Edward)
"You can never not know how to spell *my* and *is*." (Jordan)
"To cross off if you mess up." (Luis)
"Do your best writing." (Hannah)
"To use your lowercase letters and look at the lines." (Madison)
"Stretch it out." (Kearsin)
"Slow down your writing." (Madison)

Wow! Isn't that incredible after only 4 days!! Praise your children for working so hard
and encourage them to keep up the great work!! Please let me know what you notice
about their writing at home and school in the coming months . . .

Many thanks,

Lea Payton
(grade 1 teacher)

Suggestions to Parents

- Read interesting stories (fiction and nonfiction) and poetry aloud to your child, regardless of your child's age. Reading aloud exposes children to vocabulary and language they may not yet be able to read independently. Children need to "hear" literary language before they can use it in their own writing.

- Have lots of paper, cards, stationery, markers, pens, and pencils around and perhaps a blank book that could be used as a journal. Encourage writing for real reasons; thank-you notes, invitations, lists, letters, requests, room signs.

- Write notes to your child often. Tuck a complimentary note inside the lunch box, at the bedside. Write notes on birthdays and special occasions.

- Create a photo-memory book together. Label photos with captions you write together.

- Encourage your child to read widely. Join the public library. Give books as gifts for special occasions. Help your child establish a personal home library. Be a reading model yourself. The best writers are almost always the best readers.

- Limit television, video, and DVD watching to perhaps an hour a day to allow your child to participate in other activities.

- Help your child's imagination blossom. Tell stories to and with each other. For many children, it is easier to write once they have spoken the words aloud to someone.

- Use reading and writing for pleasure, never punishment.

Understanding Nonfiction

Text _____ Date _____

Group members (circle the scribe's name): _____

_____

Summary sentences: _____

_____

_____

_____

_____

_____

_____

_____

What we think (infer): _____

_____

_____

_____

_____

_____

What we wonder: _____

_____

_____

_____

_____

(continue on back)

Writing Essentials by Regie Routman (Heinemann: Portsmouth, NH); © 2005

Writing History

WRITING RECORD					
Title/Topic	Audience	Genre	Date Started	Date Ended	What happened to the piece?

Poetry Writing Rubric

NAME _____ DATE _____	Yes	No
Title that grabs the reader's attention		
Beginning interests the reader to read on		
Put your feelings in your poem so people know that you are in the poem		
Plays around with print to make it more exciting and easier to understand for the reader. May use: • Conversation • **Bold** • Caps • Punctuation		
Uses creative word choice		
Ending wraps up the poem so the reader isn't left hanging		
Line breaks and spacing make poem look and sound like a poem		
Publishes with perfect conventions • Spelling • Punctuation • Grammar		
Writes expected amount of poems on time		

If using for a grade, allow 10% for each category; doubleweight one area. We allowed 20% for voice (putting self into poem).

Arapahoe Ridge Elementary, Westminster, CO, a shared writing with grade 4 students

Writing Essentials by Regie Routman (Heinemann: Portsmouth, NH); © 2005

Word Work Sentence Worksheet

NAME _____

DATE _____

Glue your word work sentence below:

How can you sort the words? Write 3 ways in the boxes below:

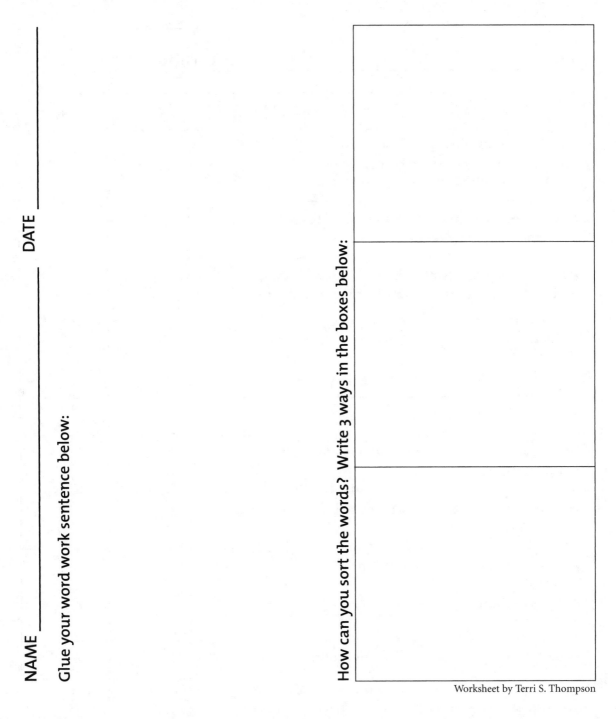

Worksheet by Terri S. Thompson

Writing Essentials by Regie Routman (Heinemann: Portsmouth, NH); © 2005

Writing Strengths/Next Steps

STUDENT NAME _____

Date	Strengths	Next Steps	I can spell these **No Excuses Words** correctly:
			about all an and are as be but by can do each for from had have
			he his how I if not of on one or said that the their there they this to was
			we were what when which will with you your up

Adapted from Patty Sherman, Vancouver, WA; Second Grade. "No Excuses" word list by Rebecca Sitton.

Writing Rubric

NAME _____ DATE _____

Category	Consistent	Inconsistent
Able to write a rough draft that reflects thought and organization		
Willingly takes suggestions from peers and teacher and revises accordingly		
Able to give helpful feedback to a peer's draft		
Attempts to use interesting language		
Demonstrates awareness of audience and purpose		
Proofreads and efficiently edits for _____		
Completes writing on time		
Writes in a variety of forms and genres		
Is learning to take meaningful notes		
Shares ideas and writing with whole group		

Comments

Writing Essentials by Regie Routman (Heinemann: Portsmouth, NH); © 2005

Grade 2, Editing Expectations

Directions

Share this sheet with an adult and explain how we use it. Show how you can do these things by yourself in your writing.

Show how your teacher uses a dot in the margin to show any line you need to go back to and check again.

Explain how if you do these things that you listed below you can get help with the rest of your writing "for free!"

After you have shared this with an adult, have the adult sign the slip below and return that slip to school as your homework assignment. KEEP THIS SHEET AT HOME TO HELP YOU!

EDITING

Spelling

1. Circle *most* misspelled words.
2. Correct *most* of them by:
   - writing it another way
   - sounding it out
   - asking another person
   - looking at words around the room
   - using a dictionary

Capitals

1. Start each sentence with a capital letter.
2. Use capitals for important names, places, and dates.

Punctuation

Use a period at the end of each sentence.

Reread to check how it sounds.

Write Neatly.

My child, _____, has explained how this sheet is being used at school and at home. He/She understands how to use these strategies to self-edit his/her work.

_____

Parent's Name

Writing Essentials by Regie Routman (Heinemann: Portsmouth, NH); © 2005

Grade 4, Editing Expectations

*Reread! (5–6 times)

Spelling
1. Circle most misspelled words.
2. Correct the spelling of most of these.
   - Look at the word carefully to see if you already know it.
   - Look for it on a sign or book cover in the room.
   - Ask a friend.
   - **Try writing it another way!**
     Put a check above the letters you know are correct.
     Make two attempts to spell the word correctly.
   - Use a dictionary (only if you already know the first three letters of the word).
3. Spell out numbers (one, thirty, twenty-five).

Punctuation
1. End every sentence with correct punctuation (., !, ?).
2. Use quotation marks when someone is talking.
3. Use commas when you list more than two things (*cat, dog,* and *iguana*).

Organization
1. Make sure sentences make sense (sound right and go together).
2. REREAD!
3. Cross out words that don't belong or are boring, and add better words.
4. Indent first paragraph.
5. Use proper format for things like friendly letters.

Capitalization
1. Start each sentence with a capital letter.
2. *I* is always capitalized.
3. Specific names and places are capitalized (Rio Grande School).
4. No capitals in the middle of sentences for words that are not proper nouns (names and places).
5. Important words in a title are capitalized.
6. Use a capital letter to begin dialogue.

Legibility
1. Make sure reader(s) can read it.
2. Use your best handwriting.
3. Make sure there are spaces between your words.
4. All letters are formed correctly and are the right height.
5. Slow down!

*REREAD

Shared Writing in Kristin Potter's Fourth Grade Class, Santa Fe, New Mexico, April 2003.

Writing Essentials by Regie Routman (Heinemann: Portsmouth, NH); © 2005

avorite Poetry Books

andra, Deborah. 1993. *Rich Lizard and Other Poems*. Farrar, Straus and Giroux.

eech, Sharon. 2004. *Heartbeat*. HarperCollins. (poetic narrative)

eech, Sharon. 2001. *Love That Dog*. HarperCollins. (poetic narrative)

etcher, Ralph. 1997. *Ordinary Things. Poems from a Walk in Early Spring*. Atheneum Books for Young Readers.

orian, Douglas. 2003. *Autumnblings*. Greenwillow. (See other books by Florian.)

orian, Douglas. 2001. *Lizards, Frogs, and Polliwogs*. Harcourt, Inc. (See all of Florian's poetry/painting books.)

eorge, Kristine O'Connell. 2001. *Toasting Marshmallows: Camping Poems*. Clarion Books.

eorge, Kristine O'Connell. 1997. *The Great Frog Race and Other Poems*. Clarion Books.

raves, Donald. 1996. *Baseball, Snakes, and Summer Squash. Poems About Growing Up*. Boyds Mills Press.

rimes, Nikki. 2001. *Stepping Out with Grandma Mac*. Orchard Books.

arrison, David. 1999. *Wild Country: Outdoor Poems for Young People*. Wordsong.

olbrook, Sara. 1996. *My Dog Ate My Homework*. Boyds Mills Press.

opkins, Lee Bennett (selector.) 2004. *Wonderful Words: Poems About Reading, Writing, Speaking, and Listening*. Simon & Schuster.

ughes, Langston. 1994. *The Dream Keeper and Other Poems*. Alfred A. Knopf.

hnston, Tony. 2000. *It's About Dogs*. Harcourt, Inc.

atz, Bobbi. (selector) 2004. *Pocket Poems*. Dutton.

evy, Constance. 2002. *A Tree Place and Other Poems*. Margaret K. McElderry Books.

ocker, Thomas. 2001. *Mountain Dance*. Harcourt, Inc.

edina, Jane. 2004. *The Dream on Blanca's Wall*. Wordsong/Boyds Mills Press. (See also *My Name is Jorge On Both Sides of the River*, 1999.)

ora, Pat. (ed.). 2001. *Love to Mama: A Tribute to Mothers*. Lee & Low Books.

oda, Takayo. 2003. *Dear World*. Dial.

eters, Lisa Westberg. 2003. *Earthshake: Poems from the Ground Up*. Greenwillow.

anger, Laura. 1995. *Laura's Poems*. Auckland, NZ: Godwit Publishing.

outman, Regie. 2000. *Kids' Poems. Teaching Children to Love Writing Poetry*. Scholastic (4-volume series for grades K, 1, 2, and 3–4).

inger, Marilyn. 1989. *Turtle in July*. Macmillan Publishing Co.

oain, Sahara Sunday. 2001. *If There Would Be No Light: Poems from My Heart*. Harper/SanFranciso.

orth, Valerie. 1994. *All The Small Poems and Fourteen More*. Farrar, Straus and Giroux.

orth, Valerie. 2002. *Peacock and Other Poems*. Farrar, Straus and Giroux.

Regie Routman with Donna Maxim

　　　　Writing Essentials by Regie Routman (Heinemann: Portsmouth, NH); © 2005

Genre Characteristics (excerpt)

Genre/Definition	Frequently Found Elements	Picture Book Exam
PERSONAL NARRATIVES **Memoirs** A record of events based upon the writer's own observation.	• Memoir may cover only one event or aspect of the author's life. • Memoir is a retrospective account of a memorable event. • Memoirs for children can be fictionalized.	*When I Was Young in the M* Cynthia Rylant, illustratio Goode. New York: Dutton *Don't You Know There's a l* James Stevenson. New Yor Books, © 1992.
Journals and Diaries A log written by an author at regular intervals	• Entries are usually dated. • Diaries and journals in series have been published as a way of sharing historical fiction. • Fictional diaries can be animal fantasies when animals write them.	*Only Opal: The Diary of a l* Opal Whiteley, selected [an Jane Boulton, illustrations l Cooney. New York: Paperst *Diary of a Worm* by Doree pictures by Harry Bliss. N Cotler Books, © 2003.
INFORMATIONAL BOOKS Factual presentations of documented knowledge.	• Nonfiction is an informational text dealing with an actual, real-life subject. • Major types include chapter books, picture books, photographic essays, and informational books with a narrative blend. • Elements of expository writing in informational books are description, time sequence, enumeration, cause and effect, and comparison/contrast. • Nonfiction picture books can serve as models for student content reports.	*Ice-cream Cones for Sale!* by Greenstein. NY: Arthur A. l © 2003. *What Do You Do with a Tai* Steve Jenkins & Robin Page Houghton Mifflin, © 2003. *Cow* by Jules Older; illustra Severance. Watertown, MA © 1997.
Essay A short literary composition that reflects the author's outlook or point of view.	• These are often of a persuasive nature. • May be found in collections • Frequently found in magazines and periodicals.	*Vote!* by Eileen Christelow. Clarion Books, © 2003. *50 Simple Things Kids Can l* *Earth* by the Earth Works (City, MO: Andrews and Mc
FICTION **Historical Fiction** Imaginative stories with fictional characters and events in a historical setting.	• May be based on dates, people, or events that really happened. • Major historical event may be an essential. • Accuracy of the historical detail is evident. • May include author notes on research. • Categories of historical fiction are based on the time period or historical era. • Characters and time periods are lifelike. • Conflict allows children to compare the past with the present in order to better understand our world.	*White Socks Only* by Evelyn illustrated by Tyrone Geter. IL: A. Whitman, © 1996. *The Cello of Mr. O* by Jane (ed by Greg Couch. New Yor Children's Books, © 1999.

The complete Genre Characteristics table is available on the companion website, www.heinemann.com/writingessentials. Compiled Haloin with input from Gaylynn Jameson and JoAnne Piccolo. Arbuthnot, May Hill. *The Arbuthnot Anthology of Children's Literatu* Scott Foresman and Company, 1961. Hancock, Marjorie R. *A Celebration of Literature and Response: Children, Books, and Teachers in Second Edition*, New Jersey: Pearson Merrill Prentice Hall, 2004. Hillman, Judith. *Discovering Children's Literature 3rd Edition*. New J Merrill Prentice Hall, 2003. Larsen, Karen, *Handy Dandy List of Genres*, Compiled by Karen Larsen. Adams Twelve School District, V August 2003. Lukens, Rebecca J. *A Critical Handbook of Children's Literature*. Boston: Allyn and Bacon, 2003. Nixon, Norma *The Ne Literature Guide K-6*. Cherry Creek School District. Aurora, Colorado, 1991.

Writing Essentials by Regie Routman (Heinemann: Portsmouth, NH); © 2005

Weekly Professional Conversation Guidelines

Make Weekly Professional Conversations Part of School Life

Our school started a weekly support group three years ago. The purpose was to create an atmosphere where we could read professionally and share our thoughts on the selected books or articles. With our principal's encouragement it has become an integral part of our school's environment. In addition to the professional development opportunities, it has opened our lines of communication across all grade levels.

How to Start a Group and Keep It Going:

- One staff person needs to be in charge: facilitate set schedule, schedule meeting place.

- Another person takes notes and types up weekly minutes. (It is difficult to be the facilitator and secretary.)

- Publicize first meeting, date, place, and time.

- Personally invite staff members to attend, if possible.

- Bring possible books or reading selections for the group to review as possible reading materials to the first meeting.

- Don't worry about food for meetings except for an occasional special event.

- Principal helps set up meetings, but does not actively participate until fourth or fifth meeting; principal participates as equal.

- Investigate grants, district professional development funds, etc. to purchase books for group.

- If there is no money for books, discuss an article from *The Reading Teacher* or another professional journal for use at the meeting.

- Investigate the possibility of offering graduate credit or professional development contact hours to members.

- It is important to meet weekly; only cancel for really important reasons.

- Don't forget to invite the speech pathologist, guidance counselor, special education teacher, educational assistants, music and physical education teachers, and other support staff.

- Start and end on time!

- Don't worry if you experience an occasional "slump" in attendance. That will happen and it may depend on what's going on such as grade cards or even the material selected at that time. Attendance will pick back up.

By Linda Benedict, 2004, Huntsville Elementary School, Huntsville, Ohio.

Brief Definitions of Terms

The following terms may not be defined in the body of the text or are introduced before they are fully explained.

audience

The person(s) to whom the writing is addressed.

author's chair

Designated "chair" in which the author sits while reading his writing aloud to listeners/responders.

author's craft

Embracing and shaping language in a manner that entices and engages the reader.

continuum

"A visual representation of literacy development using descriptors to depict the developmental stages of learning" (Hill 2001, p. 3).

culture

"The acquired knowledge people use to interpret experience and generate behavior" (Ball and Farr 2003, p. 436, quoting J. Spradley, Participant Observation (New York: Holt, Rinehart, & Wilson, 1980), p. 6, italics in original.

differentiated instruction

Challenging and relevant instruction that is tailored to meet the needs and interests of each learner. In a heterogenous group (often whole class), students receive scaffolded, multilevel instruction across content, processes, and product that enables each student to be successful.

draft

A writer's first thinking and rethinking; getting ideas down without regard to final product.

English language learners

Students who come from homes in which a language other than English is spoken and who need some assistance in both English and academics in order to progress well in school; also called second language learners.

fluency

Deft, cohesive writing created quickly and easily.

formulaic writing

Writing that must adhere to preset rules and structure.

freewriting

A burst of stream-of-consciousness writing: the student writes without interruption for about five-to-ten minutes without concern for organization, grammar, and spelling; freewriting may be jumpstarted with a prompt; also called quickwriting.

genre

The type or form of writing, such as poetry, literary analysis, or research report. Each type conforms to specific expected rules and, often, a unique format.

grammar

The formal rules and conventional patterns of a language that speakers and writers elect to use.

graphic organizer

A visual—such as, a map, chart, diagram, or web—used to organize information so it can be more easily represented, recalled, and understood.

high-poverty school

A school in which the majority of students live in poverty (as defined by federal guidelines) and therefore are entitled to receive federally funded services such as free and reduced-cost lunch, Title 1 services, tutoring services, and extra instruction in reading and writing.

high-stakes assessment

"Assessments that involve substantial consequences for good (high) or poor (low) performance" (International Reading Association 1999) for individual students, teachers, or schools.

independent writing

On their own, writers choose topics to write about that they enjoy, understand, and/or want to explore in writing; usually, daily sustained silent writing in school together with careful teacher monitoring.

interactive writing

A shared-pen technique in which the teacher and child compose collaboratively, and the child writes the letters and elements of writing he is able to tackle on his own. (If the child makes an error, the teacher helps him fix it up so spelling and other conventions are correct.)

invented spelling

Temporary spelling children use—based on their letter–sound and word knowledge and spontaneous linguistic analysis of the orthographic system—to approximate conventional spellings; sometimes called phonetic spelling. Invented spelling is not "spell it any way you wish," but is rather the reasoned linguistic approximations that are appropriate for the child's developmental knowledge of letters and sounds.

lead

The opening to a piece of writing written with the intention of attracting the readers attention and interest.

minilesson

Explicit teaching; usually a short, focused demonstration based on what students need to become more proficient and independent as learners.

National Writing Project

A K–12 school/university partnership that was started by James Gray in 1973 on the University of California campus at Berkeley to improve student writing through better teaching of writing; federally funded, national network of teacher-learning communities that rely on close examination of effective, innovative classroom practices.

onset/rime

See *rime/onset*.

optimal learning model

A gradual-release-of-responsibility cyclical learning model that begins with demonstration (showing the learner how to do it), moves to guided practice of the specific strategy or activity, and eventually leads to independence. Depends on a safe, risk-taking, caring environment for success.

phonemic awareness

Sensitivity to and awareness of the fact that words comprise individual sounds; being able to discriminate between different consonants and to sequence each small unit of sound (phoneme) in a word.

phonics

Knowing the relationship between letters and their sounds, often called sound–symbol relationships.

portfolio

A reflective selection of writing samples and records that demonstrates student writing development over time.

prewriting

Deliberate activities that help the writer to think, talk, and plan for writing.

quickwrites

See *freewriting*.

Readers Theatre

Performing a text or part of a text orally for an audience from a script (can be written by students); often uses well-loved stories; few or no props; excellent technique to encourage repeated reading and develop fluency.

reciprocal teaching

Interactive, scaffolded instruction for strengthening reading comprehension; the teacher (or peer, older student, parent) leads a group of students through a text to understand it; involves an emphasis on four strategies—generating a question, clarifying, predicting, and summarizing. (Developed by Annemarie Sullivan Palinscar and Ann L. Brown.)

rime/onset

The rime is the part of the syllable that begins with the vowel and comes after the onset. The onset is the part of the syllable that comes before the vowel; it consists of one or more consonants. For example, in the word *play*, *pl* is the onset and *ay* is the rime. Nearly five hundred words can be derived from only thirty-seven rimes.

rubric

A list of criteria (such as organized paragraphs, interesting word choice) for determining the quality of specific writing products. Rubrics are also used to determine what's to be included in the writing (for example, an introduction and at least three important facts); rubrics are sometimes employed as scoring guides.

scaffolded conversation

Instructional conversation in which the learner is led by an expert—through specific questioning, encouragement, and modeling—to expand and clarify her thinking about story, text, concept, and so on.

scaffolding

Temporary support from a teacher, parent, or accomplished peer that enables the learner to take on and understand new material and tasks they are not quite ready to do independently. *"Scaffolding is a process that enables students to use resources they have already mastered through cultural experiences in order to understand and undertake new and more advanced academic tasks"* (Ball and Farr 2003, p. 440).

self-monitoring

The writer—and reader—is aware of the clarity and correctness of his own thinking and writing and is able to revise and "fix" gaps in meaning in the process of composing and editing.

shared writing

Students and teacher collaboratively compose a coherent text with the teacher doing the writing while scaffolding children's language and ideas; often, these texts become shared reading texts as well as published texts for guided and personal reading.

six traits

Writing traits that many writers agree make up quality writing: content and ideas, organization, word choice, sentence fluency, voice, and conventions. Also the name of a published program that details the characteristics of each trait and trains teachers in using and evaluating each of the traits in students' writing.

skills

Automatic, learned responses that are the same for each situation; for example, knowing that a letter makes a particular sound.

strategies

In-the-head mental thinking that learners construct for each unique learning situation in order to read, write, problem solve, and so on.

transitions

In writing, coherent phrases or sentences that help the reader move seamlessly to another idea; comes from the Latin word *transire*, which means "to pass from one place to another."

word sort

Grouping words into different categories based on some criterion or characteristic; for example, finding all the words in a group that have a similar pattern.

word wall

A space where frequently encountered words (that students are learning to read and write automatically) are posted; each word is listed under the corresponding letter of the alphabet that coincides with the beginning letter of the word; the words are often movable.

writing aloud

Thinking out loud and speaking the words while composing text.

writing workshop/writers workshop

A process approach to writing that includes planning, drafting, revising, editing, and publishing. The approach is not a rigid set of procedures but rather a flexible, problem-solving process that is greatly influenced by the audience and purpose for the writing.

Notes

Chapter 1

3   Henri Frederic Amiel was a ninteenth-century Swiss poet and critic. I found the quotation in Donald M. Murray's *Shoptalk: Learning to Write with Writers* (Portsmouth, NH: Boynton/Cook, 1990), p. 129.

5   The statement about the writing problem in schools is supported by Kathleen Cotton's *Teaching Composition: Research on Effective Practices,* School Improvement Research Series: Research You Can Use (Portland, OR: Northwest Regional Educational Laboratory, March 2002), p. 1.

8   The importance of collegial relationships to lasting change is the subject of Anthony Bryk and Barbara Schneider's "Trust in Schools: A Core Resource for School Reform," *Educational Leadership,* March 2003, pp. 40–44. I also discuss this topic in *Reading Essentials: The Specifics You Need to Teach Reading Well* (Portsmouth, NH: Heinemann, 2003).

9   The school mentioned is Rummel Creek Elementary, in Houston, Texas.

10   The discussion about and comments of Terry Lamp stem from a conversation I had with him in June, 2004.

12   Melinda Jennings's comments were made in an email she sent me in June, 2004.

13   "Fool with words" is Bill Moyers's term, as attributed to him by Tom Romano on page 125 of *Crafting Authentic Voice* (Portsmouth, NH: Heinemann, 2004).

13   Craft authentic voice: See Tom Romano's book, above.

14   . . . "the strategies of production are generalizable to other comparable tasks. When instruction is aimed at developing a particular narrative, students may not learn those strategies of production for use independently": George Hillocks, Jr., *The Testing Trap: How State Writing Assessments Control Writing* (New York: Teacher College Press, 2002), p. 184.

Chapter 2

17   The epigraph is from Stephen King's *On Writing: A Memoir of the Craft* (New York: Scribner, 2000), p. 249.

20   The statement that kindergartners see themselves as writers is supported by Dorothy Strickland and Joan Feeley, "Development in the Elementary School Years," in *Handbook of Research on Teaching the English Language Arts,* 2d ed., ed. by James Flood, Diane Lapp, James R. Squire, and Julie M. Jensen (Mahwah, NJ, and London, England: Lawrence Erlbaum, 2003), pp. 339–56, citing Graves (1983), Sulzby (1985a), and Temple et al. (1988). The Don Graves quote is from page 4 of his 1983 book.

21   The teacher quoted is Diane Mattern, of Westminster, Colorado.

23   The statement that stories help low socioeconomic students is supported by Cynthia Brock, Fenice Boyd, and Juel Moore, "Variation in Language and the Use of Language Across Contexts: Implications for Literacy Learning," in Flood et al. 2003, p. 450, where they cite Purcell-Gates et al. (1995).

23   The benefits of dramatizing stories are discussed in Mary Jane Wagner, "Imaginative Expression," in Flood et al. 2003, pp. 1008–25). The benefits of telling stories provides English language learners are discussed by Danling Fu in "Teaching ELL Students in Regular Classrooms at the Secondary Level," *Voices in the Middle,* May 2004, pp. 8–15.

23   The statement about boys and pop culture stories is supported by Tom Newkirk, *Misreading Masculinity: Boys, Literacy, and Popular Culture* (Portsmouth, NH: Heinemann, 2002).

24   Oral language development and literacy skills are closely linked: Jeanne S. Chall and Mary E. Curtis, "Children with Reading Difficulties," in Flood et al. 2003, p. 414.

24   *Try it. Apply it.* For demonstrations, procedures, and guidelines for journal writing, see my book *Conversations* (Portsmouth, NH: Heinemann, 2000), pp. 233–82; see Patsy Cooper's *When Stories Come to School* (Teachers and Writers Collaborative, 1993) and almost anything by Vivan Paley for great specific information regarding dramatization.

25   "I put my heart on the page when I tell the story": Kate DiCamillo, in an interview on the *Jim Lehrer News Hour* (PBS, March 30, 2004), talking about how she wrote *The Tale of Despereaux,* which won the 2004 Newbury Medal for the "most distinguished contribution to American literature for children."

27   Often the writing that students do freely at home (mostly stories and poems), which emerges from their own interests, far exceeds the quality of the work and effort they put into school writing, which they mostly see as mechanical and routine: Anne Haas Dyson and Sarah Warshauer Freedman, "Writing," in Flood et al. 2003, p. 974. Dyson and Freedman cite Janet Emig's *The Composing Processes of Twelfth Graders* (Research Rep. No. 13, Urbana, IL: NCTE, 1971). Janet Emig and many other researchers have known for at least thirty years that school writing is mostly a routine, mechanical, learned activity devoid of authentic communication and problem solving.

27   Students will spend a substantial amount of time planning, writing, and revising when they are interested in the writing: Dyson and Freedman 2003, p. 975.

27   When we tap into students' interests, they are more likely to connect with all aspects of schooling: Lisa Delpit, ed., *The Skin That We Speak: Thoughts on Language and Culture in the Classroom* (New York: The New Press, 2002).

29   Taylor's comment is from a letter she wrote me in June, 2004.

29   "We have to let children in on the secret of how powerfully they write": Ralph Fletcher, *What a Writer Needs* (Portsmouth, NH: Heinemann, 1993), p. 14.

30   The Leonard Cohen verse is from . . . "Anthem" in *The Future—1992.* Sony/ATV Music Publishing.

31   "Poetry helps us live better, helps us understand the human experience": John W. Barr, "A Passion for Poetry (and Profits): Charting a Literary Course with $100 Million," *The New York Times,* April 19, 2004, Arts sec., B4.

31   Such playfulness helps develop children's interest in language: Peter H. Johnston, *Choice Words: How Our Language Affects Children's Learning* (Portland, ME: Stenhouse, 2004), p. 49.

34   All students, and especially those who begin school with limited literacy skills, need to think of themselves as readers and writers, see the processes as meaningful, and have positive attitudes about literacy before they can successfully engage in literacy practices: Kathryn Au, "Balanced Literacy Instruction: Implications for Students of Diverse Backgrounds," in Flood et al. 2003, p. 956, also citing the "engagement perspective" (which goes beyond "how" people read and write to "why" people would want to read and write) of John Guthrie and Donna Alvermann, eds., in *Engagement in Reading: Processes, Practices, and Policy Implications* (New York: Teachers College Press, 1999).

34   More and more of our students are culturally and linguistically diverse and are at risk of educational failure, and these numbers are increasing: Arnetha F. Ball and Marcia Farr, "Language Varieties, Culture, and Teaching the English Language Arts," in Flood et al. 2003, p. 435.

34   These students are most successful with contextualized, social learning—not isolated drills and skills: Ball and Farr 2003, p. 440; also see research cited in *Writing Essentials,* Chapter 5, Do More Shared Writing.

Chapter 3

35   Cami Kostecki is a second-grade teacher in Westminster, Colorado. She made this statement in a letter to me in October, 2003.

36   Bonding as a staff is not just a "feel good" activity; staffs that are more collegial and collaborative have higher achievement in writing and reading: Roland S. Barth, *Improving Schools from Within: Teachers, Parents, and Principals Can Make the Difference* (San Francisco: Jossey-Bass, 1991); Michael Fullan and Andy Hargreaves, *What's Worth Fighting for in Your School,* 2d. ed. (New York: Teachers College Press, 1996); Cerylle A. Moffett, "Sustaining Change: The Answers Are Blowing in the Wind," *Educational Leadership,* April 2000, p. 36; Regie Routman, "Teacher Talk," *Educational Leadership,* March 2002, pp. 32–35; Joan Servis, *Celebrating the Fourth: Ideas and Inspiration for Teachers of Grade*

Four (Portsmouth, NH: Heinemann, 1999); John Simmons and Pamela S. Carroll, "Today's Middle Grades: Different Structures, Students, and Classrooms," in Flood et al. 2003, pp. 357–92.

38   When someone, regardless of age or profession, writes something of importance and reads it aloud, the audience pays attention because its members are personally touched by the writing: Donald M. Murray, *Shoptalk: Learning to Write with Writers* (Portsmouth, NH: Boynton/Cook, 1990), p. 128.

39   The Houston, Texas, teacher is Lisa Bacon. She teaches third grade.

42   Teachers find that recording ideas while they are fresh reduces planning time and increases teacher effectiveness: I quote Marnie Danielski on this subject on p. 218 of *Reading Essentials* (2003).

42   *Writing enhances thinking and helps develop it:* Robert J. Marzano, "Language, the Language Arts, and Thinking" in Flood et al. 2003, p. 691, citing Nickerson 1984; and Donald M. Murray, *Crafting a Life in Essay, Story, Poem* (Portsmouth, NH: Heinemann, 1996).

42   The Toni Morrison and Wallace Stegner quotes are from Donald M. Murray's *Shoptalk: Learning to Write with Writers* (Portsmouth, NH: Boynton/Cook, 1990). The Morrison quote is on p. 109, the Stegner on p. 113.

43   In connection with the material on connecting your reading and writing lives, see Chapter 3, "Share Your Reading Life," in my book *Reading Essentials* (Portsmouth, NH: Heinemann, 2003). A page from my notebook is shown there on p. 29.

44   Donald Murray's advice is from *Shoptalk*, p. 129.

45   "You only have to write a little bit better than your students for them to take something away from your writing": Nancie Atwell, *In the Middle*, 2d.ed. (Portsmouth, NH: Heinemann, 1998).

45   Darcy Ballentine shared her insight with me in a letter she wrote me in June, 2004.

47   The statements on recursive writing are supported by Nancy Farnan and Karin Dahl, "Children's Writing: Research and Practice," in Flood et al. 2003, p. 995, citing Janet Emig 1971; and by George Hillocks Jr., *Research on Written Composition: New Directions for Teaching* (Urbana, IL: ERIC Clearinghouse on Reading and Communication Skills and the National Conference on Research in English, 1986).

48   Even professional writers are rarely able to produce final copy in a first draft: Robert J. Marzano, "Language, the Language Arts, and Thinking," in Flood et al. 2003, p. 691, citing Perkins 1981.

50   Cindy Coronado, a first-grade teacher in Westminster, Colorado, shared her thoughts in a letter she wrote to me in January, 2004.

Chapter 4

53   Epigraph from Deborah Meier's *The Power of Their Ideas: Lessons for America from a Small School in Harlem.* (Boston: Beacon Press, 1995), p. 4.

54   I also discuss my father's stroke on pages 220 and 221 of *Reading Essentials* (Portsmouth, NH: Heinemann, 2003).

54   It is well documented that minority students as a group experience a curriculum of lowered expectations and less rigor: P. Barton, *Parsing the Achievement Gap* (Princeton, NJ: Educational Testing Service, 2003); Michael S. Knapp et al., *Teaching for Meaning in High-Poverty Classrooms* (New York: Teachers College Press, 1995); Arnetha F. Ball and Marcia Farr, "Language Varieties, Culture, and Teaching the English Language Arts," in Flood et al. 2003, pp. 435–45; Ronald Ferguson with Jal Mehta, "An Unfinished Journey: The Legacy of *Brown* and the Narrowing of the Achievement Gap," *Phi Delta Kappan,* May 2004, pp. 656–69; John H. Holloway, "Research Link: Closing the Minority Achievement Gap in Math," *Educational Leadership,* February 2004, pp. 84–86.

56   Gillian's mother made her comment in a conversation I had with her in May, 2004.

56   The first-grade teacher quoted is Lea Payton, from Vancouver, Washington.

56   All students, advantaged or disadvantaged, go through similar stages of literacy development: Jeanne S. Chall and Mary E. Curtis, "Children with Reading Difficulties" in Flood et al. 2003, pp. 413–20), p. 414.

56   Students achieve faster, more easily, and on a higher level when they find the lessons and materials interesting, relevant, and challenging: Knapp et al. 1995.

57   Gail Westbrook made these comments in a conversation I had with her in June, 2004.

64   Kelly's mother, Sheila Pearce, said this in a letter she wrote me in April, 2004.

65   Students who are excellent writers write a lot: Richard Allington, *Big Brother and The National Reading Curriculum* (Portsmouth, NH: Heinemann, 2002a).

66   And, fair or not, handwriting quality impacts how scorers rate students' writing papers: Richard E. Hodges, "The Conventions of Writing," in Flood et al. 2003, p. 1056.

66   When we raise our expectations and refuse to accept poor handwriting, kids' handwriting improves: Hodges 2003, p. 1057.

68   Research indicates that students need to be knowledgeable about styles of writing, not that cursive is preferable to printing: Hodges 2003, p. 1057.

77   . . . interactive, responsive learning . . . is the best way to attain achievement, versus telling, which does not raise one's achievement level: Barbara Taylor, Debra Peterson, P. David Pearson, and Michael Rodriguez, "Looking Inside Classrooms: Reflecting on the 'How' as Well as the 'What' in Effective Reading Instruction," *The Reading Teacher*, November 2002, pp. 270–79.

80   Margaret Phillips teaches fourth grade in Chattanooga, Tennessee.

80   "Try to focus more on what the child is trying to do and less on what we are trying to teach": Linda Labbo, James Hoffman, and Nancy Roser, "Ways to Unintentionally Make Writing Difficult," *Language Arts,* March 1995.

81   All children bring rich language and cultural resources into the classroom: Cynthia Brock, Fenice Boyd, and Juel Moore, "Variation in Language and the Use of Language Across Contexts: Implications for Literacy Learning" in Flood et al. 2003, pp. 446–58, p. 450, citing Moll 1997; Gordon Wells, *The Meaning Makers: Children Learning Language and Using Language to Learn* (Portsmouth, NH: Heinemann, 1986); Bryce Heath, *Ways with words: Language, Life and Work in Communities and Classrooms* (Cambridge, MA: Cambridge Press, 1983).

81   *"It is this teaching behavior and not the language of the child, no matter how different, that creates the problem for learners"*: Asa G. Hilliard III, "Language, Culture, and the Assessment of African American Children," in *The Skin That We Speak: Thoughts on Language and Culture in the Classroom*, edited by Lisa Delpit (New York: The New Press, 2002), p. 101. The italics are mine.

81   "Language works to *position* people in relation to one another": Peter H. Johnston, *Choice Words: How Our Language Affects Children's Learning* (Portland, ME: Stenhouse, 2004), p. 9, citing other researchers. Italics in original.

81   "Our decisions must be guided by 'What might help this writer?' rather than 'What might help this writing?'": Lucy McCormick Calkins, *The Art of Teaching Writing*, 2d.ed. (Portsmouth, NH: Heinemann, 1994), p. 228.

82   Paul O'Neill's plaque is discussed in Ron Suskind, *The Price of Loyalty: George W. Bush, the White House, and the Education of Paul O'Neill* (New York: Simon & Schuster, 2004), p. 165.

Chapter 5

83   Karen Sher is a kindergarten teacher in Shaker Heights, Ohio with twenty-five years of experience. She made this comment in a conversation I had with her in June, 2004.

83   See my book *Invitations* (Heinemann, 1994), pages 59–66, for shared writing procedures and sample lessons, and see my *Conversations* (Heinemann, 2000) for some shared writing contexts and examples of shared writing lessons.

84   Also see my story about the importance of shared experiences for learning on pp. 75–76.

84   "As teachers we have to decide *what* to be explicit about for *which* students, and *when* to be explicit about it": Peter H. Johnston, *Choice Words: How Our Language Affects Children's Learning* (Portland, ME: Stenhouse, 2004), p. 8.

85   An example of bilingual text created by a grades 1–3 class is on p.118.

85   Students who are weak in organization, structure, and form are often strong in ideas: Jeanne S. Chall and Mary E. Curtis, "Children with Reading Difficulties," in Flood et al. 2003, p. 415. Cory's writing in *Writing Essentials* on p. 79 is an excellent example. The advantages of shared experiences are listed on p. 77.

85   Social context is crucial for learning: L. S. Vygotsky, *Mind in Society: The Development of Higher Psychological Processes*, edited by M. Cole, V. John-Steiner, and E. Souberman (Cambridge, MA: Harvard University Press, 1978); James L. Collins, *Strategies for Struggling Writers* (New York: Guilford, 1998); Don Holdaway, "The Structure of Natural Learning as a Basis for Literacy Instruction," in *The Pursuit of Literacy: Early Reading and Writing*, edited by Michael R. Sampson (Dubuque, IA: Kendall/Hunt, 1986); Don Holdaway, *The Foundations of Literacy* (Sydney: Ashton Scholastic, and Portsmouth, NH: Heinemann, 1979).

91   The desire to share ideas and words is the impetus behind writing development: Collins 1998, p. 132.

91   The five principles of education relative to language-minority students are identified by Sarah Hudelson, Leslie Poyner, and Paula Wolfe in "Teaching Bilingual and ESL Children," in Flood et al. 2003, p. 423, citing Tharp 1997.

88   The teaching tip to have everyone use an individual whiteboard is from Marilyn Robbins, a kindergarten teacher in Vancouver, Washington.

89   The what-if-the-story-went-this-way idea is Taylor Campsey's. (She's ten.)

90   The strategies that writers use are constructed, not transmitted: Collins 1998, p. 63.

91   Watch Your Language: For additional ideas on language to use during shared writing, see the shared writing lessons at the end of Chapter 5 and the additional discussion of being sensitive to and respecting students' language and culture under the heading Demonstrate Respect for Students' Language and Culture, on p. 81.

97   Working with tiles: If your local tile or home improvement store doesn't stock these inexpensive one-inch-by-one-inch, shiny, nonporous tiles, you can order them through World of Tile, 9333 Wadsworth Parkway, Westminster, CO, 80221.

112   Many examples of these shared writing ideas can be found in this text as well as in *Invitations* (Portsmouth, NH: Heinemann 1994), *Conversations* (Portsmouth, NH: Heinemann 2000), and *Reading Essentials* (Portsmouth, NH: Heinemann 2003).

Chapter 6

119   The epigraph is from Jhumpa Lahiri, speaking on her book, *The Namesake.* (Seattle: University of WA, sponsored by Elliott Bay Books, October 3, 2003.)

119   The impact of writing on reading is documented in Nell K. Duke and P. David Pearson, "Effective Practices for Developing Reading Comprehension," in *What Research Has to Say About Reading Instruction,* 3d ed., edited by Alan F. Farstrup and S. Jay Samuels , pp. 205–42 (Newark, DE: International Reading Association, 2002); *Teaching Children to Read: An Evidence-Based Assessment of the Scientific Research Literature on Reading and Its Implications for Reading Instruction,* Report of the National Reading Panel, Reports of the Subgroups (Rockville, MD: NICHD Clearinghouse, 2000); Nell K. Duke and V. Susan Bennett-Armistead, *Reading and Writing Informational Text in the Primary Grades* (New York: Scholastic, 2003); Judith A. Langer, *Effective Literacy Instruction: Building Successful Reading and Writing Programs* (Urbana, IL: National Council of Teachers of English, 2002); *The Neglected "R": The Need for a Writing Revolution,* Report of the National Commission on Writing in America's Schools and Colleges, C. Peter Magrath, Chair (College Entrance Examination Board, 2003); and my *Reading Essentials* (Portsmouth, NH: Heinemann, 2003).

119   The survey is reported in Jack Cassidy and Drew Cassidy, "What's Hot, What's Not for 2003: Seventh Annual Survey Examines Key Topics in Reading Research and Practice," *Reading Today,* December 2002/January 2003. See p. 1 and p. 18.

119   . . . reading and writing are interactive, closely connected processes that support each other: Nancy Farnan and Karin Dahl, "Children's Writing: Research and Practice," in Flood et al. 2003, p. 993.

119   . . . participation in strong writing programs clearly benefits both reading and writing development: David D. Dickinson and Lori Lyman DiGisi, "The Many Rewards of a Literacy-Rich Classroom," *Educational Leadership,* March 1998, p. 24.

119   In classrooms—including those in high-poverty schools—where student achievement is high, reading and writing are routinely linked, and students have a great many writing opportunities across the curriculum: Michael S. Knapp et al., *Teaching for Meaning in High-Poverty Classrooms* (New York: Teachers College Press, 1995).

120   Our best writers are usually our best readers: Patricia M. Cunningham, James W. Cunningham, and Richard L. Allington, "Research of the Components of a Comprehensive Reading and Writing Instructional Program," draft document, September 11, 2002.

120   The Stephen King quotation is from his *On Writing: A Memoir of the Craft* (New York: Scribner, 2000), p. 145.

120   Effective teachers who have high-achieving students (including on high-stakes tests) do more writing and reading of whole texts and spend little time on "stuff"—activities about writing and reading: Richard Allington, "What I've Learned from Studying Exemplary Teachers," *Phi Delta Kappan*, 83 (2002b), pp. 740–47.

120   Clay's research is reported in *Becoming Literate: The Construction of Inner Control* (Portsmouth, NH: Heinemann, 1991) and *The Early Detection of Reading Difficulties*, third edition (Portsmouth, NH: Heinemann, 1985)

120   Growth in reading positively impacts writing, and growth in writing positively impacts reading: Mary F. Heller, *Reading-Writing Connections: From Theory to Practice*, 2d.ed. (White Plains, NY: Longman, 1995).

120   . . . poor readers tend to become poor writers: C. Juel, "Learning to Read and Write: A Longitudinal Study of 54 Children from First Through Fourth Grades," *Journal of Educational Psychology* 80 (1988), p. 415; Jeanne S. Chall and Mary E. Curtis, "Children with Reading Difficulties," in Flood et al. 2003, pp. 413–20.

120   . . . it is easier to learn to read and write words that you already understand orally: Maria Quezada, Terrence Wiley, and J. David Ramirez, "How the Reform Agenda Shortchanges English Learners," *Educational Leadership*, December 1999/Janusary 2000, pp. 57–61.

120   Integrating reading and writing leads to more authentic teaching, better reading and writing, and higher achievement on tests: David Sudol and Peg Sudol, "Yet Another Story: Writers' Workshop Revisited," *Language Arts: Revisiting the Teaching of Writing*, March 1995, pp. 171–178; Dickinson and DiGisi 2003; Duke and Bennett-Armistead 2003.

120   "When students write the literature the class reads, they bypass economically the deep split between reading and writing which afflicts classrooms from first grade forward": Marie Ponsot and Rosemary Deen, *Beat Not the Poor Desk: Writing—What to Teach, How to Teach It, and Why* (Portsmouth, NH: Boynton/Cook, 1982), pp. 147–48.

121   . . . I do not see guided reading as a necessity in kindergarten: see *Reading Essentials*, pp. 159–60.

123   "Children's writing reflects the quality of the reading they do": A few resources for finding great literature and memorable language are Bamford, Rosemary A., and Janice V. Kristo. *Making Facts Come Alive: Choosing and Using Nonfiction Literature K–8.* 2nd ed. Norwood, MA: Christopher-Gordon, 2003; Harwayne, Shelley. *Writing Through Childhood: Rethinking Process and Practice* (Portsmouth, NH: Heinemann 2001); Hepler, Susan, and Maria Salvadore. *Books Your Kids Will Talk About!* Washington, DC: National Education Association, 2003; Silvey, Anita. *100 Best Books for Children.* (Boston: Houghton Mifflin, 2004).

123   Children who read literature—well-written folktales, narratives, and trade books—become better writers than children who primarily read basal reading texts: Lee Galda and Bernice Cullinan, "Literature for Literacy: What Research Says About the Benefits of Using Trade Books in the Classroom," in Flood et al. 2003, p. 643, citing several studies to support their statement.

123   Expository writing develops more slowly than narrative writing: Anne Haas Dyson and Sarah Warshauer Freedman, "Writing," in Flood et al. 2003, p. 979, citing many researchers.

123   "Children who read nonfiction have more information with which to write . . .": A few recommended resources for writing (and reading) nonfiction are Duke, Nell K., and Susan Bennett-Armistead. *Reading and Writing in the Primary Grades.* New York: Scholastic, 2003; Kristo, Janice V., and Rosemary A. Bamford. *Nonfiction in Focus.* New York: Scholastic, 2004; Stead, Tony. *Is That a Fact? Teaching Nonfiction Writing K–3.* Portland, ME: Stenhouse, 2001; McMackin, Mary C., and Barbara S. Siegel. *Knowing How: Researching and Writing Nonfiction 3–8.* Portland, ME: Stenhouse, 2002. *The Best in Children's Nonfiction,* Latest Edition, Edited by Myra Zarnowski, Richard M. Kerper and Julie M. Jensen, (Urbana, IL: National Council of Teachers of English).

123   Children who read nonfiction have more information with which to write, have writing models at hand, and are more aware of nonfiction features such as visuals: Sharon Taberski, "Nonfiction Reading and Writing" (presentation at the Reading Recovery and Early Literacy Conference, Portland, OR, October 2003). Some useful nonfiction resources include Duke, Kristo, Stead, and McMackin.

123   Resources for Students: Aliki. *How a Book Is Made;* Bauer. *On Fiction Writing;* Fletcher, Ralph (all his texts for students such as: *A Writer's Notebook, How Writers Work, and Live Writing*).

See also Annotated Resources in the Blue Pages in Routman, Regie. *Conversations.* (Portsmouth, NH: Heinemann, 2000) and see Children's and Young Adult Literature Recommended websites and Essential Kid Lit websites.

123   *Invitations* (Portsmouth, NH: Heinemann 1994) and *Conversations* (Portsmouth, NH: Heinemann 2000) contain many ideas for using literature as a springboard to writing.

123   . . . scoured them "for clues to technique, to language, to structure, to anything that might help him learn how to write": Michiko Kakutani, "A Family Haunted by Ghosts of History," Books of the Times, *The New York Times,* The Arts, November 11, 2003, pp. B1 and B8.

123   The Gary Paulson quotation is from "Author Gary Paulsen Trusts Kids and Believes in Teachers," *The Council Chronicle* 13 (1) (September 2003), p. 3.

123   Kent Haruf . . . says that he reads daily from his literary heroes, such as Faulkner and Hemingway: John Marshall, "Everyman's Champion," *The Seattle Post-Intelligencer,* Life and Arts (Section E), May 18, 2004, p. E2.

124   Students who read more are more confident writers "because of their superior command of the written language": Stephen Krashen, *Explorations in Language Acquisition and Use: The Taipei Lectures* (Portsmouth, NH: Heinemann, 2003), p. 23.

124   And while superior writers read "good" books, the quality of what they read appears to be less important than the sheer amount of reading they do: Henry B. Maloney, "Writing's 'Revolution': Shouldn't It Begin with Reading?," letter to editor, *Education Week,* June 4, 2003, p. 32.

124   For our English language learners, the research is overwhelming that voluntary reading is a powerful means for developing language competence: Krashen 2003, p. 26.

124   "What the reader brings to the writing is at least as important as what the writer presents in the writing": Ministry of Education, *What Makes Good Writing? A Handbook for Teachers,* project manager David Fisher (Victoria, BC: Ministry of Education, Assessment, Examinations, and Reporting Branch, 1991), p. 1.

124   "I don't read in order to study the craft; I read because I like to read": Stephen King, *On Writing,* p. 145.

124   Rereading during the composing process improves the quality of the writing: Heller 1995.

125   . . . research shows that when students answer teacher-originated short-answer questions, they quickly look for the needed information and copy it, with little thought or reflection: Farnan and Dahl 2003, p. 1000.

125   Many students, especially culturally and linguistically diverse students, substantially improve their writing—content, quantity, form, fluency—as a result of keeping these journals: Arnetha F. Ball and Marcia Farr, "Language Varieties, Culture, and Teaching the English Language Arts," in Flood 2003, p. 440.

126   Paragraph beginning, Composing text and comprehending text are closely related: the statements in this paragraph are supported by Lee Galda and Bernice Cullinan, "Literature for Literacy: What Research Says About the Benefits of Using Trade Books in the Classroom," in Flood et al. 2003, p. 643; Sandra Stotsky and Cindy Mall, "Understanding Research on Teaching the English Language Arts: An Introduction for Teachers," in Flood et al. 2003, pp. 133–42; Patricia M. Cunningham, James W. Cunningham, and Richard L. Allington, "Research on the Components of a Comprehensive Reading and Writing Instructional Program," September 11, 2002; *The Neglected "R,"* 2003, p. 33.

126   Children develop meaning as they write: Lucy McCormick Calkins, *The Art of Teaching Writing,* second edition (Portsmouth, NH: Heinemann, 1994).

126   Primary-grade students who do more writing, especially content-related writing, have higher reading achievement: Dickinson and DiGisi 1998, p. 24; Duke and Bennett-Armistead 2003.

126   David Dickinson . . . found that students who had highest test scores in reading and spelling came from classrooms in which writing was integrated into many activities: "Research Notes," *Education Week,* April 8, 1998; Dickinson and DiGisi published their research in "The Many Rewards of a Literacy-Rich Classroom," *Educational Leadership,* March 1998, pp. 23–26.

127   Teaching kids how to write expository text improves their overall writing skill and their reading comprehension: Heller 1995, p. 5.

127   Kids who write nonfiction are stimulated to read more nonfiction: Tony Stead, *Is That a Fact? Teaching Nonfiction Writing K–3* (Portland, ME: Stenhouse, 2002); Taberski 2003.

127   The Accelerated Reader comment is base on Todd Oppenheimer's *The Flickering Mind: The False Promise of Technology in the Classroom and How Learning Can Be Saved* (New York: Random House, 2003).

127   One of the most effective ways to teach reading comprehension is by asking students to write summaries: James Flood, Diane Lapp, and Douglas Fisher, "Reading Comprehension Instruction," in Flood 2003, p. 937; Thomas G. Devine and John S. Kania, "Studying: Skills, Strategies, and Systems," in Flood et al. 2003, p. 946.

132   Book reviews are a form of summary writing: writing book reviews is discussed in this book on pp. 132–133. Excellent models of book reviews are included in the recurring feature "Reviews for Kids by Kids" in *Voices from the Middle,* a journal for middle school teachers published by NCTE.

133   I also discuss how I use current nonfiction articles in my reading workshops in *Reading Essentials,* on pp. 120–22.

133   Note taking causes the reader to pay better attention to the material at hand and to process the material at a deeper level: Thomas G. Devine and John S. Kania, "Studying: Skills, Strategies, and Systems," in Flood et al. 2003, pp. 945–48. The authors note many studies that support note-taking as a way to increase reading comprehension and that document that students who write summaries outperform those who copy words or take verbatim notes.

134   Having students keep a notebook or journal in which they write predictions, underline, make notes, create charts or written summaries, and ask their own questions has been found to help older students be more strategic, reflective readers: Devine and Kania 2003, p. 948.

134   Students who use graphic organizers remember more content than students who just underline text: Devine and Kania 2003, pp. 946–47.

134   When I introduced little spiral notebooks in guided reading groups in grades 1, 2, and 3, the students' comprehension greatly improved: see *Reading Essentials,* pp. 170, 171, 172, 180, 181.

135   Kristen Heine made this observation in a note she wrote to me in March, 2004.

136   Students who grapple with higher-level questions (in the context of purposeful reading and writing) get higher scores on standardized reading tests: Barbara Taylor, Debra Peterson, P. David Pearson, and Michael Rodriguez, "Looking Inside Classrooms: Reflecting on the 'How' as Well as the 'What' in Effective Reading Instruction," *The Reading Teacher,* November 2002, pp. 270–79.

137   Almost 90 percent of Texas ninth graders taking their state's high-stakes reading test in a recent year were unable to support their answers with text evidence. That is, they were unable to generate a reasonable idea from inside the text and connect it to text evidence that strongly supports that idea: Victoria Young, presentation on assessment and state writing tests at the twentieth-anniversary conference of the National Writing Project, Houston, TX, February 7, 2004.

138   . . . it's good instruction that helps students perform best on state tests, not an isolated focus on skills that will be assessed: Kathleen Kennedy Manzo, "Schools Stress Writing for the Test," *Education Week,* December 12, 2001, p. 18.

138   Powerful connections between reading and writing help accelerate students' knowledge and skills in both areas: Gay Su Pinnell, "Helping Children Read, Understand, and Think About Text," state literacy conference session, Greensboro, NC, January 2004.

Chapter 7

141   The epigraph is from Mem Fox's *Radical Reflections: Passionate Opinions on Teaching, Learning, and Living* (New York: Harcourt Brace, 1993.), p. 30.

142   Imagine having all the pieces of a large puzzle on the floor in front of you but never seeing the picture on the lid of the box: Judie Thelen made this analogy in her literacy workshops, and Andrea Butler made it public on a national scale in her literacy presentations.

142   For specific examples of and procedures for teaching poetry, see my *Kids' Poems: Teaching Children to Love Poetry Writing* series (Scholastic 2000). There are separate volumes for kindergarten, grade 1, grade 2, and grades 3–4.

142   . . . decades of research show that drills do not improve student writing: George Hillocks, *The Testing Trap: How State Writing Assessments Control Learning* (New York: Teacher College Press, 2002).

142   "Programs that focus too much on the teaching of letter-sounds . . .": National Reading Panel, "Alphabetics Part 2: Phonics Instruction" (Chapter 2), in *Report of the National Reading Panel: Teaching Children to Read: An Evidence-Based Assessment of the Scientific Research Literature on Reading and Its Implications for Reading Instruction: Reports of the Subgroups,* Rockville, MD: NICHD Clearinghouse, 2000, p. 2-97. Italics in the original.

143   . . . "skill instruction should intrude as little as possible upon students' ongoing efforts at constructing meaning from text": Kathryn Au, "Balanced Literacy Instruction: Implications for Students of Diverse Backgrounds," in Flood et al. 2003, p. 963.

143   . . . until a child understands that words can be broken into sounds, teaching "*p* is for paint" has no meaning for them: Jana M. Mason, Steven A. Stahl, Kathyrn H. Au, and Patricia A. Herman, "Reading: Children's Developing Knowledge of Words," in Flood et al. 2003, p. 916.

146   "Voice is the single most important element in attracting and holding a reader's interest": Donald M. Murray, *Crafting a Life in Essay, Story, Poem* (Portsmouth, NH: Heinemann, 1996), p. 39.

146   Voice is the writer's unique personality on paper: Ralph Fletcher, *What a Writer Needs* (Portsmouth, NH, 1993).

146   The quotation is from Amy Tan's *The Opposite of Fate: A Book of Musings* (New York: Putnam, 2003), p. 296.

147   They often have to start all over again in learning how to compose interesting, well-written pieces: Katie Hughes, letter to the editor under the heading "Would You Trust a Computer to Grade Emerson?," *The New York Times,* Editorials/Letters, May 22, 2004, p. A24, in response to "Indiana Student Essays Being Graded by Computers," *The New York Times* Education Page, May 19.

147   Voice is in the details: Donald Graves made this point in an email exchange he and I had in February, 2004. He said, "Voiceless writing is like soup with no seasoning," during that same exchange.

149   The term "efficiency of context" was coined by first-grade teacher Gail Westbrook, of Vancouver, Washington.

150   From one school district's guidelines. Evergreen, Washington Public schools.

151   From scoring rubric, level 4 (out of 4) on WASL (WA Assessment of Student Learning in Writing) on OSPI (Office of Superintendent of Public Instruction) website, www.k12.wa.us/curriculuminstruct/writing/annotations/4grad Annotations.aspx/WASL

153   The California standards are from the California Department of Education's *Reading/Language Arts Framework for the California Public Schools: Kindergarten Through Grade Twelve* (California Department of Education, Sacramento, 1999).

153   It's impossible to define a sentence in a way that helps students produce one; the best and fastest way to teach what good sentences is to call attention to them in the context of students' good writing: Marie Ponsot and Rosemary Deen, *Beat Not the Poor Desk: Writing—What to Teach, How to Teach It, and Why* (Portsmouth, NH: Boynton/Cook, 1982), pp. 134–35.

154   "In mini-lessons we teach *into* our students' intentions": Carl Anderson, *How's It Going? A Practical Guide for Conferring with Student Writers* (Portsmouth, NH: Heinemann, 2000), p. 139; italics in the original.

156   "Of course anything must be revised if you really want it to work for an audience": Peter Elbow, *Writing with Power: Techniques for Mastering the Writing Process,* 2d ed. (New York: Oxford University Press, 1998), p. 125. Elbow is a professor of English and the director of the writing program at the University of MA, Amherst.

157   "The more you zero in on the precise meaning you have in mind . . .": Elbow 1998, p. 134.

159   "With the fresh eyes of a reader" is Peter Elbow's phrase; it's also on p. 134 of *Writing with Power.*

159   . . . "if you want to take revising seriously . . . you need to write plenty that you don't revise": Elbow 1998, p. 127.

160   . . . when teachers overemphasize correctness when students write, writing quality declines: Nancy Farnan and Karin Dahl, "Children's Writing: Research and Practice," in Flood et al. 2003, p. 1002, citing several studies.

161   . . . punctuation "directs you to read, in the same way musical notation directs a musician how to play": Lynne Truss, *Eats, Shoots & Leaves: The Zero Tolerance Approach to Punctuation* (New York: Gotham, 2004), p. 20.

161   Being able to spell makes writing easier, as the writer can focus on meaning and audience: Shane Templeton, "Spelling," in Flood et al. 2003, p. 747.

161   . . . "the most recent research supports the need for most learners to experience words through reading, writing, and focused examination": Templeton 2003, p. 747.

161   In *Conversations* (Portsmouth, NH: Heinemann 2000), I set out in detail the elements of an effective comprehensive spelling and word study program. The Blue Pages in *Conversations* list excellent annotated spelling resources. Other recommended resources include Bear et al., *Words Their Way* (Upper Saddle River, NJ: Pearson, 2004); and Marten, *Word Crafting* (Portsmouth, NH: Heinemann, 2003).

161   [Competent spellers] also write more and do it better and more easily: Debra Viadero, "Studies Back Lessons in Writing, Spelling," *Education Week,* November 20, 2002, p. 8.

161   Students who struggle mightily with spelling or worry unnecessarily about perfect spelling do not write fluently or easily: Templeton 2003, p. 747.

162   Children who have the opportunity to use invented spelling to infer how the spelling system works become better spellers than students who learn to spell by rote: Kathryn Au, "Balanced Literacy Instruction: Implications for Students of Diverse Backgrounds," in Flood et al. 2003, p. 960.

163   First graders who are encouraged to use invented spellings write more words and spell more of them correctly than students who are focused on correct spelling: Richard E. Hodges, "The Conventions of Writing," in Flood et al. 2003, p. 1058, citing L. K. Clarke, "Invented Versus Traditional Spelling in First Graders' Writings: Effects on Learning to Spell and Read," *Research in the Teaching of English* 22 (1988), pp. 281–309.

163   And teaching phonics by encouraging invented spelling is faster and more effective than teaching letter sounds in isolation: Au 2003, p. 960.

163   "Phonemic awareness is very likely to develop as a consequence of learning phonics, learning to read, and learning to write, especially when teachers encourage children to use invented spellings." Marilyn Chapman, "Straight Talk About Phonological and Phonemic Awareness," *Primary Leadership: Learning for the Love of It,* Fall 2001, pp. 33–42, citing Adams 1990; Allington and Cunningham 1996; and Snow, Burns, and Griffin 1998. (*Primary Leadership* is a publication of the British Columbia Primary Teachers Association, Vancouver, BC.)

164   Research shows that five or six misspellings in a three-hundred word text can cause the reader to say, "I can't read this": Nancie Atwell, *Lessons That Change Writers* (Portsmouth, NH: Heinemann, 2002), p. 196.

164   "Errors create the impression that a writer either doesn't care or doesn't know better": Atwell 2002, p. 213.

166   The goal of the word wall is to empower students "to independently take words apart in reading and construct words in writing": Libby Larrabee and Kathie Heap, *Taking the Words Off the Wall: How to Create and Use Word Walls* (Carlsbad, CA: Dominie, 2004), p. 37.

168   Monica Carrera-Wilburn said this in a letter she wrote me in May, 2004.

168   "Never use a long word where a short one will do": Donald M. Murray, *Crafting a Life in Essay, Story, Poem* (Portsmouth, NH: Heinemann, 1996).

169   Also, don't neglect expository writing, which struggling writers often find more interesting and engaging: Derek Furr, "Struggling Writers Get Hooked on Writing," *The Reading Teacher,* March 2003, pp. 518–25.

Chapter 8

173   The epigraph is from Somerset Maugham in Donald Murray's *Shoptalk: Learning to Write with Writers* (Portsmouth, NH: Heinemann, 1990).

173   See my book *Conversations* (Portsmouth, NH: Heinemann 2000), pp. 283–329, for more information on organizing for writing.

175   Those who write every day in a regular planned writing session produce about twice the volume and twice the number of ideas as writers who write when they feel like it: Stephen Krashen, *Explorations in Language Acquisition and Use: The Taipei Lectures* (Portsmouth, NH: Heinemann, 2003), p. 75, citing the research of Boice 1983 and reports from professional writers.

175   . . . if we don't teach writing at least four days a week for at least forty-five minutes, we shouldn't bother to teach it at all: Donald Graves, *A Fresh Look at Writing* (Portsmouth, NH: Heinemann, 1994), p. 104.

175   The National Writing Commission goes further and recommends that schools double the amount of time spent writing at every grade level (some of this time is spent writing at home): *The Neglected "R": The Need for a Writing Revolution*, Report of the National Commission on Writing in America's Schools and Colleges, C. Peter Magrath, Chair (College Entrance Examination Board, 2003), p. 26.

177   "If the teacher doesn't demonstrate choosing her own topic, kids won't understand what choice means": Don Graves said this in a conversation I had with him in May, 2004.

178   . . . "the topic is the single most important factor contributing to writer variability": Donald Graves, *Writing: Teachers and Children at Work,* (Portsmouth, NH: Heinemann, 1983), p. 263.

179   Many young writers' actual planning involves talking to themselves and drawing: Donald Graves, "Children's Writing: Research Directions on Hypothesis Based Upon an Examination of the Writing Process of Seven-Year-Old Children," doctoral dissertation, State University of NY, Buffalo, 1973.

179   Much of skilled writers' planning takes place mentally, especially when the topic is very familiar: George Hillocks Jr., *Research on Written Composition: New Directions for Teaching* (Urbana, IL: ERIC Clearinghouse on Reading and Communication Skills and the National Conference on Research in English, 1986).

181   Cami Kostecki said this to me in a letter she wrote me in June, 2004.

181   Classrooms that have more high-level talk going on have higher reading and writing achievement: P. David Pearson and Barbara Taylor, "What Really Matters: The Impact of Schoolwide and Classroom Practices on Growth in Students' Reading Achievement," presentation at the annual meeting of the International Reading Association, Reno, NV, May 5, 2004.

181   These conversations are consistent with research showing that students make higher gains when teachers ask authentic, open-ended questions and continue with probing questions about students' responses: Judith A. Langer, center director, and Janet Angelis, ed., "Effective Fourth-Grade Teachers and Their Classrooms," *English Update: A Newsletter From the Center on English Learning and Achievement* (Albany, NY: University at Albany, SUNY), Spring 2001a, p. 1, citing a 1991 study by Nystrand and Gamoran, p. 3.

182   The kindergarten teacher is Marilyn Robbins, from Westminster, Colorado. She made her comment in an email I received from her in March, 2003.

183   . . . conversation is the way most ethnic groups of color in the United States communicate, with the roles of speaker and listener being "fluid and interchange-

able": Geneva Gay, "Preparing for Culturally Responsive Teaching," *Journal of Teacher Education* 53 (2) [March/April 2002], p. 111.

184 Any "strategies that stimulate elaboration or problem solving are likely to foster better story writing": Mary Jane Wagner, "Imaginative Expression," in Flood et al. 2003, p. 1019.

184 Informal conversations among students as they write influences the amount and quality of revisions students are willing to make: Shelley Peterson, ed., *Untangling Some Knots in K–8 Writing Instruction* (Newark, DE: International Reading Association, 2003), p. 25.

184 Conversations with others help students express their ideas more fully and make them their own: Peterson 2003, p. 19, citing her own work and Wells and Chang-Wells 1992.

184 Judith A. Langer and Janet Angelis, "Raising the Level of Student Engagement in Higher Order Talk and Writing." *English Update,* Fall 2001, p. 3.

184 Telling students the criteria without their input is likely to be less effective in promoting high achievement: Barbara Taylor, Debra Peterson, P. David Pearson, and Michael Rodriguez, "Looking Inside Classrooms: Reflecting on the 'How' as Well as the 'What' in Effective Reading Instruction" *The Reading Teacher,* November 2002, pp. 270–79.

184 For more information on teaching with a sense of urgency, see Chapter 4 in *Reading Essentials* (Portsmouth, NH: Heinemann, 2003), pp. 41–62.

184 Better classroom managers are more likely to teach for meaning and less likely to have mastery of discrete skills as their main instructional goal: Michael Knapp et al., *Teaching for Meaning in High-Poverty Classrooms* (New York: Teachers College Press, 1995), pp. 157–8.

189 Bryna Osborne said this in a note she wrote to me in June, 2004.

192 There is no research that suggests what particular genres are most effective to teach: Nell K. Duke,and V. Susan Bennett-Armistead, *Reading and Writing Informational Text in the Primary Grades* (New York: Scholastic, 2003), p. 37. The three broad genre categories are also suggested in this book, on p. 35.

194 "You learn to write by grappling with a real subject that truly matters to you": Ralph Fletcher, *What a Writer Needs* (Portsmouth, NH: Heinemann, 1993), p. 4.

194 "The most effective essays, I believe, are those that find a way for the writer to reveal a process of thought that invites the reader to think alongside the writer": Donald M. Murray, *Crafting a Life in Essay, Story, Poem* (Portsmouth, NH: Heinemann, 1996), p. 75.

194 "Make one argument thoroughly, point by point; the more detail the better. If you try to do too much you can wind up with an article that, in striving to say everything, ends up saying nothing." David Shipley, "And Now a Word from Op-Ed," *The New York Times,* Op-Ed, February 1, 2004, p. 11.

196 Expository writing develops more slowly than narrative writing: Anne Haas Dyson and Sarah Warshauer Freedman, "Writing," in Flood et al. 2003, p. 979, citing many researchers.

196   At the same time, it's important not to overload students with nonfiction writing that requires a lot of research skills: Judy Davis and Sharon Hill, *The No-Nonsense Guide to Teaching Writing: Strategies, Structures, and Solutions* (Portsmouth, NH: Heinemann, 2003), p. 165. This text contains many good ideas about teaching writing.

200   "There is no substitute for letters, handwritten, pulsing with the vitality of the moment": Nichols Fox, "Our History Is in Our Mail," Op-Ed, *The New York Times,* November 3, 2001, p. A23.

202   . . . gratitude has been found to be a key component of happiness and well being: "Gratitude Visits," *The New York Times Magazine*, December 12, 2003, p. 73. This article describes the work of Martin E. P. Seligman, a professor of psychology at the University of Pennsylvania, whose research "suggests that gratitude is a key component of personal happiness."

204   Do More Publishing: Nationwide Learning (www.studentreasures.com) custom-publishes hardbound books of children's writing. The cost is about $17.00 a book, but it's a fabulous motivation for writing and a wonderful way to savor the great writing your class has done. Treetop Publishing (www.barebooks.com; 1-800-255-9228) sells hard-covered, fully bound books with twenty-eight blank pages (fourteen sheets). All books are constructed with quality white paper and are suitable for crayons, watercolor markers, colored pencils, and other writing and coloring materials. Some helpful publishing resources include *Real ePublishing, Really Publishing: How to Create Digital Books by and for All Ages,* by Mark Condon and Michael McGuffee (Portsmouth, NH: Heinemann, 2001) and *Publishing with Students: A Comprehensive Guide,* by Chris Weber (Portsmouth, NH: Heinemann, 2002).

Chapter 9

205   Epigraph: Don Graves said this in a conversation I had with him in May, 2004.

206   The structure of a writing conference includes conversations about the writing work the child is doing and how the child can become a better writer: Carl Anderson, *How's It Going? A Practical Guide for Conferring with Student Writers* (Portsmouth, NH: Heinemann, 2000).

206   "When I realized that conferencing didn't have to be . . .": Millie Rable said this in an email she sent to me on March 12, 2004.

217   The roving conferences teaching tip is Millie Rable's.

220   . . . peer interaction, especially when it is spontaneous, informal, and not heavily teacher directed is likely to help writers progress: John Simmons and Pamela S. Carroll, "Today's Middle Grades: Different Structures, Students, and Classrooms," in Flood et al. 2003, p. 380; Anne Haas Dyson and Sarah Warshauer Freedman, "Writing," in Flood et al. 2003, p. 971.

220   "Frontloading" is a term first used by Linda Hoyt in *Make It Real: Strategies for Success with Informational Texts* (Portsmouth, NH: Heinemann, 2002) in reference to reading.

221   "Frontloading definitely assured success . . .": Sue Mikulecky said this in a note she wrote to me in April, 2004.

222   Expecting students to manage their own behavior so we can focus on conferences has to be modeled and practiced: see *Reading Essentials*, pp. 163–67, "Model Exactly What You Expect Students to Do."

224   "... compliments showed me what I could do ...": Penny Kittle, *Public Teaching, One Kid at a Time* (Portsmouth, NH: Heinemann, 2003), p. 56.

225   And again: when we comment first on mechanics (spelling, handwriting, grammar), we may give the message that students' ideas are secondary to correctness: Dyson and Freedman 2003, p. 973, citing Petty and Finn, 1981.

226   ... writers often experience writer's block and lose their concentration when editing concerns become a focus too early in the process: Stephen Krashen, letter to the editor, *Education Week*, December 11, 2002, in response to Steve Graham, "Studies Back Lessons in Writing, Spelling," *Education Week*, November 20, 2002.

Chapter 10

238   The epigraph is from Richard J. Stiggins, "Assessment Crisis: The Absence of Assessment *for* Learning," special section on assessment, *Phi Delta Kappan*, June 2002, p. 761. Emphasis in the original.

238   "Furthermore, standardized tests tend to focus on readily accessed features of the language . . .": National Council of Teachers of English, "Positions and Guidelines," *Writing Assessment: A Position Statement* (Urbana, IL: NCTE, 1995).

239   More troubling, standardized test results are often used to make inaccurate statements about students' learning, especially minority students: NCTE 1995.

239   ... these conclusions come from impromptu writing completed in fifteen minutes: Anne Haas Dyson and Sarah Warshauer Freedman, "Writing," in Flood et al. 2003, p. 974.

239–240 "Assessment to improve instruction requires active learning communities that sustain productive conversations about teaching and learning that are based on data": Peter H. Johnston, "Assessment Conversations," *The Reading Teacher*, September 2003, p. 92.

240   "Traits are the qualities—ideas, organization, voice, etc.—that define good writing. Criteria are the language we use to define how those traits look at various levels—beginning, developing, proficient—along a continuum of performance": Vicki Spandel, *Creating Writers Through 6-Trait Writing Assessment and Instruction* (New York: Addison Wesley Longman, 2001), p. 21.

240   While students' test scores may be higher when their teachers adhere strictly to a set of writing traits, the writing is often "vacuous": Linda Mabry, "Writing to the Rubric: Lingering Effects of Traditional Standardized Testing on Direct Writing Assessment," *Phi Delta Kappan*, May 1999, p. 678.

240   Rubrics often fail to measure the development of ideas, overall coherence, and relevance of evidence presented, which sends a message to students that writing to the formula matters, not the content: Mabry 1999; George Hillocks, *The Testing Trap: How State Writing Assessments Control Learning* (New York: Teacher College Press, 2002).

240   Rubrics also "fail to provide a *demonstration* of the reading process that can later be internalized by the writer": Tom Newkirk, "A Mania for Rubrics: Will the Standards Movement Make Satire (and Good Writing) Obsolete?," Commentary, *Education Week,* September 13, 2000, p. 42.

242   "Although rubrics promote reliability, they may simultaneously undermine validity, the more important determinant of the quality of an assessment": Mabry 1999, p. 675.

243   Writing involves "complex subprocesses that occur interactively as writers work their way from the beginning of a writing to its culmination": Nancy Farnan and Karin Dahl, "Children's Writing: Research and Practice," in Flood et al. 2003, p. 995.

243   The original quote (which is paraphrased in this book) reads: "The very authoritative language and format of rubrics, their pretense to objectivity, hides the human act of reading. The key qualities of good writing (organization, detail, a central problem) are represented as something the writing *has*—rather than something the writing *does*." by Thomas Newkirk in "A Mania for Rubrics: Will the Standards Movement Make Satire and Good Writing Obsolete," *Education Week,* September 13, 2000, p. 42.

244   Also, a narrow focus on skills does not yield high scores on state tests: Kathleen Kennedy Manzo, "Schools Stress Writing for the Test," *Education Week,* December 12, 2001, pp. 1, 18 & 19.

244   . . . only about 20 percent of state departments of education adequately align standards with curriculum: *The Neglected "R": The Need for a Writing Revolution,* Report of The National Commission on Writing in America's Schools and Colleges, C. Peter Magrath, Chair (College Entrance Examination Board, 2003), p. 29.

244   . . . teachers tend to overfocus on what is tested rather than the skills and strategies that underlie writing competency: George Hillocks, *The Testing Trap: How State Writing Assessments Control Learning* (New York: Teacher College Press, 2002).

245   Research shows that *high achievement and high test scores result when what is tested is woven into daily teaching and challenging curriculum in a relevant manner.* Judith A. Langer, *Effective Literacy Instruction: Building Successful Reading and Writing Programs* (Urbana, IL: National Council of Teachers of English, 2002); John T. Guthrie, "Preparing Students for High-Stakes Test Taking in Reading," in *What Research Has to Say About Reading Instruction,* 3d ed, edited by Alan E. Farstrup and S. Jay Samuels (Newark, DE: International Reading Association, 2002), pp. 370–91.

245   Kari Oosterveen's comments are from a letter she wrote to me in October, 2003.

244–246 Kids who write a lot develop higher-order thinking and understanding that translates to higher achievement on all types of tests: Kim Marshall, "Test Prep: The Junk Food of Education," *Education Week,* Commentary, October 1, 2003, p. 34.

246   Linda Rief's *100 Quickwrites* (New York: Scholastic, 2003) contains great suggestions for freewrites.

248   I developed the ideas about how to reduce test anxiety in conjunction with Kari Oosterveen.

249   *Try it. Apply it.* . . . test performance is only slightly impacted by knowing the format in advance: Guthrie 2002, p. 377.

250   Richard Allington mentioned these longitudinal displays when he responded to a draft of this chapter in June, 2004. He got the idea from a talk given by Rob Tierney, a Dean at the University of British Columbia.

251   Parents are able to put high-stakes testing in perspective when we teachers are rigorous about classroom assessment and clearly communicate the quality, benefits, and results of our assessments to parents and the public: James Hoffman, Scott Paris, Rachel Salas, Elizabeth Patterson, and Lori Assaf, "High-Stakes Assessment in the Language Arts: The Piper Plays, the Players Dance, But Who Pays the Price?" in Flood et al. 2003, p. 628.

252   When we put too much emphasis on grading, we spend our time looking to justify the grade rather than helping students learn how to become better writers: Dyson and Freedman 2003, p. 973.

252   "To become reflective writers, students must take communication, not grades, as their end goal": Dyson and Freedman 2003, p. 973.

252   . . . keep in mind that exemplary teachers rely more on effort and improvement in assigning grades than on simple achievement: Richard Allington, "What I've Learned from Studying Exemplary Teachers," *Phi Delta Kappan* 83, pp. 740–47.

Chapter 11

259   The first epigraph is from Joan Wink and Dawn Wink, *Teaching Passionately: What's Love Got to Do with It?* (Boston: Pearson/Allyn and Bacon, 2004), p. 157. The second epigraph is from *The Neglected "R": The Need for a Writing Revolution,* Report of the National Commission on Writing in America's Schools and Colleges, C. Peter Magrath, Chair (College Entrance Examination Board, 2003), p. 26.

260   Literacy is "a social practice that varies according to the particular use to which it is put in each context": Arnetha F. Ball and Marcia Farr, "Language Varieties, Culture, and Teaching the English Language Arts," in Flood et al. 2003, p. 438.

260   Instead of providing staff development that focuses on excellent teaching, they focus on raising test scores through formulaic, step-by-step writing: Samuel Totten, "Completing the Paradigm Shift to Process Writing: The Need to Lead," *The Quarterly,* Winter 2003, p. 11.

261   It's a fact that teachers who employ meaning-centered approaches get results and test scores that are "significantly higher" than teachers who employ more traditional, skills-based techniques: Richard Valencia and Bruno Villarreal, "Improving Students' Reading Performance Via Standards-Based School Reform: A Critique," *The Reading Teacher,* April 2003, p. 618.

261   "Rules made by men that restrict the realization of human potential . . . should be changed." Paul O'Neill, as quoted in Ron Suskind, *The Price of Loyalty: George W. Bush, the White House, and the Education of Paul O'Neill* (New York: Simon & Schuster, 2004), p. 214.

261   Teachers can't be expected to be accountable if they are told specifically what to do: Richard Allington, *Big Brother and The National Reading Curriculum* (Portsmouth, NH: Heinemann, 2002).

261   The best teachers are "not followers" and have an "independent spirit." Based on their professional and moral knowledge and judgment, they override directives when something else will work more effectively: Gerald G. Duffy, "Visioning and the Development of Outstanding Teachers," *Reading Research and Instruction* 41 (4) (Summer 2002), p. 333.

261   *Try it. Apply it.* "We recommend that the nation's leaders place writing squarely in the center of the school agenda and that policymakers at the state and local levels provide the resources required to improve writing": *The Neglected "R": The Need for a Writing Revolution,* Report of the National Commission on Writing in America's Schools and Colleges, Peter C. Magrath, Chair (College Entrance Examination Board, 2003), p. 26.

262   "Research is crystal clear: Schools that do well insist that their students write every day and that teachers provide regular and timely feedback with the support of parents": *The Neglected "R, 2003,"* p. 28.

262   Unfortunately, many teachers, principals, and superintendents, not to mention school board members, are unfamiliar with both the research on the teaching of writing and recommended practices for teaching it: John Simmons and Pamela S. Carroll, "Today's Middle Grades: Different Structures, Students, and Classrooms," in Flood et al. 2003, p. 387; Samuel Totten, "Completing the Paradigm Shift to Process Writing: The Need to Lead, *The Quarterly,* Winter 2003, pp. 8–13 & 38.

262   Only a few states require courses in writing for certification: *The Neglected "R, 2003,"* p. 23.

262   . . . the amount of research available on the subject of writing is about half the amount of what's available for reading: Nancy Farnan and Karin Dahl, "Children's Writing: Research and Practice," in Flood et al. 2003, p. 993.

262   . . . researchers and educators acknowledge that most students do not and cannot write well: Kathleen Cotton, *Teaching Composition: Research on Effective Practices,* School Improvement Research Series: Research You Can Use (Portland, OR: Northwest Regional Educational Laboratory, 2002), p. 1.

263   . . . the main purpose of research is not to direct how we teach but to allow us to be more thoughtfully deliberate in our instruction and assessment: Sandra Stotsky and Cindy Mall, "Understanding Research on Teaching the English Language Arts: An Introduction for Teachers," in Flood et al. 2003, p. 135.

267   . . . students who were introduced to language activities in connection with direct teaching of phonics learned more: G. Camilli, S. Vargas, and M. Yurecko, "Teaching Children to Read: The Fragile Line Between Science and Federal Education Policy," (Camden, NJ: Education Policy Analysis Archives, National Institute for Early Education Research and Rutgers University, May 8, 2003).

268   . . . "the more peer interaction was spontaneous and less teacher directed, the better the outcomes in the writing progress": John Simmons and Pamela S. Carroll, "Today's Middle Grades: Different Structures, Students, and Classrooms," in Flood et al. 2003, p. 380.

268–269   The less knowledge teachers have about teaching writing, the more the "testing system tends to become the knowledge base for teaching writing," and this is particularly true in high-poverty schools: George Hillocks, *The Testing Trap: How State Writing Assessments Control Learning* (New York: Teacher College Press, 2002), p. 102.

269   The level of professional talk in a school impacts test scores; so does the level of teacher collegiality: R. Allington, P. H. Johnston, S. Guice, and G. Brooks, "Moving to Literature-Based Instruction: A Multilevel Study of Curriculum Reform," *Peabody Journal of Education* 73 (1988), pp. 81–103; B. F. Birman, L. Desimone, A. C. Porter, and M. Garet, "Designing Professional Development," *Educational Leadership* 57 (2000), pp. 28–32; Regie Routman, "Teacher Talk," *Educational Leadership,* March 2002, pp. 32–35.

269   Linda Benedict and Diane Gillespie made their comment in a conversation I had with them in June, 2004.

269   *Try it. Apply it.* Start your own professional conversations group: Two useful resources are Diane Sweeney, *Learning Along the Way: Professional Development by and for Teachers* (Portland, ME: Stenhouse, 2003) and pp. 520–31 in my book *Conversations* (Portsmouth, NH: Heinemann, 2000).

274   Outstanding teachers analyze situations, know the research, rely on their heart and spirit as well as experience and professional knowledge, and make wise instructional decisions for their students: Gerald G. Duffy, "Visioning and the Development of Outstanding Teachers," *Reading Research and Instruction* 41 (4) (Summer 2002), pp. 331–43.

274   Melinda Jennings's comments are from a letter she wrote to me on October 13, 2003.

275   And once those decisions have been made, the beliefs and practices behind them need to be communicated to parents and caregivers effectively: See my *Literacy at the Crossroads* (Portsmouth, NH: Heinemann, 1996) for many ideas about enlisting parents as advocates for change.

275   Nor is there is any research supporting a skills-first approach to teaching writing or demonstrating that adopting a writing program will improve the quality of students' writing. George Hillocks Jr., *Research on Written Composition: New Directions for Teaching* (Urbana, IL: ERIC Clearinghouse on Reading and Communication Skills and the National Conference on Research in English, 1986) and *The Testing Trap: How State Writing Assessments Control Learning.* (New York: Teacher College Press, 2002).

275   . . . when 70 percent of the schools in Tennessee implemented AR in the 1990s, scores across the state generally declined: Todd Oppenheimer, *The Flickering Mind: The False Promise of Technology in the Classroom and How Learning Can Be Saved* (New York: Random House, 2003), p. 291.

275   . . . scores on the National Assessment of Educational Progress (the "nation's report card") went up slightly for top students but fell for low-performing students: Oppenheimer 2003.

275   Even the National Reading Panel weighed in on AR and other "incentive" programs and found no effect on achievement: National Reading Panel, *Teaching Children to Read: An Evidence-Based Assessment of the Scientific Research Literature on Reading and Its Implications for Reading Instruction,* Report of the National Reading Panel (Rockville, MD: NICHD Clearinghouse), p. 3-3.

275   Does the program develop teacher expertise for teaching writing? Richard Allington and Patricia Cunningham suggest this question in the third edition of *Schools That Work* (Boston, MA: Allyn & Bacon). Any program that is worthwhile should increase teacher knowledge in a way that promotes excellent teaching, learning, and assessing. If it doesn't, we shouldn't be using it.

276   Formulaic writing leads to boredom; students are stifled by the rigid format: Mark Wiley, "The Popularity of Formulaic Writing (And Why We Need to Resist"), *English Journal* 90 (1) (September 2000), p. 63.

276   They also often have a hard time breaking free from the rigid structure: Michael Winerip, "A Touchstone for the High School Essay," On Education, *The New York Times*, March 3, 2004, A23.

276   English language learners, like all students, do best with high expectations, interesting and challenging work, an interactive teaching style, and lots of opportunities for conversation: Judith Lessow-Hurley, *Meeting the Needs of Second Language Learners: An Educator's Guide* (Alexandria, VA: Association for Supervision and Curriculum Development, 2003).

276   If students are going to acquire a second language, what they hear must make sense. Second language learners can pick up conversation pretty easily. However, academic language takes at least several years to acquire: Joan Wink and Dawn Wink, *Teaching Passionately: What's Love Got to Do with It?* (Boston: Pearson/Allyn and Bacon, 2004), p. 125.

277   Grammar for second language learners is best learned through revising authentic writing and reading widely: Karen Hornick, "Teaching Writing to Linguistically Diverse Students," *ERIC Digest* (New York: ERIC Clearinghouse on Urban Education, ED275792, No. 32), p. 2; Stephen Krashen, *Explorations in Language Acquisition and Use: The Taipei Lectures* (Portsmouth, NH: Heinemann, 2003); W. B. Elley and F. Manghubai, "The Impact of Reading on Second Language Learning," *Reading Research Quarterly* (19) (1983), pp. 53–67.

277   They may well learn the discrete skills but are unable to transfer them to reading and writing actual texts: Michael S. Knapp et al., *Teaching for Meaning in High-Poverty Classrooms* (New York: Teachers College Press, 1995); Ardith Davis Cole, *When Reading Begins: The Teacher's Role in Decoding, Comprehension, and Fluency* (Portsmouth, NH: Heinemann, 2004).

277   . . . classroom teachers have little or no knowledge about what happens in special education resource rooms: Knapp et al. 1995, p. 109.

280   Ongoing, effective communication with families is a necessity if you are going to have their support and advocacy: see my *Literacy at the Crossroads* (Portsmouth, NH: Heinemann, 1996) for lots of ways to communicate with family members and enlist them as advocates.

Chapter 12

281   The epigraph is from Henry Miller in Jon Winokur's, *Writing on Writing* Philadelphia, PA: Running Press, 1990.

281   Most teachers understand that extensive opportunities for sustained writing are essential if all students are to become fluent and willing writers who do well in

school: Michael S. Knapp et al., *Teaching for Meaning in High-Poverty Classrooms* (New York: Teachers College Press, 1995).

284   Teachers' comments on students' papers do little to improve writing, even if the comments are positive ones: George Hillocks, *Research on Written Composition: New Directions for Teaching* (Urbana, IL: ERIC Clearinghouse on Reading and Communication Skills and the National Conference on Research in English, 1986).

284   . . . when comments are limited, students are more likely to pay attention and make some improvement: Nancy Farnan and Karin Dahl, "Children's Writing: Research and Practice," in Flood et al., p. 1002 (Mahwah, NJ, and London: Lawrence Erlbaum, 2003), citing Hillocks 1986.

285   Having more reading experiences positively impacts growth in writing skills: (Kathleen Cotton, *Teaching Composition: Research on Effective Practices*, pp. 1–18, School Improvement Research Series: Research You Can Use (Portland, OR: Northwest Regional Educational Laboratory, 2002), citing Stotsky 1983.

285   . . . there is no research that shows that doing isolated skills work improves writing (or reading): Gerald Coles, *Misreading Reading: The Bad Science That Hurts Children* (Portsmouth, NH: Heinemann, 2000); Knapp et al. 1995.

285   "Those taught well enough to complete grammatical exercises without error do not therefore write either better or more accurately": Marie Ponsot and Rosemary Deen, *Beat Not the Poor Desk: Writing—What to Teach, How to Teach It, and Why* (Portsmouth, NH: Boynton/Cook, 1982), p. 130.

285   *Try it. Apply it.* Teachers whose students do lots of extended writing (and have high achievement) do not spend a lot of class time teaching discrete skills: Knapp et al. 1995.

Write Your Own Ending

288   The teacher's name is Beth Petrie. She lives and teaches in Vancouver, Washington.

References

Allington, Richard. 2001. *What Really Matters for Struggling Readers*. New York: Longman.

———. 2002a. *Big Brother and The National Reading Curriculum*. Portsmouth, NH: Heinemann.

———. 2002b. "What I've Learned from Studying Exemplary Teachers." *Phi Delta Kappan* 83: 740–47.

Allington, Richard, and Patricia Cunningham. 2002. *Schools That Work: Where All Children Read and Write*. 2d ed. Boston: Allyn and Bacon.

Allington, R., P. H. Johnston, S. Guice, and G. Brooks. 1988. "Moving to Literature-Based Instruction: A Multilevel Study of Curriculum Reform." *Peabody Journal of Education* 73: 81–103.

Amiran, E., and J. Mann. 1982. *Written Composition, Grades K–12: Literature Synthesis and Report*. Portland, OR: Northwest Regional Educational Laboratory.

Anderson, Carl. 2000. *How's It Going? A Practical Guide for Conferring with Student Writers*. Portsmouth, NH: Heinemann. An excellent, explicit text.

Angelillo, Janet. 2003. *Writing About Reading: from Book Talk to Literary Essays, Grades 3–8*. Portsmouth, NH: Heinemann. Very useful book with lots of great ideas.

Atwell, Nancie. 1998. *In the Middle*. 2d ed. Portsmouth, NH: Heinemann.

———. 2002. *Lessons That Change Writers*. Portsmouth, NH: Heinemann.

Au, Kathryn. 2003. "Balanced Literacy Instruction: Implications for Students of Diverse Backgrounds." In Flood *et al.*, 955–66. Mahwah, NJ, and London: Lawrence Erlbaum.

"Author Gary Paulsen Trusts Kids and Believes in Teachers." 2003. *The Council Chronicle* 13 (1) (September): 3.

Ball Arnetha F., and Marcia Farr. 2003. "Language Varieties, Culture, and Teaching the English Language Arts." In Flood *et al.*, 435–45. Mahwah, NJ, and London: Lawrence Erlbaum.

Barr, John W. 2004. "A Passion for Poetry (and Profits): Charting a Literary Course with $100 Million." *The New York Times,* April 19, the Arts, B1 and B4.

Barth, Roland S. 1991. *Improving Schools from Within: Teachers, Parents, and Principals Can Make the Difference*. San Francisco: Jossey-Bass.

Barton, P. 2003. *Parsing the Achievement Gap.* Princeton, NJ: Educational Testing Service.

Bear, Donald B., Marcia Invernizzi, Shane Templeton, and Francine Johnston. 2004. *Words Their Way: Word Study for Phonics, Vocabulary, and Spelling Instruction.* 3d ed. Upper Saddle River, NJ: Pearson.

Berson, Misha. 2003. "The Secret Life of Suzan-Lori Parks." *The Seattle Times,* August 31, Entertainment & the Arts, K1 and K5.

Birman, B. F., L. Desimone, A. C. Porter, and M. Garet. 2000. "Designing Professional Development." *Educational Leadership* 57, 28–32.

Boice, R. 1983. "Contingency Management in Writing and the Appearance of Creative Ideas: Implications for the Treatment of Writing Blocks." *Behavioral Research Therapy* 21 (5): 537–43.

Bond, G. L., and R. Dykstra. 1997. "The Cooperative Research Program in First-Grade Reading Instruction." *Reading Research Quarterly* 32: 345–428. Originally published in 1977.

Brock, Cynthia, Fenice Boyd, and Juel Moore. 2003. "Variation in Language and the Use of Language Across Contexts: Implications for Literacy Learning." In Flood *et al.,* 446–58. Mahwah, NJ, and London: Lawrence Erlbaum.

Bryk, Anthony, and Barbara Schneider. 2003. "Trust in Schools: A Core Resource for School Reform." *Educational Leadership* (March): 40–44.

Burke, Jim. 2003. *Writing Reminders: Tools, Tips, and Techniques.* Portsmouth, NH: Heinemann. Written by a gifted high school teacher and chock full of ideas for teaching writers of all ages.

California Department of Education. 1999. *Reading/Language Arts Framework for the California Public Schools: Kindergarten Through Grade Twelve.* Sacramento: California Department of Education.

Calkins, Lucy McCormick. 1986. *The Art of Teaching Writing.* Portsmouth, NH: Heinemann. 2d ed.n 1994.

Cambourne, Brian. 2000. "Conditions for Literacy Learning—Observing Literacy Learning in Elementary Classrooms: Nine Years of Classroom Anthropology." *The Reading Teacher* 53: 512–15.

Camilli, G., S. Vargas, and M. Yurecko. 2003. "Teaching Children to Read: The Fragile Line Between Science and Federal Education Policy." Camden, NJ: Education Policy Analysis Archives, National Institute for Early Education Research and Rutgers University.

Cassidy, Jack, and Drew Cassidy. 2002/2003. "What's Hot, What's Not for 2003: Seventh Annual Survey Examines Key Topics in Reading Research and Practice." *Reading Today,* December 2002/Janusary 2003, 1 and 18.

Chall, Jeanne S., and Mary E. Curtis. 2003. "Children with Reading Difficulties." In Flood *et al.,* 413–20. Mahwah, NJ, and London: Lawrence Erlbaum.

Chapman, Marilyn. 2001. "Straight Talk About Phonological and Phonemic Awareness." *Primary Leadership: Learning for the Love of It.* Fall, 33–42.

Clay, Marie. 1991. *Becoming Literate: The Construction of Inner Control.* Portsmouth, NH: Heinemann.

————. 1985. *The Early Detection of Reading Difficulties*. 3d ed. Portsmouth, NH: Heinemann.

Cole, Ardith Davis. 2004. *When Reading Begins: The Teacher's Role in Decoding, Comprehension, and Fluency*. Portsmouth, NH: Heinemann.

Coles, Gerald. 2000. *Misreading Reading: The Bad Science That Hurts Children*. Portsmouth, NH: Heinemann.

Collins, James L. 1998. *Strategies for Struggling Writers*. New York: Guilford.

Cotton, Kathleen. 2002. *Teaching Composition: Research on Effective Practices*, 1–18. School Improvement Research Series: Research You Can Use. Portland, OR: Northwest Regional Educational Laboratory.

Cunningham, Patricia M., James W. Cunningham, and Richard L. Allington. 2002. "Research [on] the Components of a Comprehensive Reading and Writing Instructional Program." Draft document.

Davis, Judy, and Sharon Hill. 2003. *The No-Nonsense Guide to Teaching Writing: Strategies, Structures, and Solutions*. Portsmouth, NH: Heinemann. An explicit, helpful guide for teaching writing in a workshop setting using writer's notebooks.

Delpit, Lisa, ed. 2002. *The Skin That We Speak. Thoughts on Language and Culture in the Classroom*. New York: The New Press.

Devine, Thomas G., and John S. Kania. 2003. "Studying: Skills, Strategies, and Systems." In Flood *et al.*, 942–54. Mahwah, NJ, and London: Lawrence Erlbaum.

DiCamillo, Kate. 2004. Interview by Jim Lehrer. *Jim LehrerNews Hour*. PBS, March 30.

Dickinson, David D., and Lori Lyman DiGisi. 1998. "The Many Rewards of a Literacy-Rich Classroom." *Educational Leadership* (March), 23–26.

Duffy, Gerald G. 2002. "Visioning and the Development of Outstanding Teachers." *Reading Research and Instruction* 41 (4) (Summer), 331–43.

Duke, Nell. 2000. "3.6 Minutes Per Day: The Scarcity of Information Text in First Grade." *Reading Research Quarterly* 35 (2) (April/June): 202–24.

Duke, Nell K., and V. Susan Bennett-Armistead. 2003. *Reading and Writing Informational Text in the Primary Grades*. New York: Scholastic.

Dyson, Anne Haas, and Sarah Warshauer Freedman. 2003. "Writing." In Flood *et al.*, 967–92. Mahwah, NJ, and London: Lawrence Erlbaum. A review of the research on writing.

Elbow, Peter. 1998. *Writing with Power: Techniques for Mastering the Writing Process*. 2d ed. New York: Oxford Universtiy Press.

Elley, W. B., and F. Manghubai. 1983. "The Impact of Reading on Second Language Learning." *Reading Research Quarterly* 19: 53–67.

Farnan, Nancy, and Karin Dahl. 2003. "Children's Writing: Research and Practice." In Flood *et al.*, 993–1007. Mahwah, NJ, and London: Lawrence Erlbaum.

Fay, Kathleen, and Suzanne Whaley. 2004. *Becoming One Community: Reading and Writing with English Language Learners*. Portland, ME: Stenhouse.

Ferguson, Ronald, with Jal Mehta. 2004. "An Unfinished Journey: The Legacy of *Brown* and the Narrowing of the Achievement Gap." *Phi Delta Kappan* (May): 656–69.

Fletcher, Ralph. 1993. *What a Writer Needs.* Portsmouth, NH: Heinemann. Still one of my all-time favorite books on teaching writing.

Flood, James, Diane Lapp, and Douglas Fisher. 2003. "Reading Comprehension Instruction." In Flood *et al.,* 931–41. Mahwah, NJ, and London: Lawrence Erlbaum.

Flood, James, Diane Lapp, James R. Squire, Julie M. Jensen, eds. 2003. *Handbook of Research on Teaching the English Language Arts.* 2d ed. Sponsored by the International Reading Association and the National Council of Teachers of English. Mahwah, NJ, and London: Lawrence Erlbaum.

Fox, Nichos. 2001. "Our History Is in Our Mail." *The New York Times,* November 3, OP-ED, A23.

Freeman, Yvonne S., and David E. Freeman, with Sandra Mercuri. 2002. *Closing the Achievement Gap: How to Teach Limited-Formal Schooling and Long-Term English Learners.* Portsmouth, NH: Heinemann.

Fu, Danling. 2004. "Teaching ELL Students in Regular Classrooms at the Secondary Level." *Voices in the Middle* (May): 8–15.

Fullan, Michael, and Andy Hargreaves. 1996. *What's Worth Fighting for in Your School?* 2d ed. New York: Teachers College Press.

Furr, Derek. 2003. "Struggling Writers Get Hooked on Writing." *The Reading Teacher* (March): 518–25.

Galda, Lee, and Bernice Cullinan. "Literature for Literacy: What Research Says About the Benefits of Using Trade Books in the Classroom." In Flood *et al.,* 640–48. Mahwah, NJ, and London: Lawrence Erlbaum.

Gay, Geneva. 2002. "Preparing for Culturally Responsive Teaching." *Journal of Teacher Education* 53 (2) (March/April): 106–16.

Gentry, Richard. 2004. *The Science of Spelling: The Explicit Specifics that Make Great Readers and Writers (and Spellers).* Portsmouth, NH: Heinemann.

Graves, Donald. 1973. "Children's Writing: Research Directions on Hypothesis Based Upon an Examination of the Writing Process of Seven-Year-Old Children." doctural dissertation, State University of New York, Buffalo.

———. 1983. *Writing: Teachers and Children at Work.* Portsmouth, NH: Heinemann.

———. 1994. *A Fresh Look at Writing.* Portsmouth, NH: Heinemann.

———. 2001. *The Energy to Teach.* Portsmouth, NH: Heinemann.

———. 2004. "What Does It Take to Change a School's Story?" Institute presentation at the annual meeting of the International Reading Association, Reno, NV, May 2.

Guthrie, John T. 2002. "Preparing Students for High-Stakes Test Taking in Reading." In *What Research Has to Say About Reading Instruction,* 3d ed., edited by Alan E. Farstrup and S. Jay Samuels, 370–91. Newark, DE: International Reading Association.

Harwayne, Shelly. 2001. *Writing Through Childhood: Rethinking Process and Practice.* Portsmouth, NH: Heinemann.

Heard, Georgia. 2002. *The Revision Toolbox: Teaching Techniques That Work.* Portsmouth, NH: Heinemann. Very useful text for teaching revision more effectively.

Heath, Bryce Shirley. 1983. *Ways with Words: Language, Life and Work in Communities and Classrooms.* Cambridge, MA: Cambridge Press.

Heller, Mary F. 1995. *Reading-Writing Connections: From Theory to Practice.* 2d ed. White Plains, NY: Longman.

Heubert, J. P., and R. M. Hauser, eds. 1999. *High Stakes: Testing for Tracking, Promotion, and Graduation.* Washington, DC: National Research Council.

Hill, Bonne Campbell. 2001. *Developmental Continuums: A Framework for Literacy Instruction and Assessment K–8.* Norwood, MA: Christopher-Gordon.

Hillocks, George. 1986. *Research on Written Composition: New Directions for Teaching.* Urbana, IL: ERIC Clearinghouse on Reading and Communication Skills and the National Conference on Research in English.

———. 1984. "What Works in Teaching Composition: A Meta-analysis of Experimental Treatments." *Americal Journal of Education* 93: 133–70.

———. 2002. *The Testing Trap: How State Writing Assessments Control Learning.* New York: Teacher College Press.

Hillocks, George, and Michael W. Smith. 2003. "Grammar and Usage." In Flood *et al.*, 591–603. Mahwah, NJ, and London: Lawrence Erlbaum.

Hodges, Richard E. 2003. "The Conventions of Writing." In Flood *et al.*, 1052–63. Mahwah, NJ, and London: Lawrence Erlbaum.

Hoffman, James, Scott Paris, Rachel Salas, Elizabeth Patterson, and Lori Assaf. 2003. "High-Stakes Assessment in the Language Arts: The Piper Plays, the Players Dance, But Who Pays the Price?" In Flood *et al.*, 619–30. Mahwah, NJ, and London: Lawrence Erlbaum.

Holdaway, Don. 1979. *The Foundations of Literacy.* New York: Scholastic.

———. 1986. "The Structure of Natural Learning as a Basis for Literacy Instruction." In Sampson, ed., *The Pursuit of Literacy: Early Reading and Writing* (Dubuque, IA: Kendall/Hunt).

Holloway, John H. 2004. "Research Link: Closing the Minority Achievement Gap in Math." *Educational Leadership,* February, 84–86.

Hornick, Karen. 1986. "Teaching Writing to Linguistically Diverse Students." *ERIC Digest* 32. New York: ERIC Clearinghouse on Urban Education. ED275792.

Hoyt, Linda. 2002. *Make It Real: Strategies for Success with Informational Texts.* Portsmouth, NH: Heinemann.

Hudelson, Sarah, Leslie Poyner, and Paula Wolfe. 2003. "Teaching Bilingual and ESL Children." In Flood *et al.*, 421–34. Mahwah, NJ, and London: Lawrence Erlbaum.

Hughes, Katie. 2004. Letter to the editor. *The New York Times,* May 22, Editorials/Letters, A24. Written in response to "Indiana Student Essays Being Graded by Computers," *The New York Times,* May 19, Education Page. The writer is an instructor of university undergraduate composition courses.

International Reading Association. 1999. *High-Stakes Assessments in Reading: A Position Statement of the International Reading Association.* Newark, DE: International Reading Association.

Jago, Carol. 2002. *Cohesive Writing: Why Concept Is Not Enough.* Portsmouth, NH: Heinemann.

Johnston, Peter. 2004. *Choice Words: How Our Language Affects Children's Learning.* Portland, ME: Stenhouse.

———. 2003. "Assessment Conversations." *The Reading Teacher* (September): 92.

Juel, C. 1988. "Learning to Read and Write: A Longitudinal Study of 54 Children from First Through Fourth Grades." *Journal of Educational Psychology* 80: 434–47.

Kakutani, Michiko. 2003. "A Family Haunted by Ghosts of History." *The New York Times,* November 11, Books of the Times, The Arts, B1 and B8.

King, Stephen. 2000. *On Writing: A Memoir of the Craft.* New York: Scribner.

Kittle, Penny. 2003. *Public Teaching, One Kid at a Time.* Portsmouth, NH: Heinemann.

Knapp, Michael S., *et al.* 1995. *Teaching for Meaning in High-Poverty Classrooms.* New York: Teachers College Press.

Krashen, Stephen. 1996. *Under Attack: The Case Against Bilingual Education.* Culver City, CA: Language Education Associates.

———. 2002. "The Reading-Spelling Connection: Krashen Looks at a Century of Spelling Research," letter to the editor, *Education Week,* December 11. Written in response to Steve Graham, "Studies Back Lessons in Writing, Spelling," November 20. Krashen makes the points that good writers delay editing concerns until final draft, that "premature editing" can lead to writing block, and that a feel for correctness in spelling comes from extensive reading.

———. 2003. *Explorations in Language Acquisition and Use: The Taipei Lectures.* Portsmouth, NH: Heinemann.

Kristo, Janice V., and Rosemary A. Bamford. 2004. *Nonfiction in Focus: A Comprehensive Framework for Helping Students Become Independent Readers and Writers of Nonfiction, K–6.* New York: Scholastic.

Labbo, Linda, James Hoffman, and Nancy Roser. 1995. "Ways to Unintentionally Make Writing Difficult." *Language Arts* (March): 164–70.

Lahiri, Jhumpa. 2003. A talk on her book *The Namesake.* University of Washington, Seattle. Sponsored by Elliott Bay Books, October 3.

Langer, Judith A. 2002. *Effective Literacy Instruction: Building Successful Reading and Writing Programs.* Urbana, IL: National Council of Teachers of English.

Langer, Judith A., center director, and Janet Angelis, ed. 2001a. "Effective Fourth-Grade Teachers and Their Classrooms." *English Update: A Newsletter from the Center on English Learning & Achievement* (SUNY, Albany) (Spring).

———. 2001b. "Raising the Level of Student Engagement in Higher Order Talk and Writing." *English Update: A Newsletter from the Center on English Learning and Achievement* (SUNY, Albany) (Fall).

Langer, Judith A., with Elizabeth Close, Janet Angelis, and Paula Preller. 2000. *Guidelines for Teaching Middle and High School Students to Read and Write Well.* Albany, NY: National Research Center on English Learning and Achievement.

Larrabee, Libby, and Kathie Heap. 2004. *Taking the Words Off the Wall: How to Create and Use Word Walls.* Carlsbad, CA: Dominie Press.

Lessow-Hurley, Judith. 2003. *Meeting the Needs of Second Language Learners: An Educator's Guide.* Alexandria, VA: Association for Supervision and Curriculum Development.

McGee, L. M., and V. Purcell-Gates. 1997. "So What's Going On in Research on Emergent Literacy?" *Reading Research Quarterly* 32 (3): 310–18.

McIntire, Mike. 2003. "In Teacher Training Class, a School for Skeptics." *The New York Times,* August 6, A19. University of Pennsylvania researchers found in a study published in 2002 that less than half of teachers in a random sample "fully applied what they had learned" in a series of literacy workshops.

McNeil, Linda. 2000. "Creating New Inequalities: Contradictions of Reform." *Phi Delta Kappan* (June): 732.

Mabry, Linda. 1999. "Writing to the Rubric: Lingering Effects of Traditional Standardized Testing on Direct Writing Assessment." *Phi Delta Kappan* (May): 673–79.

Maloney, Henry B. 2003. "Writing's 'Revolution' Shouldn't It Begin with Reading?" letter to editor, *Education Week,* June 4, reporting on research project that identified superior ninth-grade writers based on organization, maturity of insight, word choice, and style.

Manzo, Kathleen Kennedy. 2001. "Schools Stress Writing for the Test." *Education Week,* December 12, 1, 18 and 19.

Marten, Cindy. 2003. *Word Crafting: Teaching Spelling Grades K–6.* Portsmouth, NH: Heinemann.

Marshall, John. 2004. "Everyman's Champion." *The Seattle Post-Intelligencer,* May 18, Life and Arts, E2.

Marshall, Kim. 2003. "Test Prep—The Junk Food of Education." Commentary, *Education Week,* October 1, 30 and 34.

Marzano, Robert J. 2003. "Language, the Language Arts, and Thinking." In Flood *et al,* 687–716. Mahwah, NJ, and London: Lawrence Erlbaum.

Mason, Jana M., Steven A. Stahl, Kathyrn H. Au, and Patricial A. Herman. 2003. "Reading: Children's Developing Knowledge of Words." In Flood *et al.,* 914–20. Mahwah, NJ, and London: Lawrence Erlbaum.

Ministry of Education. 1991.*What Makes Good Writing? A Handbook for Teachers.* Project manager, David Fisher. Victoria, BC: Ministry of Education, Assessment, Examinations, and Reporting Branch. A feature analysis of writing samples taken from English 12 provincial examinations.

Moffett, Cerylle A. 2000. "Sustaining Change: The Answers Are Blowing in the Wind." *Educational Leadership* (April): 36.

Moll, L. 1997. "The Creation of Mediating Settings." *Mind, Culture, and Activity* 4 (3): 191–200.

Murray, Donald M. 1989. *Expecting the Unexpected: Teaching Myself—and Others—to Read and Write.* Portsmouth, NH: Boynton/Cook.

———. 1990. *Shoptalk: Learning to Write with Writers.* Portsmouth, NH: Boynton/Cook.

———. 1996. *Crafting a Life in Essay, Story, Poem.* Portsmouth, NH: Heinemann. One of my favorites, full of good writing advice and a great read.

National Center on Education and the Economy and the University of Pittsburgh. 1997. *Performance Standards: English Language Arts, Mathematics, Science, Applied Learning.* New Standards. Vol 1, Elementary School. Pittsburgh: National Center on Education and the Economy and the University of Pittsburgy. Provides national standards and accompanying work samples with commentary to illustrate standard-setting performance.

National Council of Teachers of English. 1995. "Positions and Guidelines." *Writing Assessment: A Position Statement.* Urbana, IL: NCTE.

National Reading Panel. 2000. "Phonics Instruction" (Chapter 2), Part II, Alphabetics. In *Teaching Children to Read: An Evidence-Based Assessment of the Scientific Research Literature on Reading and Its Implications for Reading Instruction.* Report of the National Reading Panel, Reports of the Subgroups. Rockville, MD: NICHD Clearinghouse.

The Neglected "R": The Need for a Writing Revolution. 2003. Report of the National Commission on Writing for America's Families, Schools, and Colleges, C. Peter Magrath, Chair. College Entrance Examination Board.

Newkirk, Thomas. 2002. *Misreading Masculinity: Boys, Literacy, and Popular Culture.* Portsmouth, NH: Heinemann.

———. 2000. "A Mania for Rubrics: Will the Standards Movement Make Satire (and Good Writing) Obsolete?" *Education Week,* Commentary, September 13, 42.

Nickerson, R. S. 1984. "Kinds of Thinking Taught in Current Programs." *Educational Leadership* 42: 26–37.

Nystrand, M. and A. Gamoran. 1991. "Instructional Discourse, Student Engagement, and Literature Achievement." *Research in the Teaching of English,* 25, 261–290.

Oppenheimer, Todd. 2003. *The Flickering Mind: The False Promise of Technology in the Classroom and How Learning Can Be Saved.* New York: Random House.

Pearson, P. David, and Barbara Taylor. 2004. "What Really Matters: The Impact of Schoolwide and Classroom Practices on Growth in Students' Reading Achievement." Presentation at annual meeting of the International Reading Association, Reno, Nevada, May 5.

Perkins, D. N. 1981. *The Mind's Best Work.* Cambridge, MA: Harvard University Press.

Peterson, Shelley, ed. 2003. *Untangling Some Knots in K-8 Writing Instruction.* Newark, DE: International Reading Association.

Petty and Finn. 1981. "Classroom Teachers' Reports on Teaching Composition." In *Perspectives on Writing in Grades 1–8,* edited by S. Haley-James, 19–34. Urbana, IL: National Council of Teachers of English.

Pinnell, Gay Su. 2004. "Helping Children Read, Understand, and Think About Text." Session at state literacy conference, Greensboro, North Carolina, January.

Ponsot, Marie, and Rosemary Deen. 1982. *Beat Not the Poor Desk: Writing—What to Teach, How to Teach It, and Why.* Portsmouth, NH: Boynton/Cook.

"Power Point Makes You Dumb." 2003. *The New York Times Magazine,* Third Annual Year in Ideas, December 14, 88.

Quezada, Maria, Terrence Wiley, and J. David Ramirez. 1999/2000. "How the Reform Agenda Shortchanges English Learners." *Educational Leadership*, December/ January, 57–61.

Quindlen, Terrey Hatcher, ed. 2003. "Expanding Writing's Role in Learning: Teacher Training Holds Key to Change." *Curriculum Update* (Summer). Alexandria, VA: Association for Supervision and Curriculum Development.

Ray, Katie Wood, with Lisa B. Cleaveland. 2004. *About the Authors: Writing Workshop with Our Youngest Writers.* Portsmouth, NH: Heinemann.

Rice, M. L. 1989. "Children's Language Acquisition. *American Psychologist* 44: 149–56.

Rief, Linda. 2003. *100 Quickwrites.* New York: Scholastic Teaching Resources.

Romano, Tom. 2004. *Crafting Authentic Voice.* Portsmouth, NH: Heinemann. Don't miss this one! Terrific text on all aspects of writing well.

Routman, Regie. 1993. "The Uses and Abuses of Invented Spelling." *Instructor,* May/June, 36–39.

———. 1994. *Invitations: Changing as Teachers and Learners K–12.* Portsmouth, NH: Heinemann.

———. 1996. *Literacy at the Crossroads: Crucial Talk About Reading, Writing, and Other Teaching Dilemmas.* Portsmouth, NH: Heinemann.

———. 2000b. *Kids' Poems: Teaching Children to Love Writing Poetry.* New York: Scholastic. Separate volumes for kindergarten, grade 1, grade 2, and grades 3–4.

———. 2000a. *Conversations: Strategies for Teaching, Learning, and Evaluating.* Portsmouth, NH: Heinemann.

———. 2002. "Teacher Talk." *Educational Leadership,* March, 32–35.

———. 2003. *Reading Essentials: The Specifics You Need to Teach Reading Well.* Portsmouth, NH: Heinemann.

Routman, Regie, and Donna Maxim, eds. 1996. "Invented Spelling: What It Is and What It Isn't." *School Talk* 1 (4) (April): 1–6.

Ruiz, Nadeen T., Eleanor Vargas, and Angelica Beltran. 2002. "Becoming a Reader and Writer in a Bilingual Special Education Classroom." *Language Arts* (March): 297–309.

Schallert, Diane Lemonnier, and Debra Bayles Martin. 2003. "A Psychological Analysis of What Teachers and Students Do in the Language Arts Classroom." In Flood *et al.* Mahwah, NJ, and London: Lawrence Erlbaum, 31–45.

Servis, Joan. 1999. *Celebrating the Fourth: Ideas and Inspiration for Teachers of Grade Four.* Portsmouth, NH: Heinemann.

Shanahan, Timothy. 2002. "Reading Report's Unending Debate." *Education Week,* May 22, Letter to editor, 38.

———. 2004. "Critiques of the National Reading Panel Report: Their Implications for Research, Policy, and Practice." In *The Voice of Evidence in Reading Research,* edited by P. McCardle and V. Chhabra, 235–66. Baltimore, MD: Paul Brookes.

Shipley, David. 2004. "And Now a Word from Op-Ed." *The New York Times,* February 1, OP-ED, A11.

Silvey, Anita. 2004. *100 Best Books for Children.* Boston: Houghton Mifflin.

Simmons, John, and Pamela S. Carroll. 2003. "Today's Middle Grades: Different Structures, Students, and Classrooms." In Flood *et al.*, 357–92.

Slackman, Michael. 2003. "Harriet Tubman's Family Seeks Civil War Pension." *The New York Times,* November 1, The Arts, B17.

Slavin, R. E. 1991. "Reading Effects of IBM's 'Writing to Read' Program: A Review of Evaluations." *Education Evaluation and Policy Analysis* 13 (1): 1–11.

Spandel, Vicki. 2001. *Creating Writers Through 6-Trait Writing Assessment and Instruction.* New York: Addison Wesley Longman.

Stead, Tony. 2002. *Is That a Fact? Teaching Nonfiction Writing K–3.* Portland, ME: Stenhouse. A very useful book with lots of specifics.

Stiggins, Richard J. 2002. "Assessment Crisis: The Absence of Assessment *for* Learning." *Phi Delta Kappan*, June, special section on assessment.

Stotsky, Sandra. 1983. "Research on Reading/Writing Relationships: A Synthesis and Suggested Suggestions. *Language Arts* 60: 627–42. Reviews the research on reading and writing.

Stotsky, Sandra, and Cindy Mall. 2003 "Understanding Research on Teaching the English Language Arts: An Introduction for Teachers." In Flood *et al.* 133–42. Mahwah, NJ, and London: Lawrence Erlbaum.

Strickland, Dorothy. 1998. *Teaching Phonics Today: A Primer for Educators.* Newark, DE: International Reading Association.

Strickland, Dorothy, and Joan Feeley. 2003. "Development in the Elementary School Years." In Flood *et al.*, 339–56. Mahwah, NJ, and London: Lawrence Erlbaum.

Sudol, David, and Peg Sudol. 1995. "Yet Another Story: Writers' Workshop Revisited." *Language Arts: Revisiting the Teaching of Writing* (March): 171–78.

Suskind, Ron. 2004. *The Price of Loyalty: George W. Bush, the White House, and the Education of Paul O'Neill.* New York: Simon & Schuster.

Sulzby, Elizabeth, and W. H. Teale. 2003. "The Development of the Young Child and the Emergence of Literacy." In Flood *et al.*, 300–13. Mahwah, NJ, and London: Lawrence Erlbaum.

Taberski, Sharon. 2003. "Nonfiction Reading and Writing." Presentation. Reading Recovery and Early Literacy Conference, Portland, Oregon, October.

Tan, Amy. 2003. *The Opposite of Fate: A Book of Musings.* New York: Putnam.

Taylor, Barbara, Debra Peterson, P. David Pearson, and Michael Rodriguez. 2002. "Looking Inside Classrooms: Reflecting on the 'How' as Well as the 'What' in Effective Reading Instruction." *The Reading Teacher* (November): 270–79.

Templeton, Shane. 2003. "Spelling." In Flood *et al.*, 738–51. Mahwah, NJ, and London: Lawrence Erlbaum.

Tharp, R. 1997. *From At-Risk to Excellence: Research, Theory, and Principles for Practice.* Santa Cruz, CA: Center for Research on Education, Diversity, and Excellence.

Tompkins, Gail, and Eileen Tway. 2003. "The Elementary School Classroom." In Flood *et al.*, 501–11. Mahwah, NJ, and London: Lawrence Erlbaum.

Totten, Samuel. 2003. "Completing the Paradigm Shift to Process Writing: The Need to Lead." *The Quarterly* (Winter): 8–13 and 38.

Truss, Lynne. 2004. *Eats, Shoots & Leaves: The Zero Tolerance Approach to Punctuation.* New York: Gotham. Deals with the (British) rules of punctuation in a humorous, easy-to-understand manner.

Troia, Gary A., and Mary Maddow. 2004. "Writing Instruction in Middle Schools: Special and General Education Teachers and Students." *Exceptionality.*

Valencia, Richard, and Bruno Villarreal. 2003. "Improving Students' Reading Performance Via Standards-Based School Reform: A Critique." *The Reading Teacher* (April): 612–20.

Viadero, Debra. 2002. "Studies Back Lessons in Writing, Spelling." *Education Week* (November): 20, 8. Cites findings by researcher Steve Graham that suggest "that systematically teaching handwriting and spelling might actually help some students write more and do it better."

Vygotsky, L. S. 1978. *Mind in Society: The Development of Higher Psychological Processes,* edited by M. Cole, V. John-Steiner, and E. Souberman. Cambridge, MA: Harvard University Press.

Wagner, Mary Jane. 2003. "Imaginative Expression." In Flood *et al.*, 1008–25. Mahwah, NJ, and London: Lawrence Erlbaum.

Weaver, Connie. 1996. *Teaching Grammar in Context.* Portsmouth, NH: Heinemann.

Wells, Gordon. 1986. *The Meaning Makers: Children Learning Language and Using Language to Learn.* Portsmouth, NH: Heinemann.

———. 1978. *Processes.* Cambridge, MA: Harvard University Press.

Wells, G., and G. L. Chang-Wells. 1992. *Constructing Knowledge Together.* Portsmouth, NH: Heinemann.

Wilde, Sandra. 1991. *You Kan Red This! Spelling and Punctuation for Who Language Classrooms, K–6.* Portsmouth, NH: Heinemann.

Wiley, Mark. 2000. "The Popularity of Formulaic Writing (and Why We Need to Resist")" *English Journal* 90 (1) (September): 61–67.

Winerip, Michael. 2004. "A Touchstone for the High School Essay." *The New York Times,* March 3, On Education, A23.

Wink, Joan, and Dawn Wink. 2004. *Teaching Passionately. What's Love Got to Do with It?* Boston: Pearson/Allyn and Bacon.

Young, Victoria. 2004. Presentation on assessment and state writing tests at the twentieth anniversary conference of the National Writing Project, Houston, Texas, February 7.

Index